SEVEN DAYS IN HELL

ALSO BY DAVID O'KEEFE
One Day in August: The Untold Story behind Canada's Tragedy at Dieppe

SEVEN DAYS IN HELL

CANADA'S BATTLE FOR NORMANDY AND
THE RISE OF THE BLACK WATCH SNIPERS

DAVID O'KEEFE

HarperCollinsPublishersLtd

Published by HarperCollins Publishers Ltd

First edition

HarperCollins Publishers Ltd
Bay Adelaide Centre, East Tower
22 Adelaide Street West, 41st Floor
Toronto, Ontario, Canada
M5H 4E3

www.harpercollins.ca

Library and Archives Canada Cataloguing in Publication information is available upon request.

ISBN 978-1-4434-5477-3

Map on page *x* and chart on page *xi* by Mike Bechthold (mbechthold@wlu.ca)

Printed and bound in the United States of America
LSC/H 9 8 7 6 5 4 3 2 1

For those who no longer speak

Contents

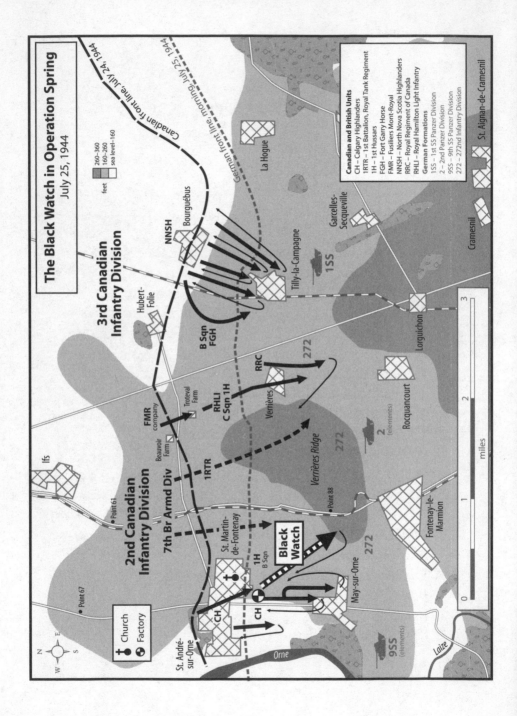

The Black Watch in Operation Spring
July 25, 1944

feet
- 260–360
- 160–260
- sea level–160

3rd Canadian Infantry Division

2nd Canadian Infantry Division

Canadian front line, morning July 24, 1944

German front line, morning July 25, 1944

Ifs

St. André-sur-Orne

• Point 67

• Point 61

7th Br Armd Div

St. Martin-de-Fontenay

Beauvoir Farm

Troteval Farm

Church
Factory

CH

CH

1H B Sqn

Black Watch

1RTR

FMR company

RHLI C Sqn 1H

Verrières

RRC

272

272

Verrières Ridge

Point 88

272

May-sur-Orne

Fontenay-le-Marmion

Rocquancourt

Lorguichon

2 (elements)

9SS (elements)

Orne

Laize

Hubert-Folie

B Sqn FGH

Bourguébus

NNSH

La Hogue

Tilly-la-Campagne

1SS

Garcelles-Secqueville

Cramesnil

St. Aignan-de-Cramesnil

Canadian and British Units
CH – Calgary Highlanders
1RTR – 1st Battalion, Royal Tank Regiment
1H – 1st Hussars
FGH – Fort Garry Horse
FMR – Fusiliers Mont-Royal
NNSH – North Nova Scotia Highlanders
RRC – Royal Regiment of Canada
RHLI – Royal Hamilton Light Infantry

German Formations
1SS – 1st SS Panzer Division
2 – 2nd Panzer Division
9SS – 9th SS Panzer Division
272 – 272nd Infantry Division

N W E S

miles
0   1   2   3

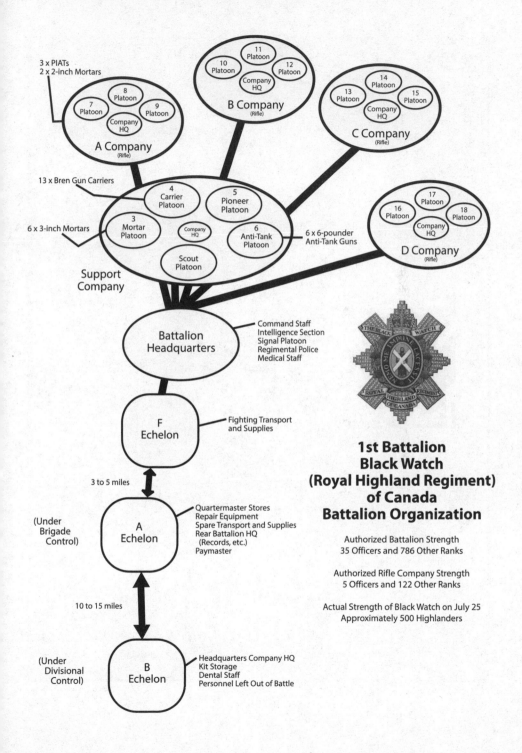

3 x PIATs
2 x 2-inch Mortars

8 Platoon
7 Platoon
9 Platoon
Company HQ

A Company
(Rifle)

11 Platoon
10 Platoon
12 Platoon
Company HQ

B Company
(Rifle)

14 Platoon
13 Platoon
15 Platoon
Company HQ

C Company
(Rifle)

13 x Bren Gun Carriers

4 Carrier Platoon
5 Pioneer Platoon
3 Mortar Platoon
Company HQ
6 Anti-Tank Platoon
Scout Platoon

6 x 3-inch Mortars

6 x 6-pounder Anti-Tank Guns

Support Company

17 Platoon
16 Platoon
18 Platoon
Company HQ

D Company
(Rifle)

Battalion Headquarters

Command Staff
Intelligence Section
Signal Platoon
Regimental Police
Medical Staff

F Echelon

Fighting Transport and Supplies

3 to 5 miles

(Under Brigade Control)

A Echelon

Quartermaster Stores
Repair Equipment
Spare Transport and Supplies
Rear Battalion HQ
 (Records, etc.)
Paymaster

10 to 15 miles

(Under Divisional Control)

B Echelon

Headquarters Company HQ
Kit Storage
Dental Staff
Personnel Left Out of Battle

1st Battalion
Black Watch
(Royal Highland Regiment)
of Canada
Battalion Organization

Authorized Battalion Strength
35 Officers and 786 Other Ranks

Authorized Rifle Company Strength
5 Officers and 122 Other Ranks

Actual Strength of Black Watch on July 25
Approximately 500 Highlanders

AUTHOR'S NOTE

WHEN I FIRST WALKED THROUGH THE DOORS OF the "Castle on Bleury Street," the Black Watch armoury in the heart of Montreal, in the late winter of 1991, I had no idea where my journey would lead. At that time, the first Gulf War had just erupted, and I had decided that the time had come to follow in the footsteps of my grandfather, my father, uncles, great-uncles and cousins who had served during both World Wars, Korea and the First Gulf War, a service to the country that would extend into Bosnia and Afghanistan.

My tenure as a young subaltern with the Black Watch was both brief and thoroughly undistinguished, and I left the uniform after two years to pursue my passion for military history. Over the next two decades, I maintained my association with the Department of National Defence, working as a researcher with the Directorate of History and Heritage before returning to the Black Watch, where I served as regimental historian. During that period, I penned a series of academic articles concerning the experiences of the 1st Battalion in 1944–45 and interviewed (formally and otherwise) most of the men quoted directly in this work. Many of those men went on to be lifelong friends, and as a fan of military history, I stood in awe of their courage and fortitude, but as a historian, I remained professionally distanced and detached, objective, questioning and critical. I made this distinction clear upfront and told them I was sworn to tell it as the evidence portrayed it, rather than simply as they saw it. To a man, they respected that caveat, and they responded openly and honestly—sometimes, as you will read in the pages, painfully so.

Sadly, all of these men are now gone, as the ravages of time wait for no man. For whatever reason, the snipers in the battalion's scout platoon enjoyed greater longevity than their brethren in the rifle companies, and as such, their story began to dominate the Black Watch narrative, leading one rifleman to quip, "Bloody scouts think they won the damn war!" Indeed, the scouts were, as Corporal Jimmy "Hook" Wilkinson recalled, "the eyes and ears of the battalion," and over time they had developed a distinct sense of themselves, in part due to their longevity, in part their unique, almost bohemian role in the battalion, but more importantly, the fact that they had come through the bloodbath on Verrières Ridge in that half-forgotten summer of 1944 and lived to tell their tales.

Memory, of course, is a fickle beast, and I have relied on their recollections primarily for tone and atmosphere, or to convey impressions or express their intensely personal experiences or inner thoughts. Any claims of fact that have an impact upon the overall narrative, I have cross-referenced with the archival record to verify historical accuracy and reduce the degree of bias associated with any historical venture.

To avoid a flood of repetitive references, all the direct quotations (unless otherwise noted) have come from these conversations. Some of these men, as you will notice, were enlightened, eloquent and highly educated; others, not so much. But all of them opened up in a straightforward fashion and entrusted with me their emotive recollections, which in some cases they had withheld from families or friends, awaiting the proper context for their unveiling.

I have also employed the narrative style; as a professor of history, I have taught in classrooms, on battlefields, on television and in monograph and journal form, and have not found any other vehicle that can deliver a multitude of complex, interlaced, nuanced and layered concepts in a simple (but never simplistic) fashion. In this respect, I have dared invoke the spirit of Cornelius Ryan and Stephen Ambrose, whose oral history tradition has thrilled and captivated millions over the last five decades, though I have anchored my work in a deep and thorough corpus of research whose scope remains both broad and deep, and provides evidence that organically shocks, amazes, electrifies and magnetizes the public conscience. What has evolved in this work, and has been the main constant throughout my career in history, is that truth is, indeed, stranger than fiction.

My view on military history falls in line with that of the pre-eminent military thinker and historian Sir Basil Liddell-Hart, who believed that military history should never fall into the realm of the "sentimental treasure," where our understanding and engagement are limited to an annual polishing of our national historical trophies. Ideally, history should, through the engagement of unsettling facts, teach us about those hard-earned experiences so that we may develop an understanding and, above all, empathy for those who went before us. This is the main focus of the book.

As such, themes of heroism, courage, determination, resilience and friendship walk hand in hand with cowardice, frailty, chaos and horror throughout the following narrative. I have made a point of not sugar-coating what befell these men in July 1944. Telling their story in an unvarnished fashion was the only option, given their openness and honesty; the only way to justly honour their memory.

With that said, on the one hand, I stand in awe of what these men endured, and they have my undying respect; on the other, I do not wish for one second to see my children bear what they had to. After all, if we cannot learn and draw from history—particularly military history—then what is the point?

Perhaps the first word in this work should go to Hook Wilkinson, who for decades was a stalwart at every Black Watch regimental function, from parades to battlefield pilgrimages, funerals, mess dinners and veteran association gatherings. Over that time, his stories poured forth—some true, some embellished and oft-repeated, leading most to politely chalk up his claim as "the best shot in the regiment" to visions of glory distorted by time. "I'm sure you were, Jimmy" or "Wow, that's great, Jim" tended to be the polite yet all too patronizing response to his boast.

Then, in 2015, while filming the documentary *Black Watch Snipers* with Yap Films for History Television, our brilliant director Robin Bicknell had a creative brainstorm: Why not gather up the surviving Black Watch snipers and take them to a range to reunite them with their best friend, their Lee-Enfield No. 4 Mark I sniper rifle, for a day of target practice?

Three of the four remaining Back Watch snipers agreed to participate, including Hook Wilkinson, but one remained steadfast in a vow he made when the war ended to give up the killing, dying and misery of war, and to never touch a weapon of any kind again. Seven decades later, he remained true to his word.

However, at the age of ninety-two, and not having touched the Lee-Enfield since he left the army seven decades earlier, Hook took aim and proceeded to put the entire clip down range in less than a dozen seconds, packing four out of his five rounds together in a tight two-inch grouping at a distance of one hundred yards. His performance brought the crowd at the range to stunned silence. The old boy still had it, and nobody dared dismiss his claims out of hand again.

SEVEN DAYS IN HELL

INTRODUCTION

==

VERRIÈRES RIDGE, NORMANDY, JULY 25, 1944, 0930 HOURS—H-HOUR

NONE OF THE MEN IN THE 1ST BATTALION OF Canada's Black Watch had seen the sun for a week when it pierced through a thin veil of overcast to beat down upon their position at the foot of Verrières Ridge. As they quickly surmised, its warm rays did little more than taunt and torment, for nothing could relieve the tension and gut-gnawing dread that had ballooned during their week-long baptism of fire that now reached its crescendo.

Each of the 320 hollow-eyed, grimy and grim Highlanders, all that remained of four battered rifle companies, sat, knelt or crouched in a muddied, vacant beet field, waiting for the next move. Their heavy woollen battledress, smeared with mud, plaster dust, ash and splatters of blood, sported sweat-soaked armpits, groins and necklines that bore witness to their week-long macabre dance with the unholy trinity of sweltering heat, intense combat and waves of soul-destroying fear and anxiety.

Having learned to take nothing for granted in the moments before battle, some of the men fumbled with buttoned flies or webbed belts to relieve themselves from what the ancient Greeks termed "watery bowels," while others chose to suck back a freshly rolled cigarette or wolf down a slice of hardtack, washed down with a hidden stash of rum, to help steady overly taut nerves. Men of a more religious bent silently muttered prayers or fondled rosary beads, while those suffering from the vagaries of crushing fatigue built up over the last seven days sat despondent and stone-faced, staring aimlessly into a swath of flaxen-coloured wheat fifty or so yards ahead. Racked by fatigue that clouded minds, impaired judgment and left them ragged and sapped of strength, some toyed with trading near-paralytic exhaustion for death.

The northern slope of Verrières Ridge, coated now with thick, tall wheat standing shoulder high, rose from beyond a curtain of grain. Shimmering impressively in the prevailing breeze, it accentuated the long, slow and gentle slope that led to the main line of German resistance concealed behind its crest.

In the wake of the four Black Watch rifle companies priming for the second phase of Operation Spring, the largest Canadian Army set-piece attack since Vimy Ridge a generation earlier, lay the battle-scarred artifacts that chronicled the latest chapter of Canada's most storied regiment.

A thousand yards behind sat Hill 61, a slight rise that the Black Watch called home for four gruelling days and nights. Littered with singed wheat, smashed vehicles and hundreds of abandoned slit trenches, the pitted and scarred landscape testified to the constant cascade of shells unleashed by two rival armies locked in desperate battle. Sitting exposed to enemy observation, they dodged constant German sniper fire and the thunder of rocket, mortar and artillery shells that crashed down in torrents of white-hot steel and high explosive while fending off enemy patrols that used the blanket of wheat as cover to infiltrate their lines by day and by night.

They took the pounding devoid of sleep, hot food and rum they sorely needed to steady rapidly fraying nerves. All the while they watched comrades die, collapse or disappear, irretrievably swallowed by the dirt and the grain, or consumed by imploded psyches.

In the shallow valley at the foot of Hill 61, spiralling columns of smoke eddied up from the ghostlike ruins of the conjoined towns of St. André and St. Martin. The mining and farming community, which had stood for centuries, devastated over the previous week by massive artillery stonks and close combat encounters, sat rubbled, strewn with debris and the unburied dead. Periodically, muffled explosions from unattended fires erupted, punctuating the strange, almost serene calm that befell the beet field, a development that seemed far out of step with the corps-wide battle raging across the entire front.

Off to their immediate right stood a small cluster of industrial buildings that the locals now call Cité de la Mine. Oblivious to the existence of a 1,200-foot shaft that burrowed down to the iron deposits far below Verrières, the men in the Black Watch had mistaken it for nothing more than a factory until it gave up its secrets when they had passed through moments earlier. Smouldering now from a liberal dousing of white phosphorus grenades and fistfuls of Composition C crammed into ventilation ducts and pithead openings, the corrugated steel and tin structure displayed ominous traces of the Highlanders' wrath. Wall panels and sidings that once flashed in the sunlight stood scorched and blackened, riddled with bullet holes and pockmarked by shrapnel. Doors and window frames hung limply, ripped from their hinges by blasts that left mounds of shattered glass glinting in the sun, guide ropes severed, skips alight and trolleys overturned. In almost every corner, dead and dying German grenadiers, unable to escape to burrows underground, lay slumped in grotesque attitudes on conveyor belts and refuse heaps, while others dangled from power pylons atop the thirty-foot-high tipple used to load the iron deposits.

Not a single man spoke in the beet field—or if they did, nobody remembered. Nightmares festering from the recent fighting bubbled to the surface and clashed headlong with their bid to husband whatever fumes of courage remained for their final assault. They wondered in the back of their minds if the attack would indeed go on. After a series of nasty surprises and fatal encounters with the Germans in St. Martin, the battalion was now four hours behind the schedule of the tightly timed corps plan, which left the men in a most unenviable predicament. Instead of pushing up the wide-open slopes of Verrières in the haze of the pre-dawn light, they now faced the unnerving prospect of a matinee performance.

The nature of their objective, lying just over a mile on a straight line through the wheat field ahead, weighed heavily on their minds. Tucked into the reverse slope of Verrières, only a handful of the men knew the town by name, and fewer cared. All the villages south of the Norman capital of Caen featured fieldstone houses ringed by high dirt mounds crowned with dense hedges and thickets, all converted over the previous ten days into potent fortresses brimming with automatic weapons and anti-tank guns supported by artillery, rockets, mortars and battle groups (*Kampfgruppen*) from elite panzer divisions. With the capture of this village considered vital for the success of the entire corps plan, the men in the Black Watch harboured no doubts that its fanatical defenders would fight tooth and nail to hold out at all costs.

Getting to their objective, however, was their immediate problem. As with previous attacks that week, they expected to have a squadron of Sherman tanks in support, which would pepper the objective with direct fire while the artillery dropped an indirect curtain of steel and high explosive fifty yards ahead of their position, steadily creeping forward as they advanced. Smoke would shroud the battlefield in a great, thick mist to their right, cutting off enemy observation from the heights across the Orne River to the west. But as H-hour arrived, none of these elements so crucial for success had materialized.

Undaunted, the acting commanding officer waved his right arm and 320 men rose to their feet in unison like a fleet weighing anchor. Following a slight pause, the mass of soldiery lurched forward on his cry of "Black Watch advance" and embarked upon the most contentious chapter in their regiment's long and storied history.

Clomping through the mud with rifles across their chests at the ready and bayonets fixed, the Highlanders momentarily dipped into the sea of wheat and discovered the going more trying than first imagined. Rationing in England had prohibited training in this type of terrain, and although they had had a brief taste earlier in the week, it proved nothing compared with the almost labyrinthine world they now entered, with command and control reduced to a limited series of verbal cues.

Cutting telltale paths into the grain as they bounded up the northern slope of Verrières, the Highlanders continued to move slowly up the gentle rise that in centuries past had hosted the armies of William the Conqueror and King Henry V, but now masked a more sinister horde. Spread out in a loose configuration and carefully concealed in slit trenches and skilfully placed weapons pits, Wehrmacht and SS panzer-grenadiers, snipers, machine guns, panzers and anti-tank guns, from some of the best units Hitler still had to offer, waited patiently, baiting their quarry into a carefully crafted killing field.

To a man, each of the 320 Highlanders wading up the slope came from the ranks of the citizen-soldier, men who volunteered for service and left the relative safety of their homes to cross an ocean to fight someone else's war. Although known as a Montreal regiment, one-third of the men heading towards their destiny on the ridge came from all parts of Canada, the British Isles and Nazi-occupied Europe, and included a contingent of Americans who had arrived before Pearl Harbor to ensure that they got in on the action.

Slogging steadily through the wheat, prairie boys, longshoremen and lumberjacks strode side by side with men from the working and middle classes, the wealthy and the powerful. Former bookkeepers, truck drivers, bartenders, machine-shop fitters and general labourers joined with saints, sinners and rogues. Caucasian, African Canadians and First Nations men moving seamlessly with Jews and gentiles, communists and socialists, capitalists, conservatives and liberals. Shepherded by captains of industry, college athletes, lawyers, stockbrokers and private-school prefects, the men maintained an unyielding faith and obedience to authority underscored by their devotion to principle, duty, friendship and the ironclad concept of "regiment"; all now set for bonding and branding by Verrières Ridge.

Plowing through a horseshoe-shaped draw under enemy observation from the centre and both flanks, only the hushed *snick snick* of German sniper bullets cutting through the thick stalks met the advance. On occasion, deafening clanks signalled that they had found their mark, while the growl from section commanders and platoon sergeants to "keep together" rose above the clamour of the shuffling and the cursing.

Fifty yards into the field, the feathery whine and muffled crumps announced the arrival of mortar-ranging shots falling behind the trailing rifle companies. Soon a screen of high explosive and white-hot shrapnel arrived, erasing any notion of escape or withdrawal. In quick succession, German artillery observers, dug in on the crest and the heights across the Orne River valley, zeroed in on the ten-foot whip antennas of the battalion's wireless sets, waving madly above the wheat. In quick succession, the crackle of wireless traffic ceased as German mortar shells found their mark. With communications cut, the men in the Black Watch could not have been more alone.

A hundred yards into their advance, German machine guns, sitting snugly in camouflaged hides lining the flanks as well as up on the ridge, barked to life. Firing on fixed lines, their bright green-and-yellow tracer ripped into the field from three sides, cutting deadly swaths into the wheat with scythe-like precision, their searing-hot rounds tearing flesh, tissue and tendons, leaving organs and bones shattered. The Highlanders, devoid of cover, bobbed and weaved in the chest-high grain, desperately seeking any channel to avoid the accurate and deadly German fire pouring down, each man hoping not to draw the short straw in this morbid game of "fate or luck."

One by one, however, the men started to fall, swallowed by the wheat that reduced command and control to almost nil. The cadence of the few officers and NCOs still left on their feet, once calm and firm, now rose sharply with an increased sense of urgency. With no hope of stopping, of withdrawal or of mercy, they could only continue to chide: "Stay in step! Keep it together! Keep moving, men; keep moving forward!"

Any trepidation built up in the moments before the attack had vanished, replaced now by a scorching rush of adrenalin injected into ever-tightening veins. With their hearts now racing, throats burning and the near-deafening tone of carotid arteries pounding in their ears, only the cries from the wounded and the dying rose above the racket. Once smooth and controlled, their collective glide hastened in pace, turning rapidly into a frantic gallop as they slammed headlong into the German picket halfway up the ridge. Hidden beneath the grain, any defender naive enough to offer surrender received no quarter when the Highlanders overran their slits.

German rocket and heavy artillery fire joined the choir just yards from the crest, and a hurricane of steel and fire greeted the mass of humanity scurrying through the wheat. The normally pleasant scent of petrichor, kicked up from the soggy soil with each blast, mixed paradoxically with the bleach-like stench of cordite, the charcoal-like smell of singed flesh and the sulphuric stink of melted hair. With every step, the ground shook; bodies and body parts flew in all directions, striking those still pushing forward up the ridge.

The only reward for the intrepid Highlanders who reached the crest came in the form of elite panzers and *Panzergrenadiers* who opened fire at point-blank range. Within seconds, shredded bowels and punctured bladders unleashed the pungent, metallic scent of blood and the rancid pong of feces and urine. From beneath the grain, earth-curdling screeches from the wounded and dying, calling out in vain for a medic, a stretcher-bearer or their mothers. In short order, cries turned to whimpers and then, mercifully, irreversible silence.

Drenched in sweat and wild-eyed with rage and terror, the Highlanders who were still on their feet continued to press through the withering fire and the carnage, spurred on by desperate "do or die" calls from their acting commanding officer, whose repeated pleas to push on rose above the cacophony. "C'mon, men! Keep moving! We can reach the objective."

I

LA VOIE SACRÉE

We have been inspected by General Eisenhower and General Foulkes lately.
General Foulkes said that we might be home by Christmas—if we do a good
forceful job—hope he is right. Optimism is abundant over here, but it is tem-
pered by cold, calculating logic and the determination to hit hard and well.
— LETTER FROM LIEUTENANT COLONEL S.S.T. CANTLIE
TO COLONEL PAUL P. HUTCHISON

TO PRIVATE MIKE BRUNNER, THE ENGLISH CHANNEL
off Juno Beach seemed "busier than Montreal's Ste. Catherine
Street on a Saturday night." Perched along the rail of the
Landing Ship Infantry *Isle of Guernsey* and saddled next to his
fellow scouts from the 1st Battalion of Canada's Black Watch, the
twenty-one-year-old, saggy-eyed sniper stood gobsmacked by the
sheer magnitude of the spectacle. No photograph, newspaper article or embroidered news report could justly articulate the scene.

One month to the day after one of the greatest amphibious
forces in history crashed ashore on five invasion beaches along
the Normandy coast of France, close to a million American,
British, French and Canadian troops serving under British general Bernard Law Montgomery's 21st Army Group stood locked
in desperate battle with over 400,000 of their German foe. Under
the overall command of the Allied supreme commander, American

general Dwight David Eisenhower, Montgomery's multinational force formed the tip of the spear in what he coined an Allied "Crusade in Europe."

Entirely sober to the far-reaching gravity of his mission, "Ike," as the men called Eisenhower, had told the Black Watch just weeks before that he had planned the invasion of Europe without any alternative, save ultimate victory. The vista now on display from the deck of the *Isle of Guernsey* did little to belie his vow.[1]

Hundreds of destroyers, frigates, patrol boats and trawlers, all painted in a multitude of camouflage schemes, ran frantic search patterns for U-boats that threatened the endless collection of vulnerable Allied Liberty ships queued to deliver their consignments ashore. Each of these vessels sprouted barrage balloons tethered to their sterns to thwart German low-level air attack. They sat low-slung in the water, full with food, vehicles, tanks, guns and ordnance of all calibres destined for the front line, twelve miles inland from the Juno Beach sector.

Flanked as usual by the Wilkinson brothers, Brunner and his best friend, Private Dale Sharpe, observed the massive logistical tail of the greatest invasion force ever assembled. With each ship anchored tightly together, it appeared to Brunner that, given a chance, "a man could run the entire length of the landing zone without once touching water or sand." In sharp contrast, scores of smaller tenders and amphibious vehicles scurried about, shuffling material from ship to shore with worker-bee determination while cranes on makeshift jetties swivelled unendingly to offload equipment and supplies.

Peering through the detached sniper scopes of their Lee-Enfield rifles, which they kept tucked into the bulging pockets of their camouflaged sniper smocks, Brunner and Sharpe could make out endless winding columns of diesel-belching trucks, tanks, carriers and jeeps queued behind bulldozers, busily carving escape paths through the dunes. Marching on each side, men from the Calgary Highlanders and Régiment de Maisonneuve, who were brigaded with the Black Watch in the 2nd Canadian Division's 5th Brigade, trudged forward, conforming to shrill blasts from the beach master's whistle. Long lines of dishevelled and dejected German prisoners of war under armed guard snaked their way along the smooth sand towards a collection of makeshift barbed-wire enclosures.

The British battleship HMS *Rodney*, at station not far from the shoreline, set the backbeat for this display, unleashing thunderous salvos from its nine 16-inch naval guns at regular intervals, flinging mammoth high-explosive shells towards German lines just north of the Norman capital of Caen.

High above the beach on this crystal-clear day, the scouts spotted all types of Allied aircraft, suitably painted with broad black-and-white invasion stripes for easy identification, soaring at a multitude of levels on an equal number of missions. White contrails from the supercharged engines of heavy bombers, barely visible at 20,000 feet, left telltale signs that an unsuspecting German city had only hours to spare before it reaped the whirlwind from a mixture of blockbuster and incendiary bombs.

German retaliation came in the form of Hitler's latest vengeance weapon unveiled after D-Day: the pilotless V-1 flying bomb, dubbed the "buzz bomb," "doodlebug" or "robot bomb" by the Allied press due to the drone of its rocket engine. A V-1 would periodically glide past at 3,000 feet on course for England, with a pair of Royal Air Force fighters in pursuit, aiming to catch and kill the missile before it struck the London area.

Directly above the beach, at 10,000 feet, squadrons of rocket-firing Typhoon fighter-bombers from British and Canadian squadrons circled and soared, ready to pounce on German panzer columns, artillery positions, trains, bridges and supply dumps—

anything that would help the Allied advance or hinder the German ability to rush reinforcements to their ever-congealing front line. For Corporal Jimmy "Hook" Wilkinson, nothing proved more exhilarating than the violent lurch forward of each plane as it dove on its prey with engines whining and rockets screaming. As each aircraft disappeared below the horizon, the scouts engaged in a bluster of speculative comment about the results of these hawk-like endeavours. Soon the reappearance of the Typhoons, roaring past at what seemed a yard or two above the field of barrage balloons, told the tale. Each sported empty rocket rails and clean-sounding engines that testified to their successful escape from German flak guns liberally distributed across the area. Much to the delight of the scouts, one cocky and confident pilot wagged his wings as he raced past overhead, on his way to a newly minted grass landing strip to rearm, refuel and return later that day.

Brunner, awestruck and frozen by the spectacle, struggled to find the words to articulate his raw emotions but knew full well that he and his Black Watch mates now stood at the precipice of history. After four long and tedious years on defensive duty in southeastern England, punctuated only by the disastrous Dieppe raid in 1942 and the odd barroom dust-up with rival units in the 5th Canadian Infantry Brigade, their time to "get at 'em" had finally arrived.

No sooner, however, had this schoolboy excitement erupted than Sharpe spotted a pocket of debris kicking up in the backwash off the port quarter. Hook Wilkinson, having returned to the rail at Sharpe's request, took in the spectacle floating atop the Delft-hued surf. Empty ammunition boxes, canvas tenting, wooden crates, discarded margarine and bully beef tins, torn battledress tunics and other trappings of war drifted slowly past, all victims of the ferocious battle ashore and a mighty gale-force tempest that had pounded the invasion beaches two weeks earlier.

Soon, large splinters from wood timbers cloaked with seaweed and draped with shards of discarded fabric bubbled to the surface. Hook noticed the carcass of a dead mongrel, followed by one distinctly human in form. Still intact despite grotesque bloating, it was anyone's guess whether this soldier was friend or foe. The cadaver scratched the camouflaged hull and permanently dipped beneath the waves. It took concussive salvos from the guns of the *Rodney* and the equally jarring, high-pitched howl of their platoon sergeant, Bernard "Barney" Benson, to shake the scouts loose from their morbid daze and return them to the job at hand.

The exhilaration and trepidation of the Juno Beach sector and its parallel with Montreal's main drag struck a primal chord in Brunner, who had spent many nights staring at the pulsating glow of its neon lights blanketing the ceiling of the family's overcrowded flat in the city's Chinatown district. The draw of the strip's trolley cars, taxicabs, cinemas, diners and five-and-dimes adorned with glowing signs advertising Sweet Caporal cigarettes paled in comparison with the intimidating nature of its pool halls, lounges, nightclubs, brothels and gaggles of working girls planted on each corner.

The oldest of five children, Brunner spoke little more than a rural dialect of German when his family arrived in Canada following the collapse of the Austro-Hungarian Empire. He found it difficult to fit into a neighbourhood where he would hear Cantonese as often as English, Ukrainian, Polish, Russian, Hungarian, Yiddish or *joual*, the incumbent Quebecois French slang endemic to working-class Montreal.

The Great Depression robbed Brunner, as it did most men in the ranks of the Black Watch, of his secondary education, which he reluctantly forfeited to help his family survive. After toiling as a delivery boy and then as a collection agent for a garment factory in Montreal's usually vibrant *shmatte* trade, he worked for two years in a brush factory close to the Black Watch Armoury, earning less than fifty cents per hour. Brunner, thoroughly fed up with his predicament, enlisted in the army in the fall of 1942 but balked at joining the Black Watch, fearing he would not make it in such an elite regiment. Instead, seduced by an article in *Maclean's* magazine, the "short, stocky" candidate, who the recruiting officer noted possessed a "friendly, but rather unimpressive personality," joined the Canadian Parachute Battalion.[2]

Within a year, his dream of earning his jump wings and distinctive maroon beret ended when he suffered a punctured eardrum in training, which prompted a transfer, by chance, to the Black Watch. Now, as Brunner sucked back one last smoke and readied his pack for disembarkation, he quietly relished the irony of the move; once derided for his accent and bastardized German, his linguistic skills now made him indispensable to the scout platoon for translation and interrogation.

UNLIKE BRUNNER, THE WILKINSON BROTHERS HAD COME of age on separate paths on the "strip" in Montreal. Raised, like many men in the ranks of the Black Watch, in an English-speaking, working-class neighbourhood, the Wilkinson brothers came from Verdun, a rough, predominantly Irish borough that shared its name with the horrific bloodbath in France during their father's Great War.

Verdun, a spiritual and romantic symbol of French defiance and sacrifice, also served as the anvil that tested and tempered manhood. If a young man had not journeyed up the Voie Sacrée (the Sacred Way) that led to the frontline trenches to be baptized by the crimson waves of blood in this meat-grinder battle of attrition, then somehow he had failed, not only as a Frenchman, but more importantly, as a man. By extension, although never presented in such melodramatic prose, if as a Canadian one had not weathered a similar purgatorial rite of passage at Ypres, the Somme or Passchendaele, or stood atop the holy mount of Vimy Ridge, he somehow remained unproven and, to some, unworthy.

Short of combat, pilgrimages to and from the strip provided the Wilkinson brothers with a personal Voie Sacrée where they navigated perilous channels of cheap booze, gambling, petty crime and the ever-present spectre of destitution.

When war came in the summer of 1939, Jim Wilkinson viewed it as his contemporaries did, as salvation from the Depression. His mother, however, like most mothers, did not see it quite that way. His enlistment in 1940, followed a year later by his brother's, brought her waves of anguish and a sense of premature loss. Despite her vehement and passionate protests, their father said little. The son of a Boer War veteran himself, Old Man Wilkinson had suffered horribly in the trenches from a gas attack in the Great War, which left him with chronic blistering and a fatalistic outlook on life. When Hook enlisted, his father offered no words of wisdom, nor sage advice. "He knew exactly where I was heading and what the situation would be," Hook lamented, "but all he said was 'good luck.'"

Perhaps sensing that nothing he said would change their minds, let alone adequately prepare them for what lay ahead, Old Man Wilkinson, like his father before him, quietly passed the torch and watched his boys embark on their tortuous journey towards manhood.

The reasons young men such as Brunner, the Wilkinson brothers, Dale Sharpe and hundreds of thousands of others in Canada volunteered to fight proved complex and multi-faceted.

Traditionally, sense of duty and desire for adventure topped the list, but for many young men gripped by the economic woes of the Dirty Thirties, it offered a steady job—and, as Brunner put it, one that "needed to be done."

For Hook Wilkinson, who drew upon his father's hatred for the Hun, it came down to principle. "It wasn't a pleasant situation," he declared, "we were fighting a people who were killing babies and old people and putting them into slave labour camps."

Dale Sharpe, a twenty-six-year-old father of three from Belleville, Ontario, had other reasons for enlisting. Pragmatism, interlaced with a sense of duty, motivated him. With the provisions of the National Resources Mobilization Act in full swing, he reckoned it would not be long before full-fledged conscription compelled him to leave his job as a truck driver, and he decided to beat the government to the punch. In the fall of 1943, he reluctantly enlisted and left his wife, June, to explain to their young children that their father, like many other fathers, had gone off to work but would be home as soon as the job was done.

Underlining their practical, romantic or principled reasons for answering the call, many men sensed their world around them had slipped into an abyss socially, morally and economically. Ill-equipped to understand the nuanced elements of this existential crisis, let alone articulate them, they nonetheless felt that the seductive draw of service to one's country, and the promise it offered, was the elixir for their woes. Joining an elite and exclusive club like the Black Watch also helped, for its ironclad structure and purpose elevated their sagging pride and masculinity, much needed in an era of intellectual, ideological and cultural poverty. Joining the Black Watch guaranteed three square meals a day and a steady source of honest money, and they could signal their virility with the sharp cut and flash of their distinctive and most manly Scottish Highland uniform.

Comprising the distinctive government tartan kilt, khaki tunic and striking red hackle—a feathered regimental battle honour perched askew on their balmoral headdress—the uniform restored, unbeknownst to them, an aspect of their masculinity the Depression had usurped. Their uniform was *the* symbol of belonging and represented a place where they fit in and found respect. Indeed, the Black Watch provided the surrogate family they longed for, and as a result they struck an unwritten social contract: in exchange for respect and salvation, they would give their minds, bodies and, if necessary, young lives for the sake of the country and, perhaps more importantly, the regiment. Not surprisingly, it wasn't long before men like Hook Wilkinson would be found boasting in the mess after a few cold ones that his "body did not carry normal blood," but rather, "Black Watch blood."

Jimmy Wilkinson earned the sobriquet "Hook" the moment he joined the Black Watch in part for the prominent proboscis planted firmly in the centre of his face, but also for its bowed angle, the result of a nasty hockey injury that required twenty-five stitches to close.

By the time he arrived off Juno Beach, Hook, now twenty-three, had five years of military service behind him and had risen to the rank of corporal. The self-proclaimed crack shot of the regiment—thoroughly backed by top marks in a pair of sniper courses—Hook was a natural for the new scout platoon when it formed in early February of 1944. In short order, he became the right-hand man of Barney Benson, the scout platoon sergeant, tasked with canvassing the unit for suitable candidates.

Scouts and snipers had long been part of the order of battle with infantry battalions since the days before the Great War. Traditionally, the scout/sniper was merely the company's best shot, who roamed the battlefield employing his deadly arts in ad hoc fashion. But the exceedingly effective and coordinated German sniper effort in North Africa and Italy, which created a degree of despondency, confusion and paralysis far disproportionate to their numbers, prompted a fundamental shift in Allied thinking.

In early 1944, the British and Canadian armies sought a more professional approach to rival the Germans, and that manifested itself in the creation of a dedicated scout platoon for infantry battalions. Carved out of the existing establishment, the newly crafted Black Watch scout platoon that Hook and Benson cobbled together had the dual role of scouting and sniping. The original cadre called for a platoon of thirty men, with twenty trained as scouts and the other ten qualified as snipers. By the time the Black Watch set foot in Normandy, only twenty-two had made the stringent cut, but of these, all but two had qualified as both scouts and snipers.

Their main job consisted of patrolling by day and night and conducting reconnaissance, listening and liaison patrols, all of which came with their inherent dangers. Infiltrating enemy territory was never easy, and the constant stress associated with dodging enemy sentries, patrols, land mines and even their own trigger-happy sentries upon return weighed heavily. At times, the scouts would also undertake highly dangerous fighting patrols and advanced guard work when the battalion was on the attack or consolidating newly won ground. Here, they operated as sentinels—or human tripwires, as Wilkinson put it—pushing out in front of the lead companies to stir up trouble, forcing the enemy's hand and nullifying surprise and limiting casualties to the rest of the battalion. As Hook saw it, "We were the ears, eyes and nose of the battalion. It was our business to get as much information as possible and keep the commanding officer informed." As such, they entered into a close collaboration with company and platoon commanders, the intelligence section of battalion and brigade headquarters, and the scouts became, as

Hook noted, "the proverbial flies on the wall" when plans took shape and decisions came down.

Unlike German snipers, who roamed the battlefields as lone wolves, the Canadians worked in teams while patrolling and sniping. Taught to emulate the *shikaris* of India, the hunters of the European forests or trappers of the Canadian north, all of whom pitted themselves against wild animals, they strove to combine the art of the hunter with the "wiles of a poacher" underscored by steadfast determination to hunt down the enemy and kill him with one round.[3]

Although the army honed the soldiers' skills to stalk and kill, they paid little attention to their ability to cope. Most of the snipers couched the fruits of their deadly vocation in terms of a necessary evil generated by the grander scheme of war. None of the snipers in the Black Watch made soldiering a career; all had been peaceful and normally law-abiding citizens before the war who had had parts of their humanity stripped away by basic training that refashioned them to soldier, to fight and to kill. At first, the army expected it would be harder for men from urban environments, unfamiliar with the harsh life of the rural recruit. They were wrong. Basic training, later amplified by their advanced sniper course, taught them how to suppress feelings of overt remorse, compassion, sympathy and pity—treating their job as a grand game—or purged them altogether. None, of course, expected that the hunter at times could also become the hunted.

To varying degrees, each man succumbed to the process of dehumanization designed to make it easier to pull the trigger and kill another human being. They never considered (at least in the moment) the man between their sights, whose life screeched abruptly to a halt following a bullet to the brain or heart—that he was somebody's brother, father, son, friend or lover, possessing, as they did, hopes and dreams, fears and fantasies, compassion, creativity or empathy. He was "just a target" and one-dimensional. He did not possess a family or first name or even a unique identity; he was "the Hun," "the Boche," "Fritz," "Heinie" or that "Nazi bastard," and in no measure did he resemble them. In their minds, he was a beast, a murderer who had provoked killing in cold blood, which they saw as warranted, justified and ultimately forgiven. "After all," as Hook put it bluntly, "he had it coming."

The primary requirement for any of the snipers was the ability to shoot accurately. "You had to learn to group your shots," Hook recalled. "If they're spread all over the place, that means you're a rotten shot and you don't belong in the scouts." To qualify, the candidate had to hit a man's head at two hundred yards, or his torso at four hundred yards, with a grouping of five shots no wider than two and a half inches, nine times out of ten.

But it was more than pure marksmanship that made a prime scout or sniper. In addition to keen eyesight and night vision, a scout/sniper had to possess the right type of character to conduct operations of this nature. Given that the work was solitary, Hook found that the best candidates were men who liked to play alone or work in small groups, and all had "intelligence beyond the usual recruit; someone who could take the initiative, as you would be your own master in the field on many occasions."

In theory, no terrain was off-limits for a scout/sniper, and they had to be ready to endure swamps and mosquito-infested forests, shallow streams, muddy shell holes, manure piles or any location that no person in their right mind would ever enter. At times, the prevailing conditions compelled them to live an animalistic existence, forced to urinate and defecate where they lay and suffer through extremes of cold and heat, hunger and thirst. To Hook, "patience was the name of the game." They had to lie silent for hours on end, in the most uncomfortable and inhospitable hides, often surrounded and behind enemy lines. They chewed

SEVEN DAYS IN HELL

gum to tackle restlessness and popped "pep pills" (five-milligram Benzedrine tablets) or "confidence drugs" to stay awake. "We had rum or Scotch to keep us steady," Hook recalled. "We were well stocked."

To build up the platoon, Hook stayed close to home, combing his former rifle company for men he knew and could trust. One of the first he approached was Private Frank Balsis, a strapping and extremely aggressive twenty-two-year-old Lithuanian who passed his downtime in the boxing ring or reading detective novels. Quick with his fists, Balsis came as part of a package deal that also landed his sparring partner, the 2nd Canadian Division's middleweight boxing champion, Private Harold Burden.

Hook skimmed off the company's best shots, grabbing his mates Paul Welligan, Syd Ayling and Jackie Jack. Then he raided the other companies for their marksmen as well. In no time, he landed Privates Arthur Bowmaster, Bill Pugh and Bobby Williams, along with highly devout Lance Corporal Tommy Latham, whose kid brother Jim, an RCAF gunner, was killed in March over Nuremberg on his first bombing mission.

Benson found Brunner and Sharpe in C Company and later added the slight Charlie Lee, who, at just five foot one and 111 pounds, barely made the cut for the army. Small but alert and highly athletic, Lee, who had just turned twenty-two before he arrived in Normandy, was the only man in the scout platoon besides Barney Benson who spoke French fluently, and, like Brunner, became indispensable for liaison and reconnaissance.

The majority of the men recruited were in their early twenties and single, but there were exceptions. Lance Corporal Melvin Cameron was the old man of the platoon at age thirty, while Dale Sharpe was twenty-six. Private Fred Delutis, who recently celebrated his twenty-eighth birthday, arrived in Normandy just weeks after his wife and children had narrowly escaped death when a Liberator bomber en route to England from Canada crashed near their flat in the Griffintown district of Montreal, killing all aboard as well as eight of their unsuspecting neighbours on the ground.

In short order, Hook scooped up a diverse assortment of characters for the platoon—"all self-reliant, non-conformist types," as he put it. "There was no doubt; we had our loners, our free-thinkers, and men with a will of their own—all who danced to their own tune." What this collection of personalities had in common was the desire to hunt down the enemy and kill him, and either like doing so or learn to live with it. As Hook viewed it, "Sniping was not for everyone; in war, you need your heroes, but sometimes you just need your killers."

THE ONE MAN HOOK AVOIDED, DESPITE HIS IMMENSE natural talent, was his kid brother George, who proved equally deadly with a scoped .303 Lee-Enfield. Saddled unimaginatively with the derivative moniker "Young Hook," George was slightly taller and thinner, and unlike his brother boasted chiselled features. Despite their bloodline, they had an estranged relationship.

No matter what their age, the brothers never saw eye to eye, and the rancour continued throughout their time in the army. Hook was brash, severe and direct, with a penchant for self-righteousness; he was frightfully unforgiving of others for what he perceived to be their failings. In Jim's opinion, his kid brother was the epitome of what he detested: an inconsiderate loner, carefree to the point of recklessness, and always on the hustle.

One of George's redeeming features, however, and something Jim could not deny, was that he "had guts" and plenty of them, earned in the hard school of Montreal's main drag. While Hook spent his hard-earned half-dollar catching a Canadiens hockey game at the Forum or a Royals baseball game at Delorimier Downs, the collection of matchboxes the roguish-looking George hoarded testified to his cavorting in the nightclubs and pool halls that his brother scorned, and which men like Mike Brunner proved too impoverished and timid to enter.

Hook's hesitation stemmed from his belief that his brother's "guts" would translate into "fool's courage" once the fighting started. Dreading the moment their mother's heart would shatter upon learning that George had caught one in battle—a victim, no doubt, of a self-centred and impulsive misadventure—Hook had no desire to take on the weighty responsibility of policing his kid brother. To assuage any guilt, Hook protested vehemently to Benson, then to the scout platoon commander, Lieutenant Stan Duffield, and finally to the support company commander, Captain Ronnie Bennett, to have his brother sent back to his rifle company after Sergeant Tommy Garvin snapped up Young Hook for the scout platoon just before D-Day. His gripe went for naught, but after arguing that he wanted to spare his mother from a crushing "Sullivan brothers" scenario should both brothers die on the same patrol, Hook wrestled a gentlemen's agreement out of the battalion that forbade the brothers from working together in the field.

Despite Hook's misgivings, George quickly took to army life in a way few expected. After two years in uniform, he had developed an affinity for roughing it in the outdoors and genuine respect for the hard-slogging nature of life in the PBI—the poor bloody infantry. More surprising, perhaps, was his vow that when the war was over, he would leave the city and flee to some unnamed spot in northern Canada to cut his path as a fur trapper for the Hudson's Bay Company. As for what he thought about his brother's opinion of him? George really could not care less.

• • •

IMMEDIATELY UPON FORMATION, THE SCOUTS BEGAN TO tout themselves as an elite unit within the framework of the Black Watch. In their minds, they had come from the best platoon in the 1st Battalion and had siphoned off the top shots in the other companies to form an all-star squad. "As soon as they formed," recalled Corporal Gordy Donald from A Company, "they strutted around as though they'd won the bloody war!"

Bravado, hubris and arrogance were indeed par for the course, given the nature of their job, but not every Highlander who joined the platoon came with a stellar pedigree. Some company commanders proved unwilling to part with their best men and instead pawned off the ill-disciplined, the malcontented and those who, for whatever reason, did not fit into the tightly woven fabric of a frontline rifle company.

One of the first offered up was the notoriously clumsy Private Alex Duncan, plagued by a short attention span and a long series of gaffes on his record. The last straw came when he bounced a live grenade off the sill of an open window during a training exercise that not only exploded in his face but nearly exterminated his entire section. Left with nothing more than a permanent twitch in his left eye, the hapless Duncan found himself transferred to the scout platoon before his discharge from the aid station.

Another prime candidate was Private Kenneth Giviens, who matched Hook step for step as the battalion's best shot. Giviens was a star high-school running back from upstate New York who had turned down a university football scholarship to come north and join the Canadian Army before the Japanese attacked Pearl Harbor. Brimming with "piss and vinegar," as Hook put it, and most eager to get into battle, the static nature of defensive duties assigned to the Black Watch in England did not sit well with the feisty Giviens. On the same day that the orders arrived to organize the scout platoon, a field general court-martial handed the serial truant a six-month sentence to military prison for going absent without leave nearly ten times in less than two years, meaning he could not join the battalion until August at the earliest.

Not everyone Wilkinson approached had the right makeup to become a scout, however. Recalling accounts of Francis Pegahmagabow, the legendary Canadian sniper of the Great War credited with 378 kills on the Western Front, coupled with Dale Sharpe's tales of hunting with the Tyendinaga from the Napanee area, Hook decided to recruit every "Indian" he could find, expecting them to be naturals for the scout platoon.

What he found instead was Private Carmen Barnhardt, a Mohawk band member from the Six Nations Reserve in Caledonia, Ontario. Of medium size but powerfully built, the former truck driver and aspiring violin virtuoso appeared the perfect candidate, until Hook quickly discovered the hollow nature of his racially inspired assumption. Barnhardt, although highly skilled with a two-inch mortar, possessed horrible eyesight and a permanent twitch in his neck and the fingers of his right hand, the result of a childhood febrile attack that made pinpoint aiming of any rifle impossible under the best conditions. Thwarted in his effort, Hook could only lament, "He could fire a mortar and play a mean fiddle, but Hell knows he couldn't hit the broadside of a barn at ten paces."

ALTHOUGH THE SCOUT PLATOON SERVED ALONGSIDE THE mortar, pioneer, carrier and anti-tank platoons as part of the specialized support company under the command of Captain Ronnie Bennett, from its inception it developed a distinct subculture within the battalion. Part of this phenomenon had to do with its assigned role, which proved much more individualistic than life in the traditional rifle company. Working as they did in small groups, and usually at all hours of the day, the scouts were always on call, whether the battle raged or not. As a result, strict attention to discipline and deportment, two hallmarks of the Black Watch, tended to slacken to counterbalance the constant fatigue and stress. "The scouts lived a bohemian existence," remembered Gordy Donald. "They dressed differently, used different equipment, shaved their heads and played by their own rules; they even had their own cook!"

The pillars of the scouts' identity came in part with their job description, but also with their uniform and equipment, which separated them from the men in the rifle companies. The first was their much-coveted Denison smock, camouflaged with swaths of maroon, light-brown and drab paint. Initially designed for British and Canadian paratroopers, the heavy twill garment was warm and wind-resistant, and was intended to be worn over equipment to prevent interference with a parachute harness during a drop. The sniper's variant came with specialized pockets to squirrel away emergency rations, water, Benzedrine inhalers, field dressing and a morphine ampoule, folded maps, compass, sketchbook and grease pencils. The snipers also carried their stock of ammunition: fifty rounds of ordinary "ball," five of tracer and five of armour-piercing.

The tent-sized smock tended to swamp the average-sized man, but the opposite held for Dale Sharpe, whom Hook characterized as a "Big Fella—wide as a bull and strong as one too." Sharpe stood close to six feet and carried two hundred pounds of tightly packed muscle on a frame of sizable girth. Few could forget how snugly the smock fit over Sharpe's shoulders and biceps. Impressed with Sharpe's obvious brute strength, Brunner chalked him up as "a guy you would . . . follow anywhere."

The scouts also displayed a penchant for bladed weapons and carried both their standard-issue Lee-Enfield bayonets and either a commando-style Fairbairn-Sykes knife or a Nepalese Gurkha kukri, if they could get their hands on one from the black market, or win one by rolling dice or playing poker.

Their heads were cleanly shorn, against tradition in a regiment that prided itself on being clean-shaven and immaculately groomed. Unlike the famous Mohawk cuts of the American 101st Airborne Division (the Screaming Eagles), who donned them as symbols of virility and martial prowess, the Black Watch scouts did so out of pure practicality, to accommodate the mesh veil that covered their heads and faces while on patrol or in a sniper hide. The scouts pulled the veils, made of mesh spaced just wide enough to permit a view of the ground ahead while maintaining concealment, over their faces and shoulders to eliminate the sheen from their cheeks, chin and forehead and to break the sharp lines of the body to help them blend into the natural surroundings. Doubling as a battle scarf, it provided extra warmth in chilly weather and blocked out choking clouds of diesel and dust, the stench of death on the battlefield or the noxious fumes found in a heavily frequented latrine. When not in use, the scouts tucked it up under the helmet, but as Brunner and his mates soon discovered, its extra warmth necessitated that they "keep clean and cool," and so the clippers came out. These ingenious garments became the scout platoon's unofficial tribal headdress, much to the delight of Dale Sharpe, whose helmet brought on chronic, blinding migraines, and to army photographers constantly trolling for fresh story angles in a sea of olive-drab uniformity.

Their signature item, however, came with their tool of the trade, the Lee-Enfield No. 4 Mark 1 (T) sniper rifle. Primarily, this was the same rifle issued to the regular soldiers, a bolt-action, ten-shot weapon with an eight-inch spike bayonet that resembled a long nail rather than a knife. "The men liked the rifle," wrote Captain John Kemp, the second-in-command of D Company.

"They understood it, they could use it, they trusted it; it was a very good weapon, and they'd done a lot of shooting with it." Reliable, steady and extremely accurate, it was what every front-line soldier needed: a pig of a weapon able to get down and dirty and still come up firing accurately every time without jamming.

Their sniper variant was slightly different from those issued to the men in the rifle companies, however. The *T* stood for *telescopic*, which denoted that it had successfully passed a craftsman's selection process that saw it picked off the production line by a keen-eyed armourer and then sent to an expert fitter to ensure that the barrel and the specially crafted No. 32 Mark I sniper scope aligned precisely. The delicate nature of the rig made scouts overattentive, far beyond the average infantryman's love for his weapon, and their relationship bordered on the obsessive. "When you weren't sniping," recalled Bill Pugh, "you protected your weapon because they were a little class above the average rifle. The scope received special care, and you carried your scope inside a bag inside your smock . . . Nothing was going to damage that."[4]

What the scouts loved the most about the Lee-Enfield was its bolt action, which ran fast and smooth and permitted reloading in a split second without the shooter needing to move off his sights until the stripper clips emptied. Equipped with a specially mounted wooden cheek rest that increased accuracy, the rifle provided the ability to rapidly engage multiple targets, allowing the scouts to fire faster and more precisely than their German counterparts, an advantage that at many times would prove the difference between victory and defeat, life and death.

STAN DUFFIELD, A BRITISH-BORN LIEUTENANT WHO HAD transferred into the battalion from the Victoria Rifles in 1942, took the reins of the scout platoon upon its inception. A highly skilled rifle platoon commander and tactician, Duffield had recently guided his platoon, which included Hook, Benson and Garvin, to victory in a division-wide battle drill competition where his prize for beating over one hundred competitors took the form of his appointment to command the fledgling unit.

Duffield, whom others begrudgingly respected for his immense tactical prowess, was a twenty-three-year-old bank teller with an aloof personality that did not blend well with his platoon of free spirits.[5] The men viewed him as a "cold fish" and a bit of a snob, and suspected that their overly ambitious lieutenant, who seemed to have taken his appointment as a demotion, already had one foot out the door, aiming for a return to a rifle company at a moment's notice. As a result, the men gravitated more than usual towards their platoon sergeant, Barney Benson, who, having shared the same struggles as they had growing up on the north side of Montreal's strip, was very much "one of them." In short order, the "popular and prominent" NCO had achieved such a tight grip on the men that most in the battalion, including the officers, referred to the platoon simply as "Benson and his scouts."[6]

Benson had left school as a young teenager, after his mother died, to provide for his family. Bouncing from one dead-end job to another, he landed work as an apprentice machinist in the fall of 1939, but within months his "sense of duty" led him to join the Black Watch. Over the next two years, he progressed steadily up the ranks, training first as a wireless operator and then developing his expertise with land mines as part of the pioneer platoon under Lieutenant George "Booby Trap" Buch.[7] Unlike his men, however, Benson had no formal training in scouting or sniping, but that was not his primary job. He brought an abundance of pure leadership that provided the glue for the nascent unit.

Traditionally, company sergeants major and platoon sergeants, the linchpins of the battalion who bridged the gap between officers and men and ensured that discipline, deportment and orders were carried out to the fullest, tended to be a stern and sarcastic lot. Each presented a godlike figure for their men, and many chose to employ fear as their motivator of choice: fear of them, fear of regiment and fear of God—and usually in that order. Benson, on the other hand, took a different route. Unlike his tightly wound brethren who would scold and growl, the scout platoon sergeant was unusually soft-spoken and possessed an almost comedically high-pitched voice. "Benson, I liked right away," Brunner related. "He was relaxed and always ready to laugh. He was a lot of fun."

Anything but traditional, the scout platoon sergeant nonetheless garnered respect from his peers and the scouts for his calm and steady approach. "You always do things for somebody you like better than somebody you don't like," one scout remembered. With little need to throw his weight around, his "suggestions" and "requests," usually delivered with a customary wink and a laugh, the scouts instantly took for orders.

Benson stood five feet, nine inches, but with two hundred pounds of muscle draped over his stocky frame, the men found him as intimidating as he was nice. Like all good combat leaders, he had an abundance of talent and courage and knew his job well. But he also had a dark side. The scouts soon learned never to do anything that would wipe the grin off his face or diminish the glint of laughter in his eye. According to Hook, Benson had "a switch" that, when flipped, would see him turn ice-cold. "He just got this look," Hook recalled. "His eyes darkened when they fixed on his target, and you knew he meant business."

This dichotomy did not diminish him in the eyes of his men; rather, it served to inspire, and as one scout later recalled, "Anybody would do anything for Barney Benson." Indeed, this group of young men, tasked to carry out a highly specialized and deadly trade, required the right type of leader: one who acted more like a big brother, father or trusted uncle rather than a despotic platoon sergeant. They got that in spades with Benson.

THE HEART OF LIEUTENANT COLONEL STUART STEPHEN Tuffnell Cantlie's battalion lay in its four rifle companies (designated A, B, C and D), each of them 120 strong, that would do the battalion's heavy lifting—the fighting. Each, commanded by a major with a captain as his second-in-command, was subdivided into three rifle platoons of thirty-six men, led by a lieutenant.

On the eve of embarkation for France, Cantlie assured the regimental elders he had found "good officers" and "red-blooded men" to take the battalion into combat. By all indications, after years of sifting and weeding, his company commanders were the pick of the litter, all extremely talented and highly trained—destined, it appeared, for greatness.

The best of this stellar lot was Major Eric Motzfeldt, who commanded C Company. Tall and fair-haired, the extremely charismatic "Great Dane," as both his fellow officers and men called him, had immigrated to Canada from Denmark in 1929 to open a thriving brokerage firm in downtown Montreal. Having learned of the Black Watch through the widely publicized exploits of Lieutenant Thomas Dinesen, a fellow Dane who earned the Victoria Cross with the 42nd Battalion in World War I, and later through the Scottish heritage of his wife, Louise Drynan Fraser, he joined the regiment in 1940 at the age of thirty-three.[8] A mature and steadying type, Motzfeldt spoke Danish, Norwegian, English and Swedish fluently and had more than a working knowledge of French and German. A qualified sniper instructor, he trained many of the Black Watch snipers in their basic course and had served as the battalion's intelligence officer before assuming command of his company in 1943.⁹ Revered for his tactical acumen and stern leadership, he doubled as Cantlie's trusted advisor, or "battle adjutant." The Black Watch CO seldom made a move without his consultation.

Like Motzfeldt, Majors Alan Stevenson (B Company) and George "Pudge" Fraser (D Company) were both older and mature types and supremely talented. Each had spent time as course instructors or commanders at a multitude of Canadian and British army training establishments and battle schools.¹⁰ Like Motzfeldt, they knew their stuff.

The A Company commander, Major Phillip Griffin, was something of a phenom within the Black Watch. Just twenty-six, he was a decade younger than his fellow company commanders. Listed at a touch under five feet, eight inches and 140 pounds, Griffin, known privately amongst his family as the "Little Major," was wiry and highly athletic and always managed, no matter the circumstance, to look as though he had just come off parade. With glowing white teeth that contrasted sharply with his deeply tanned face, his penchant for aviator sunglasses and whipping around the English countryside with Ronnie Bennett on a pair of Norton motorbikes, he appeared the "typical college boy," as Bruce Ducat related, "but Jesus, he was tough as nails."

A thoroughly gifted company commander, Griffin inspired confidence in everyone around him and enjoyed an unparalleled run of professional success and a meteoric rise through the officer ranks. By the time he reached Normandy, he found himself on the fast track for a battalion command.¹¹

Stern, exacting and demanding, Griffin was self-assured about his professional abilities, but on a personal level he was shy and reserved, which many mistook for conceit and pretentiousness. As Captain John Kemp, who served with Griffin for four years, noted, "Phil was excellent . . . absolutely first class (and) a terribly interesting, slightly introspective individual. I admired him hugely (but) I can't say I ever knew him very well."[12] Indeed, with the exception of Motzfeldt, his brother Shirley, who served as Cantlie's intelligence officer, and Ronnie Bennett, very few penetrated his tightly affixed mask of command.[13]

Although from the same vintage, the support company commander, Captain Ronnie Bennett, was like Pudge Fraser and Stevenson: a "mature type" who, according to his superiors, was "keen, capable and efficient" and possessed "brains." Over his years of training, he had proved himself thoroughly "reliable and steady" and was considered by all to be an "excellent officer."[14]

Like Cantlie, Bennett came from the elite of Canadian society, where family obligations, expectations and duty meshed seamlessly with the ethos of the regiment. The nephew of Viscount R.B. Bennett, Canada's eleventh prime minister, Ronnie had moved from the family estate in Sackville, Nova Scotia, as a young teen (followed by his kid brother Harrison) into the hallowed halls of Bishop's College School (BCS), an exclusive educational institution in the lush Eastern Townships outside Montreal. He went on to McGill University to complete a degree in political science and economics, pledging (like many Black Watch officers) the Alpha Psi chapter of the Zeta Psi fraternity, whose alums included Henry Ford, Percival Molson, Victoria Cross recipient Fred Fisher and Dr. John McCrae, who penned the eternal "In Flanders Fields."[15]

Unlike the men under his command, Bennett (and his fellow officers) did not have to forgo his education to help his family survive; little had changed in the social sense for the upper echelons of Canadian society. College courses, fraternity gatherings and drinks at the posh Berkeley Hotel before a McGill–Queen's grudge match on the gridiron all continued unabated, as did summer vacations at exclusive Métis Beach and escorting the city's most eligible debutantes to the St. Andrew's Ball each fall.

35

Following his time at McGill University, Bennett attended law school at Osgoode Hall in Toronto and articled with McCarthy and McCarthy, the country's leading law firm.[16] When war broke out, he followed in his brother's footsteps and joined the Black Watch in the spring of 1940, and within a few weeks he had shipped out to England—but not before marrying Dorothy Janet Dobell, a descendant of politician and business magnate R. Reid Dobell. Their spring wedding was the toast of the country's society pages.[17]

The Bennetts' connection to the Black Watch started as teenagers, during their tenure at BCS. Although not a military academy, the boarding school—founded in 1836, more than thirty years before Confederation—had a long and storied military tradition. By the time the Second World War rolled around, nearly a thousand BCS "old boys" had gone off to war, including former 1st Canadian Army commander General Andrew McNaughton; Lieutenant General Ken Stuart, the Canadian chief of the general staff; Brigadier Bob Moncel, who at the age of twenty-seven was the youngest to hold that rank in the Canadian Army; and Major Sydney "Rad" Radley-Walters, who had become Canada's leading tank ace in Normandy.

On its centenary in 1936, the BCS cadet corps officially allied with the Black Watch to work as a feeder for the regiment's officer corps.[18] By the time the 1st Battalion arrived off the shores of Juno Beach, a sizable portion of its officers had been groomed by BCS and now held key appointments within Cantlie's battalion.

In addition to Bennett, who controlled the scout, pioneer, anti-tank, carrier and mortar platoons in his support company, Lieutenant George Buch commanded the pioneer; Captain John Kemp was the second-in-command in D Company; and Captain Campbell Stuart worked as Cantlie's battalion adjutant. Lieutenant Alan Robinson, a star cricket player, was Griffin's most trusted platoon commander in A Company, while the renowned artist

George MacKay, who had resigned his commission early in the war to ensure that he saw action, served as a lance corporal and platoon mate of Corporal Bruce Ducat in Stevenson's B Company. Even Captain Bill Doheny, Brigadier William J. Megill's intelligence officer, called himself a BCS old boy.[19]

The central force in their upbringing during these most formative years was their headmaster, the highly prominent and influential Major Crawford Grier. A former artillery officer in the Great War who not only ran the school but commanded all army cadets in Canada and was active in the Boy Scouts, Grier was known as a "builder of men."[20] Gruff and steadfast, loved and hated, "the Bear," as the boys called him, was a firebrand who was not reluctant to take his feelings about the sluggish Canadian war effort public.[21] On Thanksgiving Day 1941, he publicly condemned the King government's failure to pull out all the stops in the present war, arguing for conscription before it was too late. Likening the current climate in Canada to that found in Abel Gance's film masterpiece *J'accuse,* where the current generation had failed to live up to the sacrifices of the Lost Generation in the trenches, he chastised politicians and citizens alike for their lack of urgency and proportionate response to Hitler, tyranny and fascism.

Wounded at the Somme, Vimy Ridge and Passchendaele, Grier was the very personification of duty, courage and sacrifice, and he wielded immense influence and power while shaping his pupils. Although few could argue with the altruistic nature of his "prod to the Canadian conscience," his methodology was rooted in his experiences on the battlefield in the Great War, where sacrifice formed the foundation of honour, something he expected his boys to achieve and, more importantly, maintain.[22]

No student could forget the symbolism on display throughout the school. In the junior library, a portrait of BCS old boy Wyatt Rawson greeted the teens—bare-headed, sword drawn, mortally wounded, gallantly piloting the Highland Brigade forward in the face of withering fire and certain death at Tel-el-Kebir in Egypt in 1882. As former pupil Bob Moncel, who would serve as the operations officer of the 2nd Canadian Corps in Normandy, stated, "We feel he is one of us, and that represents the true BCS spirit."[23]

Any trembling pupil who dared enter the Bear's office came face to face with yet another emblematic portrait. Over his desk hovered a painting of sixteen-year-old Jack Travers Cornwell; it encapsulated the BCS spirit and provided the context for any subsequent discussion within the chamber. A former Boy Scout, "Jutland Jack" was forever ensconced in naval lore as the third-youngest recipient of the Victoria Cross, which had been awarded to him posthumously for remaining at his gun on HMS *Chester* during the Battle of Jutland in 1916, despite intense enemy fire that resulted in mortal wounds that eventually took his life.[24]

In retrospect, George Buch lamented, "We never stood a chance, really. We knew what was expected of us," and as it did for family and regiment, "honour came in the shape of duty, obedience and sacrifice, and that was it."

FOLLOWING CLOSE BEHIND A LONE PIPER BELTING OUT "Australian Ladies," the 1st Battalion of the Black Watch, led by the scout platoon, made a dry landing on Juno Beach, marking the first time since the guns fell silent on November 11, 1918, that the regiment had a full battalion in a combat zone. Behind the scouts and the wailing pipes came the four rifle companies and the support company that formed the 1st Battalion, shaking out for their march towards their bivouac area before heading south towards Carpiquet airfield, a former Luftwaffe base outside Caen whose capture the BBC had announced earlier that morning.

To Hook Wilkinson, life on Juno Beach resembled "organized chaos," as "if somebody was trying to stir up a riot. Nobody appeared to know what they were doing." Everywhere, trucks and jeeps teeming with ammunition, petrol and supplies jockeyed for position with Bren gun carriers towing anti-tank guns, while engineers, hard at work to remove the debris of war, strove to fix temporary bridges, clear barbed wire and lift land mines and booby traps from the sand and scores of abandoned German bunkers. The Black Watch cleared the dunes faster than expected, and as Hook put it, "army normalcy" suddenly returned.

The fields to either side of their line of march seemed to be in use for miles, crowded as they were with tented hospitals, camouflaged ammunition and petrol dumps, repair parks for half-cannibalized vehicles and emergency landing strips for the air force. Signposts adorned with skulls and crossbones and scrawled with "Achtung Minen" appeared almost every half mile or so. The Germans had carefully sown the route with anti-personnel Schu mines, nasty "Bouncing Bettys" and powerful anti-tank Teller mines, designed to castrate or obliterate any intruder.

The thin, claustrophobic road, lined with the traditional Norman hedgerows and dotted at intervals with burly provosts directing the flood of traffic moving towards the front, quickly gave way to the fertile, lush and windswept fields beyond the beach. Here, orchards of stunted apple and pear trees intermingled with patches of wheat that, having gone unharvested, stood shoulder high, rustling in the saltwater breeze. This serene portrait transported Private Jimmy Bennett, a nineteen-year-old rifleman in C Company, marching behind the scouts. He reminisced about more peaceful times on the family farm that sat a few "country miles" outside Melville, Saskatchewan, on Canada's equally lush and windswept prairies.

Bennett, a high-strung twenty-two-year-old inflicted with chronic anxiety, noted the great paths torn into the wheat by

tanks, guns and infantry that resembled those slashed by trac-
tor and scythe at home. Periodically, the ground appeared torn
and pockmarked by shell and bomb craters, littered with slit
trenches and indistinct debris. Rabbits, attempting to find new
burrows amid the hollowed pastures, ran wildly about, spur-
ring memories for Bennett of chasing gophers with his ten siblings in tow. He slipped into a welcomed and calming stream of
thought. Enthralled by military history—particularly the works
of Will Bird, who served with the Black Watch in the trenches
on the Western Front—Bennett envisioned himself now walking
alongside his own ghosts with warm hands, hoping that someday
people would learn about his adventures with an equal sense of
foreboding, empathy and awe.

Then they came upon fields laced with the dead, almost all
German, who remained unburied. Bloated in the sweltering July
heat, the corpses jittered with maggots busy scouring flesh and
marrow while dark clouds of flies gathered above, searching for
sanctuary. Beyond them, newly dug graves for Canadian soldiers
lay in a checkerboard pattern of small dirt mounds with bone-
coloured crosses affixed to each, crudely marked with name,
rank, service number, regiment and date of death. "You hadn't
gone very far when you ran into a bunch of temporary graves
from the North Nova Scotia Highlanders," remembered Gordy
Donald, marching with A Company. "It was very upsetting to see
the number of people killed on the beach."

The only interruption in the pace of the Black Watch trek
came when a dispatch rider on a Norton motorbike weaved
through, or a jeep ambulance, stacked with a quartet of supine
patients, parted their lines in a bid to make the evacuation centre
on Juno Beach.

Occasionally, a thin trickle of civilian traffic plodded by: an
old woman on a bicycle, a farm labourer pushing a cart and a

team of horses harnessed to a plow, all attempting to maintain the rhythm and semblance of normality while the battle raged. Some villages they passed seemed barely touched by the war; others were grey and grim, with only rubble to attest to their existence, prematurely stomped out by speculative artillery stonks or air strikes conducted for the vilest of reasons: expediency.

Periodically, pockets of dead cattle and horses littered the fields, most on their backs, bloated and rigid, legs pointing to the sky, each besieged like their human counterparts by maggots and flies. For Bennett, neither the freshly marked graves of his Canadian brothers in arms nor the decomposing corpses of the enemy dead matched this obscenity. Dead humans Bennett could rationalize, for humans are deterministic, capable of making decisions that influence or shape their fate to varying degrees. But these poor, innocent beasts took no part in the quarrel and did not deserve to share man's fate. Horseback riding had always been Bennett's escape from the daily grind on the farm. Now, however, the sight of their faces, teeth bared, wild-eyed and frozen in fear, etched a permanent scar on his psyche. With all vestiges of his romantic interlude quashed, Bennett started to reel as his anxiety blossomed and the encroaching reality and suffocating indignity of war unleashed a series of rapid-fire questions akin to a condemned prisoner: What's happening here? Am I dreaming or is this the truth? How am I going to get out of this mess? Only the sudden and merciful approach of desperate locals diverted his attention from the refrain constantly beating in his head.

In a bid for psychological self-preservation, Bennett shifted his focus to the predicament of the French. "How in Heaven's name," he wondered, "would the locals get back to a reasonable semblance of life when the fighting was done?" Everywhere he looked, civilians worked feverishly to corral scattered livestock, repair shattered roofs and walls of their homes or mend torn fences. Some farmers, saddled now with excess meat from cattle cut down by artillery, streamed forward to hawk their excess meat before it turned.

At one point, a coven of elderly women approached the men in D Company, offering a purple, rock-hard substance purported to be candy. Sergeant MacGregor "Mac" Roulston, fearful that the gift might contain poison, ordered his men to decline the offer, but not before they had issued their sweets to a collection of grimy schoolchildren who supplanted the British idiom "Any gum, chum?" with a bastardized "Avez-vous de gum, chum?"[25]

Although Roulston expected the wild revelry of liberation that greeted the 3rd Canadian Division troops in the days following D-Day, the French civilians the Black Watch encountered remained restrained and noncommittal. A month into the invasion, the pace of the Allied offensive had slackened, and with it came the spectre of stalemate, which stoked fears among the French that Nazi reprisals would be swift and furious should the Germans wrestle the Allies to a standstill or push the invaders back into the sea. But fear of the Germans was not the only thing that muted the French in this region of Normandy. Some civilians harboured a quiet contempt for the Allies due to the destruction wrought by their pre-invasion bombing raids, and now their incessant artillery fire. Although the local population longed for freedom from their occupiers, they preferred that some other spot in the country have the honour of sacrificing homes, families and friends for the glory of Allied victory and French liberation.

The scout platoon crossed paths with another batch of prisoners of war marching under armed guard, making for the enclosures on the beach as they neared the bivouac point. To Hook Wilkinson, his first glimpse of Nazi prisoners left him with the impression that a whole generation of German manhood had gone missing. The "rabble on display" included only the very young or the very old, with most over forty or under eighteen, and as Hook related, "some looked much younger as most couldn't even shave."

Brunner, eavesdropping on snippets of their conversations, chuckled at the wild speculation concerning their impending fate. Many wondered if they'd end up in England, Scotland or the United States, while others, seeing the Canadians march past, feared they would end up in the Siberia-like "gulag" system in northern Canada that Nazi propaganda had invented and taught them to dread.

The other thing that surprised Brunner was just how few of these men spoke proper German, as a sizable portion hailed from the conquered regions of eastern Europe and Russia. These *Ostfront* soldiers, men captured by the Nazis who then either volunteered or were pressed into battle, all wore Wehrmacht uniforms but spoke regional dialects endemic to Poland, Hungary, Romania, Poland, Czechoslovakia, Yugoslavia or the Baltic states. At one point, Hook noticed a small group of Mongolians and Koreans whom the less-than-worldly men around him collectively referred to as "Japs." All of them, in Hook's assessment, "were weedy specimens," evidence no doubt that Hitler had failed in his crusade to produce anything close to his vaunted "master race." Then the Hitler Youth prisoners appeared.

Striding past the Black Watch columns, these tall, blond, sinewy teenagers, who had survived the nasty fighting for the battered and blackened Carpiquet airfield outside Caen, wore the distinctive pea-dot camouflage smocks with *Hitlerjugend* embroidered on their cuffs. Members of the fanatical 12th SS Panzer Division, each of these teenagers remained thoroughly committed to Nazi doctrine despite their recent defeat and impending incarceration.

Mere infants when Hitler took power in 1932, they grew up fully immersed in Nazi racial ideology and the bravado of Hitler's triumphs, and above all, they oozed a genocidal self-righteousness that manifested itself in the murder of nearly two hundred Canadian and British prisoners in the days immediately following the invasion.[26] As one war correspondent later opined, "They were poured into that mould at the age of six and removed from it as perfect Nazis when they were sixteen. As the finest flower of the Hitlerian experimentation, much superior to the non-conditioned Nazis, their cold, cruel mind does not recognize the difference between war and murder."[27] Led by hard-bitten veteran officers and NCOs transferred from the 1st SS Leibstandarte Division (Hitler's bodyguard) fresh from the Russian front, where laws of war had no place and execution of prisoners was commonplace, their adolescent fanaticism meshed readily with their mentor's murderous intent.

Captain John Taylor, second-in-command of D Company, informed the regimental elders that "we take bloody good care never to be on the receiving end of their treachery," for "unlike the Hun" of the Great War, these "are a fanatical, sneaky, sulky bunch of bastards" who "knew every dirty trick and used them all."[28]

This resilience, outright defiance and refusal to yield, which these child prisoners maintained despite their precarious predicament, left a lasting impression on the men. Bound for captivity and forced re-education, the young Highlanders bombarded the SS prisoners with a steady volley of insults that grew in bandwagon measure. Rude hand gestures that promised the insertion of rusty objects into sensitive areas gave way to broadsides of mucus-laden spit, followed by verbal and gesticular assurances that they would be carnally entertaining their mothers and sisters in the Fatherland before long. This torrent of invective, delivered with buckshot precision, hit a fever pitch until one surly SS teenager shot back—in perfect English with an all-too-confident smirk—"Don't worry, we'll get you next time." The stunning retort quieted the mob instantly, leaving Hook Wilkinson to wonder, "Christ! What did he mean by 'next time'?"

THE BLACK WATCH REACHED ITS BIVOUAC AREA IN ONE of the hundreds of nondescript farmer's fields not far behind Juno Beach on the morning of July 7. The four rifle companies, made up of three platoons of thirty-six men each, hunkered down as they traditionally wound in a box formation with battalion head-quarters in the middle of the pack. As per routine, Lieutenant Colonel S.S.T. Cantlie ordered Captain Ronnie Bennett to parcel out the elements of his support company throughout the pos-ition, with sniper teams and guns from the anti-tank platoon dug in on either flank, and his mortar and carrier platoon in the cen-tre near battalion headquarters.

Unlike in England, where digging in lacked a sense of urgency, the aerial show overhead, the battle-scarred land, the constant rumble of artillery fire and the freshly dug graves made the exer-cise self-evident for most.

For the infantryman, the safest place on earth was in the ground with his slit trench, which served as his home away from home and his fortress where, as Gordy Donald described, "we ate, slept, shaved, fought, and sometimes died." Although most men shared a slit with one standing guard while the other slept in two-hour bursts, many preferred to go it alone.

Within minutes of their arrival, the men had set about excav-ating the ground, building up the foundation and tilling the bot-tom to absorb rainwater or, in an emergency, an enemy grenade. Scrounging the nearby ruins, they pillaged wood planks or straw to use as flooring or impromptu bedding and corrugated steel or an old door for a roof. Covered with shovelfuls of dirt, it not only provided concealment but offered extra protection from airborne bursts of red-hot shrapnel.

The holes were dug no more than shoulder-width and body-length. The men drilled down as far as time and the terrain would allow. "We wanted our slits as deep and tight as possible," Hook recalled, for it "cut down the odds of being hit." Although at times lonely, cold and wet, with vile dampness that penetrated to the marrow, they proved "snug and as comforting as the womb when the shelling started," Gordy Donald recounted. "As the men had learned in training, only a direct hit would knock it out, and this was never a function of location but rather, fate or luck."

Digging into the Normandy dirt, however, did not prove easy; the sweltering heat and alternating bouts of torrential rain left anything below the soft topsoil akin to Roman concrete. Bruce "Duke" Ducat, the diminutive, straight-talking corporal from B Company and self-proclaimed "lazy bastard," took the easy route and employed a nearby drainage ditch as a ready-made slit. Smug and secure in his choice, he drew his rain cape across his body and drifted off, finally getting some sleep after nearly forty-eight hours on the move. A few hours later, Ducat awoke in horror to find "rats running over him" and that mosquitoes had taken liberties with his face and hands. Fighting off the rodents with the butt of his Sten gun, he discovered that his cheeks, his forehead and the backs of his hands were swollen and riddled with insect bites. At a loss for what attracted the squirming horde that now came at him in waves, Ducat discovered a long-forgotten chocolate bar in the pouch of his webbing and tossed it the length of the ditch, unleashing squeals of delight as the vermin descended upon their prey and devoured it whole. From then on, Ducat always dug in.

As expected, men who had never faced combat before were a bit jumpy on the first night in the beachhead, and they needed time to acclimatize to their surroundings, a process the army called "inoculation." Few men other than Ducat slept the first night, as even in the quietest moments their battlefield remained awash in eerie white noise punctuated on occasion by a distant shot or explosion, the bark of a dog or a lone rooster crowing. At daybreak, the skies cleared and the sun streaked in over the city of Caen, twelve miles to the southeast. Then the bombers came.

For nearly half a millennium, the cultural, political, financial and spiritual capital of western Normandy had remained unmolested following its sacking by a marauding English army under King Edward III in the fourteenth century. In peacetime, the eleventh-century home of William the Conqueror housed nearly 60,000 civilians, but after a series of air raids that started on D-Day, coupled with the approach of the ground fighting, only 25,000 intrepid citizens remained in and around the environs by early July.[29] Late on the evening of July 7, another British force arrived, this time to plunder from above as the dramatic and lethal overture in the latest Allied bid to capture the city.

Three miles to the northwest, Mike Brunner and Dale Sharpe emerged from soggy slit trenches just before 2200 hours, summoned by a drone that resembled a thunderstorm but whose rhythm was all man-made. A series of Pathfinder aircraft buzzed overhead at top speed, dropping green flares to mark the target area for a swarm of black dots that followed. Slowly, these transformed into the silhouette of aircraft, revealing a force of 467 heavy bombers (Lancaster and Halifax types) from RAF Bomber Command, strung out in an elongated stream, soaring on a course for Caen.

The appearance of these aircraft, customarily employed to eradicate German cities, over the bridgehead marked a new, experimental role for these heavy bombers: carpet bombing of enemy positions to aid the advance of the ground troops.

Designed with the massive artillery barrages of the Great War in mind, the scheme called for the annihilation of the Wehrmacht, Luftwaffe and SS positions that Allied intelligence suspected lay in the fields on and around the northern outskirts of the town.

The plan, which looked most plausible on the map, required the bombers to lay down a tightly boxed blanket (or carpet) of high-explosive and fragmentation bombs, some with delayed fuses designed to explode hours later, on the German main line of resistance (*Hauptkampflinie*) north of Caen. Joined soon after by the fire from hundreds of artillery pieces and the sixteen-inch naval guns of HMS *Rodney*, they designed this impressive collection of firepower to blind, bewilder and obliterate the defender while at the same time bolstering the killer instinct and sagging morale of the veteran British and Canadian forces that had fought continuously since D-Day. At least on the latter point, the plan succeeded: their timely arrival transformed the atmosphere instantly from static to electric.

As Hook Wilkinson noted, "Not a single enemy fighter rose up to meet the Armada." Only anxious squirts of tracer fire from German anti-aircraft guns lining the outer ring of Caen offered a feeble challenge, which accounted for only one bomber. From the ground, Hook could see the unlucky victim dropped from the pack, engines sputtering and belching smoke while its pilot fought with the controls to level out the craft that twisted directly over their heads. Somehow the enterprising captain regained stability, forcing it to climb before it turned towards the English Channel. An explosion in the starboard engine sealed its fate, and the Lancaster plunged into the sea and exploded on impact, but not before the crew had bailed out, descending safely just behind Juno Beach.

There is nothing that excites the soldier buried deep in a man's soul than when he witnesses the unbridled power of his side dishing it out to the enemy with overwhelming and almost apocalyptic force. When the descending ordnance first came into sight, Jimmy Bennett stood transfixed, eagerly anticipating the first eruption. When the convulsive impact of the first bombs sent violent plumes of dust, dirt and debris skyward in jagged yellow, grey and black plumes as the carpet unfolded, the men around him burst in wild revelry, which unleashed a rush of adrenalin in the young private from the prairies. The sound waves from the eruptions took almost a second to reach Bennett, compressing his sternum and rendering his bowels uncomfortably weak. In the rush of excitement, the men around him cheered and shouted as the aircraft flew overhead, waving their helmets or balmorals in a show of support and gratitude while one young officer, whom Bennett did not know, eagerly cheered the fate of the German defenders with a schoolboy's glee: "They're not liberating—they're liquidating!"

When the dust clouds dissipated before the second wave arrived, the mood changed swiftly from the sanguine to the horrified. Something had gone horribly wrong. Instead of the air strike hitting German lines north of Caen, they followed the Pathfinder's flares as they drifted to the east of their intended mark and now flickered directly over the city itself. Seconds later, the bombers began delivering their deadly payloads directly into the centre of the old city in a most dreadful case of targeting error.

The disaster that unfolded before his eyes thrust Bennett into a moral paradox, forcing him to reconcile his initial blood lust with the unmitigated horror unleashed inadvertently upon the civilian population. Abruptly, his new-found sense of pride, power and fledgling confidence vanished amidst the conundrum that few convincingly reconciled as the "price of victory"; in just forty minutes, two-thirds of the thousand-year-old city lay in ruins, and speculation moved to the likely number of French civilians who undoubtedly perished in the maelstrom: Hundreds? Thousands? Tens of thousands? It was anyone's agonizing guess, but the sudden change in fortune left Jimmy Bennett crestfallen and sickened. "That was unnecessary," he told himself, reflecting on the repugnant utterance of the young officer. "It sure wasn't liberating . . . it was liquidating. That's exactly what it was."

2

ALBATROSS

The Esprit de Corps one finds in a regiment is built up and kept alive by the feeling that the members of it are part of an organization that has a background in history that such members can be proud of and look up to. This instills a feeling in the members that they must not let the Regiment down or do anything that will sully its good name.

—Colonel Paul P. Hutchison,
Regimental Commandant, the Black Watch, 1944

WITH PIPE IN HAND AND HIS LEATHER BINOCULAR case dangling above his Sam Brown belt, his balmoral fluttering in the breeze, Lieutenant Colonel Stuart Stephen Tuffnell Cantlie cut a striking figure most befitting a Black Watch commanding officer. Tall and slender with thick brown hair, hazel eyes and exquisitely groomed moustache, he possessed the self-confidence and arrogance to match his supreme talent, silver-screen looks and Errol Flynn panache. "There was no doubt that Cantlie was a first-class prick," Corporal Bruce Ducat explained, "and thank God for that!"

Known to the men as "SST," "The Colonel" or "The Boss," and privately among more senior officers as Stew, Cantlie was a youthful thirty-six, despite being an "old Black Watcher" well into his nineteenth year of service with the regiment. Dutifully responding to family tradition, SST began his military career as a teenage cadet and followed his father (class of 1893) and older cousin Stephen Cantlie (class of 1925) into the Royal Military College in Kingston, Ontario, where he earned the prestigious Sword of Honour for outstanding conduct and discipline upon graduating in 1929. Viewed by his group of exceedingly impressive peers as a "leader of men . . . chosen to guide the destinies of this class," Cantlie was every bit an upper-class "man's man" for his time. Intelligent, courageous in thought and action, he came from the mould of the classic officer and gentleman who remained persuasive and tactful but ready to settle any dispute in the boxing ring, where, as the RMC yearbook quintessentially chimed, "many a man felt the full force of his argument."[1]

Instead of taking up a post in the tiny permanent force of the Canadian Army, Cantlie chose to return to the Black Watch upon graduation, viewing it as his destiny to one day take command—something expected of a Cantlie. His sense of legacy, tradition and noblesse oblige was rooted in his wealthy Scottish ancestry and upbringing in Montreal's Golden Square Mile. The family name was equally synonymous with the regiment and with the elites of Canadian industry, finance and politics; his clan included Lord Mount Stephen, Lord Strathcona and Richard B. Angus, all past presidents of the Bank of Montreal, co-founders of the Canadian Pacific Railway and driving forces in Canadian Confederation.

His uncle George Cantlie, the "father" of the regiment and its current honorary colonel, who presided over the regimental elders in Montreal, had raised the legendary 42nd Battalion and led them to fame in the trenches during the Great War. His son Stephen, who graduated from RMC four years before SST, took command of the 1st Battalion in 1942, but a year later was relieved of duties and sent home in disgrace, crushed by the immense pressure to equal, if not surpass, the regiment's Great War performance and add to its stellar legacy.[2]

Convinced that family pedigree and regimental nepotism, rather than talent, played a large part in Stephen Cantlie's rise and fall, Canadian Army High Command pushed for an outsider (or "stranger," as the Black Watch elders called them) with no regimental entanglements to whip the 1st Battalion back into fighting shape. Few in the Black Watch took this seriously at first, until Brigade produced a candidate; in record time, regimental ranks closed, favours were asked and granted in Masonic fashion, and SST got the nod.

Unlike his cousin, Stew Cantlie possessed a wealth of passion, energy and drive, and more importantly, the supreme confidence needed to take the helm of a unit whose elders kept a keen eye on their prized commodity through a regimental mafia interlaced within the Canadian defence establishment.[3]

Few could argue with his appointment; High Command got the strict disciplinarian it demanded, while the regiment maintained tradition and ensured that a stranger would never take the reins of a Black Watch battalion.

Upon learning of his appointment in the spring of 1943, SST could not contain his delight, despite his cousin's misery. "This unit has always been my first love," he crowed to the regimental commandant. "I have 18 years of service in it now—and to be picked to return to command it was a tremendous triumph to me."[4]

When Cantlie arrived to take the reins, he discovered just how "stale" the unit had become and could sense the "feeling of general tiredness." Confiding his thoughts in a letter home to the regimental commandant, he characterized the situation as "a sad affair" and a classic example "of a unit living on its past glories and efficiency." In his mind, the remedy came with reinvesting in their legacy so that the regiment could "once more take its rightful place" within the division—"or else," he warned, "it will pass into discard."[5]

The Black Watch had emerged from the blood and the mud of the trenches on the Western Front as the undisputed stars of the Canadian Expeditionary Force. In just three years, the regiment had raised an unprecedented three battalions (13th, 42nd and 73rd) that sent 12,000 men off to war. Collectively, they garnered the most battle honours (twenty-six) and individual decorations (over eight hundred, including six Victoria Crosses for valour) in the Canadian Corps. More importantly, the Black Watch developed an unimpeachable reputation for courage, obedience and dependability on the field of battle.

Their exploits, trumpeted at full volume by anyone associated with the regiment, soon became the stuff of legend. In regimental lore, the Black Watch had stood tall during the first large-scale use of poison gas at the Second Battle of Ypres in 1915, suffered through the slaughter on the Somme in 1916, stood atop Vimy Ridge and Hill 70 in 1917, and then endured the butchery of Passchendaele that fall. In the summer of 1918, they broke the German line at Amiens, ushering in the "last hundred days," and crowned this with the capture of Mons on November 11, 1918, the day the guns fell silent.

Culturally, the common denominator in these actions, drummed into every Black Watch officer, came down to navigating the slippery concepts of honour, shame and sacrifice. In this case, it meant all members of the regiment had to maintain regimental and personal honour and avoid shame at all costs, usually through the "ecstasy of sacrifice"—men's lives were redeemable in return for success on the battlefield.

In the Great War, three-quarters of the 12,000 men who donned the red hackle paid in numerous ways for that formula. Of these, 2,163 died for king, country and regiment, while many more, like Old Man Wilkinson, came home with unhealed scars that they proudly wore as thorny crowns to justify and mute their suffering long after hostilities ended.[6]

But the battlefield on which Cantlie's battalion would fight had transformed over the last generation, and so had the understanding of sacrifice. Gone, for the most part, were the days of continuous, linear and static trench lines and the straightforward "infantry bash" that dominated the Western Front. The battalion commander of 1944 would face a far less symmetrical front; his men could expect to meet the enemy out ahead, off to the sides, from behind and above—and sometimes all at the same time. Mobility had returned in unprecedented forms, and command of an infantry battalion had become a more sophisticated and dynamic animal when it came to mindset, technology and tactical responsibilities. Air power, tanks, armoured personnel carriers, anti-tank weapons (towed, self-propelled and hand-held), mobile artillery and air-cooled machine guns, all fuelled and fed by a mechanized support system underpinned by cutting-edge military intelligence, brought about a fluidity and tempo to operations only dreamed of in the Great War.

In this transitional era of warfare, infantry battalions needed to co-operate with all arms of service to get the job done in as economical a fashion as possible. As such, their officers, NCOs and men needed to understand how to attack, defend, probe and advance to contact, protect flanks, wheel on a dime, bounce rivers and other obstacles, consolidate gains quickly, fend off inevitable enemy counterattacks and then resume the fight, all the while tackling evolving natural and human terrain and the volatile climatic challenges at hand.

As a result, an infantry commander's decision-making cycle— his ability to think, act, react and implement action—now moved at lightspeed compared with the plodding, laboured approach

55

found on the Western Front a generation earlier. Armies of the Second World War moved in bounds of tens or hundreds of miles at a clip rather than mere yards; meanwhile, conservation of men's lives, rather than their expenditure, had increasingly become the bellwether for success in battle.

Midway through the second great conflagration of the twentieth century, the concept of sacrifice, which formed a central thread in regimental ethos, had begun to evolve, due in large part to the transformative nature of the battlefield, but also the backlash against the hefty butcher's bill and the "château generalship" of the Great War. With sacrifice increasingly viewed as incidental rather than intentional, it rubbed against the grain of the Black Watch elders, who continued to maintain intense pressure to sustain the regiment's good name through the only measurement of success they understood. As a result, both officers and men of the Black Watch had two battles to fight: one against the Germans and the other against the proverbial albatross placed firmly around their necks.[7]

OPERATING AS PART SOLDIER, PART PHYSICIAN AND PART exorcist, Cantlie arrived intent on cleansing the scores of sinful habits picked up over the previous year. Within days of taking command, he ushered in a gruelling year devoted to the "sweat and strain of training," much to the chagrin of his officers and men.[8]

Determined to set the battalion on the correct path, Cantlie embarked on what he euphemistically termed his "treatment," which came in the form of meticulous attention to detail, physical hardening and the sharpening of all infantry skills needed to excel on the modern battlefield. His intensive plan to regain the battalion's "spark of pride" comprised a series of long route marches and multi-day exercises to increase fitness and mental stamina; endless range exercises to improve weapons handling and marksmanship; more route marches; commando training; patrolling; sniper courses; longer route marches; and frequent snap inspections to keep them on their toes.[9] To test and hone the mettle of his officers and men, he pitted his companies and their commanders against each other, employing their innate competitive nature and ambition, challenging them constantly to reach a bar he set at almost unreachable heights.[10]

Failure to achieve or comply with SST's treatment led to transfer; those who could not measure up or simply fit into the ever-tightening battalion clique found themselves shipped to training establishments or units fighting in Italy, or were seconded to a British unit as part of the CANLOAN scheme.

What the men appreciated was that they always knew where they stood with the Boss and exactly what to expect, and he engendered trust with his "above average amount of common sense" and his ability to excel under pressure, which seemed always to produce the right results.[11] In short order, he fundamentally recalibrated the context in which the battalion trained and operated, clinging to the traditional Black Watch ethos that eschewed mediocrity and failure and rewarded success instantly. "The day will come," he confidently predicted, "when the enemy will find himself face to face with us—only by utilizing energy, determined resolve and cunning knowledge of all our parts will it make it possible for us to see that that particular enemy never gets away to fight another day. I don't know when that time will be, but none of us can afford to be complacent—time is precious, and perfection is the only standard in which to aim."[12]

As D-Day drew closer, the nature of training turned to specialized tasks the battalion would perform once they reached the Continent. Battle-drill courses designed to teach an instinctual response to fire and manoeuvre tactics when the bullets started to fly topped the list, as did intensive storm boat training in anticipation of assault crossings of rivers and canals. From there, it was on to village clearance and street-fighting schemes for each company, while Cantlie took part in the inaugural class of the British Army's night fighting school, which, although "pretty strenuous," made him feel "quite at home in the dark." Cantlie boasted, "I would like us to become really proficient at that work [for] the Black Watch gained their name from their night work [and] I would like to make us the best night fighters in the Canadian Army. It will certainly help the men's morale to have that confidence."[13]

Indeed, in short order, Cantlie's ability to instruct, shape, mould and re-instill a sense of pride in the red hackle fostered a renewed unit cohesion that dovetailed with a rise in morale and, more importantly, confidence. As Lieutenant George Buch, the oval-faced, bespectacled pioneer platoon commander related, "The CONFIDENCE we had just before we reached Normandy that we would be the first regiment to reach the Seine was second to none."

Soon, Cantlie's methods paid handsome dividends, and the Black Watch swung back into form, excelling in a series of punishing schemes and exercises that resurrected its reputation and reclaimed what he felt was its "rightful position as the pride of 5th Brigade."[14]

Still, many continued to curse him for his relentless, pedantic and at times condescending approach. Lieutenant Jock McLennan—the spider-like platoon officer who at six feet, four inches towered over everyone in the battalion—wrote home that the "training of late had been very interesting if a little on the strenuous side" and acknowledged that his "men grumble a bit at this, but in their moments reluctantly allow that it is a good thing."[15] Even the cantankerous Bruce Ducat agreed, reasoning, "You need a strict army. You need discipline. You must know what you are doing. Cantlie knew what he was doing." Although the cursing never faded and many believed he was indeed a "Son of a Bitch," they all agreed he was the type of son of a bitch they needed to lead them into battle after four long years of waiting.

LATE IN THE AFTERNOON OF JULY 7, THE 1ST BATTALION of the Black Watch began its move towards the tiny hamlet of Francqueville, located next to the ancient Abbaye d'Ardenne, which sat only a couple of miles from Caen's northwest quarter. With pockets of the city still burning, an acrid haze covered most of the march and thickened when they reached their destination just before sunset.

Benson led the battalion into the abbey grounds where, two days earlier, the eleventh-century monastery, which doubled as the headquarters of the 25th SS Panzergrenadier Regiment from the 12th SS Panzer Division, had fallen to the Regina Rifles; it still displayed the unhealed scars from the nasty fight. Surrounding the abbey grounds, which also contained a manor house, a barn and a well-concealed garden, stood the remnants of a six-foot-high wall punctured by fleeing SS panzers. Both of its twin towers, used by the SS to observe the Canadian advance since the first hours of D-Day, remained erect, but the heavily battered east end of the massive structure had collapsed under the weight of German artillery fire, called down by the cornered SS Panzergrenadiers in a final, desperate act of defiance.

Following close behind the scouts, Bill Booth, a twenty-one-year-old private who joined the Black Watch after leaving Miami, Florida, and now served as a clerk in the intelligence section, noted, "The Abbaye gave us our first sight and lasting impression of the aftermath of battle." Although the Canadian dead had received a proper, albeit cursory, burial, the fast pace of the fighting left dozens of corpses from the SS strewn around the farmyard and inside the structure itself. Most lay in various states of decay and undress, some with extremities severed or bowels disgorged, which offered a most forceful reminder that in war there is seldom, if ever, dignity in death.

Like Booth, Captain John Kemp found himself for the first time in intimate contact with the carnage of a battlefield and profoundly moved by the foreboding nature of the scene. He reported, "This was the first place we began to sense the reality. With bodies all over the place and a couple of burned out tanks, you began to realize you were in the war [and] it wasn't going to be an easy push through."

In one corner of the farmyard sat a knocked-out German Mark V Panther tank, its hatches closed and its green-and-tan summer paint scheme spoiled by blackening on every aperture, which testified to the ferocious fire that had immolated all trapped inside. Near the collapsed abbey wall, Booth observed a fully functioning Sherman tank sitting in reserve, its main gun slightly traversed off centre, shadowing its crew. Dressed in their customary black berets and oil-smudged coveralls, they paid little attention to the arrival of the Black Watch. Instead, almost catatonic, they stared ahead while they continued to chew hardtack and bully beef and sip black tea, utterly indifferent to the sight and stench of the bloated bodies of the dead teens.

Across the farmyard, Booth noticed the burnt-out remains of another Canadian Sherman, presumably their squadron mate. "It had been knocked out, and alongside there was something that seemed burnt to a crisp," he recounted. C Company commander Major Eric Motzfeldt, ushering the men through the grounds to their company positions in an adjacent field, hurriedly waved them past like a highway cop at a road accident. His less than convincing ploy, that the lump was nothing more than "a sheep," fooled nobody; as Booth put it, "we all knew better."

The army had indeed prepared these young men to kill and to "soldier," but left them on their own to cope with the gruesome reality and the indignity of war. Humour, particularly of the irreverent variety, proved the initial coping mechanism that the men mustered to fend off the intense fear, disgust and, to a lesser extent, guilt that emerged when they encountered the carnage on the abbey grounds.

Passing one corpse, still clad in his prized SS camouflage smock but naked from the waist down, the legs folded back over a bloody stump that once anchored his head to his shoulders, one bald-faced rifleman no older than his target said, "Don't lose your head now, Fritz!" His comment set off a chain of laughter and progressively cruder comments, most centred on the proportions of the dead man's genitals.

Despite the presence of the dead and the odd bursting shell, the daily routine on the farm adjacent to the abbey carried on and provided comedic material for the men. The arrival of the farmer's daughter with a cow in tow for servicing by the bull, which remained completely uninterested, elicited an immediate broadside of catcalls. One man suggested the butcher could quickly solve her problem in a tasty fashion, while another offered up his platoon mate to satisfy the cow, while yet another offered to skip the bovine and go directly to the farmer's daughter. Flustered and no doubt intimidated by the onslaught that became progressively misogynistic, she left the cow and beat a hasty retreat with the indifferent bull in tow.

The other ritual that provided some escape was the time-honoured, but all too repugnant, souvenir hunts that soldiers from the beginning of recorded history have engaged in. After digging in, the men fanned out in all directions, swarming the abbey grounds in search of quarry. Inside the monastery, they found the smashed and ransacked remains of Brigadeführer Kurt Meyer's signals centre and his bedroom on the third floor, plus the collection of civilian vehicles parked below ground, stolen from the French by the SS.[16] Seeking a German pistol, preferably a Luger, the prime currency for barter, Mike Brunner discovered that the other units had picked the grounds clean. Finding little to scavenge, Sergeant Mac Roulston turned to his bayonet to sever the distinctive SS sleeve eagles and the Hitlerjugend band off the pea-dot smocks of the dead to send home to his girlfriend as a war trophy.[17]

What they didn't discover in their pursuit of prizes, however, were the shallow graves of twenty murdered Canadians buried behind the walls of the abbey's overgrown garden. Rumours had swirled for weeks about the criminal activities of the SS in general and the fanatical Hitlerjugend, who had murdered Canadian and British captives in the days following the invasion, in particular.[18]

In one case, they bayonetted wounded prisoners, including a padre, while in another they lined up a group against a wall at a nearby château, shot them down, dragged their bodies into the road and ground them into a fine pulp with the tracks of their tanks. Another report told of three dozen captives murdered on the Caen–Bayeux road when a section from the Hitlerjugend advanced in a skirmish line from behind with Schmeisser sub-machine guns blazing. In all, close to two hundred British and Canadian prisoners died at the hands of the 12th SS in the days following the invasion, including twenty either bludgeoned to death or shot in the head with a pistol on the abbey grounds.[19]

No doubt the nascent nature of the invasion, which hung in the balance in the first forty-eight hours, encouraged the SS to act out. Planning to drive the Allies back into the sea, they never expected their crimes to come to light. But as the Allies gained a foothold and slowly and painfully expanded it, they overran the murder sites and ironclad evidence appeared that got the blood up within Canadian ranks. What enraged the Canadians was that none of these murders took the form of "heat of battle" killings where men let boiling tempers and a rush of adrenalin and blood lust get the better of them, something both sides engaged in. These were unarmed prisoners of war in German hands for hours or days, and as such warranted the full protection from harm under the provisions of the Geneva Conventions. Instead, the SS seized their papers, subjected them to brutal interrogation and then shot or clubbed them to death in cold blood.

According to Robert Rogge, an American from Glen Osborne, Pennsylvania, who joined the Black Watch in the summer of 1941 but later transferred to the Stormont, Dundas and Glengarry Highlanders and landed on Juno Beach on D-Day, his intimate experience in combat against these teenagers left him unequivocal. "The SS . . . were unmitigated bastards in every sense of the word. They were all psychopaths, totally imbued with the filthy Nazi credo and remorseless killers of both prisoners and wounded. They were hated by their Wehrmacht almost as much as by us—and all allied troops. The ordinary Jerry would fight one Hell of a battle, but if all were lost, he would surrender, or retreat. Not the SS. They fought to the death—and so they were killed, as they deserved."[20]

The legacy of the SS, and particularly the Hitlerjugend division the Canadians dubbed the "Murder Division," led officers like B Company second-in-command Captain John Taylor (one of the only Black Watch officers to have seen previous combat) to use their actions in his carefully crafted "hate talks" designed to whip up the killer instinct in his men. Stopping short of murder, he eschewed the taking of SS prisoners, and when they did, he advocated holding them to the lowest threshold possible.[21] As one of his sergeants eagerly boasted, "They know what they get if they make a wrong move!"[22]

REPORTS OF ENEMY SNIPER ACTIVITY IN THE TINY VIL-lage of Verson, four miles west of Caen, put the Black Watch on operational alert for the first time since their arrival in Normandy. Initially, brigade intelligence dismissed the notion of active snipers, attributing the fire to a rearguard of the 12th SS that had forged its way through the village of 750 inhabitants as it retreated from Carpiquet airfield. When the firing continued, however, further inquiries revealed that the British infantry unit that liberated the village had failed to investigate and clear it properly. As a result, Brigade now suspected that the harassing fire emanated from a "stay behind" sniper working in tandem with a masterfully concealed artillery spotter hidden somewhere in the town.

When the call came down for a fighting patrol, Cantlie seized upon the opportunity to get one of his companies into action. Immediately, he tapped Major Phillip Griffin's A Company to carry out the operation, aided by the scout platoon and elements of a field engineer company and a field security section. The orders were straightforward: sweep and clear the village of any "undesirables" and hunt down and eliminate any snipers or observation posts operating in the village.

Before he joined the Black Watch, Griffin had commissioned in the Seaforth Highlanders in his native Vancouver, where he served briefly with his oldest brother, Robert, before transferring to the 15th Field Artillery Regiment of the Royal Canadian Artillery, where another brother, Herbert, served as a forward observation officer.[23] In the spring of 1939, he came east to Montreal to pursue his PhD in biochemistry, hoping to devote his life and his immense intellectual talents to pioneering cancer research. When Hitler's armies invaded Poland that fall, he, like so many others, put those plans on hold and went off to war, viewing it as nothing more than a temporary setback.[24] Although Griffin displayed great aptitude for the military arts, finishing top of his class in several courses, he never harboured a strong affinity for the profession of soldiering. "He didn't like it," John Kemp remembered. "He wanted to get back to civilian life, but he was a dedicated soldier. This was the same with everybody; nobody wanted to be a soldier."[25]

But as soon as he walked through the armoury doors on Bleury Street, the Black Watch regimental elders knew they had a winner on their hands, lauding him as "one of the most efficient subalterns we've ever had." By early 1943, he had shot up the rungs of the officer corps to reach the rank of major, on the strength of his "outstanding ability and knowledge" of tactics and his "equable and well-balanced temper."[26] Highly respected for his ability to outrun, outclimb and outperform his contemporary officers and subordinates in all fields, Griffin would never ask his men to do something he was not prepared to take on himself. As George Buch related, "He would never say, 'You guys go, and I'll be right behind you.'" But what his men appreciated most was his sizable military IQ, which allowed him to get into the tactical picture quickly, coupled with the tight grip he exercised over his company.

Operating like a good teacher, he would communicate both his orders and the essence of the job at hand, clearly laying out the steps for accomplishing the mission in no uncertain terms. "The three days I spent with A Company," remembered scout Private Bill Pugh, "left no doubt in my mind who the Company

Commander was, and when you left Major Griffin's orders group, you knew exactly what was going to take place and what he wanted you to do."

Not everyone, however, was a fan of Major Griffin. Corporal Gordy Donald, a section commander who served under him for years, found him "far too strict" and "somewhat of a snob." Even the stodgy Black Watch elders noticed this trait and feared he would prove far "too regimental" with the men, as he tended to stand on station at all times and micromanage rather than delegate, which led to many run-ins with subordinates.[27]

"Griffin's greatest fault," according to Donald, lay with his "resistance to quit or at the very least, know when to ease off the gas," as witnessed when he took his company on a training scheme to the legendary commando base in Achnacarry, Scotland. Trying to impress, Griffin drove his men harder than usual, pushing them far past the point of exhaustion in a bid to best the elite commandos at their own game. When he refused to yield, it took the personal intervention of the base commanding officer to bring Griffin to heel amidst fears he would liquidate his entire company.

Donald, unimpressed, suggested that beneath his straitlaced veneer lay something other than his drive for perfection. Based on what he witnessed over his time in A Company, Donald suspected that a ruthless ambition underpinned Griffin's actions, and in his mind "there was no doubt that the young major," like his fellow company commanders, "was out to make his mark."

MAJOR GRIFFIN'S PLAN FOR THE SEARCH OF VERSON WAS characteristic of the man: a textbook operation of war, meticulously worked out, with little, if anything, left to chance. "Because the search was to find a trained sniper," he recorded, "it had to be very thorough, both in the town and in the environs."[28] As such, he methodically carved up the village, which housed in peacetime over seven hundred inhabitants, into three areas of operation—one for each of his three rifle platoons. Following a brief background on the intelligence picture, he took his officers and NCOs through each step of his plan in succession to ensure all landed on the same page.

First, Benson and the scouts would guide the force to its target, weaving down the road leading from the Abbaye d'Ardenne, past the battered Carpiquet airfield to the railway line that formed the northern perimeter of Verson. Because this route came under German observation, Griffin planned to move at night and would bivouac in a thicket to the north of the railway so that his rifle platoons could descend upon the village at dawn, taking any defenders by surprise.

Second, the scouts would break down into two reconnaissance parties, each with an "observer-sniper" team in the mix. Both would patrol areas north and south of the town before first light to prevent interference or surprises. As Griffin told Benson, "Nobody gets in, and nobody gets out."[29] With this completed, Benson would leave the snipers in overwatch positions and move into Verson to patrol the village itself, and upon his all-clear, the third phase would kick in.

Following Benson's signal, Griffin would order his three rifle platoons to pounce. Swarming into the village in unison, they would head for their preordained sectors as Griffin, advancing down the middle of the main road in Benson's wake, would join the scout platoon sergeant near the mayor's house and market square to set up his command post.

Once in the town, the rifle platoons would divide into clearing and cover groups for the sweep, with the former breaching the structure to flush the sniper out. The latter would establish a killing zone with their Bren guns webbed into a more extensive network that could provide covering fire for the entire company at a moment's notice.

Finally, the engineer teams, supported by Lieutenant Buch's pioneer platoon, would rush into each house following the breach and clear, ready to capture or destroy enemy weapons and supply caches or defuse booby traps so that the field security section could scoop up any worthy intelligence material.

Expecting to be back that night, Griffin permitted the men to take only the barest of essentials: main weapon, helmet, webbing, bandoliers stuffed with extra grenades, magazines for the Bren guns and shells for the PIAT (Projector Infantry Anti-Tank weapon). The weapon of choice for house clearing was the hand grenade, so each man in the clearing group had at least four grenades clipped to his belt, in a nasty assortment of high-explosive, fragmentation and white phosphorus types. The latter, extremely useful for this type of operation, was a particularly cruel device; when it exploded, it showered the area with white-hot fragments of phosphorus that burned at 5,000 degrees Fahrenheit. Fed by oxygen and impossible to douse with liquid of any kind, the fire would burn relentlessly into flesh, bone and beyond, inflicting the most painful and hideous death one could imagine.

The centrepiece of firepower for each rifle section in a platoon came with the Bren Mark 2 light machine gun. Traditionally operated by teams of two (one man firing while the other swapped its thirty-round magazines or flipped the barrel for another when it heated up), the gun could be fired prone, using its bipod, or from the slung position while kneeling, standing or advancing, providing covering fire for the rest of the section to close with and kill the enemy.

The men loved the Bren for its dependability, but as is the case with any form of technology, it proved a double-edged sword.

Far slower than the German MG 34 or MG 42, the Bren could only fire five hundred rounds a minute from a series of thirty-clip magazines, compared to over a thousand rounds a minute fired from its belt- or drum-fed German brethren. What the Bren lacked in this area, it made up for with supreme accuracy at medium to long ranges, able to put a tight grouping of rounds together consistently at distances greater than four hundred yards. However, its remarkable accuracy was also a weakness; it had trouble spraying, or hosing, the enemy in tight situations. This is where the Sten submachine gun, issued to officers and NCOs, came into play.

Unlike the Lee-Enfield, the Sten was one of the most detested weapons in the Canadian Army. "They called it a plumber's abortion," recalled Corporal Bruce Ducat. "I hated the damn thing—always kept breaking down when you needed it the most." Ducat's derision was indeed widespread, for its low cost and mass production resulted in numerous teething problems. In theory, this was the weapon used for close-quarter fighting in conjunction with grenades, when clearing a room, bunker or trench, but the men found it was sorely underpowered and highly inaccurate at anything over a hundred yards. Although light and easy to carry, the snub-nosed 9-millimetre weapon, which fired thirty-two rounds, suffered from several other potentially deadly drawbacks. First, many of the ammunition clips, which had been rushed into production, proved ill fitting, which led to frequent jams, usually at the worst possible moment. Second, the Sten proved temperamental when covered in dust, mud and dirt. But what alarmed soldiers the most was its nasty tendency to go off at the slightest knock, even with the safety on, which prompted the men to suggest that, "instead of using a grenade to clear a house, you just throw in your Sten and duck!"[30] Perhaps it was not surprising, as Captain John Kemp noted, that many of the officers, including Phil Griffin, carried a Lee-Enfield as a failsafe for their Sten.

The potential political implications of this seemingly insignificant action made it a much more difficult exercise than anything the men had encountered in training. Nobody knew how many French civilians remained in the village, but after the bombing of Caen there was a heightened sensitivity when it came to collateral damage. But there was another tricky and potentially unsettling aspect to deal with that required their attention.

Since the invasion, Allied intelligence had periodically reported that the deadly sniper fire the invaders encountered was not emanating strictly from German sources. As the Allies soon learned, some young French women had indeed taken up arms and operated as *francs-tireurs* against them. Although such actions were by no means widespread, intelligence soon discovered that they were not prompted by nationalistic, ideological or political concerns. Rather, as the Allies soon found out, after four long years of German occupation, many of the local girls had come of age with their occupiers and had engaged in what the French termed "*collaboration horizontale.*" Confronted now by their lovers' imperilment and imminent incarceration, or death, they acted out in fits of rage and passion to either defend their man or seek retribution on those who took him away.[31]

GRIFFIN'S FORCE MOVED OUT AT LAST LIGHT ON JULY 15 in single file along the road that skirted Carpiquet airfield. By this time, the rain had stopped, but it remained overcast and there was no moon. A slight breeze did blow from the northwest, bringing with it the lingering odour of the horrific battle on the Luftwaffe base nearly a week before. The overpowering mixture of petroleum and putrefied flesh that wafted past testified to the fanatical defiance that the teenagers from the 12th SS maintained until Churchill Crocodile tanks spewing jets of blazing gelatinous gasoline moved in and expeditiously consigned them to the flames.

By 0300 hours, nothing had interfered with the march and Griffin's company reached the bivouac point unmolested. There, they enjoyed an uneventful night. At 0600 hours, the scouts moved out, and the search of Verson began.

Sergeant Barney Benson, with the barrel of his Lee-Enfield cloaked in burlap scrim, took one patrol along the northern bank of the narrow Odon River south of the town. Hook Wilkinson, his face veil fashioned like a balaclava, took the other in the shadows of the railway embankment to the north. Each moved east in twenty-yard clips, pausing to listen and scrutinize the terrain through their binoculars and telescopes before moving on to the next bound. Nothing appeared out of order. A brazen rooster went about its sunrise ritual, announcing a new day. Other than this, Verson remained blissfully tranquil.[32]

At the western extremity of the town, both patrols halted. They waited and watched. So far, they had moved without trouble and now had a perfect vantage point from which to observe the environs for any signs of movement. Trained to pick out a concealed man at a little over a mile through their telescopes, each scanned the area looking for the slightest signs of life. They found none. While Hook's patrol stayed in overwatch to the west, Benson's patrol turned and headed back east, retracing their steps to ensure they missed nothing and that nobody had slipped in behind to turn the tables on his men.

Satisfied that all was clear when he reached the eastern fringe, Benson set out alone to commence the "tripwire" method. In combat, it was better to lose one man than an entire platoon, company or battalion to an enemy force in hiding; to avoid that calamity, somebody had to be the bait and stir things up.

With his rifle at the ready, the scout platoon sergeant sauntered right down the centre of the main road. With the dawn light now streaking in from behind, Benson had to keep a careful watch on the road ahead for land mines and booby traps. He followed the natural terrain with his eyes, carving up the road visually into five-yard swatches of ground. He carefully examined the cropped hedges, sidewalks and garden walls, looking for any signs of enemy activity before he made his next bound.

Benson's sniper teams kept him covered from both ends of the town, scanning the upper windows, roofs, hedges and garden walls for possible hides or for any movement, glimmer or noise. If the enemy sniper proved well trained, he would remain concealed and maintain his fire discipline, waiting for a more tantalizing and vital target to come into view. If so, Benson had a better chance of survival, but if the sniper was inexperienced and jittery, or a civilian spurred by passion or personal vengeance, he likely would be dead in seconds.

John Kemp, who witnessed Benson's method of soldiering in Normandy, saw him on numerous occasions "expose himself to draw fire from a gun we had been unable to locate," adding "there was no job too difficult or dangerous for Barney to have a try at it . . . he was completely fearless."[33]

For a scout, this was the trade-off between going into battle in a rifle company and facing the full brunt of enemy mortars, automatic weapons fire, tanks and artillery and taking your chances in the middle of a road in some insignificant village in France, offering to exchange your life for the common good.

Concealed in the wooded terrain at each end of the village, the sniper teams kept watch in a 360-degree arc for any sudden

SEVEN DAYS IN HELL

movement. With their scopes pre-zeroed at a uniform 400-yard range, each sniper knew precisely how to manipulate his weapon for any sudden movement. "If the target appeared at this distance, we fired directly into his chest," Hook recalled. "Any closer, and you quickly adjusted your aim for his knees or his groin, or his feet. At ranges between 450 and 600 yards distant, you aimed high, above the top of the target's head, and dropped the round on him." Distances above 600 yards were considered "a waste of ammunition" unless a sniper was skilled enough, intrepid enough and, more importantly, lucky enough to pull it off.

The other factor to consider was the rapid movement of their mark. "If our target were stationary, then we'd aim for the heart," Hook recalled. "If he moved at a walking pace, we aimed for the leading edge of his body, but if he were running, we'd fire about an inch and a half ahead and lead him into the bullet." None of this was science. It was skill, and craft; it was the deadliest of arts.

While Benson continued to work his way down the main road in Verson, Griffin, who had deployed his platoons in the dead ground and the scrub north of the village, ordered them to make their approach using the ditches and hedges for cover. Griffin, satisfied they had achieved surprise after Benson turned to signal, launched his three 36-man platoons, who immediately swarmed into the tiny streets, fanning out to their designated sectors.

Verson itself had missed most of the heavy fighting, and the bulk of the town's buildings still stood. A few, however, displayed visible signs of battle damage: pockmarks from bullet holes in the walls, rust-coloured shingles torn from roofs, painted shutters riddled with shrapnel and dangling from upper-storey windows, leaving piles of masonry sprinkled on the gardens and sidewalks below.

The sudden bark of the platoon sergeants putting their officer's orders into action broke the stillness, and sleepy Verson came to life. The clatter of boots stomping on cobblestone and the chatter of the company wireless joined the clangs of rifle bolts dutifully responding to the confirmatory shouts of "ready" from Griffin's men. Within seconds, his Bren guns had rolled into place to provide an overarching base of fire on the streets adjacent to the buildings targeted for the search. Then the cover groups for each platoon crept into position with rifles and Sten guns at the ready to spray any opening on the target building and pick up the pieces if something went wrong when the clearing groups went in for the sweep.

Corporal Gordy Donald commanded one of the cover groups. Bren gunner Private Anthony Barbagallo, an Italian kid from Montreal, was part of his team, as was Rifleman Thanning Carl Anderson, an evangelical Christian from Edgerton, Alberta, with Norwegian heritage, and Reuben Gorodetsky, a Jew from Bessarabia and a card-carrying member of the Communist Party of Canada. None of them had any clue what to expect on the other side of the door. Since the operation kicked off at 0600, five minutes past sunrise, there was a good chance they would encounter any civilians who might have remained in their dwellings rather than fleeing over the previous week. The clearing group now faced the prospect of a very real German sniper or a terrified French family. Taking few chances after the accidental bombing of Caen, the clearing groups dispensed with the usual drill of lobbing grenades through windows and doors, followed by a violent entry after they exploded.

Civilians, however, proved only one of the many challenges for the men. The Germans, masters of the booby trap, traditionally wired any building they used for an observation post or sniper's hide, leaving behind a series of nasty surprises designed to kill, maim and demoralize. They had to open doors gently, and carefully examine floorboards, furniture and debris for tripwires, turning over anything suspicious to the engineer teams.

The scouts watched the proceedings unfold as the riflemen scurried to get into position. They watched the men breach, clear and then repeat the effort. From above, everything seemed uniform, except for the gangly Lieutenant McLennan, whose massive figure hovered above the rest. "The process of sweeping through from house to house and tearing each building apart from attic to cellar went on systematically," Griffin wrote, but added with great disappointment, "no snipers were located in the search."[34]

The sweep did not go for naught, however, as they discovered evidence of recent German activity in the town and some useful intelligence. "Plenty of documents were found," Griffin reported, which the eager field security section quickly snapped up. From the personal letters and other documents collected, they managed to establish that infantry and artillery components from the SS had occupied the village for a short spell, as had some from the Luftwaffe, who, given the proximity to Carpiquet airfield, likely used it as a rest area. They found nothing, however, to link the artillery personnel to any operations originating from within the town, as they discovered no signs of land lines, radios or telephone sets. They speculated that this SS unit might have rested briefly in the village before pulling back south of Caen. The sweep did have merit, however, as Griffin found that "some rooms were sandbagged which indicated that they had at one time been used as sniper posts." They, like their comrades, were long gone by now.

The commotion in the town woke up the few remaining French civilians who still called Verson home. Within minutes, the eager field security section detained seven civilians, but after a brief interrogation, aided by the linguistic talents of Charlie Lee and Mike Brunner, they cleared five of the bewildered and increasingly "resentful" group, but detained two others, both women, who they suspected had worked as snipers. Although Griffin believed each had "a plausible story to explain their presence," he noted that "some parts required additional checking." Fully satisfied with the results of the sweep, Griffin signalled back to 5th Brigade: "Clearing Verson complete. No snipers. Seven Civilians investigated. All OK except two women who are being checked by the Field Security Police. No Booby Traps. Some documents collected. The company will be back by midnight."[35]

3

INOCULATION

The study of war should concentrate almost entirely on the actualities of war—the effects of tiredness, hunger, fear, lack of sleep, weather . . . The principles of strategy and tactics, and the logistics of war are really absurdly simple: It is the actualities that make war so complicated and so difficult.

—Field Marshal Lord Wavell

T HE BLACK WATCH POSITIONS SPRAWLED IN THE field near the abbey had come under fire for the first time shortly before Griffin's company departed for Verson. This did not surprise Hook Wilkinson; when they first arrived in the fields near the Abbaye d'Ardenne days before, it seemed "very flat" with little cover, and he thought to himself, "my god if they send the air force over, we're dead ducks." Apparently, Luftwaffe High Command agreed.

The unannounced arrival of two German Focke-Wulf 190s at treetop level sent everyone scrambling into nearby slit trenches or ducking for cover wherever they could find it. Mike Brunner dropped to the bottom of his slit, clawing at the dirt, hoping to bury himself as deep as possible when the first fighter came in for his strafing run.

In an instant, the sole lecture about air attacks he had attended came back to him in a rush. Waiting for the sound of the engine to reach a high pitch and the guns to chatter, he slid towards the near end of his slit, facing the sound of the oncoming aircraft. At first blush it seemed counter-intuitive, but his manoeuvre cut down the angle and reduced the chances of a cannon round striking home. "In combat," Brunner professed, "it was all about cutting down the odds. From then on you knew you were in the war."

When the fighter-bomber soared past and pulled off to come around for a return pass, Brunner leaped back to the other end, ready for a repeat performance. The game ended prematurely when Dale Sharpe crashed over the precipice of his slit and landed squarely on top of the diminutive Brunner. Finding his trench far too shallow and open for his liking, Sharpe had decided to seek deeper shelter and pancaked Brunner, leaving both wedged together like Russian nesting dolls. Brunner, as he lay pinned under the two-hundred-pound Sharpe, said feebly, "You're a big fella!" Sharpe, trying to burrow even deeper as the din increased, screamed back, "No shit! I wish I were smaller!"

The enemy aircraft made several passes before a volley from an Allied 40-millimetre anti-aircraft gun set one of the planes alight, forcing it to crash in the neighbouring sector held by the Régiment de Maisonneuve. The Luftwaffe pilot managed to escape, coming down hard in his parachute and breaking his leg following his eleventh-hour bailout. Members of the Régiment de Maisonneuve (nicknamed "Maisies" by the anglophone units), who rushed forward from their slits to take in the spectacle of the burning Focke-Wulf fighter, became targets for his vengeful wingman, who burst in on the scene at treetop level, guns blazing.[1]

Just after midnight, a second air raid came in with even more intense ferocity. This time, nobody moved. Sharpe, who had found his way back to his hole after prying himself off Brunner, made necessary improvements to his slit and then fell asleep.

Brunner remained glued to the floor of his slit, staring up at the sky from under a peeled-back portion of his rain cape. "The sky was simply spectacular," he recalled, and he marvelled at the twinkling green of the flares dropped by German intruder aircraft to illuminate the area for their photo-reconnaissance planes and for their predatory night fighters, which bounded in seconds later. Except for the engines and the hacking of the anti-aircraft guns and tracers shooting skyward, there was an odd beauty to it all.

Then the bombs dropped.

"The earth started shaking," a terrified Brunner recounted. "It lasted for a little while, and then everything went dead silent . . . I remember praying, and I don't know what language, but I prayed." Fighting nerves and mounting exhaustion, Brunner fell into a coma-like sleep when the raid passed. At dawn, only the whine of the bagpipes, a Black Watch tradition, shook him from the dead to find he was "half-covered with dirt." Pulling himself up out of his slit, Brunner looked around and saw "craters all over the place." Satisfied with his narrow escape, the young sniper took it as a sign, reckoning, "I think I'm going to be okay."

Then the rain came.

The usual dry Norman summer heat, tempered by the occasional breeze, surrendered as it usually did to a rotating series of prolonged cloudbursts that transformed the concrete-like ground into a slithery quagmire within minutes. Rain capes pulled across the openings of slits kept most of the rain at bay but did not stop groundwater from penetrating. In some slits, the water rose past the level of newly excavated sumps, forcing men to employ helmets or teacups to bail water. Removing the rain cape to engage in this process made it a thoroughly self-defeating exercise, so the men, as their fathers had before them, sat there and took it. Cold, wet and tired, Captain John Kemp managed to pen a quick note to his mother: "The climate is simply bloody . . . It only rains about one out of every five hours; tell Dad that I am beginning to understand when they talk about the mud of Flanders."[2]

News that the 2nd Canadian Corps commander was on his way down to deliver a pep talk to all three battalions in the 5th Canadian Infantry Brigade failed to mitigate the dark mood. Heavy showers had returned with a vengeance, and none were impressed with the order to strip rain capes from their slits to wear during the address. Their disquiet quickly turned to discontent bordering on insubordination following a forty-five-minute wait, during which they stood in the driving rain until Major General Charles Foulkes and Brigadier William J. Megill from 5th Brigade arrived, followed by Lieutenant General Guy Granville Simonds, who appeared in his Staghound armoured car.

The British-born Simonds, known in his RMC days as "The Count" for his aristocratic bearing and appearance, was not only the youngest general in the Canadian Army, at the age of forty-one, but the youngest Allied corps commander in Normandy.[3] Lean and spry, he appeared more youthful than his age and could easily pass for a classmate of SST's, despite graduating five years earlier. The first thing that struck the men was his overt resemblance to British general Bernard Montgomery: slim physique, well-trimmed moustache, piercing blue eyes, pale skin, jet-black hair, and his black beret sporting a Royal Canadian Artillery cap badge, his branch of service.

In army slang, Simonds was a "gunner" who advocated the primacy of firepower on the battlefield supplied by the artillery to set the backbeat for operations. In this connection, he subscribed wholeheartedly to Montgomery's operational concept whereby the army would grind out Great War–style battles of attrition to soften up the enemy, leading to one giant "colossal crack," which would split the enemy wide open and produce victory. It had worked for Montgomery in his grand triumph in the desert at El Alamein in Egypt two years earlier, and in his eyes it had never let the side down.[4]

Standing on the jeep that brought Foulkes and Megill to the meeting, Simonds spun slowly to address the men, but his talk was far too laboured for the mood of the men or the weather. He discussed the attritional struggle and the nasty fighting that lay ahead, their upcoming role in crossing the Seine, their need to consolidate their positions promptly after taking an objective— all salient points, though they were thoroughly uninspiring and went miles over the men's heads. As Brunner recalled, "It went in one ear and out the other. It was another pep talk from a general— we got lots of those."

According to Montgomery's assessment of men, Simonds, who had a reputation for ruthless efficiency, was "the only Canadian General fit for high command."[5] General Miles Dempsey, the commander of the 2nd British Army, under whom Simonds's 2nd Canadian Corps now served, readily agreed with this assessment, marking him as "the best of his corps commanders." Indeed, Simonds liked to keep everyone at arm's length, and although the men respected him for his ability, on a personal level he proved far too cold to win their hearts. As one of his oldest friends and RMC classmates, General Chris Vokes, pointedly put it, Simonds might have been "the finest Canadian general we ever had," but he was not worth "a pinch of coonshit" as "a leader of men."[6]

As historian Doug Delaney makes clear in his assessment, "If Simonds had a weakness it was not his aloofness . . . it was his pride. Supremely confident, driven to succeed, and fiercely competitive, he hated being anything but the best, and his desire to prove himself and his troops got the best of him now and then."[7] Demanding, exacting and frightfully unforgiving, Simonds, in the words of his chief of staff, Brigadier Elliot Rodger, was not an easy man to work for. He expected everything yesterday, and tended to rule rather than command 2nd Canadian Corps.[8] Wielding his experience as a division commander in Italy like a maestro's baton, the corps commander treated his subordinate division and brigade commanders as little more than funnels to transmit his orders to units at the front. Reduced to the status of functionaries—notably when they lacked combat experience, as was the case with Foulkes and Megill—their mortal sin came with any attempt to decide, initiate or even to think. As Brigadier Bob Moncel, Simonds's operations officer, related, "Simonds fought the battle by visiting with the commanders and making changes on the spot—he used to hammer it home to me: 'You follow the music; I will play the variations.'"[9]

Little pushback came from the "vain, egotistical" Charles Foulkes, who was the most hated senior officer in the Canadian Army.[10] Few could explain his rise from company to division commander in just five years, and most attributed his success to smoke and mirrors and time served in the tiny Permanent Force, something that could only have happened in army starved for command talent. Continually damned with faint praise by his fellow generals as a "skilled bureaucrat and accomplished careerist" who "spent his time determining what was good for Charles Foulkes," his course reports, which listed his strengths as "reliability, obedience to command and attitude towards superiors, loyalty, tact, and leadership," betrayed a man who had nearly perfected the art of the sycophant.[11]

Simonds, however, was no fool when it came to his division commander, and he had sized Foulkes up long before his division went into battle. Foulkes, too, knew he was on the hot seat heading into Normandy and planned, as usual, to do what he could to keep the boss happy. As a result, a toxic and thoroughly dysfunctional atmosphere at 2nd Canadian Division developed where the culture of blame reigned supreme, and few took full responsibility for their actions.

Of course, none of this was apparent to the men standing ankle high in water and mud, nor did Simonds share the broader context of the predicament facing the Allies a month after D-Day. Despite Montgomery's assurances at the time and in his memoirs that all had gone "according to plan," the Allies were in fact struggling more than expected for elbow room in the bridgehead. Initially, the Allies expected to face a series of massive German panzer-led counterstrikes around the landing beaches, designed to drive them back into the sea. With his tanks and infantry supported by masses of naval gun support and tank-busting fighter-bombers vectored in by cutting-edge ultra-secret intelligence derived from Allied code-breaking efforts, Montgomery expected the showdown to come in a two-week-long dogfight with Rommel's panzers around Caen.

But one month into the campaign, his forces sat deadlocked, upending his plan. The Allies' deception operation, Operation Fortitude, had convinced the Germans that the Normandy landings were nothing more than a diversion and that the main landings would come in the Pas de Calais. It was a plan that succeeded beyond the Allies' wildest dreams. With fighter-bombers being much more efficient at knocking out bridges, railways and panzers than ever expected in pre-invasion estimates, the impact of air power on the bridgehead also exceeded expectations. Hitler refused to commit his entire panzer reserve to Normandy, while the air interdiction campaign proved so effective that it slowed the panzers down too much and they arrived in a drawn-out, piecemeal fashion, a development Montgomery failed to work to his full advantage.

These developments thwarted Montgomery's plans for a grand Götterdämmerung, a winner-takes-all battle, which had been so successful at El Alamein in 1942 when he defeated his archrival, General Erwin Rommel, the infamous Desert Fox. Although the Allies' first bout in the desert led to a knockout of the German opponent, the rematch in Normandy had turned into a full-blown fifteen-round heavyweight slugfest by early July, with neither fighter showing any signs of hitting the canvas imminently.

The lack of a decisive victory by this point, coupled with the costly, incremental progress witnessed so far by the Allied armies in Montgomery's 21st Army Group, had put the British commander's career in jeopardy. The worst-case scenario, next to the Germans driving the invasion force back into the sea, was a stalemate that would prompt a series of attritional battles, which ran the risk of stirring up the ghosts of the slaughter and futility of the Somme and Passchendaele in the Great War. By the end of the first week in July, that is precisely where the Allies found themselves.

To make matters more trying, the lack of success in the bridgehead brought the knives out for Montgomery, as his political enemies and rivals started to call for his head. The Allied press inflamed the issue, becoming increasingly enamoured of the spectacular Soviet victories in the east, where advances came in the hundreds of miles rather than the sputtering and incremental gains measured in the hundreds of yards in Normandy. The tone of these articles reflected the frustration and the war-weariness of the British home front and, more alarmingly, pointed to the same malaise found in such veteran units as the 7th Armoured Division—the famed Desert Rats—and the 50th Northumbrian and 51st Highland Divisions.[12]

Increasing the pressure, Eisenhower continued to chide Montgomery to move more quickly and decisively. Ike's call came in part due to his desire to see his crusade through to the end, but more practically, President Franklin Delano Roosevelt had just announced that he would seek an unprecedented fourth consecutive term in office.

THE FIRST BURST OF A MEDIUM-CALIBRE GERMAN ARTILLERY shell did not alarm anyone, and the men wondered if what they had just witnessed was, in fact, real. When more shells arrived in a widely spread and irregular pattern, as if in slow motion, they at first viewed the harassing fire as little more than a game or even a fraternity initiation.

Thoroughly amused by the slapstick results of the bursting rounds, Captain John Kemp told his mother, "Today we are all very tired and are having a quiet time except for the fact that Jerry every now and again mortars or shells us, and there is a wild scramble by the people resting outside their slits to get back home on time which always causes a lot of amusement." Kemp continued for a few more lines until another salvo forced an impromptu sidebar: "Considerable laughter at that point as the C.S.M. who had risked going to an 'outsider' latrine was forced to beat a very hasty and very undignified retreat."[13]

Within a few days, however, the shells, which had yet to inflict any human damage, became old hat. To some, like Jock McLennan, who admittedly did not "share the instincts of a snake," found it hard to "fold" his six-foot, four-inch frame into his slit. "As you see from our new address," he told his father, "we have at last made the leap and landed in France [and] have become expert at leaping into our slit trenches when Jerry drops the occasional shell in our direction."[14] Focusing on the humorous aspects, McLennan continued, "This morning at breakfast one of his air burst shells came over us and exploded. I was standing issuing the rations to platoon HQ and by the time I realized what it was and flopped on what a minute before had been clear ground, I landed on top of my HQ personnel. One chap had a mess tin over his head, and another had tried to dive into a campo box."[15]

During the intermittent shelling, Jimmy Bennett remained tucked into his slit trench, reflecting on the hardening process that had started once they touched down in Normandy. "I was only in that business a week, and I could kick a body over with my boot and take his wallet. It didn't matter. You get used to it, you get hardened. War changes your whole personality."

In theory, this was not the first time Bennett had served in a combat zone, but it was the first time he experienced dead bodies, enemy fire and the destructive nature of war. A year earlier, Bennett had taken part in the invasion of Kiska Island in the Aleutians as part of the Canadian contingent in an American-led invasion force sent to reclaim the island chain from the Japanese. Expecting to break the ice against the Japanese and their suicidal fanaticism, which surpassed even that of the SS, he stormed ashore to find that his potential foe had slipped away quietly days before, redeploying to the Kuril Islands.

Bennett struck up with Private Elie Desormeaux, a twenty-three-year-old French-Canadian prospector from Elk Lake, Ontario, with a sallow complexion and a robust build. Their friendship helped him weather the storm of anxiety during the operation. Desormeaux, who was four years older and chock full of experience and street smarts, offered big-brotherly comfort, which soothed and bolstered Bennett.[16] They were separated briefly when Bennett transferred into the Black Watch six months before Desormeaux followed suit. Now, back with the regiment and in Normandy, Desormeaux was one of over a hundred Black Watch reinforcements left out of battle near Juno Beach and would only reach the battalion after the fighting started.

When another salvo of heavier calibre landed only yards away, Bennett's anxiety and disquiet returned. Sitting knee to knee with Private Tommy Watt, whom he barely knew, did not help matters, and the more he thought about his current predicament, and what lay ahead, the more his heart raced and the fear of losing control enveloped him. Losing control within the construct of masculinity, the culture of the army in general, and the highly traditional and unforgiving Black Watch equated to mortal sin. The panic that seized a man's sanity for even a brief moment would permanently strip him of his manhood in the eyes of his comrades, which gave Bennett reason to panic, and the miserable circle accelerated.

What Bennett started to feel was the most natural of all human responses when confronted with fear, which soldiers had dealt with from the beginning of time. When not in combat, the anxiety built up, and by his own admission, Bennett "couldn't sleep, couldn't eat, [and was] worried all the time," but when the fighting started, everything returned to normal. This paradoxical roller-coaster ride was the natural condition in war. While the body is awake, it is in a state of balance or homeostasis. But when fear encroaches and does so rapidly, the sympathetic nervous system, or "fight or flight response," kicks in and all bets are off. The pupils dilate; the heart rate increases as oxygen and nutrients shoot into the brain to prepare the muscles for a fight. The liver goes into overdrive and secretes glucose into the bloodstream for extra energy to power the muscles. Breathing quickens, and bronchial passages in the lungs dilate to allow more oxygen to enter the blood to sustain the demands of the muscles. All this occurs in the immediate response to danger and fear, but over more extended periods, the body brings in its failsafe backup plan, the adrenal glands, which secrete epinephrine and norepinephrine, which help reinforce and sustain the response to danger. Digestive activity

87

shuts down, the mouth dries out and the bowels weaken, ready to excrete to prepare the body for battle.[17]

The more Bennett wrestled with his anxiety, the tighter his slit trench became. He was racked with anxiety and terrified he would lose it. He began to feel faint and to gulp for air as if drowning. "I don't know why I just panicked, I just about lost it," he recalled. However, as quickly as it came on, his anxiety dissipated when his adrenalin kicked in, returning his heart rate and blood pressure to functional levels. As with everyone who endures this roller coaster, Bennett then experienced a backlash, or "adrenalin dump," when the danger passed and fell into a short but blissful sleep.

When Bennett awoke, all was still—except for Watt, who was scrawling a letter home to his wife and kids. A full two decades older than the young prairie boy, Watt had left his job as an operating room attendant at the Montreal Children's Hospital to join the Black Watch. Having grown up in the predominantly Irish-Catholic neighbourhood of Pointe-Saint-Charles (or "the Point," as locals like Bruce Ducat called it), where strong republican sentiments surpassed even those of Catholicism and rivalled a good pint, his Protestant roots from Northern Ireland led to many a clash.

It dawned on Bennett that he had yet to let his own mother know that he had arrived in France. He was planning to rectify this gross oversight when a sudden commotion at the crossroads thirty yards away erupted.

The arrival of the battalion's transport trucks stirred the Black Watch positions to life. The sudden appearance of the trucks, with their engines growling, brakes squealing and gears grinding, was a welcome sight, for they brought ammunition, supplies and the first mail call since the men had arrived in Normandy.

Trailing the pack at the end of the tiny convoy came an enormous flat-faced Chevrolet C6oL, converted into a field cooker. This unique, underappreciated and all too important piece of military hardware gave a clear indication that the men were about to receive their first "home-cooked" meal since leaving England. It also raised speculation that they were being fattened up for something big in the offing, rumoured to be an assault crossing of the Orne River in Caen.

Popping his head out of the slit like a prairie dog, Watt spotted another vehicle parked next to the cooker that housed the unit shoemaker. "I need new boots!" he told Bennett, and he darted out of the slit, beckoning for Bennett to follow. Bennett, who didn't need a new pair but was too anxious to remain in his slit alone, hopped up and joined Watt on his quest.

The regimental shoemaker, a Quebecois *cordonnier* named Private Jean Jacques Bleau, held court with a small group of men, doling out replacement boots, including the pair of brand new size 6As that Watt scored. Soon, the mundane exchange gave way to a conversation about the shoemaker's collection of sleeve eagles and German stamps, liberated from the SS dead. This left Bennett cold, and he abandoned Watt and returned to his trench to finish his letter home.

As he approached the slit, the feathery whine of another approaching mortar stonk sent Bennett diving into his hole, crashing awkwardly on his left shoulder as the salvo hit. All the rounds burst harmlessly except for the last, which plunged dead centre at the crossroads and the idling cooker, sending flame, searing shards of steel and glass rocketing through the air. The blast ripped through Bleau, Watt and another private, Robert Garrett, leaving the trio disoriented and gasping for their last breaths. All attempts to provide aid proved futile. Ambulance jeeps stacked with stretchers arrived from the 18th Field Ambulance. Heaps of torn field dressing packs, bloodied swabs of cotton, discarded bits of uniform and empty morphine ampoules swirling in oblong pools of blood rendered the verdict.

When Padre Rod Berlis arrived minutes later, the medics had wrapped each body in a beige blanket tied only at the bottom in preparation for his final inspection. Berlis, who did not shy away from sharing a drink or two with the men in the mess, knew all three well. After a quick prayer, the young padre snipped the red identification discs from around their necks and left the green, octagonal one on the bodies for the burial team. Dutifully, he proceeded to examine their identification discs to register their service numbers and respective faiths and scratched a modest notation next to their names on a blank casualty chit: "Died of Wounds."[18] When he finished, Berlis signalled the attendees to draw the upper portion of the blankets over their faces and secured each with a strap, and then ordered graves dug and set the burial service to follow later that evening.

With the first part of his grim task accomplished, Berlis proceeded to B Echelon near the beaches to hand-deliver the administrative details to the quartermaster, who oversaw the preparation of the casualty lists, official notification of death to the unsuspecting next of kin, and inventory of their personal belongings.

Taking stock of their kit, some of which Berlis recovered from Bennett's slit, the quartermaster jotted down the last worldly possessions of each man: SS sleeve eagles, German stamps, pocket mirrors and snapshots for the shoemaker Bleau; pay book and a heart-shaped frame containing a photo of an attractive woman for Garrett; an unfilled dance card, fountain pen and unfinished letter home for Watt, along with pictures of his wife, Kathleen, and their two children, Billy, who was eleven, and Florence, seven.[19]

Pulling the groundsheet over his slit, Bennett prepared to write his mother but could not shake off Bleau's death and the carnage he just witnessed, especially the realization that a matter of seconds either way and it could have been him. "That scared me," recalled Bennett. "I thought if this is the way this is going to be, I don't have too much of a chance here." He thought to himself, "How long am I going to last?" After a long pause to compose himself, Bennett put pen to paper on the long-overdue letter to his mother. "I didn't tell her what had happened," he admitted. "I never did."

THE ORDERS GROUP FOR THE ORNE OPERATION CAME earlier in the day at the behest of Brigadier William J. Megill, who was about to take his 5th Canadian Infantry Brigade into battle for the first time. Megill, who had just celebrated his thirty-seventh birthday before embarking for France, had served for nearly two decades in the Canadian Army after joining the signals corps as a teenager in the 1920s. Late in that decade, after a brief sabbatical to obtain his degree in electrical engineering at Queen's University in Kingston, he returned to take up a commission in the small Permanent Force. Bent on pursuing a career as a signals officer, he rose up the officer ranks steadily, with his technical talent and a modicum of good fortune paving the way for him to attend the Imperial Staff College in Quetta, India, a rare distinction for an officer from the dominions. When war broke out in 1939, he returned to Canada and took up a series of staff appointments, working his way up to full colonel.[20] Despite his rather substantial, if unspectacular, military upbringing, Megill never stood a chance with the discriminating tastes of the officers and men of the Black Watch.

The furthest thing from Megill's mind in the winter of 1944 was the combat command of an infantry brigade. Having displayed little intimate understanding of, let alone genuine interest in, infantry operations before his appointment, one of his greatest critics—and there were many—George Hees, who served as his brigade major in the fall of 1944, declared, "Megill was a signaller who should never have been made an infantry brigadier."[21] Even his staunchest defender, historian Terry Copp, agrees that Megill's appointment to command 5th Brigade came not so much because of talent and experience, but despite it.[22]

By early 1944, the Canadian Army had a dearth in the ranks of its senior leadership, which opened the door for Megill's appointment. He endured a rough ride as an acting brigadier for the 1st Canadian Army, under General Harry Crerar. As Copp maintains, "Megill was not a success in this posting. Crerar praised his professional abilities but reported that 'Brigadier Megill is the type of man who needs experience to know. He is not what I would call imaginative . . . his lack of field experience definitely handicaps him.'"[23]

Instead of following Crerar's sound recommendation to capitalize on his excellent administrative qualities in a non-combat command, which would cap his career progression within the Permanent Force at his present rank, Megill sought a combat command and took charge of the 1st Battalion of the Algonquin Regiment, who were prepping in England to fight in Normandy as part of the 4th Armoured Division.[24]

What Megill desperately needed was actual experience, either as second-in-command of an infantry battalion or understudying a savvy combat veteran in training. He got neither. Three months later, when 5th Brigade burned through two brigadiers in less than three months, Megill received his appointment, which came as a shock to everyone—including Megill.

Originally, the Black Watch had clamoured to have their former commanding officer, Brigadier Kenneth Blackadder, posted to 5th Brigade, but despite their best efforts, the tentacles of the Black Watch mafia only went so far. Blackadder ended up taking the reins of the 8th Canadian Infantry Brigade, which stormed ashore at Juno Beach on D-Day, with Megill posted to 5th Brigade.

According to Lieutenant George Buch, the underlying problem with Megill did not stop with his lack of experience and personality; there were also the discerning tastes and cliquish culture of the Black Watch, who had little respect for what they considered his less than stellar pedigree. Coming from the "Post Office side of the Signals Corps," as Buch put it, Megill was simply not "cut from the same cloth." In their opinion, signallers did not rate amongst the elite of military circles, where frontline infantry sat at the top of the pecking order, with armour, engineers and artillery echeloned below. Without practical infantry combat experience, or at very least a natural flair to offset what they perceived as a void in his glandular makeup, specialist officers like Megill remained at the bottom of the food chain, wedged between the crystal-ball gazers in intelligence and the log wogs in ordnance, and was deemed unworthy of a combat command.

The succeeding months of training in England did little to diminish the preordained impression the Black Watch held of their brigadier. After viewing him in operation on several schemes, Buch concluded, "You just got the impression that he was not thinking things out based on the situation. It never seemed he could read a map [and he] had no tactical knowledge of the ground." Hees concurred, asserting that "Megill lacked the imagination needed to think like an infantryman." Stinging in his indictment, Hees went straight for the jugular: "Megill could never visualize the effect of his orders on rifle companies, let alone the individual soldier. I don't know if he cared."[25]

What irked officers like Buch the most was Megill's tendency to micromanage—a sin that was forgivable (although far from desirable) if the brigade commander came from an infantry background, or at the very least had proved himself in combat. Given that this was not the case, Megill's attempts to tell Cantlie's company commanders how to go about their jobs, rather than just telling them what to do, proved self-defeating and engorged the already chasm-like divide.

Megill's "brusque and dominating Permanent Force manner," as Buch put it, had done little but inflame the issue and won him no allies, particularly amongst the unyielding personalities in the Black Watch, and, to a lesser extent, with the Calgary Highlanders and the Régiment de Maisonneuve. According to Hees, Megill "was difficult . . . the most cantankerous S.O.B. I ever came across."[26] Seldom, if ever, did Megill express satisfaction or utter a good word, despite near-Herculean efforts performed by his staff or his men. "If you wanted him to go through a door you must never say so."[27] Hees remained bitter long after the war was over. "You had to say in the strongest terms possible, 'On no account go through that door.' To spite you, he'd do it instantly."[28]

No doubt his attitude, which could be quite congenial in less stressful environments and was fostered by the natural insecurity of being placed in a role he was improperly prepared to undertake, played a large part in his approach to command, an approach fully inflamed by continual resistance from the Black Watch.

One thing that neither Hees nor the Black Watch could condemn was Megill's courage. The brigadier, as they soon found out, had little regard for his personal safety and was always near the front, driving his own jeep and risking enemy fire to crack the whip and get his battalions going. Even the most rabid member of the Black Watch could not accuse him of being a "château general." In fact, some could complain that he was at the front too much for their liking, indulging in his propensity to micromanage instead of permitting his talented and highly trained subordinates to get on with it. Soon the men realized that the kind of day they were about to have depended on the headdress Megill wore when he arrived at their headquarters. "If he wore his helmet instead of his 'brass hat,'" George Buch recalled, "you knew you were in for a very long day."[29]

Megill had what higher command, particularly Simonds and his divisional commander, Charles Foulkes, desired most as a baseline for any subordinate: the ability to carry out orders unquestioningly and see them through to the bitter end if need be. Megill was, in army parlance, a "thruster" or "hard driver," a commander who would forgo or at least mask moral considerations, ruthlessly prepared to incur casualties to accomplish his objective. "He liked to push and push—not think things through," recalled Buch. "He was a funnel for orders from above who would suddenly appear at Battalion Headquarters and relay what higher command had in mind for us and then see it through." Hees agreed with Buch's assessment, recalling with great bitterness that Megill "carried out his orders with great determination," coded language to denote Moltke's axiom that commanders who are both "dumb and energetic" are the most dangerous of all.[30]

Yet despite the clash of personality, what many failed to grasp were the broader cultural and technological shifts in the Canadian military tapestry. Despite the best efforts of well-connected infantry regiments like the Black Watch to fight the trend, technocrats from the artillery and the corps of engineers had increasingly taken control of the higher direction of the Canadian Army.

The primacy of infantry to some had gone the way of the horse and buggy, or was at least on its way out. This was a new era, one of mobility, armour, firepower, intelligence and air power combining their efforts to bring about victory on the battlefield. With the best and brightest in Canadian manhood siphoned off by the modern and technologically enticing air force and navy, the army chose to lean towards technology, giving signals officers like Megill a comfortable upper-middle-class existence in the evolving culture of the Canadian defence establishment.

The other shift came with the schism between career-minded Permanent Force officers and their Non-Permanent Active Militia counterparts in regiments such as the Black Watch. Men like Megill had made their careers out of soldiering and resented to varying degrees those who did it only in their spare time or who were drawn by notions of schoolboy romanticism, family obligation or the allure of the regiment as a vehicle for social mobility. Many PF officers held the view that militia officers simply played soldier on weekends and in summer courses, rather than living the life daily, making them less *au courant* and professional in approach and naturally less entitled and deserving of postings, promotions and commands.

However, with that came the development of a PF clique that rivalled the regimental cliques step for step in syndicalist fashion. Unlike the men of means who made up most regimental officer corps, few of the PF officers had family fortunes or business-ownership interests to fall back on if something in their army career went sour. As such, the PF tended to close ranks around their own, knowing that their man walked a career tightrope devoid of a safety net, let alone one that proved gold-laced.[31]

The potential buffer between the Black Watch and Megill came with his staff, made up mostly of officers drawn from the three battalions under his command, including two from the Black Watch. Major Gordon "Torchy" Slater became Megill's first brigade major, while George Buch's best friend, Lieutenant Bill Doheny, a Bishop's College School old boy, served as his intelligence officer. Slater, who earned his nickname in part for the mane of red hair that matched his fiery disposition, was the type of officer Megill truly admired.[32] Like Stuart Cantlie, Slater was a "hitter," army parlance for an officer eager, willing and capable of taking the fight to the enemy.[33] Doheny, considered one of the best young Black Watch officers despite his "sloppy appearance" and penchant for drink, which the regimental elders euphemistically categorized as being "Irish in many ways," had an unlimited supply of charm and always proved "most effective" and able to "get things done."[34] With both men in crucial positions, hopes remained high that they could corral—or at least channel—Megill's stubborn demeanour with a well-timed bug in his ear once the bullets and the shells started to fly and his decisions meant life or death for the 2,500 men under his command.

4

BOUNCE THE ORNE

Battle is the most magnificent competition in which a human being can indulge. It brings out all that is best; it removes all that is base. All men are afraid in battle. The coward is the one who lets his fear overcome his sense of duty. Duty is the essence of manhood.

—GENERAL GEORGE S. PATTON

THE CANADIAN ATTACK ACROSS THE ORNE RIVER would come under the umbrella of a giant blitzkrieg-style offensive codenamed Operation Goodwood, Montgomery's latest bid to terminate the deadlock in Normandy in spectacular fashion.

Planned and conducted by General Miles Dempsey's 2nd British Army, the unprecedented plan called for an enormous force of 1,400 tanks, 1,500 guns and 80,000 men, supported by 2,000 fighter and bomber aircraft to deliver the ultimate colossal crack designed first to pierce the embryonic German defences south of Caen and then drive south towards the town of Falaise.[1]

Dempsey borrowed his concept for Goodwood straight from the pages of the 21st Army Group commander's North African playbook, where he had defeated Field Marshal Erwin Rommel's Afrika Korps in a master stroke at the Battle of El Alamein two summers before. This massive battle of attrition turned the tide in the desert war and now became the blueprint for victory south of Caen. Montgomery expected nothing less than a repeat performance.

Employing yet another massive carpet bombing, Dempsey's plan called for the decimation of the German line on the Bourguébus–Verrières feature whose capture he would use as bait to lure Rommel's panzer reserves into a costly dogfight. Wielding overwhelming numerical superiority in tanks, men, guns and air power, Dempsey sought to crush any attempt by Rommel to recapture the ridge, and in the process snap the spine of the German defences. With that accomplished, his armoured divisions would flood south onto the Falaise plain, grabbing all crossings over the Orne and Laize Rivers, shutting the door on Rommel's forces facing the Americans to the west. Hopelessly trapped and facing annihilation, the Desert Fox would have little choice but to withdraw or face certain destruction.[2]

Like so many other operations of war, on paper Goodwood appeared the most promising of plans.

Far down the chain of command, Cantlie discovered that his battalion would take the division lead in the Canadian subsidiary effort, codenamed Atlantic. Designed to support Goodwood, the proportionately ambitious Atlantic would be the combat debut for Simonds's 2nd Canadian Corps, comprising the weary 3rd Canadian Division and the 2nd Canadian Armoured Brigade, who had battled the Germans since D-Day, along with Foulkes's untested 2nd Canadian Division, returning to battle for the first time since its mauling at Dieppe in 1942.[3]

At first blush, the objectives that Simonds laid down appeared modest in comparison with the British task. While British armour battled farther to the east in the Bourguébus sector, Simonds's corps would cross the narrow Orne River, which bisected Caen, pushing through the industrial suburbs of the still-smouldering city and then capturing the westernmost end of the kidney-shaped rise known as Verrières Ridge. If all went well, hundreds of British Sherman, Cromwell and Churchill tanks would be streaming towards Falaise by the time Simonds's Canadian battalions slammed into the battered and bewildered elements of the elite 1st SS Panzer Corps defending the ridge.[4]

MEGILL'S ORDERS GROUP (O GROUP) FOR THE ORNE crossing commenced at the precise moment that the German shells took the lives of Garrett, Bleau and Watt at the crossroads less than a hundred yards from his tactical headquarters (Tac HQ), not far from the Abbaye d'Ardennes.[5]

Megill proudly informed Cantlie that Foulkes had selected the Black Watch, the senior battalion in his division, to take the vanguard in the attack scheduled to start late on the afternoon of July 18, ten hours after the British assault commenced.

As the 5th Brigade commander explained, the role carved out for Cantlie's men in the overture to Simonds's convoluted multi-phase scheme called for the Black Watch to "bounce" the hundred-foot-wide Orne River using assault boats and a floating kapok footbridge to establish a bridgehead on the southeast bank. Once across, the Royal Canadian Engineers would swing into action and erect two Bailey bridges to permit the remaining brigades in Foulkes's division and the tanks of the 2nd Canadian Armoured Brigade to cross and fan out southward en route towards Verrières Ridge.

At this point, Phase I of Atlantic would begin with the Régiment de Maisonneuve and the Calgary Highlanders, supported by tanks of the Sherbrooke Fusiliers, seizing their respective objectives: the tiny town of Fleury-sur-Orne and Hill 67, a dominating rise at the northern end of a small valley that led to Verrièrcs Ridge. While this unfolded, the Black Watch would pull up its tail on the Orne and capture the village of Ifs, west of Hill 67, to protect the exposed left flank of the Calgary Highlanders and provide a firm base for Brigadier Hugh Young's 6th Brigade to swarm up Verrières in their bid to seize the ridge in Atlantic's closing act.[6]

The role for the Black Watch was indeed demanding and potentially exhausting, but Cantlie harboured few doubts that his painful "treatment," which reached a fever pitch in the last few months of training in England, would now pay hefty dividends.

Before Megill reached his concluding remarks, tragedy struck again. German mortar fire, directed with skill from concealed German observers somewhere across the Orne, found its mark. Several men, including Padre Rod Berlis, presiding over the interment of the three men killed earlier in the day, succumbed in the latest round of shellfire. Berlis was hit in the lower neck by a white-hot shard of shrapnel. Few expected the popular man of God to live when they hoisted him onto an ambulance jeep, blood gushing from his gaping wound. Quick attention by the medics and Dr. Rudy Ohkle, however, saved his life, and his miraculous escape from the clutches of death led some to suspect that divine intervention played a significant role.[7] Others, particularly those given to histrionics, took his wounding as a harbinger of things to come.

Despite the best efforts of officers and NCOs to stamp out the wild talk, whispers and scuttlebutt bubbled to the surface suggesting the Black Watch was now a cursed battalion. "I guess it's human nature," George Buch recalled. "It was what soldiers do . . . but it's the last thing you need when you are about to go into combat for the first time."

•••

AT THE BEST OF TIMES SOLDIERS, LIKE ATHLETES, ARE
an overly superstitious lot. Much of this has to do with the lack
of control they experience when consumed by the context of
combat. Facing the fear, trepidation and horror that walk hand
in hand with war, soldiers tend to turn to some good luck charm,
or engage in a series of rituals, hoping to influence their fate or
their luck.

Sergeant Fred Janes of the intelligence section, who had been
Lieutenant Stan Duffield's senior colleague at the Royal Bank of
Canada during peacetime and was now his subordinate, kept a
bank key ring clipped to his webbing.[8] Harold Burden, the division's middleweight boxing champion, tucked his good luck
charm, a rabbit's foot, into his sniper's smock, while Captain John
Kemp squirrelled away his father's Colt .45 from the Great War
in a secret pocket of his battledress tunic.[9] Private Alex Duncan,
the notoriously clumsy member of the scout platoon, maintained
complete faith in his St. Christopher's medal—he believed it had
helped him cheat death on several occasions during training.[10]
Dale Sharpe kept a souvenir coin he had picked up while on
leave in London, along with a photograph of his wife and three
children.[11] Barney Benson carried a silver flask engraved with
R.E.H., which some suggested were the initials of his mysterious
fiancée, whom they only knew as Ruth.[12] Highly spiritual men
such as sniper Tommy Latham and his former rifle platoon mate
Private Johnny Breslin, both devout Roman Catholics, preferred
to line their helmets with the text of the Ninety-first Psalm, while
the agnostic, the spiritual and the merely superstitious favoured
a simple nod from the padre to ensure that if death did come, it
would be swift and painless.

Mike Brunner never carried a good luck charm, but he did
adhere to superstition, lacing his boots in a specific pattern and
carefully clipping his grenades in a precise order from his web

buckle outwards: high-explosive, then fragmentation, and finally the dreaded white phosphorus.[13] Hook Wilkinson took to cleaning his sniper rifle twice to prevent the spit on the swab pulled through the barrel on the first attempt from making it sweat, which would reduce accuracy when he needed it the most.[14] Some of his fellow snipers took their rifles everywhere, not so much because it was a soldier's best friend, but because the walnut or beech stock allowed them to touch wood constantly.

None of these behaviours were rational, but that was not the point. Satisfying the demands of faith, spirituality and superstition brought a measure of comfort and confidence and a sense of control, which in turn bolstered them to carry on in the face of abject fear, prolonged stress and terror. With one's life constantly hanging in the balance, it was only natural for men to search for opiates of the soul, fortified no doubt by the spectre of approaching battle and now the pitiful sight of their spiritual defender laid out, gasping for air, blood pouring from his mouth.

THE TONE OF MEGILL'S PRE-BATTLE BRIEFING FOR Atlantic left Cantlie and his officers with the distinct impression that their crossing of the Orne River would be relatively unopposed, given the sudden reshuffling of the German line. Indeed, Allied intelligence, mostly from high-level, ultra-secret signals intelligence, had picked up distinct signs of an abrupt retrograde movement as German formations streamed through the rubble of Caen making for the Bourguébus–Verrières feature.[15]

To Allied High Command, these moves made a good deal of sense; the slow but steady Allied advances in recent days had rendered the city strategically irrelevant from the German point of view. Soon, reports from French civilians confirmed what the "spies of the airwaves" had disclosed: elite SS panzer divisions had already started to move south and east of the city into the sector held by General Joseph "Sepp" Dietrich's 1st SS Panzer Corps, now hard at work preparing an embryonic main line of resistance that straddled Verrières Ridge.[16]

Perhaps more salient, the significant reshuffle betrayed that the Germans had reached a strategic crossroads in the battle of Normandy and had decided to hinge their entire defensive effort on the high ground south of Caen, the same high ground that now stood directly in the path of the oncoming Anglo-Canadian onslaught.

Upon his return to battalion headquarters, the Black Watch CO and his company commanders pored over the latest intelligence overprints, aerial photos and planning maps, all duly marked by Sergeant Freddy Janes and Private Booth of the intelligence section. Cantlie's former subordinates, Torchy Slater and Lieutenant Bill Doheny, who now served as Megill's brigade major and intelligence officer, laid out the enemy picture. Although the ever-evolving nature of enemy dispositions was of great concern, they stressed that Brigade and Division felt confident that the Black Watch assault would be, for the most part, a peaceful crossing.

Major Alan Stevenson, whose B Company would lead the battalion, recalled that the picture painted by Brigade led them to believe that "Jerry was not supposed to be there."[17] Likewise, Lieutenant Stan Duffield, who had returned earlier that day from a private battlefield inoculation with the Royal Regiment of Canada, saw it as a hope-for-the-best-and-plan-for-the-worst scenario: hope the crossing would be unopposed, but be prepared just the same to turn it into a full-blown assault at the first sign of trouble.

Cantlie, however, was not so optimistic. Knowing full well that German defensive doctrine called for trading firepower for manpower, the Black Watch CO surmised that if only a thin rear-guard remained, these fanatical and cornered elements would no doubt be lousy with carefully sighted machine guns, snipers and artillery observers, backed by mortars, rockets and artillery designed to inflict the maximum damage.

As such, preferring to err on the side of caution and mollify any unexpected interference before the operation began, Cantlie requested a series of speculative stonks on likely enemy hot spots by the guns of 5th Field Regiment attached to 5th Brigade. Megill, however, turned this down flat, explaining that Foulkes feared the artillery strikes might hit the men from the 3rd Canadian Division pushing south through the Faubourg de Vaucelles and did not want to flirt with possible fratricide.[18] Cantlie pressed the issue, with Foulkes eventually agreeing to provide on-call support, but this meant that rifle companies would have to hit trouble first before they could call for help.

His limited victory, however, still left Cantlie little room to manoeuvre; hauling assault boats and bridging equipment over half a mile of wide-open terrain in broad daylight was danger-ously problematic. Captain Ronnie Bennett suggested that his mortar platoon take on the task of smoking off the crossing point to shield their approach from enemy view. Cantlie, in concur-rence with his battle adjutant, Eric Motzfeldt, nixed this idea, fearing the screen would only alert the enemy to the impending crossing and draw their fire.[19] Faced now with a tactical conun-drum that could see his men cut to shreds before they reached the waterline, Cantlie requested that H-hour be pushed back sixty minutes until the last moments of daylight. Megill, after consult-ing with Foulkes, whose staff was busy tying up the multitude of loose ends associated with opening night, readily agreed. The Black Watch would now attempt to bounce the Orne at dusk, taking advantage of the fading light on July 18.[20]

• • •

THE FINAL PLAN THAT CANTLIE AND MOTZFELDT COBBLED together called for the battalion to move out from the abbey area just after the first bomber strike on the morning of July 18, bound for a rendezvous with the Royal Canadian Engineers in the western reaches of the battered city.

Aided by a team of veteran sappers and a bulldozer, Benson and his scouts would guide the rifle companies to their assembly area inside the oval of the Stade Hélitas, where they would receive their consignment of collapsible canvas boats and the kapok. While the men prepped the boats and the footbridge for easy carrying and deployment, Cantlie would establish his tactical headquarters on the top floor of a spacious, three-storey château a half mile east down the Boulevard Aristide Briand, which held a spectacular view of the crossing point.[21] The spot they selected for the crossing was a serene tree-lined stretch of the Orne River that in peacetime hosted picnicking French families along its banks, fishing its waters on weekends and holidays.

Without a preparatory artillery shoot, the key to getting across lay in the hands of Pudge Fraser's D Company. Laden with extra Bren guns, two-inch mortars and ammunition, the popular "Old Black Watchers" platoon would infiltrate to the river through a soggy drainage ditch that ran the length of the grassland separating the Orne from the Boulevard Aristide Briand and establish a base of fire at the bend. From this vantage point, his men could hose the proposed landing ground on the far bank or tackle anything that erupted in either direction along the river.

Major Alan Stevenson's B Company would have the honour of taking the lead in the Black Watch assault. Like Fraser, an Old Black Watcher, Stevenson was a highly efficient, extremely smart and tactically brilliant company commander who enjoyed great popularity amongst the officers, but not so much with his men.[22] The personification of the stereotypical upper-class officer, Stevenson's stiff demeanour and desire to remain on station, coupled with a peculiar penchant for referring to himself in the third person, gave rise to much mocking behind his back. Despite his personal shortcomings, no one dared question his tactical abilities, and in that realm, at least, he enjoyed their full confidence.

Precisely at H-hour, Stevenson's men would hoist the ten assault boats, plus their personal and platoon weapons, grenades, ammunition, wireless sets, picks, axes and shovels, and haul them across the half-mile expanse of wide-open grassland of a former horse racetrack to the riverbank. To assist in carrying and crewing the boats, Bennett chipped in one section from Buch's pioneer platoon to help shoulder the craft and lug the 55-horsepower outboard motors, which needed to be attached at the river line.[23]

As Stevenson's company steamed across the hundred-foot-wide river with its swift current, Griffin's A Company would place the kapok footbridge roughly two hundred yards downstream. Departing just minutes behind B Company, Griffin's men, with the aid of Buch and the rest of his pioneers, would manhandle the 20 six-foot-long kapok-filled floats to the Orne. Once in position on the banks, Buch's men would pound in two anchor stakes, attach the duckboards to each float, tie them off and feather each section, one by one, across the Orne until it reached the other bank. With the kapok up and running, Griffin's company would dart across to join Stevenson's in their nascent bridgehead with the scout platoon, Motzfeldt's C Company and Fraser's D Company hot on their heels.

With the entire battalion safely across, and the overture to Atlantic finished, there would be no rest for the rifle companies. Following a quick restocking of ammunition and a sweep of the streets ahead by the scout platoon to avoid ambush, Cantlie's men would have to hightail it to Fleury to meet the tanks from the Sherbrooke Fusiliers and prepare for their assault on the hamlet of Ifs, scheduled to take place that evening.[24]

WITH THE SPECTRE OF THEIR FIRST MAJOR ENGAGEMENT less than twenty-four hours away, few men found it easy to drift off at last light on July 17 despite their mounting exhaustion. Most tossed and turned between short bouts of sleep, each fixated on his mental, physical and spiritual preparation in anticipation of his combat debut.

Privates constantly obsessed about shooting straight, reloading quickly—or quickly enough—fighting hand to hand and tossing grenades without blowing either themselves or their section-mates to pieces. Corporals worried about recalling battle-drill commands at a moment's notice, while sergeants fretted about platoon tactics, support weapons handling and how they'd compel a man to carry out orders in the face of certain death. Platoon and company commanders spent long nights agonizing about making the right decision—or rather, the best decision—when confronted with a choice of the lesser of two evils.

But beyond their immediate jobs lay the crux of their worry, as Bruce Ducat explained: "It's quite the time in a man's life when you cross that line wondering if you've got it and battle was all about finding out whether you do, or you don't."

Indeed, combat is a powerful social leveller that strips a soldier's character bare. Once the first shots are fired and a soldier enters this macabre rite of passage, any notion of station, education, race, ideology, religion, gender or even sexual orientation cease to matter. Supreme above all is the contribution they make to the group, which becomes the anvil for judgment in a phenomenon anthropologists call *communitas*.[25]

Underpinning the entire process, however, is fear—constant,

unending, grinding and gut-gnawing fear—that manifests in a multitude of ways. "Like everybody else, it eats at you a little," Captain John Kemp reflected. "It's one of those things that's there, you've got it, and you're not going to get rid of it . . . it's a very difficult thing."[26]

Some, such as Bruce Ducat, chose to deal with the fear by rationalizing or adopting a fatalistic outlook. "This is war," he reasoned, "what do you expect? You are over there trying to stop us, and we're coming over to kill you." For Hook Wilkinson, it was mind over matter: "What am I going to do? I knew it was going to come. I knew there was no choice. One of these days, it may be my turn to get killed, you never know. I just said, 'Today is not my turn.'" Mike Brunner, on the other hand, "never thought of anything; never thought of what might happen . . . I was numb about it. At that age you're invincible."

For many of the men, the fear of death did not reign supreme; most dreaded the consequences of mutilation instead. "Getting killed was nothing," Ducat related. "I was worried about ending up in a wheelchair." Jimmy Bennett echoed his sentiment, one shared by scores of his comrades: "My main objective was to stay alive, but I wasn't afraid of being killed. If I get killed, I hope I get killed outright. I was afraid of losing my eyes . . . losing my eyes was the worst thing. It bothered me all the time." Corporal Gordy Donald concurred, but listed his sensitive spot far to the south—"I was terrified of losing my balls."

Greater perhaps than the fear of death or maiming was the all-consuming stigma associated with panic, psychological break-down and the involuntary loss of control that came with its own thorny crown of cruel rewards. Fostered by the military in a bid to maintain obedience and unit cohesion, and eagerly inflamed in Black Watch ethos and lore, the loathing, shame and emasculation associated with psychological collapse meant that nobody was harder on the men before a battle than the men themselves.

Beyond the simple questions of martial skill, every soldier, no matter their rank or job description, wondered how they would take it once the bullets and shells started to fly. Would they hold it together and overcome the all too human desire to flee, or would their fear paralyze and consume them? Could they harness the beast within and push aside, at least temporarily, the morality, civility and human compassion they fought para-doxically to restore to carry out their deadly jobs? Could they rationalize their actions, or would remorse and guilt consume them? Some questions, however, did not run so deep, nor were they as complex and nuanced. For Bruce Ducat, it came down to the most pedestrian and universal of fears: "God, I really hope I don't shit myself."

DAWN ON THE MORNING OF JULY 18 CAME EARLY AND quick, disturbed as it was by the drone of heavy bombers that broke the stillness of an unusually quiet yet restless night. Roused by the familiar siren song, hundreds of bleary-eyed Highlanders emerged from muddied and cramped slits to watch a massive flock of four-engine bombers soar in from the west at an unusually low altitude of three thousand feet. Destined for their targets to the south and east of Caen, this enormous armada of over a thou-sand aircraft easily tripled the force that had obliterated the city ten days earlier. To an astonished Lieutenant George Buch, the sight of the giant swarm was "majestic, to say the least, as plane after plane came straight past us—it was bloody magnificent!"

Starting at precisely 0600 hours, the first of 15,000 bombs crashed down for forty-nine minutes on a corridor in the German lines along the Bourguébus sector, with five thousand tons of earth-shattering high explosives duly administered in less than an hour. Once again, the men witnessed brilliant yellow flashes, followed by deep-brown geysers of dirt and debris that rocketed skyward while the earth trembled incessantly across the battle-front. German defenders, caught beneath this rain of death, were crushed or eviscerated or buried alive. Their vehicles and guns, including sixty-ton Tiger tanks, were tossed in the air like dis-carded toys, leaving them twisted, abandoned and half-buried in giant craters. The centuries-old village of Cagny, which had thrived since the days of the Romans, ceased to exist by any recognizable measure.

Buch, watching from several miles away, saw the explosions and then felt the concussive waves rip into his chest and "clear through" to his spine a second later.[27] When the last bomb of the first wave fell on their targets, another wave of a thousand air-craft—medium bombers, fighters and fighter-bombers—swooped down to fire rockets and drop fragmentation and high-explosive bombs. Then, on cue, the artillery opened fire.

At 0800 hours, over a thousand field, medium and heavy artillery pieces from units in the 2nd British Army opened fire, laying a concentration of high explosives on a wide range of tar-gets ringing the perimeter of the German positions that ran the ten miles from the banks of the Orne eastward to the town of Troarn. At regular intervals, the mammoth sixteen-inch shells fired from the *Rodney*, stationed off Juno Beach, joined them, arriving "like oncoming freight trains" that slammed home with a series of deep bass thuds.[28] Augmented by the guns of the mon-itor HMS *Roberts* and the cruisers *Enterprise* and *Mauritius*, the density of the shells screaming past overhead created a warm, stiff breeze. Soon, however, nothing could dissipate the giant, dark-grey cloud laced with debris that rolled in to eclipse the clear skies and bright sunshine and covered the entire battlefront in a cloak of gritty mist. As George Buch related, "Everything appeared to come off like clockwork. The excitement was palpable, and everyone was raring to go. After so many summers, there was a sense that our time had finally come."

THE ARRIVAL OF THE BLACK WATCH IN THE WESTERN end of Caen at noon on July 18 left Jimmy Bennett near paralyzed with dread. "Caen," he recalled, "was a scary place." The Norman capital now stood as a sombre testament to the barbarity of war. Mountains of debris, some thirty or forty feet high, lined both sides of Avenue Albert Sorel, which rendered the approach march towards the assembly area in the Stade Hélitas a hard, foreboding slog.

"Caen was nothing but a pile of rubble. You couldn't even walk down the street," Bennett remembered. Everywhere, shattered glass, torn fencing, bent girders, scattered roof and floor tiles, smashed furniture, hulks of squashed vehicles and massive chunks of concrete that sprouted twisted, severed wrought iron rebar blocked the traditional routes through the city.

Stuck behind a bulldozer from the Royal Canadian Engineers, Bennett choked on the exhaust fumes that belched freely from the beast as it cut a narrow, winding path through the wreckage. No matter how thick the cloak of diesel, nothing could alleviate the reek from the dead still entombed below the rubble or churned up with each violent thrust of the excavator's blade. Blended with the blunt pong of burnt timbers, damp concrete, plaster dust and the nauseating aroma of raw excrement that spewed forth from uprooted sewage pipes, it made for a chilling spectacle that quickened Bennett's breathing. In a flash, the grisly scene brought back the excited utterances of the young officer days before that now proved more repugnant than the stench: "It wasn't liberating—it was liquidating."

"Everywhere you looked, you could see death," an equally unnerved Bruce Ducat reported. "Even ten days later the smoke from smouldering cellars and charred corpses wafted past. It was godawful."

Plodding behind at the rear of the battalion, Sergeant Mac Roulston marvelled at the ancient Abbaye aux Hommes, still standing majestically amidst the scattered rubble. The Benedictine structure, housing the tomb of William the Conqueror, had taken damage during the bombing but remained defiantly intact. Now, ten days later, it played host to a horde of desolate citizens seeking shelter, food and medical attention. Up above, "they draped a large white sheet to ward off bombers," Roulston remembered. "It had a dark-red, crimson-coloured cross that rumour had it came from the blood drawn from the cadavers stacked four high awaiting disposal."

Attached to the abbey sat the Lycée Malherbe, one of France's leading secondary schools, which housed a refugee collection centre, a hospital and a makeshift morgue for victims of the bombings.[29] In the school grounds, hundreds of displaced French citizens, lost and reeling from the destruction of their homes, stood in a long, doleful queue, hoping to secure a loaf of bread and other essentials in desperately short supply. Canadian provosts kept the pitiful pack from approaching the men on the march, and the procession of Highlanders towards the assembly area paused only when a single car pulled out of the *lycée* grounds to shuttle the dead in twos and threes down the boulevard towards a local cemetery for burial.

When the battalion arrived at the stadium, which had suffered damage during an earlier bombing, they found the assault boats and kapok bridging waiting for assembly. Major Phil Griffin, whose company would erect the kapok bridge, had trained the entire battalion in the use of assault boats and was not a fan of the equipment. The boats, which were fragile and bulky to carry and designed for eighteen men, could only handle fourteen fully equipped riflemen. The canvas siding also had the annoying tendency to rip while being manhandled or when pulled from the trucks for set-up. Their detachable 55-horsepower Evinrude engines, as Griffin found out, were highly temperamental; some were "slow starters," while others failed to catch or stalled outright, leaving occupants hopelessly stranded on shore or precariously in midstream, resorting to rifle butts or bare hands for propulsion.

To offset these potentially tragic shortcomings, Griffin suggested that the lead boats carry toggle ropes to be staked out on the friendly side at embarkation and then paid out during the crossing and secured on the far bank upon landing. These lifelines would be used to pull stranded boats across in emergencies, or by the wounded to haul themselves back across to safety.[30]

But getting the boats to the river line was another tricky chore that required skill and teamwork. To limit the damage, the men in Stevenson's company planned to hoist the boats onto their shoulders bottom-up and carry them half a mile, gunwales cutting into their shoulders until they reached the river line. This, however, was much preferable to the slow and cumbersome hulldown method, where the boats would be dragged and dropped, an approach considered far too slow for open terrain and one that increased the chance of tearing the canvas siding or snapping the wooden supports.[31]

Adding to their strain, rifles, Stens and Bren guns had to be lugged either in their open hand or slung around their heavily laden necks. To ensure smooth handling, the relative height of the men hauling the craft needed to be appropriately paired on each side to maintain balance and rhythm. The three men chosen to crew the boat followed closely behind with the outboard engine in hand, ready to slap it on the back when the craft was flipped and launched at the waterline.[32]

As could be expected, the level of anxiety started to rise as H-hour approached. As Cantlie suspected, ongoing changes on all levels, no doubt a symptom of opening night jitters, forced him to rework elements of the plan four times between noon and 2030 hours. Fed up with the constant interruptions from German shelling, which seemed to find them wherever he held his O Groups, Cantlie sent out a small patrol led by the mortar platoon officer, Lieutenant Jock Neil, to the river line, intent on pinpointing the location of the enemy observation post (OP).[33]

Beefed up with a few men from B Company who were left out of battle for the river crossing, Young Hook took point and steered the Black Watch band down the same gulley that Fraser's men would use to reach their covering point later that evening. But when the patrol reached the river line at the end of the ditch and the men broke the surface, the concealed German observation they hoped to spot noticed them first. Within seconds, a cluster of bouncing bombs, 81-millimetre mortar shells saddled with a second charge designed to blast the shell back up into the air after landing to create an airburst effect, detonated, showering the area in a cascade of lethal fragments.

From the upper floor of the château nearly half a mile away, Cantlie saw several men fall before a second deadly mortar stonk hit home, enveloping the area in a cloud of dirt and debris. Moments later, when the veil of dust dissipated, he spotted several figures lying crumpled near the river's edge. None in the clump displayed signs of life or movement, while the others on the patrol had slipped from view. A few minutes later, the first survivors from the patrol filtered back into Black Watch lines, bringing the grim account of what Cantlie and other onlookers suspected: Neil had been hit and wounded, but had made it back to the regimental aid post; Lance Corporal George MacKay, the artist from BCS, and Private Wilkinson had been killed instantly.[34]

Word of his brother's death hit Jim "Hook" Wilkinson like a thunderbolt; instantly, the young sniper's thoughts turned to his mother in Montreal. Still devastated by her husband's abandonment and his subsequent disappearance not long after Hook joined the army, George had become her pillar of strength until he too joined the Black Watch. All Hook could envision at that moment was the imminent arrival of a bicycle-bound messenger bearing the far too impersonal telegram conveying the generic regrets of the Minister of National Defence. He wondered now if his sisters could hold their mother together or whether his father would ever know that his youngest son had died following in his footsteps. Hook's grief was "intense," and at moments "overwhelming," but thankfully short-lived. Before he could fully comprehend the significance of the loss, his kid brother emerged from the gully, soaked and muddied but very much alive.[35]

Perhaps not surprising in a regiment of Scottish traditions, four Private Wilkinsons had arrived with the battalion when it landed in Normandy on July 6. One was Private Arthur Campbell Wilkinson, a tall, fair-haired, twenty-four-year-old former sergeant with the Canadian Postal Corps who reverted to a private and joined the Black Watch to ensure he saw combat.[36] A week earlier, he explained to his mother in a carefully worded note that there was little he could say about his current predicament, except that "it is a gigantic business and we are fighting a tough enemy."[37] These, as it turned out, were his last words to her, for he was the Private Wilkinson killed close to the riverbank.

The initial relief and elation Hook felt when he discovered the mix-up proved fleeting; it was solidly checked by the grim realization that "the other Wilkinson had a mother too." Indeed,

Arthur's mother, Alta, at home in Ottawa, would receive the dreaded telegram.[38]

THE RECEPTION THE PATROL GOT MADE IT CLEAR THAT the crossing was not going to be unopposed as brigade, division and corps had expected. Once again, Cantlie pressed to push H-hour back until darkness had fallen. This, however, proved futile; the entire divisional plan relied on the Black Watch getting over the Orne quickly so that the engineers could place the two Bailey bridges to open the bottleneck for the division to advance south. With little leeway, the best Megill could offer was one hour, moving H-hour back to last light at 2215 hours. Although not ideal, it was the best Cantlie could hope for under the circumstances, and it now meant that Fraser's D Company, which would move down the same ditch employed by the patrol, would need to be in place by 2200 to ensure they would be in position in sufficient time to cover the crossing.

Yet, with everything in place for the assault, Cantlie and his company commanders were alive to the fact that any plan, no matter how good on paper, no matter how tight or how well rehearsed, seldom survives contact with the enemy.

Once the starter's gun had sounded and the companies were on the move towards the river, Cantlie's influence as battalion commander, situated in his tactical headquarters, would be minimal to non-existent in the minute-by-minute battle. Success or failure of the operation would now sit in the hands of his company commanders, their platoon officers, and NCOs. Hopefully, their years of training would translate into the situational awareness needed to get into the picture quickly once the bullets and shells started to fly. Combat in its truest sense is neither strictly science nor art, but rather a deadly craft that requires seasoning and experience and what the Germans call *Fingersptizengefühl*, or "fingertip feel." Successful battlefield leaders are expected to observe, assess, act, react and make split-second decisions amid the fog of war and then push those through with flexibility, fortitude and determination, all while the enemy is trying to kill them. At this point, Cantlie, his officers and his men could learn nothing more from training or inoculation. Their finishing course could only come now, in the hard school of combat.

AT ONE MINUTE BEFORE H-HOUR, STEVENSON'S SUPERB company sergeant major, Vic Foam, one of four brothers from Deal, Kent, to follow in their father's footsteps in the service of the king, gave the order to "hoist boats." A soldier through and through, Foam's bark jolted the men into action, and in almost perfect unison, all ten assault boats lifted into the air and then promptly settled on their shoulders, releasing a cascade of grunts and curses.[39]

A shuffling of weapons and webbing followed as chest pouches, bulging with extra ammunition clips for rifles, Sten and Bren guns, clashed with picks, shovels and axes strapped to their backs or slung through their belts. All sported webbing crowded with grenades, while several carried extra projectiles for the platoon anti-tank weapon, the hand-held, shoulder-fired PIAT (Projector Infantry Anti-Tank). Just over three feet long and weighing thirty-two pounds, this ungainly beast of a bomb thrower did not so much shoot its two-and-a-half-pound projectile on targets like the rocket-firing American bazooka or German *Panzerschreck* as much as it flung it via a tightly cocked spring that ignited a propulsion charge. Highly effective at short ranges, it required nerves of steel to wait for a tank to get within its effective range of fifty to one hundred yards to pop off a shot. However, until the battalion's anti-tank gun platoon ferried across on the assault boats or the Bailey bridges allowed the Sherman tanks of 2nd Canadian Armoured Brigade to stream across, this would be the battalions' primary defence against panzer counterattack.

Ten minutes earlier, Stevenson led his men from the Stade Hélitas across Boulevard Aristide Briand to a dirt track that lined the northern fringe of the grassland. Here they paused to catch their breath and make final checks of their equipment. Crouched on one knee, Stevenson stared at his pocket watch, anxiously counting down to H-hour. With ten seconds to go, he snapped his map case shut, swung it around over his left hip and then checked his watch once more. At precisely 2115, he rose, reached behind with his right arm and held it for a beat, then waved it forward. With that, the Black Watch attempt to bounce the Orne began.

Lurching forward, the platoons of Stevenson's company plowed into the knee-high grass, struggling at first to find their rhythm with the cumbersome craft. The thumping of over 125 pairs of boots, which at first resembled the pounding sound of a team of unbridled Clydesdales, swept past Place Foch and the statue devoted to France's Great War dead off to the left flank. Finally, after a few awkward steps, the men caught their stride and the beat.

Cantlie, joined by Doheny, Benson, Bennett and Duffield, monitored the proceedings through their binoculars and telescopes, while Captain Campbell Stuart, the adjutant, worked frantically with his signaller to keep the battalion's wireless set netted to the advancing companies. Entrenched in slits on the château grounds, half of the scout platoon remained concealed, providing close protection for tactical headquarters, while the others, perched near the aid post, manned stretchers, "ready," as

Hook Wilkinson recalled, "to dart out and retrieve the wounded should the shit hit the fan."

At twenty-five-yard intervals, Stevenson, who was advancing just behind Corporal Ducat's boat, swivelled around to ensure that his men remained tightly bunched, ready to swarm across the Orne in one massed block rather than in piecemeal fashion. So far, the only sounds of battle came from the distant rumble thrown up by the massive tank clash unfolding east of Caen and from aircraft and artillery roaring overhead towards targets in the distance.

For the time being, the guns of Fraser's platoons remained silent, which Stevenson took as a most promising sign now that his company was one-third of the way towards the river. At this moment, the lead elements of Griffin's A Company broke cover at the north end of the field, hauling portions of the kapok footbridge. Private Gordy Donald, standing slightly under average size, laboured along with a six-foot duckboard strapped to his back. Protruding three feet above his heavily camouflaged helmet, he expected it would make the perfect target for even the most short-sighted of German gunners. Like his platoon mates, Donald sported pouches teeming with extra clips for his Sten gun and a daisy chain of Hawkins grenades for tackling panzers in close combat. Echeloned behind, men from Lieutenant Alan Robinson's platoon plodded forward, laden with their own burden. While some advanced saddled with shovels, axes and sledgehammers to pound in the mooring stakes, others, paired up for the job, carried the six-foot canvas floats stretched between them, ready for insertion at the water's edge.

Advancing at a slightly quicker pace and 150 yards off the left rear flank, it was not long before Griffin's company started to close the gap with Stevenson's men. Halfway across the field, everything remained on track, and Fraser's company remained blissfully silent. Only the pulsating thump of boots meeting grass, the rattle of equipment and the steadying tones of CSM Foam and other platoon NCOs urged the men to keep moving.

At that point, Motzfeldt's C Company moved across the Boulevard Aristide Briand and prepared for its dash across the grassland. A quarter mile from the riverbank, Stevenson turned to check the progress and cohesion of his platoons and instantly froze in horror. Trailing far behind Motzfeldt's men was Fraser's company. "You can imagine my uneasy feeling," Stevenson wrote, "when I got halfway across the open field thinking D company were in position only to see them breaking cover behind!" For some unexplained reason, Fraser's company now stood half a mile from its objective on the river bend, leaving the men from A and B Companies hung out to dry in a wide-open field, devoid of covering fire.

Having rehearsed river assaults for months, a mistake of this nature at this juncture was incomprehensible and thoroughly inexcusable. Fraser never made mistakes, particularly one as elementary as missing his timing. Something must have been lost when they tweaked and then retweaked plans and timetables during the series of O Groups held earlier that day. "It was impossible to think of going back," Stevenson recalled, "and anyway all you could hear was silence." Cycling through what few options he had, Stevenson realized the unsettling fact that, even before they contacted the enemy, the Black Watch plan had not survived. Worse yet, the damage was self-inflicted. As Stevenson reported, "At that moment, I did an awful lot of wishful thinking."

Boldly confronted by the old military maxim "order, counter-order, disorder," the B Company commander now had a life-or-death decision to make on the fly: Should he halt his company in the field and wait for Fraser's men to catch up, or continue to advance to the riverbank, hoping to launch his assault unscathed? Neither course of action was ideal, but such is the nature of command and decision-making in war. With little hesitation, he chose the latter course of action.

Frantically, he began to pump his fist up and down, ordering the men to move at double time. The steady refrain to keep moving turned to stern barks laced with urgency. "Pick up the pace! Pick up the pace! Move faster! Faster!" came the cries from Foam and the other NCOs. Griffin, moving at the head of his company farther behind in the field, noticed the mix-up too and, like Stevenson, ordered his men to double-time it to the river.

Less than a quarter mile from the northern bank of the Orne, both leading companies were now fully exposed. One lumbered forth with a collection of large, enticing targets propped prominently on their shoulders, and the other trundled behind, hoping to make it to cover before all hell broke loose.

Watching the spectacle unfold from his post on the upper floor of the château, Duffield recorded, "The Germans waited until the assault company got well out in the open with its boats, and then opened fire." Stevenson, now leading from the front, said, "Jerry waited till the lead boat was about 50 yards from the bank and let us all have it with light machine guns and mortars." Dug in off the right flank, a pair of deadly German MG 42s now came to life. Firing in long, ten-second bursts, their telltale ripping sound—the signature of the most feared machine gun in the world—announced the arrival of a twin torrent of bullets laced with green-and-yellow tracer fire that slammed into Stevenson's men.[40]

Through his binoculars, Duffield spotted violent puffs of grey Blanco shoot out the back of Lieutenant Bob Austin, his former mate from their days with the Victoria Rifles. Austin was struck by rounds just above both elbows, and his rifle tumbled to the ground, involuntarily released when his arms, muscles and tendons shredded, seized at right angles.[41] Two more rounds struck home in quick succession—one pierced his lower abdomen, the other his left leg, fracturing it. The tall, thin, white-collar kid from Westmount slumped onto the grass, writhing in agony, now paralyzed from the knees down, his bowels and stomach filling with blood. Given the intensity of the German fire and under orders to keep moving to the water, nobody dared stop to help.[42] Ducat, who saw Austin fall, could only hope that his twenty-three-year-old platoon commander, whom he referred to as a "real gentleman," would still be breathing when the stretcher-bearers reached him.

Racing towards the river with boats propped high on their shoulders, the men in B Company now had to contend with the German mortar fire that joined the fray. Plunging down just behind the last boat, the shells ripped up the ground, throwing grass, dirt and shrapnel in all directions, which forced Stevenson's men to charge forward through the lines of machine-gun fire. In quick succession, men and boats started to fall, torn by bullets ripping into the axis of their advance. One of the first bursts caught Stevenson in the left arm, but luckily it was a tracer round that delivered a through-and-through wound that failed to find bone, muscle or tendon. Others, however, were not so lucky.

The terrifying impact of taking fire and casualties for the first time ignited confusion throughout the lead company, and unit cohesion started to wane as NCOs and officers fell alongside their men. Hoping to save the impossible situation, Stevenson furiously waved the men to the right, ordering them to follow his lead in a mad dash for cover in the ditch. "Did you ever see an antelope running wide open?" he later recalled. "Well, that was I."[43]

But not all his men caught in the wild rush could hear his orders above the explosions and cries for medics or see his hand signals through the dust and smoke now rising from the burning grass. Corporal Johnny Watson, a gawky farm boy from the Eastern Townships south of Montreal, moving with his boat on the easternmost extreme of the company, streaked past the fire chewing up his comrades and managed to reach the riverbank with his men and boat intact.

In perfect coordination, as if on an exercise in England, they flipped their assault craft over, dumped their weapons inside and then dragged it to the water's edge, where they mounted the engine on the stern and pushed off. For the moment, luck was riding with them as the temperamental outboard fired up on the first strike. But even at full throttle, the 55-horsepower Evinrude was underpowered with the trim low in the water. Weighed down by fourteen men with a full complement of equipment, the outboard motor did not so much roar as it chugged, moving so slowly that the hundred-foot-wide Orne seemed like an ocean. The level of anxiety of the men on board increased dramatically when the machine-gun fire lifted from the field and swept to the right and settled along the riverbank, where it raked the thin tree line, tearing off leaves and branches and shattering tree trunks, showering the area with pine shards.[44]

Focused on the job at hand, Watson searched for an inviting landing spot while his men paid out the toggle rope. They failed to notice the tracer fire whipping past overhead. Just a few yards short of the touchdown on the enemy side, both the line and the luck of this gallant group ran out. German gunners had found their mark and descended upon the boat without mercy.

Bruce Ducat, who had crawled into the waterlogged ditch after the first mortar shells landed, watched in horror as the first burst decapitated the men seated aft, their torsos slumping to the bottom of the boat, leaving a large pool of blood awash on the wooden floorboards. Then the second burst hit, shredding the canvas on the starboard side near the bow, along with Watson and the rest. The violent impact of scores of machine-gun bullets heaved Watson into the murky Orne, where, mortally wounded and with nothing to clutch onto, he flailed madly until the weight of his boots, webbing and ammunition dragged him to the river-bed a dozen feet below.[45]

The unintentional sacrifice of Watson and the men in the lead boat permitted three craft carrying Lieutenant Don Menzies's platoon to land intact. Wasting no time, his men spread out and went to work cutting gaps in the barbed wire and tying off toggle ropes for the boats behind.

Back across the Orne, Menzies's company commander, Alan Stevenson, bleeding from his wounded arm, found the ditch where Ducat had huddled with two other men. Leo "Smokey" Lalonde he knew well, for the twenty-three-year-old private was as sharp a shot with his Bren gun as he was with his mouth. Four years into his military service, his impulsive and insolent talents had kept him a private.[46] Private Herb McLeod was the opposite: a quiet, reserved, but highly strung twenty-year-old, the eldest of eleven children, who joined the army to save the family farm after his father died in the fall of 1941. Sitting with his pants around his ankles, he dutifully patched up his right knee, torn open by a mortar fragment, and, as Ducat recalled, in the best Black Watch tradition, "picked up his drawers and got back into battle." This small group was all that remained of two of Stevenson's three rifle platoons and his headquarters company.

Stevenson counted thirty-six men lying prone, strung out in a line that dribbled down to the waterline next to a collection of abandoned boats scattered along their axis of advance. "Some were stone cold still, while others called or waved for a medic," Ducat recalled. "Our company," he continued, "now consisted of five men in No. 10 platoon, one in No. 11 platoon, with

No. 12 platoon [under Menzies] still intact." Of the 120 men with whom Stevenson had started the advance less than fifteen minutes before, only forty-one could carry on the fight, with thirty-seven of these on the enemy side of the river, cut off and vulnerable to German counterattack until the remainder of the Black Watch arrived.

Sensing that Stevenson was considering ordering the surviving trio out to retrieve an abandoned boat to continue the assault crossing, Ducat piped up, "If you want to get across this river, you better learn how to swim! Those boats are going nowhere, sir!" Frustrated, Stevenson reluctantly agreed with his brazen corporal, who had a series of knocks of his own on his record for mouthing off to superiors. Cut off from his signaller, who lay dying in the field next to his smashed wireless set, Stevenson stifled Ducat's impertinence with a direct order to work his way back to Tac HQ, a thousand yards behind, to deliver a situation report to Cantlie.

Realizing his chances were far better moving towards battalion headquarters than crossing the Orne, Ducat gladly took off, using the ditch, towards the château—passing Major Pudge Fraser, who finally arrived with his company in tow, twenty minutes late. Although there is no specific record describing their encounter, it is fair to suggest after reading Stevenson's account that his greeting for his old friend was, to say the least, icy. Under the present circumstances, however, there was precious little time to waste in finger-pointing, and ignoring Stevenson, Fraser dug his platoons in along the bank. In a few seconds, his Bren guns began to chatter in an attempt to suppress the German machine guns; some of their fire, however, overshot its intended target and plunged into the lines of the 3rd Division, crossing about half a mile to the east.[47] Private Carmen Barnhardt, the Mohawk mortarman from the Six Nations Reserve in Caledonia, Ontario, whose twitchy neck and shaky hand disqualified him as a sniper, went to work immediately, laying down a smokescreen to obscure the enemy's field of fire.

Farther down the riverbank on the left flank of the Black Watch assault, the heavy fire that decimated Stevenson's company turned out to be a blessing for Griffin's A Company. Moving unmolested through the field, Griffin's men reached the river and were able to pound in the mooring stakes and hitch up the first section of the kapok while the German machine guns dispatched Watson's boat.

Lieutenant Jock McLennan's platoon was first to slide its floats and duckboard into the water, followed almost robotically by those hauled by Lieutenant Tommy Dorrance's platoon. With the aid of Lieutenant Buch's pioneers, the first two sections reached out across the Orne in record time, but the third set, handled by Lieutenant Alan Robinson's men, proved problematic and slowed down the process. The men on the bank who had rid themselves of the kapok floats or duckboard had to dig in quickly when the German fire found them too.

The smokescreen laid down by Private Barnhardt had, as Cantlie and Motzfeldt feared, a double-edged effect. Although it obscured the events unfolding along the water to a certain degree, it hindered Fraser's gunners from finding their targets and magnetized the German fire to the crossing point. Although not as accurate as it was earlier in the attack, the German fire did increase in volume, with sniper fire now joining the mix from concealed positions across the river.

Periodically, German fire forced the furious work on the kapok to halt when bursts of machine-gun fire tore down the bank and out into the river, and incoming mortar rounds forced all to take cover immediately. Miraculously, none of the enemy fire inflicted casualties on A Company, but the kapok took a beating. Three-quarters of its floats suffered punctures by bullets or shrapnel, but all remained buoyant, a testimony to their legendary capacity for ruggedness and dependability under fire. With two sections firmly in place, it was now a race to finish the span before the Germans could zero in and destroy it.[48]

At tactical headquarters, Cantlie did not need a wireless message from Stevenson to realize things had gone horribly wrong. Worried now about the entire operation collapsing, the Black Watch CO grabbed a signaller and his wireless set and took off towards the river, leaving his adjutant, Captain Campbell Stuart, to run the show while he attempted to pick up the pieces on the Orne.

With darkness now enveloping the battlefield, Stuart ordered the stretcher-bearers to go to work, and several of the scouts, including Mike Brunner and Dale Sharpe, joined a small squad of pipers and drummers led by medic Corporal William Steel, who moved with stretchers in hand to bring home the wounded while under fire. By all accounts, they had their hands full. By midnight, less than two hours after the attack started, the 18th Field Ambulance had treated thirty men, but they reported ominously that more "casualties had begun to come in." Thirty minutes later, Major Letourneau, a Montreal doctor who tended to most of the men himself, recorded that another "75 casualties were admitted since [midnight] and evacuated, nearly all Black Watch [and] nearly all bullet wounds," and then noted with disgust that "too much faith had been placed in the success of the plan."[49] Steel garnered a mention in dispatches for his selfless devotion to duty hauling dozens of his comrades, including Lieutenant Bob Austin, out of the murderous fire.

Most had flesh or minor wounds, but others arrived in a "moribund" state, including Private Albert Warburton, who had taken shrapnel to his head from one of the first mortar rounds.[50]

Warburton died without regaining consciousness at 0330 on a stretcher next to Lieutenant Bob Austin, who miraculously still clung to life despite his horrific wounds. Duffield took it as a sign that his old friend would make it. Upon a more detailed examination when he reached the aid station, Letourneau discovered a third hole in Austin's lower abdomen, filled with dark blood. This was the bullet that nicked his spine and left him paralyzed from the waist down. Austin was now in grave condition and fading fast. Repeated plasma transfusions could not stabilize him, and within forty-eight hours he too was dead.[51]

While the scramble was on to reach and evacuate the wounded, Corporal Bruce Ducat finally reached Black Watch tactical headquarters to deliver Stevenson's situation report to Cantlie. Failing to find the commanding officer, the pugnacious corporal, sweating profusely and out of breath, confirmed to Captain Campbell Stuart what everyone already suspected: "I have to report that one boat got across [but] they are all dead." Unfazed by the news, which was already far out of date, Stuart told Ducat that Cantlie had "gone up to the river" with a wireless operator to sort out the mess, and ordered him to return immediately to the banks of the Orne to find the colonel.

Frustrated and exhausted, Ducat duly departed for another run down the ditch. He found Cantlie on the riverbank, pacing back and forth like a "caged animal," thoroughly incandescent, fuming at the screw-up that had needlessly cost lives and precious time.[52] The entire timetable for Atlantic was now behind schedule, and pressure from Brigade and Division to press on increased with every minute.

Cantlie, checking his pocket watch again and again, sought a solution that would speed up the pace, which proved impossible at the present moment. Next to him sat his signaller, Private Robert Stephen, soaking wet, with the battalion's No. 18 wireless set in pieces by his feet. With a rag in hand, the young private worked feverishly to dry each component of the radio, which had ended up submerged in the Orne when an enemy mortar shell, which had narrowly missed Cantlie, tossed him into the river upon arrival at the bank minutes before.[53]

With his hopes dashed for the time being of taking command of the situation on the far shore, Cantlie rounded up what few stragglers he could find to cross the Orne on anything that would float. "Stay with me," he ordered Ducat.

"Yes sir! Gladly," replied the exhausted corporal. "I will tell you one thing, sir, my Sten gun hasn't got a firing pin—it broke off. I would like to throw it in the river!" Before Cantlie could respond, a cry of success from Stephen went up that the wireless set was dried and reassembled, putting the CO back in contact with the battalion and brigade headquarters, as well as Menzies on the other side.

With everyone now on the same page and the fragile element of command and control restored, Cantlie began to call down artillery fire on the German machine-gun nests, which temporarily alleviated the pressure and provided some much-needed breathing room. At the same time, Buch had helped Robinson solve the kapok issue, and Menzies's platoon had grabbed the last section of the footbridge and anchored it to the far shore, putting the Black Watch back in business. With the cry of "kapok open," Griffin's men emerged from their hastily dug slits and scrapes and surged forward towards the tenuous span, hell-bent on crossing the Orne. But no sooner had the cry gone out than trouble descended.

On a return leg from a night reconnaissance operation, a low-flying *Schwärme* of four German FW-190s bounded in over the Abbaye aux Hommes and Black Watch tactical headquarters on a direct path for the crossing point. Whether directed by the German observation post still in action across the river or just capitalizing on the opportunity presented by the spectacular tracer fire below, the aircraft swept in fast and low, wings flashing, tracers streaming from their four 20-millimetre cannons. "Christo de la Madonna! I thought that was it!" Stevenson reported when each released its payload of four 110-pound bombs, which tumbled wildly to earth and crashed down in a random pattern from the ditch right out into the Orne.[54]

Minutes before the planes arrived, Private Jimmy Bennett reached the river line with the rest of Motzfeldt's C Company, only to find that everything was jammed up. Motzfeldt, as anxious as Cantlie to get things moving again, seized the initiative and ordered his men to salvage what few of the craft could still float and make the crossing to alleviate the bottleneck of men queuing for the footbridge.

Following a flurry of activity, Bennett found himself in the lead boat, halfway across the Orne, when the German fighters swooped in and another round of German mortar fire arrived. With adrenalin coursing through his veins, Bennett's frequently elevated level of anxiety had tapered off to manageable levels, but his initial exposure to full-blown combat was by no means an exercise in heroism in the classical sense. Self-preservation served as his driving force amidst the confusion. "Anybody that tells you they know what's going on, they don't . . . You don't know what's going on ten feet beside you. Guys could be getting killed thirty feet away, you don't see them. You don't care about them, you're trying to think about yourself."

Like Watson's craft earlier, the boats trailing behind Bennett's absorbed the worst of the cannon and mortar fire. Men not killed outright found themselves thrashing in the water, struggling to reach the nearest toggle rope to inch themselves back to shore. With too few lines in place and the injuries to the wounded sapping their strength, several men slipped beneath the surface and drowned.[55]

Bennett, fully aware of the commotion behind, could only will his boat to move faster to the far shore. In a desperate bid to cling to his fragile sanity as another wave of fear swept over him, Bennett remained blinkered, fixated on the job at hand. "I didn't look behind me, I looked in front because I was going across the river to cut the wire. Who came behind me didn't matter . . . I was too interested in keeping alive."

Downstream from Bennett's craft, mortar shells plunged down on Griffin's men readying to cross the kapok. Miraculously, the luck of A Company, which was rapidly approaching legendary status, continued to hold. George Buch, who was dug in alongside Griffin, watched in amazement as one shell landed next to Jock McLennan, whose impressive size and powerful demeanour the men had come to trust and rely upon. The blast flung the goliath high into the sky and "ass over teakettle," Buch recalled, before he descended onto the exact spot he had lifted off from a moment before.[56] Landing hard on all fours, the platoon commander stared straight into the ground and then began to search aimlessly for his helmet and rifle. The men around him, who had frozen with amazement at the spectacle that just unfolded, waited for his giant frame to collapse; it didn't. The men were awestruck as they retrieved his rifle and helmet. Seconds later, McLennan was on his feet, rifle in hand and helmet propped awkwardly on his head. The young platoon commander appeared no worse for wear, apart from an intense ringing in his ears, but seemed unusually quiet and despondent, no doubt suffering from the concussion of the blast and perhaps captivated by his narrow escape from death.[57]

But good luck does not last forever. The last shell in the latest salvo dropped dead centre on the newly completed kapok bridge, severing the lashings of the middle sections and setting them adrift. Realizing the gravity of the situation, and angered that all his arduous work would go for naught, George Buch dove into the water and swam out to the gap before it widened too far. He grabbed one section with his left hand and dragged it out to midstream until it drew taut, and then swung his feet out to hook the other section tethered to the far bank before it drifted away. With his boots entwined, he pulled the two spans towards each other, but with insufficient strength to complete this Herculean task, he sat stalemated, stretched out as a human span linking the bridge.[58]

The always-pragmatic Griffin seized upon the opportunity and ordered his men to move at full gallop, with McLennan's platoon leading the way across the bridge. One by one, they bounced off Buch's shoulders and back, using him as the linchpin to connect each side of the span until help arrived to permanently lash the footbridge together. Wet and bruised, and with his only set of eyeglasses dangling precariously from the collar of his tunic, the exhausted pioneer platoon commander swam back to shore to catch his breath and report to Cantlie that the bridge, for the time being at least, was in operation.

The men from Motzfeldt's C Company who had survived the crossing with Bennett came under sniper fire less than two hundred yards down the river, where they disembarked amid a tangle of barbed wire. Bennett fumbled with his wire cutters, dropping them twice. On the third attempt, he sank the cutters into the wire but didn't have the strength to clamp down to sever the strand. Without his combat gloves, which he had forgotten in his small pack, Bennett's hands ended up a bloody mess. Through his almost-paralytic condition, he managed on his second attempt to cut a gap, all the while thinking about the sniper's bullet with his name on it—the one he feared would take his eyesight at any moment. Yet he succeeded in opening a breach for his platoon to follow, leaving him bewildered by his relative good fortune. "I don't know how I got out of that mess, I just don't know," he later recalled.

When word came through of the initial completion of the footbridge, Duffield and Benson grabbed the scouts not involved in casualty evacuation and raced down to the riverbank to prepare for their crossing on the heels of A Company. As Cantlie had told Duffield before he departed for the river, once the companies had crossed, he wanted the scouts to launch a series of patrols that would fan out in the built-up area of Faubourg de Vaucelles and hunt for snipers, machine-gun nests and the German observation post directing the German fire at the crossing point.

Moving quickly down the ditch, they covered the ground quickly and arrived on the riverbank to find Griffin's men queuing for the bridge. Left in the open, they jumped into A Company's newly vacated slits. With everything moving so fast, there had been little time to draw up a proper patrol plan, something that Duffield and Benson went headlong into arranging when the Focke-Wulf 190s arrived and the latest mortar stonk hit.

Hook Wilkinson, who had caught a break after the apparent near-death experience of his kid brother, sat alone in his slit, flanked by fellow snipers Harold Burden, Alex Duncan and Fred Delutis. "All of a sudden," Hook recalled, "a mortar shell landed," which knocked the scout platoon corporal cold. When Hook regained consciousness seconds later, the dust had just begun to settle, and he could feel nothing. Over the pronounced ringing in his ears, he heard men screaming. Burden, who emerged from his slit in one piece, crawled over to Wilkinson and shouted, "Hook? How are you feeling?" Still stunned and terrified by the concussive effects of the blast, Hook said, "I don't know." Wilkinson patted his body to make sure everything remained in place, and continued to blink rapidly to clear his vision, which brought the fate of Alex Duncan into sharp focus.

Less than two yards away, Duncan's lifeless body lay pinned to the stump of a sheared pine tree in the sitting position, his helmetless head flung back, eyes and mouth agape, blood trickling from his ears and nose. A large, deep-red pool of blood gathered below the lower fringe of his sniper smock where his legs once joined his hips, slowly retreating into the freshly churned soil. "That's how close—that's how close," was all Wilkinson could think at that moment, until Barney Benson smacked the back of his helmet, which roused him to his senses. "Get out of here and cross the river," he barked, "or you're all dead!"

BY 0400 HOURS, THE REST OF THE BRIGADE AND LARGE parts of the division had poured over the tiny kapok or been ferried across by the Royal Canadian Engineers. Confusion and congestion reigned in the tiny bridgehead, with every conceivable unit and vehicle trying to get forward. As one forward observation officer attached to Megill's tactical headquarters reported, the "town is literally full of snipers [and] machine guns [on] some streets and there appears to be quite a large infiltration of enemy. Engineers claim snipers French. Caen being heavily shelled and mortared."[59]

Hampering operations, a handful of bedraggled German prisoners from the recently arrived 272nd Infantry Division, whose rearguard had given the Black Watch fits during the crossing, now gave up without a fight.

Once across the Orne, Private Charlie Lee, testing out his bastardized French on a small group of civilians who appeared out of nowhere to offer help to their liberators, learned that l'Église de Vaucelles, half a mile away, housed the German observation post that had harassed the Black Watch for the last twenty-four hours. Immediately, Duffield seized the initiative and set out with his patrol in the final hours of darkness, bent on revenge not only for the regiment but for the loss of Austin.[60]

Having slept little over the previous four days, the scout platoon commander and his charges had to dig down deep for the energy to proceed cautiously and rein in any impulsive urges. Moving first along the ditch of the main railway line, Duffield took them south, across Rue de l'Arquette, which snaked along the Orne, as first light broke on the morning of the nineteenth.

Tucked in along the walls of a row of three-storey apartment buildings, the patrol slunk unimpeded until they reached the last building on the block. Entering the main door of the apartment complex, they worked their way past the ground-floor flats before squeezing out the back, where they cautiously crossed a lush garden that connected to the rear of another apartment complex directly overlooking the church. Gingerly, the men made their way up the stairs towards the top floor, reducing commotion to the minimum. The stairwell, painted in institutional colours, appeared unmolested, while the apartments they breached on the top floor showed the haphazard signs of war. As Hook noted, some had shattered windows, disjointed shutters and plaster dust told the tale, while others they entered remained in pristine condition—paintings symmetrically hung, beds made and tables set impeccably for dinner or breakfast, interrupted only by the Allied bombing or a forced evacuation by the Germans. Everywhere, striped wallpaper, all the rage in pre-war France, lined the walls, but at no time did they encounter a soul, save for a cat that let out a shriek as it darted past.

Reaching the top floor, Duffield's patrol had a perfect view of the main door, ground-level windows and tower of the tenth-century church, less than seventy yards away, well within

range of their scoped Lee-Enfields. Each scout chose a carefully concealed firing position well back from the windows and
trained his sights on any conceivable point of entry and exit on
the church. Primed and ready, they hung on Duffield's order
to fire.

Peering through his scope, Hook noticed two figures in the
belfry of the circular tower, both of them busy scanning the
countryside with their binoculars. It was impossible, given that
they remained in the shadows, to pick out what branch of service the two targets belonged to, and no vehicles could be spotted
parked around the church. Logically, he suspected they'd sport the
red piping of German artillery on their collar tabs, but upon closer
inspection, something seemed amiss. Both of his potential victims
were facing to the south and east, fixated on events unfolding
along the Bourguébus–Verrières feature and paying no attention
to the Black Watch crossing point. The unpredictable nature of
their behaviour did not go unnoticed and gave Duffield reason for
concern. Traditionally, the most dangerous move a combat commander can make is to vacillate. In this case, it saved lives.

Passing from the shadows into the sunlight that now streaked
into the tower at daybreak, one of Duffield's marks moved into
clear view, donning a fawn balmoral with red hackle perched
high. Upon closer inspection, he noticed the mane of red hair partially uncovered under the headdress that proved unmistakable:
Torchy Slater, Megill's highly aggressive brigade major, who, with
Bill Doheny in tow, had moved ahead of the advancing infantry
companies to set up Megill's new brigade OP in the tower, following on the heels of the German spotters who had evacuated
moments before his arrival.

The combat initiation for the Black Watch had come at a price;
eighteen men had lost their lives, with another 105 wounded seriously enough to be taken out of the line, not to mention the two

dozen others, like Herb McLeod, who suffered minor injuries and were patched up quickly and sent back into the line.

The scout platoon lost its first man, Alex Duncan, killed not patrolling or sniping, but sitting in a slit trench, waiting to cross a river. But despite this inauspicious debut, the battalion persevered through a sticky situation that required fortitude and courage to overcome.

The green troops had made an elementary and costly mistake, but had rebounded and pressed home the crossing of the Orne while under stiff German fire. Their success paved the way for the Régiment de Maisonneuve and the Calgary Highlanders to move through the bridgehead to capture Fleury-sur-Orne and Hill 67 respectively. But with that came few rewards and no chance to rest. Within a few hours of daybreak on the morning of July 19, the rifle companies had to set out towards Fleury in anticipation of the final act in Phase I of Atlantic. Their attack on Ifs was scheduled to commence that evening.

5

IFS

Three miles or so south of Caen the present-day tourist, driving down the arrow-straight road that leads to Falaise, sees immediately to his right a rounded [hill] crowned by farm buildings. If the traveller be Canadian, he would do well to stay the wheels at this point and cast his mind back to the events of 1944; for this apparently insignificant eminence is the Verrières Ridge. Well may the wheat and sugar-beet grow green and lush upon its gentle slopes, for in that now half-forgotten summer the best blood of Canada was freely poured out upon them.

—C.P. STACEY, THE VICTORY CAMPAIGN

A T A CURSORY GLANCE, NO SOLDIER IN THE BLACK Watch suspected that the gentle slopes that rose to the crest of Verrières Ridge, four miles south of Caen, would be the Vimy Ridge and the Passchendaele of their generation. Standing no more than 290 feet above sea level at its highest point, the low-slung ridge that once entertained the armies of William the Conqueror, Edward III and Henry V now hosted the main line of resistance and the hinge of the German defences in Normandy.

Even four years into the war, the vista remained sublime and almost untouched: lush, emerald-green farmers' fields teeming with golden stalks of grain and bountiful apple and pear orchards, all sharply contrasted by a patchwork of deep hazel plots sown with the staples of the Norman diet, including peas, sugar beets,

carrots and potatoes. Everywhere, cattle roamed as their owners
had fled, evacuated at gunpoint by the SS in recent days. Despite
intermittent bouts of high heat and rain, a fresh, cool breeze
flowed in from the Channel, filling lungs and soul equally, temporarily clearing the stench of Caen's dead and seductively spur-
ring memories of life without war.

Periodically, they came upon small towns of typical Norman
construction sporting fieldstone and red-brick dwellings, adorned
with burnt-orange tiled roofs and guarded against the steady
breeze by high walls or hedgerows crowned with thickets. Most
were centuries-old farming communities mingled with a few
mining towns, all awkwardly connected by a road network of
paved and unpaved thoroughfares, small lanes, garden paths,
dirt tracks and the arrow-straight Route Nationale, known as
the Falaise road.

At first, most pilgrims to the area would have missed the
strategic importance of the ridge; its slow rise made it appear
deceptively benign. From atop, however, its local dominance was
impressive. On any given day, one could take in all the environs
of Caen to the north and the dominating Hill 112 to the west. On
a cloudless day, the field of view stretched far north of the city,
towards the invasion beaches, making it an ideal location for a
new German main line of resistance.

LIEUTENANT COLONEL CANTLIE CONTINUED TO FUME AT
the self-inflicted damage suffered on the Orne when the Black
Watch reached Fleury-sur-Orne late in the afternoon of July 19.
Gathering his officers and senior NCOs around the altar of the
neo-Gothic Église Saint-Martin, which sat smack in the middle
of the tiny town, he prepared to deliver his orders for the Ifs
attack.

"Everyone was in a dark mood," George Buch noted. "We hadn't slept in two days and had nothing to eat. Everyone sported two days' growth of beard, puffy red eyes and drawn expressions. . . . Pudge Fraser, still stewing about his screw-up, remained unusually quiet but no doubt determined to make amends."

The inauspicious debut on the Orne had indeed hit the regiment where it lived—in its pride—and the news that the Régiment de Maisonneuve, the French-Canadian regiment from Montreal, had also paid a dear price in its combat debut did nothing to mitigate the gloom. The rush of excitement leading up to the Maisies' first attack on the hamlet of Haute, just outside Fleury, saw their two leading companies devastated when they mixed up their artillery barrage line with their start line. When H-hour arrived at 1300 hours, the men in the front ranks paid dearly for someone's indiscretion when the storm of steel from the massed 25-pounder guns of a full Canadian field regiment crashed down. In the chaos and confusion, the Maisies lost one company commander, with eleven men killed and thirty-seven wounded, while twenty-seven others suffered psychological collapse and required immediate evacuation for battle exhaustion. Only the quick thinking of their commanding officer, Lieutenant Colonel Lefort Bisaillon, who took personal command and pushed his two trailing companies through to capture their objective, saved the day.

Following on their heels, the Calgary Highlanders had swooped down through the Maisies' positions to capture Hill 67 just after 1700 hours, when the Black Watch arrived in Fleury. Now, however, with reports that German artillery had begun to soften up the Calgarys' position, fears of an impending counterattack loomed large and increased the urgency for the Black Watch to get on with their attack.

Given the fluid events unfolding along the front, it was anyone's guess as to what type of reception the Black Watch would receive in Ifs. The consensus opinion around the altar suggested they would hit little more than German rearguard similar to what they had encountered on the Orne, which meant tackling a few machine-gun and observation posts, a handful of snipers and perhaps the odd anti-tank gun. Nobody could gauge the quality or the motivation of the troops defending the town, but according to George Buch, if the prisoners they captured earlier that morning in Vaucelles provided any indication, "it would be a breeze."

No doubt coloured by a profound desire to seek redemption for the near debacle on the Orne, the mounting hubris did not faze Cantlie, who remained very much alive to the fact that they could easily bump headlong into the tail end of an SS panzer division scurrying towards the cover of the reverse slope of Verrières Ridge. If so, they would instead meet the hard, fanatical resistance of a rearguard willing to fight to the finish for the glory of Adolf Hitler.

Unlike the Orne show, the Black Watch would have B Squadron of the veteran Sherbrooke Fusiliers and its fifteen Sherman tanks, along with the full weight of the 25-pounder guns from the 5th Field Regiment, to support the attack.

For this set-piece assault, Cantlie's rifle companies would advance towards Ifs in a tight box formation with two companies up and two companies in the rear. His Tac HQ would be in the middle, while support company hung back, ready to rush forward to consolidate the newly captured ground once the rifle companies had seized the objective.

Like the percussion section of an orchestra, the artillery set the rhythm and the beat for this type of operation, with the infantry and tanks inextricably wedded to its timetable. Once their barrage, or stonks, started to roll in incremental lifts designed to accommodate the infantryman's rate of advance of a hun-

SEVEN DAYS IN HELL

dred yards every three minutes, the infantry needed to lean into the plunging steel curtain fire to close the ground leading to the German positions. To increase the pressure, the tanks from C Squadron advancing on the flanks would pepper the objective with direct fire from their 75-millimetre main guns and their .30-calibre coaxial machine guns to augment the high-explosive and shrapnel rounds from the artillery that rained down from above.

The key to success lay with the infantry keeping up with the barrage so that they could spring out of the shells and descend upon the pinned German defenders the moment the barrage lifted, to despatch them in a nasty close-quarter fight where the prime goal was to kill.

Captain John Taylor, who had arrived to replace Major Alan Stevenson (his wounded arm had become infected and required emergency evacuation to England), had experienced several of these shows when he served with the 8th Battalion of the Argyll and Sutherland Highlanders in the brutal Tunisian campaign in North Africa. If the operation was conducted in a tightly coordinated and controlled manner and delivered with determined leadership—as was the case when his fellow company commander, Major John "Jock" Anderson, garnered the Victoria Cross for driving home a similar attack under withering fire at the Battle of Longstop Hill—Taylor remained convinced of its effectiveness and potential for spectacular results.

THE SKIRL OF BAGPIPES BELTING OUT "THE GREEN HILLS of Tyrol" roused Hook Wilkinson from his sleep of the dead. Still feeling the effects of his near miss on the Orne, which left him concussed, with his parasympathetic backlash in full effect after the patrol to the church, he woke up to find himself on the porch of a small house in Fleury with no recollection of how he got there. Like his comrades, he remained filthy from head to toe, uniform soiled and caked with dirt, sweat and dark-brown splatters that he suspected came from Duncan's blood. He had little time to do more than restock ammunition and shovel down a bit of hardtack before joining Barney Benson, Brunner and Sharpe for a quick belt of rum and hustling out to the battalion's form-up point in a field outside the village in preparation for the attack.

By the time he arrived, the rifle companies had already shaken out, and each man had taken a knee, waiting for the signal to advance. Not far behind, Captain Ronnie Bennett prepared to move quickly on the first sign of success. His goal was to haul up the battalion's mortars, anti-tank guns, ammunition and rum, as well as Buch's pioneer platoon, armed with a supply of land mines, to consolidate the newly captured objective. The three troops of Sherman tanks from B Squadron of the Sherbrooke Fusiliers then rumbled into position on the flanks. At nine feet high, eight feet wide and almost twenty feet long, and weighing thirty-five tons, each of the Shermans towered over the grass, the grain and the men. The regular Sherman V type, which sported a 75-millimetre main gun, fashioned extra sandbags and discarded treads welded to the hull below the driver's hatch to increase protection from German armour-piercing rounds. The Sherman "Firefly" model, parcelled out one per troop, arrived swathed in camouflage netting, which did little to soften the distinctive nature of its long and highly deadly seventeen-pounder gun. Like the Black Watch, the crews of the Sherbrooke Fusiliers looked spent, and understandably so: after the Fleury and Hill 67 operations, Ifs would be their third attack in just under seven hours.

Duffield posted teams of snipers about fifty yards ahead of the lead tanks, where they would stalk and shoot during the chaos created by the shelling, slinking undetected to within 250 yards

Group photo of the 1st Battalion Black Watch of Canada officers, taken two months before they shipped out to Normandy. Only seven of the men pictured here made it through the war without becoming a casualty. BLACK WATCH ARCHIVES (BWA)

Left to right: Major General Charles Foulkes, 2nd Canadian Division commander; Lieutenant General Guy Simonds, 2nd Canadian Corps commander; and Brigadier William J. Megill, commander of the 5th Canadian Infantry Brigade.
LAC, PA-183992, 30445 AND PA-129125

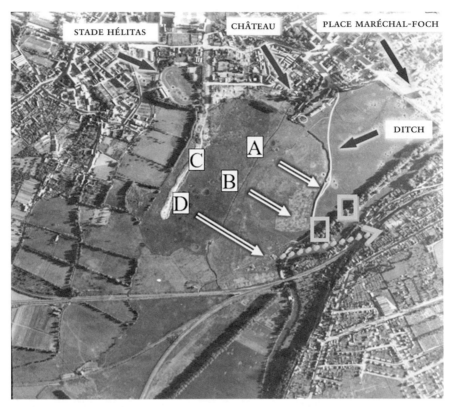

Aerial photo of the Black Watch crossing area on the Orne River, late on the evening of July 18, 1944. Laurier Centre for Military and Disarmament Studies (LCMDS)

Private Mike Brunner (*left*) and Private Dale Sharpe of the scout platoon.
BWA and Sharpe Family

PIAT (Projector Infantry Anti-Tank weapon) operators in training, taking on a Mark IV German panzer, like the ones employed by Peter Prien in May-sur-Orne. Nerves of steel were needed to close to within effective range of the tank.

Canadian soldiers on their snipers' course during the spring of 1944, displaying their distinct uniforms and tools of the trade.

Private Jimmy Bennett, from just outside Melville, Saskatchewan, joined the Black Watch after taking part in the campaign in the Aleutian Islands. A high-strung character, he had to battle his anxiety as hard as he did the Germans in Normandy. BENNETT FAMILY

Black Watch officers Lieutenant Bill Doheny (*top*), who served as Megill's intelligence officer, and Major Gordon "Torchy" Slater, the highly aggressive "hitter" who served as Megill's brigade major. BWA

Left to right: Lieutenant General Guy Simonds, going over his plan for Operation Spring during a photo op with visiting prime minister Winston Churchill, General Bernard Law "Monty" Montgomery and General Miles Dempsey at a crossroads near Ifs on July 22, 1944. IMPERIAL WAR MUSEUMS (IWM), TR 2045

Sergeant Bernard "Barney" Benson, who became the scout platoon sergeant in February 1944. Considered fearless and courageous, he was known for his rock-solid leadership and the jovial grin that nobody dared wipe off his face. BWA

Padre Rod Berlis (*left*), whose wounding before the Black Watch went into battle was seen as an omen, and his replacement, Canon E.C. Royle. BWA AND ROYLE FAMILY

A photo of the temporary graveyard in St. Martin, where the fallen from the Black Watch were buried after their retrieval from the Verrières battlefield once the ridge fell into Canadian hands in early August. BWA

The "factory" south of St. Martin shows the scars of the wrath of the Black Watch as they cleared it on the morning of July 25, before their assault up Verrières Ridge. It also shows damage from the heavy German anti-tank and artillery fire that riddled its upper reaches during the battle. LAC, 38134KB

One of several openings used by the Germans that led to the mine shafts, which descended several storeys below Verrières Ridge. LAC, PA-131353

Corporal Jimmy "Hook" Wilkinson. The "best shot" in the 1st Battalion, he was responsible for stocking the scout platoon with qualified candidates when it formed in February 1944.
BWA AND WILKINSON FAMILY

Private George "Young Hook" Wilkinson was a highly trained and skilled sniper and the kid brother of Jimmy "Hook" Wilkinson. WILKINSON FAMILY

A photo taken in the opening moments of Operation Spring, when the artificial moonlight designed to light the battlefield and ease the way for the assault units silhouetted them instead, making them easy targets for German machine gunners and artillery spotters. LAC, PA-131384

A remarkable photo of men from the Black Watch after their capture late on July 25. In the centre, one can see the experimental body armour hanging around the midsection of the man facing the camera. DIDIER LODIEU

A rare photo taken by members of the 272nd Division following their capture of those members of the Black Watch who survived the four-hour assault up Verrières Ridge. During the battle, 122 men from the Black Watch died, 100 were wounded and nearly 100 were taken prisoner. DIDIER LODIEU

A Sherman tank—most likely belonging to either Lieutenant Teddy Williamson or Lieutenant William Rawson of the 1st Hussars (6th Canadian Armoured Regiment)—knocked out in May-sur-Orne by fire from the Panthers of the counterattacking Kampf-gruppe Sterz from the 2nd Panzer Division. DIDIER LODIEU

The streets of May-sur-Orne after the town finally fell to the 1st Canadian Army on August 8 in the wake of Operation Totalize, Lieutenant General Simonds's third and final bid to capture Verrières Ridge and the ground to the south. LAC, PA-114507

of Ifs. The job called for them in part to screen the Shermans from concealed tank-hunting teams before taking up defilade firing positions overlooking the town. When the barrage lifted, it would signal what Hook termed "rush hour" for the snipers, as German infantry and gun crews emerged from their slits and scrambled to man their weapons. Concealed off to a flank by the confusion and din of the raging battle, the snipers would seek out victims with little mercy in this target-rich environment, hunting down and killing machine-gun and anti-tank-gun crews, mortar teams, runners, signallers, artillery observers and anyone barking orders or frantically signalling commands.

It was a tricky endeavour, to say the least, because it meant the snipers had to hug the artillery barrage even closer than the men in the first rank advancing with rifle companies. Because this tactic was a recent development in the Canadian Army, the scout platoon had only attempted it on the odd occasion in training, and never with live artillery. Despite this, all the snipers volunteered to give it a go.

In addition to sniping, the scouts also had another critical and potentially perilous task. Each team carried a flare pistol known as a Very light, with which they would mark larger and more immediate targets that required support from the Shermans. "Green for shoot, red for ceasefire," Hook recalled, but painting targets with flares was a dangerous game—the trail they left instantly gave away the user's location in the field, making him a prime target for German retaliation.

AT 2100—H-HOUR—JUST AS THE SUN BEGAN TO SET, THE artillery barrage commenced. At that moment, Cantlie swung his arm forward and over four hundred men rose from the grain and began their methodical glide towards the battalion's start line, which lay five hundred yards in the distance—halfway to Ifs. Once the force crossed this arbitrary Rubicon, there would be no turning back; regimental ethos shunned any thoughts of failure, let alone retreat.

Less than a hundred yards ahead of the leading ranks, and just fifty ahead of the snipers, thousands of high-explosive shells plunged with successive thunderclaps, crashing to earth in a torrent of steel that tore up the pristine field, showering the countryside with gritty soil and singed grain. In just minutes, a thin haze laced with the acrid and nauseating scent of cordite smothered the battlefield.

Bren gunners, firing from the hip, led the way, while off to the flanks the sniper teams went to work but failed to register a target in the field. Traditionally, advancing out of the sun would be a deadly mistake, as the men would be silhouetted, giving the enemy a prime target. On this occasion, however, it mattered little; the shells threw up an almost impervious curtain of steel that shielded the Black Watch from German observation.

So far, the battalion had yet to lose a man. They encountered scores of dead cattle, some with stiff legs pointing skyward, killed by the concussive blasts or disembowelled by shrapnel, leaving spatters of bright-red blood in the low-slung wheat.

Once again, German concealment and fire discipline appeared excellent, and even when the barrage lifted, the scouts failed to find sufficient targets to snipe. Frustrated, they turned to their Very lights and painted every potential hot spot with a generous coating of green flares that streaked in from the flanks and glowed bright now that dusk had arrived. Dutifully, the Shermans following behind responded, each tank pounding a series of high-explosive shells into the buildings on the fringes of town, followed by a stream of tracer fire from their .30-calibre machine guns that ricocheted spectacularly in all directions.

This immense display of firepower had an immediate and intoxicating effect on both officers and men. "My company reacted superbly," an exuberant John Taylor oozed. "Never have I felt the thrill of battle so deeply or been so proud and full of confidence as when I crossed the start line at the head of that happy, clean-cut bunch of kids whose average age was 21." The rapid injection of adrenalin, infused by the naked display of firepower, stoked a sense of invincibility and inflamed the killer instinct that now reached hubristic levels. Indeed, as they say in the regiment, "Hackles were flying high!"

On the receiving end inside the village of Ifs, Willie Wick, a twenty-four-year-old grenadier from the 980th Regiment of the 272nd Division, squeezed into his slit when the barrage rolled onto his position, "praying to God to put an end to the ceaseless fire." Wearied and drained, like his comrades who had just arrived from the Orne a few hours earlier, he had had nothing to eat for over twenty-four hours, his feet still swollen from the heat and the pounding of the hundred-mile march over five days to reach the Caen front. Once the barrage lifted, Wick emerged from his slit expecting to see the flak guns positioned in the centre of town, barking at the Shermans and the Black Watch now bearing straight for him. Instead, he discovered to his horror, as did his platoon commander, Lieutenant Adolf Thomae, that the flak crews had abandoned their weapons when the first shell landed and had scurried off south, disappearing into the wheat. Without supporting fire, Thomae noted that panic instantly seized his men, and the rout was on.

As Wick and his comrades fled out the eastern end of Ifs, the Black Watch rifle companies enveloped the village from the west, north and south, where Cantlie ordered them to dig in and then called for Bennett's support company to move up to consolidate.

Arriving in short order in the fields west of the town, Bennett, riding in the lead carrier driven by Private Jack Gemmill, expected to enter Ifs and set up shop in the town centre without a fight. A small group of desperate snipers, cornered near the church and market in the centre of Ifs, decided otherwise, and in seconds took aim and opened fire.

"You could hear the '*snick-snick*' of bullets cutting through the grain," recalled Gemmill. The fire, at first, proved nothing more than a nuisance. However, after a few minutes, the German snipers found their mark and men began to fall wounded, forcing Bennett to halt and return fire with the massed Bren guns of his carriers, while medics and stretcher-bearers went into action.

Cantlie, inundated with messages concerning the German counterattack that had now hit the Calgary Highlanders at full bore on Hill 67, had to move quickly to prepare the Black Watch lines. Immediately, he dispatched tank-hunting teams—pairs of men armed with PIATs—into the wheat to lie in wait for the approaching panzers. They dug in six-pounder anti-tank guns on each flank to replace the tanks that had retired at nightfall to replenish their fuel and ammunition for the push up Verrières the next day. The Cameron Highlanders of Ottawa, a machine-gun battalion, lent support, sending one of its companies, commanded by Ronnie Bennett's brother Harrison, to help the Black Watch.

The village, however, was stuck in the middle of the Black Watch position, and continued to pose a problem. Cantlie ordered Duffield to send in the scouts, reinforced by Bruce Ducat's under-strength platoon from B Company, to flush out the enemy once and for all. As the last shred of light faded from view near 2300 hours, the sniper hunt began.

The small task force crept into the town from the fields to the west and moved methodically from building to building, using the cover of darkness to sneak up on suspected sniper nests and hides. Bruce Ducat, who managed to scrounge up another Sten gun, moved through the streets with Lance Corporal Edmond "Tex" Richards and Bren gunner Smokey Lalonde. Unsure whether civilians still inhabited the buildings, Ducat employed a variant on what he had learned at the London Street Fighting School to clear each house. Instead of exposing a terrified French family to a deadly blast, the Black Watch corporal lobbed fist-sized boulders he scrounged from the road into the dwellings to simulate the bounce of a live grenade. Hoping the sound alone would flush the Germans out into Lalonde's field of fire, he told his mates, "You stay here, watch for them to come out back . . . when they do, kill them. Don't take a prisoner."

None of the buildings in the western end of the hamlet yielded rewards; the German snipers, sensing the approach of the Canadians, hightailed it out of the town. "Like ghosts," Ducat recalled, "they disappeared leaving discarded ration packs, bloodied bandages, empty bullet casings and wine bottles as calling cards."

Then firing started again. This time, it emanated from an adjacent orchard and wheat field off to the east, impossible to spot in the darkness. The scouts resorted to advancing through the fields in a skirmish line to flush their quarry into the open. "Their camo was excellent," a frustrated Barney Benson noted. "They would never fire if we had more than one man in the area. Whenever we swept a field in an extended line, not a shot would be fired, and our job would apparently be done, but within a half an hour they would be back sniping away from their former positions."

The cat-and-mouse game continued through the hours of darkness as the scouts chased, shot or captured a score of snipers from the 272nd Infantry Division. As Benson discovered, "their snipers seemed to be Poles or Russians who were forced to fight and fired only because they were ordered to without ever hitting anyone." When the struggle moved from the open wheat fields to an adjacent orchard, however, its haystacks, woodpiles, stone walls and wooded copses gave up their secrets. The scouts, stalking each suspected lair in quick succession, resorted to phosphorus grenades and their Ronson lighters, skilfully employing the promise of immolation with profound effect.

According to the Black Watch war diary, only ten enemy snipers were brought back to tactical headquarters for a brief interrogation, with most "in a very shaky condition." A bloody-minded John Taylor crowed, "All my advice and hate talks had their effect . . . it was really incredible how few prisoners we sent back." Indeed, each of the captured German snipers appeared worse for wear, and an irate Cantlie, suspecting his scouts of taking liberties with the prisoners, demanded an explanation about their sullied and bloodied condition. When the scouts feigned ignorance, Ronnie Bennett came to their defence and pulled no punches. As he explained: "One of Jerry's habits seems to be that his peculiar code requires that he fire some shots at the enemy before he surrenders . . . He seems to care little whether his fire is effective or not but, in many cases, it does inflict casualties on us . . . This habit is dangerous and leads to reprisals for it is difficult to act humanely with someone who fires a burst at you and then walks forward with his hands up." Cantlie, satisfied, dropped the matter at once.

The German sniper fire had only inflicted a few casualties but no deaths, yet the fear, stress and nuisance they posed reinforced some lessons learned in England that, until this point, seemed decidedly academic. Officers and senior NCOs promptly removed or muddied distinctive signs of their authority on their battledress: pips and crowns denoting rank disappeared from shoulder epaulets, as did rank badges from sleeves; Sten guns were exchanged for rifles, while moustaches, characteristic of most officers and senior NCOs, were hacked off in a bid to blend in with the average soldier. As for the scouts, who could not ditch their Denison smocks, they made sure to remove their telescopic scopes and tuck them away into their tunic pockets, knowing first-hand what type of treatment a sniper received if captured.

Nervous sentries sent up warning flares several times during the night, and there were false alarms, but no counterattack materialized on the Black Watch front in the traditional sense. Artillery spotters, conspicuously absent during the attack on Ifs, now zeroed in on the fields around the town and made up for lost time.

One of their first ranging shots to land struck the regimental aid post situated in a barn in the middle of town. Not long before, Dale Sharpe and Mike Brunner had exited the aid post following treatment for some scratches suffered in the sniper hunt. The explosion set the roof alight, threatening to incinerate those too wounded to move, trapped in the paddocks below. Sergeant William Clements, a Black Watch medical orderly, took matters into his own hands without hesitation and carried each man to safety amidst the flames and screams and cries for mercy. All made it out alive thanks to his quick work, and Cantlie made sure to recommend him for the Military Medal, which he received for his gallant actions.

DESPITE ITS PROMISING OPENING, MONTGOMERY'S MUCH-ballyhooed Operation Goodwood had ground to an ignominious and permanent halt by midday on July 20. The German gun line on the Bourguébus end of the ridge had held in spectacular fashion, inflicting grievous casualties on the British 8th Corps in what became known as the Death Ride of the Armoured Divisions. In just under forty-eight hours, the British lost nearly three hundred

Sherman, Crocodile, Stuart and Cromwell tanks. The wrecks now lay strewn across the ridge, smoking or ablaze.

Although the offensive had snatched some ground and inflicted roughly four thousand German casualties and destroyed seventy-five panzers and assault guns, Goodwood had failed to achieve its prime objective of forcing a breakthrough of the German line and trapping Rommel's forces west of the Orne valley. Montgomery, pressured to achieve success, did not help matters when he oversold the operation to the press. Promising it would rival or eclipse anything seen on the Russian front, his official communiqué, issued on the first day, led the BBC and the major dailies to erroneously report a massive breakthrough on a scale not seen since El Alamein. Now, with the evidence laid clearly before them, the press had to walk back that notion in a series of sober updates that pegged out Goodwood as one of the greatest "white elephants" of the war.

The Allied press, feeling betrayed, took to the counteroffensive. The next day, headlines trumpeted that the entire Allied effort in Normandy had bogged down on the entire front. Soon, a string of stinging editorials followed, all of which pointed to one salient fact: after six weeks of heavy fighting, Montgomery's Army Group had advanced no more than a paltry twenty-five miles inland (only a dozen in the British sector), at the cost of 100,000 casualties and rising.

There remained a small glimmer of hope, despite the dismal results. Although the British armoured drive had sputtered and stalled to the east, intelligence revealed a rupture of the German line south of Caen in the Canadian sector, and Simonds, Dempsey and Montgomery now suspected that Verrières Ridge lay open for the taking. Simonds, spurred on by this news and convinced that the Germans could find little to throw in his path, ordered Brigadier Hugh Young's 6th Brigade to go ahead as planned and pass through Megill's 5th Brigade and capture Verrières Ridge by nightfall.[1] With the ridge in Canadian hands, he would pause the following day to allow his massive array of artillery to cross the Orne before 6th Brigade would resume the advance to capture the Cramesnil Spur, a tactically dominating piece of ground on the Falaise Road just south of Verrières.[2] However, this overly optimistic assessment of the situation before his corps did not consider the inherent time lag of intelligence; what was indeed once a potentially mortal gash in the German line a day earlier had, by the afternoon of July 20, begun to congeal. Once Fleury, Hill 67 and Ifs had fallen, historian Doug Delaney believes that Atlantic should have ended, for he saw "no rationale for launching of an unnecessary attack" prompted by "Simonds's personal and national pride" that "interfered with his judgement."[3]

The 6th Brigade assault on Verrières Ridge commenced precisely at 1500 hours, however.

Cantlie, joined by his company commanders, Duffield and the adjutant, Captain Campbell Stuart, witnessed an awe-inspiring spectacle from the newly excavated observation post near Black Watch tactical headquarters. Over a thousand men from the Fusiliers Mont-Royal, the South Saskatchewan and the Queen's Own Cameron Highlanders rose from the wheat on cue and began their methodical stride over a four-thousand-yard front towards their objectives more than a mile distant. Behind them came the Essex Scottish from Windsor, Ontario, commanded by Lieutenant Colonel Bruce MacDonald from 4th Brigade and given to Young as a reserve for the assault.[4]

There was a distinct big-game feel in the air with the wireless set crackling and popping at Black Watch tactical headquarters. Cantlie and his officer strained through their binoculars to watch the proceedings, while calm and determined voices from brigade, battalion and company headquarters, and their reps from the artillery, tanks and air elements supporting the assault, methodically reported their progress.

Soon, tanks from the 2nd Canadian Armoured Brigade appeared on the scene, darting back and forth in the dead ground to take up hull-down positions along the flanks of each battalion. The first sighting reports of German panzers working along the ridge brought an instant fusillade of white-hot armour-piercing rounds from the Shermans, while Allied fighter-bombers broke through the low ceiling of the clouds to deliver rocket and bombing runs. All the while, the artillery barrage did its number on the fields ahead, and in minutes, the pristine landscape started to scar.

THE TWIN TOWNS OF ST. ANDRÉ AND ST. MARTIN, a combination farming/mining community typical of this part of Normandy, sat in the small valley that ran south between Hills 61 and 67 and the crest of Verrières Ridge. Each village, although closely linked on the map, had its own church, graveyard, mayor's house, butcher shop and bakery, while Café Voisin, not far from Garage Fontaine, vied for patrons with Café Fresnel along the Route d'Harcourt, which stretched from Fleury-sur-Orne southward to May-sur-Orne on the westernmost end of Verrières Ridge. However, by late afternoon, few of the centuries-old structures remained intact in either town. In preparation for the assault, Simonds designated the twin towns for a "murder" shoot and unleashed a fifteen-minute concentrated blitz barrage from every available gun in his corps.[5] Over 2,400 light, medium and heavy shells slammed into the towns in just over three minutes. Dust swirled, fires raged and smoke eddied up from the rubble just before the Cameron Highlanders arrived from the north.[6] The Fusiliers Mont-Royal from Montreal made good headway towards their objective, the aptly named Beauvoir Farm, on the easternmost end of the advance. In the centre of the push, the South Saskatchewan Regiment encountered some resistance during their drive up the rise of Verrières Ridge, but arrived at their objective in good order, while the Essex Scottish moved to fill in behind them at the crossroads at the southern reaches of Hill 61.

Early returns suggested Young's 6th Brigade would be in solid along the road that ran from St. André–St. Martin, south of Hill 61 and past Beauvoir Farm in short order. However, as the 6th Brigade flooded south towards Verrières, they plunged headlong into a salient that the Germans commanded from three sides and held under constant observation.

From the Bourguébus area in the east, the crest of Verrières in the centre and the high ground west across the Orne, the Germans could pinpoint almost every move made in the rolling grain fields, taking stock and sizing up the best moment to launch their counterstrike.

Then the heavens opened.

Intermittent showers that started just after H-hour quickly intensified, bringing on a series of unrelenting thunderstorms that camouflaged the noise of grouping panzers. The storm played havoc with the wireless network and grounded all air support. The Germans pounced, using the rain and a gathering mist for cover.[7]

On the flanks, both the Camerons and the Fusiliers Mont-Royal (the FMRs), who had advanced with support from the tanks of the Sherbrooke Fusiliers, had time to consolidate their positions just before the German artillery, mortars and rocket fire arrived. They withstood the initial counterthrust despite heavy casualties and vicious fighting.

In the middle, however, where the South Saskatchewan Regiment advanced without the benefit of direct fire from supporting tanks, things went off the rails almost at once. Unlike the built-up objectives on their flanks that required the direct firepower of the tanks to capture, Young, for some unexplained reason, decided to forgo armoured support for the capture of the pool table–flat piece of ground near the crest of Verrières Ridge. Exposed on a salient five hundred yards ahead of the units on the flanks, the only protection from panzers came with a troop of seventeen-pounder anti-tank guns sent to augment the battalion's six-pounders. Neither, however, had unlimbered when the first SS panzers suddenly appeared out of the mist.

Before the men of the South Saskatchewan Regiment had a chance to dig more than a few spadefuls of dirt, the cry went up: "Tanks!" Major John Edmondson, commander of B Company, who survived one massacre at Dieppe in 1942, now faced another on the slopes of Verrières. "One tank came right into my left forward platoon, driving right over top of people it didn't shoot," he recalled. "I was hollering at the platoon sergeant when the tank fired a high-explosive shell which struck him in the back. He disintegrated into pieces before my eyes."[8]

The calm, steady voices on the brigade radio net quickly became strained and then desperate, pleading with Young's brigade for immediate support. "We are being attacked by tanks! We need help from the tank counterattack coming from the SOUTH." Unbeknownst to Cantlie, the *cri de coeur* was the final utterance of Edmondson's acting commanding officer, Major Reg Matthews, whose tactical headquarters exploded seconds after the message was sent.

Thoroughly skilled after three years of mortal combat on similar terrain on the steppes of Russia, the SS Panther and Mark IV panzers plunged forward, showing no mercy, targeting command and control elements that left Edmondson's battalion staggering from the first blow. With the battalion wireless sets knocked out, the panzers then fixed on the battalion's anti-tank guns, most of which were still moving forward. They destroyed each limbering or partially deployed gun in succession, leaving the infantry devoid of protection from the panzers, which proceeded to pick off anyone in the fields ahead.

Edmondson reported, "The tanks, once they had no easy targets sprayed the wheat fields with machine-gun fire and turned in circles through the wheat to crush the men or flush them into the open so they could be fired upon."[9] The hardened German panzer veterans showed little mercy, overrunning the forward companies and forcing the South Saskatchewan men to scatter in all directions. "Once the men went to ground in the 3- to 4-foot high wheat," Edmondson related, "control was almost impossible because we could not see them or us. Our span of control was limited to voice which could be heard only by those in the immediate vicinity."[10] Panzers preyed upon the men, who were unable to dig in. The anti-tank weapons were knocked out, and the South Saskatchewan Regiment were cut off from communication with brigade headquarters, with no hope of air, tank or artillery support. Edmondson concluded he "had but one duty left, to save as many lives as possible."[11] Quite independently, his surviving company commanders had reached the same conclusion.

Streams of bedraggled men, some walking wounded, some carried, some crawling, all soaked, muddied, exhausted and terrified, worked their way through the thick flaxen stalks, headed for the Essex Scottish positions on Hill 61.

Brigadier Hugh Young at 6th Brigade headquarters did not immediately grasp the seriousness of the situation unfolding at the front. He dismissed the desperate calls for support as overexcited offerings from men fighting their first battle. At first, there appeared some merit in this interpretation; even the veteran Sherbrooke Fusiliers noted that men from 2nd Division "were a bit jumpy in the first real action, constantly getting their 'wind up'—everything was exaggerated—cries of counterattack, over-estimation of enemy strength and intent were all symptomatic."[12]

What Young and Foulkes chalked up as misperception soon became a reality when the retreating men of the South Saskatchewan Regiment collided with Essex Scottish arriv-ing at the southern foot of Hill 61. Without sleep or a meal in over twenty-four hours due to a series of logistical screw-ups in their secondment to Young's brigade, the Essex Scottish became unnerved by the tales of the murderous panzers now making straight for their unprepared positions. Their situation was compounded by the sight of the bloodied, bewildered and terrified state of Edmondson's remaining men filtering through their lines.

It should not have come as a shock that the Essex Scottish flinched, as they had no tank, artillery or air support. They buckled and finally broke when the panzers of the seasoned 1st SS, supported by infantry and artillery, struck near dawn on July 21.

The mounting fear that had gone unchecked now approached panic. Soon, frantic reports of Essex men flooding towards the rear streamed in over the wireless. As the war diary of the 2nd Anti-Tank Regiment recorded: "Big scare of our front collapsing. Essex streaming back with tales of big attack . . . wounded flying off carriers landing into mud face down and no one trying to pick them up, in other words, panic."[13]

These accounts sent a shock wave right up from brigade, through to division and corps. Instead of capitalizing on the opportunity to roll up the German defences on Verrières Ridge as Simonds demanded, Young and Charles Foulkes now feared they had a full-scale rout on their hands, with a major German counterattack descending upon their front.

Foulkes, terrified of Simonds's retribution in an atmosphere that espoused a culture of blame, was sure the corps commander would have his head, so both he and Young began scheming to distance themselves from the debacle by offering up the Essex Scottish commanding officer, Bruce MacDonald, as their sacrificial lamb.

The case against MacDonald began even as the drama along the ridge continued to unfold, with Young noting the orderly "withdrawal to reorganize" of his South Saskatchewan Regiment while recording the movement of MacDonald's battalion from 4th Brigade as "out of control."[14]

Young, genuinely concerned with the state of panic that gripped both units, noted that he ordered "patrols established" to "stop any further movement of the Essex Scots." He turned to Foulkes and requested the Black Watch from 5th Brigade act as a counterattack force to check the German advance and restore the line. More importantly, he expected Cantlie's men to stiffen the backbone and resolve of all the 2nd Division battalions, and to serve as a shining example of obedient and effective Canadian soldiery.

The call for immediate action caught Cantlie and his men off guard. With little time to rest after the Ifs attack, Cantlie sent word to his company commanders to attend an emergency orders group. "First thing we heard was that the Germans had attacked the Essex Scottish and that they were breaking," recalled Lieutenant George Buch. "We had to get up there fast and stop the Essex Scottish and the Germans." Bruce Ducat, fresh off the sniper hunt with Smokey Lalonde and Herb MacLeod, had no idea what was unfolding until a military policeman asked, "Did you see the Essex Scottish coming through here?" He told the trio that their commanding officer had taken off, along with the rest of the regiment. Whether that was true or not, Ducat neither knew nor cared; word quickly arrived that the Black Watch had to rush south to restore the line south of Ifs.

Hurriedly, men checked weapons, stuffed pockets and pouches with extra rations and shoved clips of ammunition into their tunics, tightened webbing and rushed to their company form-up point, sensing that the mounting tension and frantic energy meant the situation was indeed serious and urgent. Indeed, all the companies in the battalion, including Bennett's support company, would advance with artillery and tank support in the following hour to recapture the crossroads at the foot of Hill 61 and restore the Canadian line.

Returning from his meeting with Young at 6th Brigade, a determined-looking Cantlie revealed what the brigadier had in store for the battalion. Young, entirely taken with the Black Watch reputation, had stroked their ego to maximum effect, calling upon their skill, history, pride and fortitude to restore the sagging Canadian line, materially and morally. With Black Watch tradition centred around faithful obedience in the face of overwhelming odds, wedded to the self-imposed motto of "never retreating," Young expected them to be an example for the entire division to follow. He called upon Cantlie's men to stop the fleeing Essex and stem the German counterattack and regain the line using the most extreme measures necessary.

Echoing Young's instructions in the mounting tension, Cantlie turned to his officers and ordered: "If you have to stop the Essex by shooting them, then shoot them. Nothing gets by— nothing!"[15] The drastic measure caught Buch off guard, not for the moral implications of such a sanguine order, but rather the urgency and desperation of the moment. To Buch, the directive, which nobody questioned, made perfect sense with the resolve of some units wavering and fear contagious.

Left with a fraction of the usual time to plan an operation of this nature, Cantlie sent his adjutant, Campbell Stuart, ahead to marshal up the rifle companies at the form-up point a few hundred yards south of Ifs. As with the previous attack, they would advance in box formation, but this time with support and headquarters companies right on their tail in the initial assault.

"Everyone went up," Buch remembered. "Support is not apt to be on the front line as it were, but we were all up there. Everyone was rushed up. We went up as infantrymen." With no time to carry out reconnaissance, the scouts joined the companies and would fight this battle as regular line infantry.

Every artillery piece in the 2nd Canadian Corps and some of Dempsey's medium and heavy regiments chimed in with barrage set to roll from the start line south of Ifs over the thousand-yard stretch to Hill 61. Unlike the South Saskatchewan and Essex Scots, the Black Watch would have full support from the tanks of the Sherbrooke Fusiliers for their advance. Once on the objective, forward observation officers from the artillery units supporting the attack (who joined the advance as well) would be available to call down concentrations to fend off expected German counterattacks. With speed and ease of communication essential, each of these young "FOOs," as the men called them, needed intimate knowledge of the infantry plan so that they did not call down fire on friendly units on the flanks. Additionally, this intimacy gave Cantlie extra flexibility as he arranged a "private" fire plan for emergencies instead of the time-consuming six-digit grid reference. Each relied on one number only to call down fire on targets of opportunity.[16]

Stitching these elements together ate away at precious time, forcing Cantlie and his company commanders to miss the start of the show. With their attack wedded to artillery fire plan, it would take an eternity to retime if they missed the initial H-hour for any reason. As such, Cantlie extended permission for Captain

Campbell Stuart and the company sergeant majors to take the attack in on Hill 61 when H-hour came at 1805 hours. The Black Watch CO, Motzfeldt, Taylor and Griffin would have to catch up with their charges midstream.[17]

Bill Booth, the young intelligence section private tasked with situating Cantlie's observation post on Hill 61, hung close to one of the Sherbrooke Fusiliers' Shermans during the assault as he glided through knee-high grain. The racket made by the beast's thundering main gun, growling engine and grinding gears surpassed even that of the falling shells, which gave the whole spectacle, in Booth's opinion, "an air of unreality, as though it were a movie."[18]

Halfway through the advance, Booth witnessed his friend Lance Corporal Rod Hudson, a twenty-three-year-old sketch artist in McLennan's platoon, perish instantly when a Canadian shell fell short. His body was flung high into the air before it crashed violently back to earth, swallowed by the grain. Hudson was not the only one to fall to friendly fire in the barrage. "The Artillery gave us a tremendous shoot," recalled Campbell Stuart, who grimly added that "at least two or three of the men went down with each salvo fired by Canadian guns." This was a necessary evil in war, and proved the lesser of all evils. It was a relatively small price to pay for overall success on the battlefield.

Captain Ronnie Bennett had a ringside seat to two distinct battles unfolding simultaneously from his Bren gun carrier, moving close behind the rear rifle companies. A mile and a half away, far past the barrage that tore up the ground in support of the Black Watch assault, he could see armour-piercing rounds ricocheting, bouncing off the thick armour of at least six Panther tanks from the 1st SS Panzer Division that were pressing home their attack on the FMRs at Beauvoir Farm. His driver, Private Jack Gemmill, fixated on the debris and destruction littering their axis of advance. "The whole area between Ifs and Hill 61 was littered with tanks, guns and trucks that had been destroyed." Indeed, haze from smouldering shell holes and burning grain blanketed the area, creating a macabre, ghostlike landscape strewn with abandoned personal equipment, rifles, PIATs, Bren guns, kits, helmets, webbing and unopened ammunition boxes intertwined with knocked-out carriers, jeeps and anti-tank guns. Bill Booth recalled the unworldly feeling he had entertained earlier in the advance suddenly "vanished in the shock of seeing Canadian dead, the Essex Scottish, lying on the ground. Seeing Hudson fall did not have the effect on me of seeing the sleeve patch of the Second Division on the uniforms of those killed."

Due to the German preoccupation with the continuing struggle for Beauvoir Farm and St. André–St. Martin, the Black Watch reached the objective without encountering a single German. However, as George Buch recalled, there were "plenty of Essex Scottish men who [had] wasted little time moving to the rear." Later that morning, Buch heard tales that some members of the Black Watch had indeed doled out the most extreme form of punishment to the fleeing men, but the pioneer platoon commander vehemently rejected that notion, chalking it up as nothing more than "wild talk" of hubristic young men.[19] From Brigadier Young's perspective, however, the Black Watch had delivered "a textbook operation of war."

6

HILL 61

Attrition has undermined something deeper than the renewable parts of man. You know the great upset in the general economy, the policies of states and the very lives of individuals: distress, uncertainty, and apprehension are everywhere. The mind itself has not been exempt from all this damage. The mind is in fact stricken; it grieves in men of intellect, and looks sadly upon itself.

—Paul Valéry

CAPTAIN RONNIE BENNETT WAS LEFT COLD BY THE spot inherited by the Black Watch on Hill 61. Foulkes's headquarters had chosen the area after a cursory reading of the map with little, if any, reference to the actual terrain. The freshly repossessed plot of land gave Bennett a new-found appreciation for the struggles faced by the men from the Essex Scottish and South Saskatchewan Regiments earlier that day.

Griffin's A Company and Fraser's D Company straddled the rise, entrenched on the forward slope. Motzfeldt's C Company, Taylor's B Company and Bennett's own support company lay dug in on the reverse slope, with Cantlie's tactical headquarters burrowed into the crest in the middle of the box formation. The entire position, however, came under direct enemy observation and fire from both Verrières Ridge to the south and the heights across the Orne to the west. The shoulder-high wheat, which covered the rise and stretched down into the valley and up Verrières Ridge, provided limited concealment from prying enemy eyes, but it failed to shield the men from enemy shells or patrols that infiltrated into Black Watch lines over the undulating ground. George Buch, whose pioneers had blown the cavernous hole in the cement-like ground for Cantlie's headquarters, thought their position was at best "a dicey thing," while the laconic Captain Ronnie Bennett stated simply it "was not ideal."

Within minutes of their arrival on the hill, a series of ranging shots from German artillery and mortars plunged down, sending everyone scurrying for cover. Corporal Bruce Ducat, who as usual adopted the most expedient solution, dove into the closest slit, only to discover it occupied by the ashen-faced corpse of an Essex Scottish rifleman who had been killed just hours earlier. "It was too bad; he was a good-looking fella," Ducat recalled. "He didn't stand a chance." Hopelessly glued to his spot with German shellfire careening towards them, the Black Watch section commander lamented, "I couldn't move, and I couldn't drag him out, or I'd end up like him."

Ducat found it impossible to carve out a prime piece of real estate at the bottom of the slit that now doubled as a tomb. Expecting that little else could make snuggling up to a dead man worse, he cursed the moment he was born when the skies broke into a torrential downpour, leaving the pair to stew in the tepid deluge.

Despite his morbid conundrum, Ducat's main worry centred on what awaited after the shelling had stopped. Fears of an impending German counterattack continued to run high and increased the tension with each round that landed. "There's nothing you can do but just stay in your slit when the shells arrive and pray one doesn't find you," he recalled. "The tough part is when it lifts, and you find yourself face to face with a Jerry."

Ducat's concern did not come to fruition; the aggressive response by the 1st SS Panzer Division in the centre of the 6th Brigade push did not turn into the major counterstrike that Foulkes or Young had feared. Once the SS *Kampfgruppen* despatched the South Saskatchewan and Essex Scottish Regiments, and their reconnaissance battalion had chased the Canadians as far back as the fringes of Ifs, they pulled back when the barrage for the Black Watch attack started.[1] Tucked away for the time being in their lairs on the reverse slope of Verrières, they turned the defence of the area over to their artillery, which had pounded the Calgary Highlanders on Hill 67 and now found the Black Watch.

The Germans did not recognize at that moment that Goodwood and Atlantic had shot their respective bolts, and they suspected that the Allies planned to renew their push at daylight. To make life miserable, they now called down fire from both the 1st SS and 2nd SS Panzer Corps, which had moved to the Orne area, in the heaviest bombardment the Germans had delivered to date in the Normandy campaign. To counter the German plans, Allied artillery opened up as well, delivering shoots along Verrières Ridge and into the valley before them, while periodically laying smoke to obscure German observation. The Black Watch company commanders worked feverishly with their assigned forward observation officers to organize a defensive fire program to rebuff the German ground attack that they expected to arrive seconds after the German artillery lifted.

FOR HOOK WILKINSON, THE FIRST STRIKES EVOKED memories of his father's stories, which intimated that the ultimate rite of passage for any infantryman came with enduring concentrated, accurate and prolonged enemy artillery barrages designed to obliterate mind, body and soul. "Nothing ever prepared us for this hell," Wilkinson recalled. "We had machine guns fired over our heads while we crawled through the mud in training, grenades and flashbangs tossed near us to simulate enemy shells, and watched our tanks and artillery dish it out, but nobody and nothing prepared us for this."

Gordy Donald was dug in on the forward slope with Griffin's A Company. "The first thing you hear is the whine of the shells coming in, then the blasts, followed by the echo and the twang, twang of shrapnel whipping past. A second later you hear the rattle of rocks, mud and debris crash back to earth. It's terrifying!"

George Buch, settled in among the pioneers on the crest, felt "the ground shake" in step with the intensity of each salvo. "The odd shell will startle you," he recounted, "but concentrated blasts will suck the air right out of your lungs and leave you woozy." Buch was describing the whiplash effect of the concussive blast (or overpressure), followed immediately by the intense shock wave that forces air from the lungs and shoots blood from the organs and arteries into the brain. Depending on proximity to the blast, it can bring on nausea and disorientation, ruptured eardrums or instant death. "It's claustrophobic," Buch explained. "You gasped for air, you felt like you were suffocating and all you wanted was for it to end—and you don't care how."

Above the fury of the shells, Sergeant Mac Roulston could hear men around him "scream for a medic" or "just yell at the top of their lungs" to combat the deafening noise from each blast. "Some cursed the shells as if challenging them to a fight," while others, deafened by the explosions, "just shrieked unintelligibly."

Mortar fire proved particularly unsettling, due primarily to its accuracy. Highly skilled German crews could drop a shell with precious little warning directly onto an unsuspecting gun position, truck, carrier or turret of a tank and either decapitate the commander or obliterate the vehicle through its open hatch.[2] Likewise, any time the battalion or company radios piped up or Cantlie gathered his officers and NCOs for an O Group, accurate German mortar stonks followed. Mortars were difficult to spot, firing as they did from behind Verrières Ridge, and they became a frustrating and deadly nuisance. Their impact increased dramatically when German rockets joined the fray.[3]

The multi-barrelled German Nebelwerfer rocket launcher, coined the "Moaning Minnie" for its distinctive banshee shriek, telegraphed the arrival of its 150- or 210-millimetre projectiles. The Minnie caught the men off guard at first, and the sound and blast radius shook them to their core.

Private Jimmy Bennett scrunched down in his trench, trying to ride out the mortar fire by penning the oft-interrupted letter to his mother. He heard the first rocket round wailing down onto his company position. "All of a sudden, I could hear it coming; it hit right in front of my trench and blew my kit bag on the lip apart, destroying all my stuff. The shrapnel went sideways and wounded the guys in the slits on each side of me. One had his hand just about cut off, the other wounded in the side of his head, but it never touched me at all!"

Despite its enormous size, the destructive force of the rocket shell proved far less than artillery or heavy mortars and penetrated but a mere six inches into the ground. Only if a slit received a direct hit were you "a goner," Bennett recalled. "Usually it would blow your legs off." With time and exposure to the new commodity, John Kemp noted that initial fear wore off quickly when the men discovered its "bark was worse than its bite." "The men got to know how close the shell was going to land by the sound," Kemp chronicled. "If dug in, they had little problem with them."[4] Mike Brunner, sharing a slit with Dale Sharpe near the A Company positions on the forward slope, concurred with

Kemp's assessment. "After a while, you just numb them out, it was all you could do."

Nothing, however, equipped the men for the high-velocity shells fired from German panzers, anti-tank guns and flak cannons. The "88s," as high-velocity rounds were known, gave no warning. The shell would slam into its unsuspecting target. "The only way to avoid its lethal projectile," Hook Wilkinson warned, "was to remain concealed under cover and hunkered deeply into your slit—if you were lucky enough to survive the first one that went off, that is."

With no practical way to combat the shells without punching back directly at the source, a virulent strain of fatalism developed to overcome the dread and stress. One shell slammed next to Hook, onto the slit he shared with Harold Burden. The blast killed Private Charles Mayall, an American from Middletown, Connecticut, and Alvin Roberts, a thirty-eight-year-old stone-cutter from Montreal. Hook said to himself, "There's nothing you can do about it. One of these days it may be your turn." Jimmy Bennett, riding out the kinetic energy from each blast that shook the fine, talcum-like dust from the walls of his slit, muttered a similar refrain. "If you hear a shell coming, don't worry. It's not going to touch you. It's the one you can't hear you watch out for."

A TROOP OF SEVENTEEN-POUNDER ANTI-TANK GUNS, MOR-tars and Vickers machine guns from the Cameron Highlanders of Ottawa relieved the tanks of the Sherbrooke Fusiliers and made the Black Watch's arrival on Hill 61 complete. It marked the end of Simonds's Operation Atlantic.

Casualties in the corps commander's opening act in Normandy proved heavy. In just three days of combat, the units in the 2nd

Canadian Corps suffered nearly two thousand casualties, which included over four hundred killed. This staggering number rivalled the "death ride" of the British armoured divisions during Goodwood. As the history of the Royal Canadian Army Service Corps framed it, "Losses to both sides have been very heavy indeed, but on our side losses in men and equipment can be replaced from a tremendous reserve, whereas German reserves both of men and equipment no longer exist."[5] Everywhere this spirit of attrition and its pyrrhic heart reigned supreme, particularly at higher headquarters and with units not tasked with implementing that stratagem at the sharp end. It signalled that the struggle for Verrières had become very much a bean counters' war.

Two alarming trends appeared in the quartermaster's ledgers, which marked the traditional totals of killed, wounded and missing.[6] The first saw disproportionate losses suffered by the highly trained infantry arm. With a surplus of armour in the bridgehead, British and Canadian High Command expected to sacrifice tanks for men in pursuit of their attritional goals. The nature of the terrain and the sluggish fighting, exacerbated by the inexperience of Foulkes's 2nd Canadian Division and his questionable leadership, resulted in losses of trained infantrymen that soared to unforeseen and unplanned-for levels.

More alarming, the operation had resulted in an unprecedented spike in "psychological casualties" in frontline units, which conservative estimates placed at one-quarter of all non-fatal battle casualties, leaving commanders and medical professionals scratching their heads for answers. So far, there seemed to be a correlation with heavy or prolonged artillery strikes, something the Black Watch would come to realize over the coming days. As Captain John Kemp recorded, "Men appeared to be able to stand almost any amount of physical fatigue, but when in defensive positions under heavy mortar and artillery fire and the men were unable to hit back at anything, mental fatigue became very noticeable and had to be watched carefully."[7]

With men confined to their slits by day and forced to stand watch for German patrols and counterattacks by night, sleep was a rare commodity. The men slept briefly and restlessly. Jimmy Bennett, desperate for sleep, now viewed the fight with the Germans as secondary to his battle to stay awake and alert. A lack of sleep will kill a soldier faster than lack of food because it breaks down the body's defences and saps the will to carry on. Pep pills only masked the symptoms temporarily, and could not fix the problem since they could not replenish the stores. As a result, each man in the Black Watch started to decline. Over the next few hours and days, the ordeal would grind them down incrementally, leaving Bennett and his comrades ripe for break-down and collapse.

Recognized today as post-traumatic stress disorder, it was known to soldiers of the Great War as shell shock. During the Second World War, the Allied armies officially designated psychological breakdowns as combat fatigue or battle exhaustion, while the less astute called it "bomb happy" or "bomb whacky."[8]

In the First World War, its effects had led at times to extreme punishment, including execution for cowardice or desertion. Officially, these practices had ceased by the Second World War, with the evolving realization that the condition was medical rather than disciplinary in nature and was much more complex and complicated than simply the result of a poor upbringing or lack of moral fibre.

Despite progress, however, the stigma attached to combat breakdown remained, particularly in frontline units where tight cohesion stood paramount to success and survival in battle. Unofficial punishment for breakdowns at this level came in the form of ridicule, scorn, loss of respect and ostracism from the group, along with the immediate forfeiture of manhood in the eyes of peers. "Some of the men . . . were ruthless," George Buch remembered sullenly. "They wrote you off as a man if you went that way . . . It [was] terrible really."

No level of training, regimental pride, stoic demeanour or "manning up" made a soldier immune from the genuine physiological impact that fear and other stressors brought. In the evolving understanding of the army's medical authorities, every man had his limit. Still, to receive any compassion, a soldier had to pay his dues and then some in order to earn his breakdown. Generally, only prolonged exposure to battle conditions or massive acute trauma met with any degree of pity, let alone understanding and empathy. Breaking down in the first action or first week of combat denoted heresy and a fundamental weakness of character, and was seldom forgiven and never forgotten.

In just the first twenty-four hours of their stay on Hill 61, thirty-one reported cases of psychological breakdown appeared in the Black Watch alone, although more went unreported, including some within the ranks of the reinforcements who had just arrived.[9]

Just hours before the attack on Ifs, one terrified young soldier, no older than eighteen, who had just arrived with the look of a man sentenced to death row ended up in the slit next to Jimmy Bennett and Elie Desormeaux. Even in his high-strung state, Bennett reached out to offer some comfort to the teenager. Seeing someone worse off than him had a calming effect on him, and he told the terrified teenager, "Don't worry about it, you stick with me. I've been here for quite a while, and I'm not dead, and I intend to keep living." No sooner had he extended the hand of camaraderie and friendship than Bennett came to regret it. "I just wanted to cheer him up, just let him know he wasn't going to get killed immediately. I shouldn't have said that because no matter where I went, he just followed me, right behind me . . . [He] never would leave from my side . . . he was just scared."

Concerned for both the teenager's psychological disposition and his fragile mental state, Bennett took an extraordinary step and snuck off through the wheat between barrages to seek help from his platoon sergeant, Tommy Garvin, who was on loan from the scout platoon to D Company to make good their recent losses. "That kid is not going to last here," he told the less than sympathetic NCO. "He's gonna die of fright." Pleading to have the kid removed from the front line, Bennett continued to press Garvin. "You don't have to send him home, but he's not the type of person to be in the front lines. Also, he's going to drive me crazy!" Unmoved, Garvin put any attempt at jailhouse lawyering to bed by ordering Bennett to return to his slit immediately, and the private promptly obeyed.

Now that his appeal had gone for naught, Bennett settled back into his hole and tried to get some sleep while Desormeaux stood guard in the rain that continued to pour down. Not long after, another short, fierce German barrage woke Bennett. When it lifted moments later, he noticed a ruckus stirring in the next slit. The young private bolted straight out of his hole, thoroughly petrified and in panic. "I'm not staying here!"

Bennett was alarmed but not surprised. "Where are you going?" he shouted.

Tossing his helmet in the field ahead, the young man replied, "I don't know, but I'm going to get the hell out of here!"

When Bennett demanded again to know his intended destination, it provoked an ominous and tectonic change in the teenager's demeanour that remained emblazoned on Bennett's memory. With a wide, asylum-like grin, he exclaimed, "I'm going to leave." Then, as Bennett stared in amazement, he laughed and howled, "then took off into the dark at night . . . we never saw him again."

• • •

In A Company's sector, where Brunner and Sharpe kept watch over the valley, they could see the fires burning in St. André and St. Martin. Periodically, flashes of machine guns in the town were followed a millisecond later by the corresponding burp. The fight for the twin towns remained a going concern. Isolated panzer-led counterattacks continued to probe Canadian lines, and they watched tank-hunting teams armed with PIATs wade out into the grain to wait in ambush. Mulling over their predicament relative to the men in the grain, Brunner and Sharpe readily agreed they had the better bargain.

Although the cumbersome thirty-two-pound PIAT could destroy almost any panzer in the German arsenal, it took nerves of steel to wait until the prey reached the optimal fifty-yard range before unleashing its two-and-a-half-pound warhead, which it flung rather than shot towards its target via a tightly coiled spigot. Likewise, the weapon's peculiar traits could at times be as deadly for the operator as for his target. Sometimes the automatic recocking system of the spring-loaded mechanism failed to engage after a shot, leaving the operator to recock it himself. Fighting against great tension, he had to stand and place his feet on the shoulder rest like an air pump and pull. He could also roll over on his back and cock it with feet in the air, but neither option proved ideal in the middle of a firefight. As Brunner witnessed, the weapon had a nasty and deadly surprise for the operator. The propulsion charge at the end of the shell, intended to recock the spring, tended to blow back metal and debris into the operator's face. The men were instructed to wear their helmets to protect against injury or death when firing from a prone position. But as Brunner witnessed in training, one Black Watch officer disregarded these instructions and, wearing his balmoral instead of a helmet, paid for his indiscretion with his life when shards from the blast blew back and pierced his skull.

The whine of rockets and mortars interrupted Brunner and Sharpe's conversation and forced both down into their slit. When this salvo passed, the now-habitual screams for stretcher-bearers went up, and one familiar voice screamed unintelligibly.

Less than forty-eight hours earlier, Lieutenant Jock McLennan had survived a direct hit while readying to cross the Orne. Since that moment, the ordinarily thoughtful, reflective lieutenant with an artistic flair had displayed a noticeable despondency that most assumed came as the result of the concussive blast—and to a lesser extent, his near-death experience. He was unusually quiet in the hour that followed Few thought much of the Goliath-like platoon commander's dutiful and robotic manner during the attacks on Ifs and Hill 61, but now all the pieces came together in frightening fashion.

Seeking cover in the overly tight confines of his slit, the six-foot, four-inch McLennan fought the claustrophobic cruelty of each blast of a shell that taunted and threated to smother and suffocate him. Resisting the urge to run, his anxiety built to the boiling point. Then his slit blew up again.

McLennan, the victim of yet another direct hit, awoke from his momentary bout of unconsciousness to find himself on his back, buried chest-deep in the ground; his ears, eyes, nose and mouth were packed with soil. He gasped for air as he clawed at the dirt, then staggered upright from his would-be grave.[10]

McLennan was physically fine after the blast, with all limbs and digits intact, but his sympathetic nervous system went into complete overdrive and he was in full-blown panic. He bolted out of the trench and tore straight out into no man's land, running in wild, mad circles in the wheat until he reached a state of delirium and collapsed. Lieutenant George Buch watched in horror from the crest near Tac HQ as his fellow officer crumbled. "It was awful . . . The last thing you wanted to see was an officer, and a big one like him, break down. You could feel it rippling through the men . . . We had to jump on him quickly and get him to the rear."

The horrific sight of their commander, their pillar of confidence and authority, psychologically shattered acted as a contagion that spread quickly through his platoon. Six other men broke down as well. Some ran away; others sank into their slits, hyperventilating, crying and convulsing. One man just passed out. Jimmy Bennett watched as one of McLennan's men "went crazy, stumbling around, didn't know what he was doing, didn't know what he was saying."

Paradoxically, McLennan's close calls in recent days had bought him a reprieve from the scorn attached to such episodes, but that didn't apply to his men, who received little compassion. Brunner and Sharpe, emerging from their trench to scoop up the discarded weapons and kit after the stretcher-bearers arrived, noticed one of McLennan's men "lying on the ground sobbing," his body heaving. Having had it drilled into them that a combat breakdown equated weakness, that it amounted to "letting down the side," for Brunner and Sharpe the man in extreme distress had all the appeal of a leper.[11] Unsure of what to do—their rudimentary first aid training only dealt with conventional wounds—they ignored him and went about their task. "We didn't even stop," remarked Brunner. "We just walked by."

Bennett, watching from his slit, empathized, knowing full well how close he stood to the edge. "He couldn't stand the pressure, and he went crazy," he recalled with regret. "Then they say he's a coward. He's not a coward; his system cannot handle that," he added. However, terrified more of the stigma attached to "courting weakness" for a man stripped of his masculinity, Bennett never left his slit to offer a hand.[12]

• • •

JIMMY BENNETT SHARED HIS SLIT WITH ELIE DESOR-
meaux, who had arrived with the first batch of reinforcements to
make good the losses on the Orne. Bennett's chronic anxiety had
subsided, due in large part to his two weeks of battle inoculation,
the brotherly presence of his best friend and the leadership exercised by the officers and NCOs on Hill 61.

Instead of hunkering down in their slits, the Black Watch
company commanders, platoon commanders, CSMs and platoon
sergeants were ever-present, moving from slit to slit after a heavy
enemy stonk, checking on the well-being of the men. Private Bill
Booth recalled, "Major Motzfeldt did much to boost the morale
of those around the command post by strolling among the slit
trenches with his Balmoral and its red hackle on his head," a
tactic that all the officers matched in the attempt to check the
mounting tension with a calm, controlled air.

The only bright spot on this extremely bleak day came with
the news that a group of high-ranking German Army officers had
attempted to assassinate Adolf Hitler in his Wolf's Lair in East
Prussia the day before. This astonishing turn of events unleashed
speculation that the war might soon be over. It stirred up the
ghosts of the Battle of Amiens in August of 1918, which broke
the German line and ushered in the last hundred days, leading
to the collapse and surrender of Imperial Germany in November
of that year.

Hopes disappeared when the artillery gave way to ferocious
German probes that hit their lines repeatedly over the next few
days, and life for the men of the Black Watch on Hill 61 progressively deteriorated.

During a very brief lull in the enemy fire near twilight on the
evening of the twenty-first, Hook Wilkinson, trying desperately
to get some sleep, heard a calming and familiar voice calling for
him from above his slit. Peering from a crack through his rain

cape, he noticed Major George Fraser, balmoral and red hackle proudly perched on his head, glaring down at him through the drizzle. The steady and mature demeanour of the "Old Black Watcher" proved a welcome sight for Wilkinson. Fraser was a hard, quiet type of officer, a man who readily inspired confidence and always had "grip."

"They need you back at Tac HQ as they have something for you," he told the young scout, lifting the cape to allow him re-entry onto the soggy ground. Hook thanked the major for delivering the message personally and dutifully grabbed his rifle and helmet and trudged towards the command post. All the while, he cursed about the lack of a hot meal—brewing up in their slits gave their positions away, and the shelling prevented the new battalion cooker from getting anywhere near the front. More importantly, Brigadier Young cut off their rum ration, citing the warm temperatures. That left the men devoid of their spiritual and psychological pacifier. Many suspected the temperance had more to do with the recent problems with the South Saskatchewan and Essex Scottish Regiments. Having to sit there and take it, without the ability to respond to the Germans guns, was tough enough, but going dry in a combat zone, particularly without a hot meal, stood akin to heresy.

Hook did not relish the idea of another contact patrol. He had already come off one after their consolidation on Hill 61 and was not thrilled about another. "I was more terrified coming back into our lines, having feared I forgot the password . . . They were trigger-happy guys out there." Less than thirty seconds after Hook checked in with Sergeant Barney Benson and Lieutenant Stan Duffield, both SS Panzer Corps unleashed the full weight of their massed guns across the entire 2nd Canadian Division front.

The shriek of the latest round of incoming rockets sent Wilkinson diving into the nearest hole. The cluster of explosions that followed lasted no longer than half a minute, tapering off into sporadic harassing fire as the lion's share moved to the FMR's positions at Beauvoir Farm and the Camerons' in the rubble of St. André–St. Martin.

Hook crawled out into the open, realizing with complete disgust and dismay that his impromptu refuge had once housed a latrine. Preoccupied with his predicament, he failed at first to notice the approaching jeep ambulance bouncing through the mud towards the command post. As it passed, Hook fixed on the ashen face of George Fraser. The D Company commander was without his fawn balmoral. His uniform smouldered; his right foot and left leg above the knee were missing. The battalion medical officer, Captain Rudy Ohkle, worked to stabilize Fraser, but he faded away and died not long after, at 2120 hours.

Nobody fathomed that a man like Fraser could die. It was indeed a naive notion in war, but one all too human. Like the other company commanders, officers and senior NCOs, Fraser was a pillar of stability, the epitome of what "Black Watch" meant. He had the intrinsic value everyone took for granted the way a child would a parent or an older sibling—until, of course, they were gone.

Few had time to process the loss, let alone mourn Fraser's death. The alarm went up yet again to take cover. Expecting shells to crash down and the SS to appear out of the blackness at any moment, everyone stood at the height of readiness, fully alive and prepared to meet the onslaught. However, this time the habitual sounds of incoming shellfire failed to materialize, suggesting at first a false alarm. For close to ten minutes, an eerie quiet befell their immediate front while the sounds of skirmishes farther down the line continued to rage.

At first, only the thunder from yet another downpour disturbed the scene, until the battalion wireless suddenly jolted to life with a stream of urgent messages that flooded the airwaves from both the Camerons and FMRs off to each flank. While the former were engaged in a pitched battle in the streets and ruins of the twin towns of St. Martin and St. André, the latter, locked in close combat around the Beauvoir Farm, reported that the 1st SS had overrun their lead company under Major Jacques Mousseau. Desperately pleading for support and instructions, only one message followed from Foulkes: "HOLD THAT LINE!"[13]

OVER THE PREVIOUS TWENTY-FOUR HOURS, THE FIRST IN a series of powerful SS *Kampfgruppen* from General Wilhelm Bittrich's 2nd SS Panzer Corps had arrived south of Verrières to bolster Dietrich's 1st SS Panzer Corps holding the ridge. Taking full advantage of the inclement weather that grounded Allied fighter-bombers, the spearhead of the 9th SS Hohenstaufen Panzer Division, Kampfgruppe Koch, had reached the crossroads in the village of May-sur-Orne, overlooking the western end of Verrières Ridge, by early morning on July 22.

The Germans maintained a commanding view of the fight for St. André–St. Martin and Black Watch lines on Hill 61, almost two miles to the northeast, from the church tower and atop the buildings on the northern fringes of May. Cantlie, suspecting that the Germans had employed the church tower to call down artillery fire, ordered one of the supporting seventeen-pounder anti-tank guns from E Squadron of the 2nd Anti-Tank Regiment to take it out at last light. By the time the reconnaissance units of Kampfgruppe Koch arrived, the steeple had disappeared, testifying to the marksmanship of the Canadian anti-tank gunners.

Waiting for the tail of his column to catch up, Koch ordered Oberscharführer Hermann Wehrle to take his panzer platoon of three Mark V Panther Gs on a reconnaissance patrol of

Canadian positions. Wehrle, a grizzled forty-year-old Nazi who joined the SS in 1933 and had seen combat on the Russian front with the 3rd SS Totenkopf Panzer Division, made a quick recce on foot, returning to his tank after discerning the best approach route. Following a winding path that took full advantage of the rolling nature of the ground, the SS staff sergeant lost his bearings in the early morning twilight dimmed by rain. He had no idea how far he advanced, and had doubts "whether an enemy was actually there since the advance seemed to be going so smoothly."[14]

Moving in bounds, he halted his platoon once more to check his course. He popped the hatch but found it difficult to situate himself in the pre-dawn darkness. When the light slowly increased in the next few minutes, he noticed infantry, anti-tank guns and other support vehicles in the area surrounding his platoon. As he strained through the half-light to ascertain whether he had landed in the lines of 1st SS or the 272nd Division (both known to be operating in the area), a further glance cleared up the situation.

To his shock, Wehrle realized he had overshot his target and had stumbled into Black Watch lines on Hill 61. At this point, not one man in the Black Watch noticed the three Panthers idling in the wheat. Coolly, the seasoned SS veteran radioed his location and demanded immediate reinforcements, then ordered his panzers to button up and attack.

Panther hatches slammed shut in unison, and their 650-horsepower engines roared to life, drawing the attention of every man on Hill 61. "Like a lightning bolt from a clear sky," Wehrle reported, he opened fire with his 75-millimetre main gun and the MG 34 that chattered away below in the bow. "Everyone in the area scattered, with men jumping into slits, firing back with their rifles, Brens, Stens and PIATs."

Immediately, Major Phil Griffin dispatched Lieutenant Tommy Dorrance to get a handle on the situation unfolding up front. Sensing that it was too dangerous to send a subordinate, Dorrance ventured out alone. Skirting a small hedge that shielded his platoon's position in the wheat just north of the crossroads, he came face to face with one of Wehrle's Panthers. In a flash, the platoon commander who had skilfully guided his men through the clearing of Verson, the crossing of the Orne and the attacks on Ifs and Hill 61 was dead, killed instantly by a point-blank blast from a 75-millimetre shell that burst between his feet.[15]

The explosion off the flank caught the attention of Bennett and Desormeaux, but they failed to locate the ten-foot-high monster in the tall wheat. Resorting to blind firing, the duo pumped round after round from their rifles into the veil of grain until one Panther suddenly broke through into a thin, open corridor that lay out ahead. Taken by surprise, both froze in fear as the panzer squealed to a halt no more than than thirty yards away, its right side offering the perfect target for a defilade shot. With no means at hand to combat the panzer other than a few Hawkins grenades that lay dribbled out ahead of their slit, they hoped for a sabot round from an anti-tank gun or a PIAT shell fired by one of the tank-hunting teams to light up the idling Panther, but nothing happened.

After just a few seconds, which felt more like an eternity for Bennett, the seventy-ton panzer, drizzled with crimson, dark-emerald and mustard-yellow paint and generously draped with branches and leaves for camouflage, lurched back to life. The driver gunned the engine, shifted gears and swung the beast to the right in a violent pirouette that churned up mud and crops and spat dirt from the treads. The panzer began its advance towards the petrified pair. Desormeaux yanked Bennett below the lip of the slit by his webbing and urged him to prepare for the tank to overrun their position, hoping that its two-foot-wide treads would straddle their slit rather than hitting them head-on, crushing their earthen fortification and entombing them alive.

With the ground trembling in equal measure to his hands, Bennett felt the slit tighten. The rapid approach of the panzer, now no more than twenty yards away, proved too much for the 150-pound private to bear. In a desperate bid for salvation, he popped his head above the lip in search of an escape route and found himself staring straight at the nose of the 100,000-pound armour-plated behemoth bearing down on him. "Holy Christ! He's going to run over me or shoot me!" Bennett thought, and he started to scramble out of the slit.

Desormeaux, sitting with his head between his knees, failed to notice the escape attempt. "I was going to make a break," Bennett recalled, and then, at the last moment, "the thing suddenly started to turn, and he went left."

Few of the anti-tank guns still reeling from the shock and surprise could get into action quickly, let alone find Wehrle's Panthers in waist-high grain. The one or two that managed to get a shot off sent their shells screaming in all directions, slicing the heads off wheat stalks as their armour-piercing rounds streaked past above the dug-in Highlanders.

Screams, confusion and near panic continued for the next ten minutes, and in the estimation of the boastful SS veteran Wehrle, had the reinforcements he requested arrived in time, he could have broken through the Black Watch lines and driven them back to Ifs. However, with the bulk of the 9th SS Panzer Division still moving in piecemeal fashion across the Orne and Laize Rivers, no reserves were available to exploit his good fortune, and after expending his ammunition in the target-rich environment, Wehrle ordered his platoon to pull back to ambush positions on the ridge near May-sur-Orne to await replenishment and support.

In the meantime, the respite gave Cantlie time to get his battalion under control and consolidate his position. He reported to Young at 1005 hours that they had been attacked by three or four panzers and perhaps "some infantry which have not been seen," but "Everything OK."[16]

7

MAESTRO

In all military history, to force an able commander to expend his reserves there has been discovered no alternative to the "holding attack." To effect its purpose, such an attack must be directed against an objective about which the enemy is highly sensitive and for the protection of which he is certain to react. In the Normandy bridgehead, the "Caen Hinge" was just such an objective.
—LIEUTENANT GENERAL GUY GRANVILLE SIMONDS, JANUARY 1946

LIEUTENANT WILLIAM MACKENZIE-WOOD TRIED DESperately to keep his seat in the back of the snub-nosed 15-hundredweight Chevrolet truck that trundled down the inundated, corduroy roads winding their way between Juno Beach and Ifs. The young subaltern, who had just arrived in Normandy following an overnight journey from England, regretted very much the moment he thumbed a ride in the Black Watch hauler as diesel fumes and the constant buffeting and banging of the truck's suspension had brought on an intense bout of motion sickness. At first, he praised the moment when the truck slowed and then crawled to a halt at the crossroads between Fleury and Ifs. He soon thought otherwise. The ditches on either side of the road were swollen from the recent torrential downpours, and a group of white-gloved provosts dashed any thoughts he entertained of escaping to continue his trek on foot.

Relishing the momentary stillness, he dared not question why the truck had failed to resume its journey after idling for what seemed an eternity. He was curious about the heavy military police presence and peered out from behind a stack of ammunition boxes. He spotted Lieutenant General Guy Simonds and his aide-de-camp, Captain Marshal Stearns, standing next to the 2nd Canadian Corps commander's specially modified Staghound armoured car among a fervent pack of army photographers and staff officers who "flittered about."[1] Transfixed by the inordinate amount of brass on display, the young Black Watch officer had no explanation until a drab Humber Snipe open-top staff car pulled into sight and drew everyone's attention as it splashed to a halt at the crossroads.

General Montgomery leaped out of the front passenger door sporting a light-coloured hunting blazer, corduroy trousers, his traditional black beret adorned by two cap badges and a camouflage scarf fashioned as an ascot. The tall, sinewy figure of the 2nd British Army commander, General Miles Dempsey, dressed in traditional battledress with his red-banded brass hat on high, jumped down to join him. Simonds, their long-time subordinate, rushed across to greet the pair and received a hearty handshake and warm smiles following a cursory salute.

The sole figure that remained in the back seat, clad in a black peacoat and dark trousers and sporting a naval officer's cap, a cigar crooked in his mouth, toddled down from the staff car onto the Normandy soil. Winston Churchill, the rotund, sixty-nine-year-old British prime minister, ignored the pack and swept past to the ditch. He slipped off his black leather gloves and promptly proceeded to relieve himself. Caught off guard by the developments, the embarrassed group spent the next two minutes "slapping their legs with their swagger sticks, pretending not to notice."[2]

The young reinforcement officer chuckled to himself as the

truck resumed its journey. As it plowed slowly down the traffic-clogged road towards Ifs, his focus turned to the Black Watch, who sat locked in a deadly struggle to maintain their precarious hold on Hill 61, unaware of the machinations going on farther up the chain of command that would shape their fate in the coming days.

The deadlock in Normandy, coupled with Goodwood's less than stellar results, had prompted the visit by the prime minister, whose sudden arrival convinced everyone on Montgomery's staff that the bulldog of a war leader had come for the head of their chief. No sooner had he arrived, however, than news broke of the attempt on Hitler's life, which no doubt played a role in saving Monty's head but did not extricate him from the hot seat.

General Dwight D. Eisenhower, the supreme commander, faced his own set of pressures during an election year in the United States. He had teed up Operation Cobra, a breakout operation by General Omar Bradley's 1st US Army, in the west of the bridgehead around St. Lô, which he planned to kick off on July 20 just as Goodwood and Atlantic reached their zeniths. The heavy rain, however, forced its postponement to July 24. As a result, the supreme commander now turned to Dempsey's Anglo-Canadian forces to keep the German panzer reserves, who were at that moment hammering Foulkes's 2nd Canadian Division, pinned down along Verrières Ridge and away from American forces. The day before Churchill arrived, Ike sent a note to Montgomery, urging him to press Dempsey to act more aggressively. "As Bradley's attack starts, Dempsey's should be intensified," he suggested. "Certainly, until he gains the space and airfields, we need him on that flank."[3]

Eisenhower's specific reference to the need for airfields set off alarm bells with Montgomery, who suspected that "curious undercurrents" might be at play in Ike's directive. Indeed,

Dempsey's failure to grab the Falaise plain south of Verrières Ridge had unleashed another round of attacks by his arch-nemesis, Air Marshal Sir Arthur Tedder, and Air Chief Marshal Sir Arthur Coningham in an ongoing feud that stretched back to their time in the North African desert.

The most recent chapter came in the wake of Montgomery's pre-D-Day promise to deliver this much-coveted land so that the RAF could build advanced airstrips for its tactical air forces by June 24 at the latest. However, almost two months after the landings, the area remained in German hands, and the air barons pounced, using the delay and the legitimate need for elbow room in the bridgehead as ammunition to settle old scores.[4] On extremely thin ice and already given one reprieve, the 21st Army Group commander felt obliged to lance what had become a nasty, festering boil.[5]

Montgomery confided in his diary that there "was no real objective at the moment [southeast] of Caen."[6] However, with this bottleneck behind the 2nd British Army, and pressed for immediate action, Monty shifted gears and ordered Dempsey to create the conditions for a breakout by engaging in a series of attritional assaults designed to wear down and "write off" the German panzer reserve as a precursor to another colossal crack in early August.[7]

In response to this directive, Dempsey concocted what he euphemistically dubbed his "Tennis over the Orne" approach, in which he planned to bat German panzer divisions back and forth over the Orne and Laize Rivers in a series of right-left, right-left blows. The first, set to begin in less than two days, stemmed directly from the renewed breakout operation currently in its final planning stages at Simonds's headquarters.[8]

Originally codenamed Operation Springtide, this plan was Simonds's attempt to renew the breakout called for in Atlantic.

However, as the weather turned, the German line along Verrières thickened, and Foulkes's division stumbled out of the starting gate. Montgomery's new directive allowed the Canadian Corps commander to recast and rechristen the operation as Spring.

The new plan, which continued to evolve until it kicked off in the early morning hours of July 25, had all the hallmarks of what Eisenhower desired and Montgomery felt obliged to deliver. At its core, Spring was a battle of attrition designed to pin down and "write off" German panzer reserves, while at the same time delivering the long-sought-after space for the airfields south of the ridge.

To bolster Simonds's corps for the attack, Dempsey provided two British armoured divisions, the 7th Armoured and the Guards Armoured, to augment his two Canadian infantry divisions and the 2nd Canadian Armoured Brigade.

In theory, the concept for Spring appeared straightforward: pierce the main German line on the western end of Verrières Ridge with the infantry, and then push the armour through to imperil the 1st SS Panzer Division dug in to the east. As with the Battle of Verdun in the First World War, when the Germans attempted to "bleed France white," the seizure of the Verrières feature per se was not the end game; instead, that came with the cost associated with the German reaction. With the precarious fate of Hitler's prized bodyguard serving as bait, the full weight of Allied artillery, air power, tanks and anti-tank guns would be brought to bear to crush the German panzer reserves attempting to rescue their trapped brethren.

The method for achieving this result proved anything but simple. Going against his own advice that a plan should be "sound and simple," Simonds instead created a monster of a plan that became the epitome of "war by timetable," which proved typical of the Maestro's command style.[9] Unnecessarily complicated,

Spring relied on an overcentralized command structure and strict adherence to tight timings for each component where his forces would indeed follow the music while Simonds—and only Simonds—played the variations.[10]

To effect his goal, Simonds designed his plan in three major movements, or phases, with the first calling for his two infantry divisions to storm up Verrières in the middle of the night to capture the German line near the crest running from May-sur-Orne to Verrières village and onwards to Tilly-la-Campagne. Phase II would commence at dawn with his infantry, supported by tanks of the 2nd Canadian Armoured Brigade, breaching the main German defence line on the reverse slope of Verrières to capture Fontenay-le-Marmion and Rocquancourt. Once in Canadian hands, these two key towns would form the solid shoulders of the breach that would allow the two British armoured divisions to push through in Phase III to capture the Cramesnil Spur and the town of Garcelles, a move that would turn the flank of 1st SS Panzer Division and threaten it with impending doom. At that point, Simonds would consolidate on the ground gained and unleash the overwhelming power of the Allied tactical forces, his 1,500 artillery pieces and nearly 1,000 tank and anti-tank guns, to absorb the inevitable German counterattack, hoping to inflict fatal losses on General Sepp Dietrich's 1st SS Panzer Corps.[11]

Hopes of reaching the final phase, however, came into question by the time Simonds held his orders group for the attack on the morning of July 23. Thanks to the penetrating work of Allied intelligence, the 2nd Canadian Corps commander knew that several battle groups from at least three panzer divisions and a pair of heavy SS Tiger battalions had arrived to bolster the 272nd Infantry Division defending the west end of the ridge and the 1st SS to the east.[12] By conservative estimates, Dietrich had amassed 275 panzers and assault guns, with approximately another 200 en route, all backed by panzer-grenadiers and the artillery, mortars, rockets and anti-tank guns of both 1st SS Panzer Corps and 2nd SS Panzer Corps on the flank.[13]

Buoyed to a certain extent by the suggestion that this number represented only the paper strength, and that recent fighting had reduced the actual strength by as much as two-thirds, it still posed a formidable threat and left no doubt in anyone's mind that the entire centre of gravity of the German defences in Normandy had shifted east of the Orne to rest now on the Bourguébus–Verrières feature.[14] As one post-battle report put it, "There could be no doubt at all that such ground offered the Germans defensive possibilities which they were supremely well qualified as tacticians to exploit. Across these exposed and enfiladed slopes our troops, many of them with only slight experience in battle, were to assault the strong positions of a wily, resourceful and determined enemy."[15]

This realization was not lost on Dempsey, and it gave the 2nd British Army commander cause for concern that did not echo as loudly at 2nd Canadian Corps headquarters.[16] With hopes of a clean breakthrough resulting from the attritional struggle likely dashed, Simonds steadfastly expected that, despite the odds, his divisions would at the very least come away with the ridge and perhaps even more. Dempsey, however, did not share his subordinate's optimism and imposed a deadline that gave his exuberant subordinate until noon on July 25—just eight and a half hours after the attack began—to complete Phase II with the capture of Fontenay and Rocquancourt or he would shut the operation down cold. Unfazed by the added pressure and determined to capture the ridge even with the clock ticking, Simonds ordered that "troops must drive on wherever there is a gap," as there would be "no waiting for George" under any circumstances.[17]

• • •

"STAY IN YOUR SLITS! STAY IN YOUR SLITS!" CRIED THE unmistakable voices of Majors Eric Motzfeldt and Phil Griffin. The tumult shook Private Bill Booth awake at 0400 hours on July 23. Seconds later, more screams ensued, this time in both English and German, followed by a muffled crump from an explosion near Cantlie's headquarters. Then Harrison Bennett's massed Vickers machine guns opened fire, ripping right across the Black Watch positions on Hill 61.

Staring up from the bottom of his slit, Booth watched as the green, yellow and red tracer fire tore past overhead in a sweeping arc, searching for the German patrol that had used the pouring rain, the mist and night as black as pitch to slip between A and D Companies near the crest.

Before he dove down to join Dale Sharpe, Brunner, who had stood watch for the last two hours, had caught a quick glimpse of one figure, no more than ten feet away, slithering madly towards a neighbouring slit when the machine guns opened up. Brunner had no clue whether the man was friend or foe. The torrents of machine-gun bullets that cut through the stalks above like a swarm of angry wasps prevented any investigation, until an earth-curdling cry rising above the din from fellow sniper Private Frank Balsis in the next slit solved the mystery.

A German soldier who had been searching for refuge landed on top of the athletically built twenty-two-year-old pugilist, knocking the dog-eared copy of Dashiell Hammett's *The Thin Man* from his chest. Balsis was now face to face with the surprised and equally terrified enemy, clad in his distinctive Zeltbahn rain cape and clutching an MP 40 submachine gun. Balsis frantically patted the top of his boot in a futile search for the handle of his dagger, while the German scrambled to find his. Neither could find their weapon in the tight confines. Only a few feet away, Brunner and Sharpe sat pinned by the threat of friendly fire, forced to endure the sounds of the two men locked in a primal struggle for survival.[18]

Engulfed by fear, rage and animalistic instinct, Balsis kicked, bit, gouged and squirmed, managing to work his way from underneath the German into a position where he could clutch his opponent's throat. With thumbs clasped on the man's Adam's apple, Balsis squeezed without cessation. The German, with his arms trapped at the elbows by the tight dirt walls, could not break free and his body slackened. Terrified that his opponent's limp posture might be a ruse, Balsis took no chances and maintained his ironclad grip for another half minute, until his uncontrolled twitching and the pungent smell of vacated bowels delivered the final verdict. Brunner, unable to intervene while the fire continued above, remained psychologically scarred and tormented by the convulsive gasps from Balsis, who sobbed uncontrollably.[19]

Cantlie, meanwhile, escaped death when a German rifle grenade scored a direct hit on his headquarters. When the firing stopped, both sides found themselves in a tense ceasefire, with only the thin stalks of grain separating the foes.

At dawn, Corporal Oscar Bulow, dug in with his anti-tank gun about a hundred yards off to the flank, shouted out in fluent German demanding the surrender of the German patrol. At first, his efforts produced nothing but silence, but Bulow pressed the issue and eventually coaxed the remnants of the German patrol to surrender, which took the Black Watch by surprise. "Suddenly," as George Buch recalled, "out of the mist the Germans emerged with their hands up . . . Three feet in front of some of our men . . . Half of us did not know they were right there!" Bill Booth was thoroughly astonished. "The Germans who had survived walked toward us, hands on their heads and calling out, 'Kamerad' and all wore field caps, in lieu of steel helmets."

On first impression, the intelligence clerk noticed that, even though seventeen of their comrades lay dead around them, none of the prisoners appeared dismayed about falling into Canadian hands. One private, who appeared at least in his late forties, startled Booth with his pleasant, welcoming demeanour and fluency in English. Responding to Booth's cursory interrogation in a calm, polite manner, the prisoner, obviously a worldly sort, asked with a smile, "*Amerikanisch*?" Ignoring his question, Booth continued to rifle through the man's pockets. He found little of obvious intelligence value at first, though the bulging left pouch on the prisoner's tunic produced a shaving kit, which Booth thought strange, given that the man was on patrol and expected back in a few hours. Then it clicked. Intelligence had suspected that the 272nd had been forcibly bolstered by roaming SS units in the wake of the attempt on Hitler's life. "Perhaps the patrol was for him a way of resigning from the war?" Booth wondered.

Brunner, called in to glean what information he could from the prisoners, could barely understand anything uttered at first by men who proved more than willing to talk. As he soon discovered, a portion of the 272nd was made up of men pressed into service from German-occupied nations who had seen previous action on other fronts—"some for, some against, and others both [for and against] Germany."[20] All brought stories of their long journey to Normandy and the devastating impact of Allied air power and artillery, and how the SS were operating as battle police, stiffening the resolve of Wehrmacht units by employing lethal means to ensure they remained obedient to Adolf Hitler and the Nazi cause.[21]

At first glance, it appeared that the Black Watch had got off lucky in the wild exchange of gunfire in the dark—until Benson realized that Private Charlie Lee, farmed out to D Company to man one of their observation posts, had failed to report.

Immediately, Benson dispatched the scouts, who carried out a meticulous search, but when daylight broke and German sniper and mortar fire increased, they called off their efforts until nightfall.

Twelve hours after the German patrol stumbled into Black Watch lines, the scouts found Lee, slumped in his slit, motionless and unconscious but still breathing. Unable to rouse him, neither the scouts nor the medics who arrived to stretcher him out noticed a small bullet hole, the size of a half dollar, in the back of his head just above his left ear.[22] Apparently, not everyone had heeded the warning to stay in their slits, and it was anyone's guess whether he had been hit by friend or foe. As no exit wound appeared on part of Lee's skull, the medics rightly suspected the bullet remained lodged in his skull, and they quickly placed the diminutive sniper onto a carrier destined for the regimental aid station and immediate evacuation to England for life-saving brain surgery. Two days later, having failed to regain consciousness and unresponsive to treatment, Charlie Lee slipped away in St. Margaret's hospital in Swindon, England. Quietly interred in Brookwood Cemetery, the news of his death never reached his fellow scouts during their fight in Normandy.[23]

To PREVENT A REPEAT OF THE NIGHT'S SURPRISE, CANTLIE ordered up two standing patrols to head down the forward slope leading into the valley near St. Martin that night. The first, led by Sergeant Mac Roulston, would slip out into the wheat just after dark. The other, made up of reinforcements and led by a less than enthusiastic Corporal Duke Ducat, would depart fifteen minutes later. Ducat, incensed that the CO had called his number again, complained bitterly on his way back from Taylor's command post to anyone who would listen. "I was tired, I was fed up, and I was bloody mad," he explained, and going out with six new men on a patrol did not seem fair. However, as he would realize later, the testy corporal had nobody to blame but himself for his present predicament, and that is what angered him the most.

With the imminent threat of German counterattack looming, Ducat and his trigger-lipped confrere Smokey Lalonde sat in their slit, brewing up a much-needed spot of tea when the fresh-faced Mackenzie-Wood hastily approached their slit, looking for company headquarters. The young lieutenant, twenty-two years of age, looked sixteen and had all the natural authority of a high school hall monitor. He was slightly built, overly polite, diplomatic and always correct. He was short of anything related to street smarts, and the pair of self-proclaimed Dead End Kids sized him up with one glance.

The young officer made the mistake of asking the two men what they were doing. "Don't you know the Germans are coming over that hill with Tiger tanks?" In deadpan response to his skittish tone, Ducat shot back, "Yes, I know that. I got a Sten gun, and he's got a Bren gun, and he wants his cup of tea. Now fuck off . . . sir!" Flustered as much by the wanton use of foul language as the corporal's impertinence, the blushing Mackenzie-Wood scurried off. "You are going to go up on charges." Smiling wryly at Lalonde, Ducat shouted back as the officer departed, "Go ahead—ding me." Then he went back to his tea.

The incident was long forgotten by the time Ducat arrived at Taylor's command post early in the evening after the resumption of heavy shelling. The hole in the ground that constituted the company headquarters left little room, as Benson and Duffield had joined Taylor and John Kemp, who had replaced Fraser at the helm of D Company, to prepare the night's patrol program. As the Germans dominated the area by day, patrolling proved impossible until darkness fell, and the group pored over map traces and the latest aerial photographs, discussing the relative merits of infiltration and exfiltration points and ambush spots. As Ducat approached, Taylor turned slightly to acknowledge him with a nod and then motioned the corporal towards the company's new platoon commander, who had arrived to take the place of Bob Austin, who had been killed on the Orne. All Ducat remembered as he stared straight at Mackenzie-Wood was Taylor's voice, which rang with delicious irony. "Have you two been formally introduced?"

Captains John Taylor and John Kemp had arrived in Normandy as the seconds-in-command of their respective rifle companies, but within two weeks of landing, both found themselves thrust into command and promoted on the spot to acting majors.

Kemp, the same age as Mackenzie-Wood, had four years of seasoning under his belt and seemed long overdue for promotion and command of a company. Next to Griffin and Motzfeldt, Cantlie considered Kemp, an engineering student from McGill University, a "first-class officer and a natural leader." George Buch, his Bishop's College School old boy chum, stood in wholehearted agreement with this widely held assessment of Kemp, noting he "was a rather serious fellow; nothing was done without his heart and soul." Major George Fraser, whose death vaulted Kemp into command, had echoed this sentiment in earlier assessments, noting that, although "very cooperative" and "continually thinking of the well-being of his men," Kemp came across as a thoroughbred who had "a will of his own and quite a quick temper." Certainly, in the early days of the war, when he was just eighteen, his mercurial temper got the better of him, but as he matured, his legendary outbursts became less frequent, although they did from time to time rear their unprepossessing head. As

DAVID O'KEEFE

Buch recalled, "Kemp had a serious temper [and] didn't brook any nonsense . . . he wasn't a guy who just pushed his weight around . . . he was well respected but very hard."

John Taylor, who turned thirty-four the week before the battalion arrived in Normandy, was a different matter. Tall, fair-haired, charismatic and remarkably fit, the B Company second-in-command (2ic) took immense pride in keeping up, step for step, with his fellow officer, who was a decade or more his junior. Like Fraser, Stevenson and Cantlie, Taylor was an "old Black Watcher" with sixteen years of service in the regiment. He had started the war with the rank of temporary major, but reverted back to captain to proceed overseas with the Black Watch when they left for England in 1940.

By 1944, his natural career progression should have put him in line directly behind Cantlie and the battalion deputy commanding officer, Major Frank Mitchell, for command of the unit, but despite successive postings, courses and eventually three months of combat experience in North Africa, he remained stuck at captain while the new crop of Black Watch talent, including Griffin, Kemp, Motzfeldt and Bennett, had caught up and then surpassed him. "There was no doubt Taylor had a chip on his shoulder," Buch remembered. "He had been in the regiment a long time." And, despite drawing rave reviews for his ability to train men, he did not measure up to "Black Watch standards" when it came to the tactical handling of his formation in the field. As Phil Griffin noted in his diary after commanding Taylor for several months before he left for North Africa, he was a "sound egg," but "lacked drive," a verdict echoed in his evaluations. In a regiment that prided itself on "excellence," being merely damned good did not measure up.

Taylor, however, was extremely popular with the men, which proved a double-edged sword. As his sergeant, Mac Roulston, remembered, unlike the other Black Watch officers, "he was down to earth—you could talk to him." But in the class-conscious world of the Black Watch, his fraternization with the men drew heavy scorn and criticism, which led to an increased overemphasis on any of his perceived weaknesses. Inflaming matters, Taylor turned down several opportunities to sharpen and hone his skills by taking command of a company in another regiment. He was stubbornly bent on making it within the Black Watch. Friction developed with some fellow officers, who, like George Buch, found him rather "prickly." Even the normally brusque and less than timid Phil Griffin noted that he had to "overlook Taylor's weaknesses," as their relationship proved "far too delicate" and he "didn't have the confidence to tick him off."

Eventually, Cantlie farmed Taylor out to the British so he could obtain much-needed combat experience in North Africa, where, by all accounts, he handled himself admirably over three months of intense combat in Tunisia. However, his combat schooling had come at a heavy cost. Having encountered "some frightful sights" on the battlefield in Tunisia, he admitted to "drinking heavily" since his return to deal with recurring nightmares. Noticing that Taylor's manner had become quick and jumpy when he returned to the Black Watch in the late spring of 1943, Dr. Rudy Ohkle, the astute regimental medical officer, intervened and got Taylor back on the rails, but his invisible wounds took a severe toll on his health, reputation and career.[24] How much this set him back is impossible to assess, but it is safe to say that when he took the reins of B Company from the wounded Stevenson, he was, like his fellow company commanders, not only trying to make his mark but, unlike his contemporary, seeking a form of redemption as well.

The immediate concern for both Taylor and Kemp was two-fold: how to successfully launch their standing patrols without getting the men killed out of the chute, and how to make sure that the reinforcements that arrived were up to snuff. "Even at that point," Kemp would later recall, "many were untrained, and the NCOs were instructed to go around and show them how to prime grenades and show them how to use their basic weapons." Kemp pointed out that this had a "disconcerting" impact because every officer "expected reinforcements would be fully trained by the fourth year of the war." Motzfeldt was equally alarmed when he noticed deficiencies in the quality of infantry reinforcements on July 20, when he "received one draft of about 40 men half an hour before the attack on Hill [61]." Later, he discovered that "one man had less than six weeks' training in Canada and one week in England, while another only had three months of military service in total." Kemp, unimpressed and genuinely concerned, reported that "all any battalion could do was to do their best and get on with it. You couldn't stop the war for six weeks and train them."[25]

Saddled with this flawed instrument, Kemp and Barney Benson endeavoured to produce a scheme for the night's patrols. At last light, both patrols would sneak out into the wheat, armed with Bren guns, PIATs and Hawkins grenades, to lie in wait for unwary German patrols. After several hours in no man's land in the valley, they would work their way back to Canadian lines about thirty minutes before daybreak, arriving at an alternate location from where they first exited hours before.

MAC ROULSTON HAD TAKEN MANY PATROLS OUT IN training and a few contact patrols with the scouts since the arrival in Normandy, but this would be his first standing patrol. His biggest worry was not the enemy, but rather his creaky memory for details. "The code word was a joint one—STRIKE—and the answer was supposed to be A MATCH." He had gone two weeks without more than two or three hours of sleep, and was convinced he would forget it.

Precisely at 2200 hours, both heavily laden patrols made their first attempt to wade into the fields ahead of A Company, but somehow, even in the dark, the Germans spotted them and sniper fire drove them back into their lines. In a bid to out-fox the Germans, Kemp sent out a Bren gun team on the right flank to draw enemy fire so that his patrols could slip through. The fracas drew the German fire. The first effort by an exceedingly nervous gun crew miscarried, for they failed to venture far enough out in the valley. Firing at a sustained burst, the scheme rapidly backfired and evoked a heavy concentration of German mortar and artillery fire that careened down on top of the less than delighted forward companies. About an hour later, a renewed ruse succeeded when Kemp, frustrated by the timid nature of the gun team, ordered them to poke their noses out 250 yards ahead and slightly off to the right flank for the second effort. This time the ploy worked, and both patrols slipped away, into the night.

ALTHOUGH ALL MEN IN THE BATTALION COULD BE called upon to go out on patrol, not every man was cut out for patrolling, as Ducat soon learned not long out into no man's land.

With yet another German counterattack on Cameron's positions in St. André providing a spectacular backdrop, Ducat found a suitable spot in the wheat where he planned to set up shop for the next four hours. Within the first hour, however, stress among the new arrivals experiencing their first patrol became an issue. Their anxiety level increased with every eerie sound a battlefield makes at night; they sat in the dark, not knowing what to expect or where the enemy roamed. "I thought several would have near-fatal coronaries from panic and fright," Ducat recalled. Sensing that more than half of his small standing patrol would snap and give away their position at any second, he ordered his men to return to Black Watch lines earlier than expected.

When they arrived, Ducat reported straight to the intelligence officer, Shirley Griffin, with two of his men in a desperate state in tow. "I explained [that] I had come in off patrol and that these two men [had] broken down." Exhausted, fed up and unable to cope with their psychological distress, Ducat noted, "I just left them there . . . that's all I could do."[26]

Ducat, finally back in his slit, planned to catch some sleep while Smokey Lalonde stood watch. Before the exhausted corporal could drift off, an outpost to their immediate front at the junction between B and C Companies challenged someone moving in the water-filled ditch ahead. "Strike," the sentry called. Silence followed. "Strike!" he called again, louder and more sternly this time. Nobody responded. Everyone in the Black Watch lines went on high alert. Bren and Vickers machine-gun bolts slammed home, and without hesitation they opened fire. Tracer fire tore into the area ahead from the front and flank, cutting a scythe-like swath through the wheat. The steady fire continued unabated for a full two minutes as flashes from the barking MGs lit the area in strobe-like fashion.

When the call came to cease fire, the water-cooled Vickers belched steam while piles of discarded magazines lay strewn beside each Bren gun, ushering in the first silence in days. Then bedlam ensued when someone from the direction of Cantlie's command post shouted that Roulston's fighting patrol had failed to return on time.

• • •

EARLIER IN THE EVENING, WHILE DUCAT'S PATROL HAD proceeded without incident, Roulston's moved southwest in the direction of St. André and St. Martin and ran into trouble almost immediately. The Black Watch sergeant had to halt on several occasions to check his location on the map, hounded by the rain and mist in the moonless night. Suspecting he had reached the point selected for the standing patrol, he ordered his men to go to ground in an all-around defensive position. The night was unusually quiet, except for the occasional cracks and pops from fires burning in the twin towns, or sporadic sniper fire. Digging more than a few inches risked drawing enemy fire. Having sighted their Brens and PIATs and laid out the daisy chain of Hawkins grenades twenty yards ahead, Roulston's men lay prone in their shallow scrapes, straining to hear any little noise. They fought off fatigue and insects while waiting for a German patrol that never came.

Poking his head around for what seemed like the millionth time, hoping to find anything to shoot at, Roulston suddenly noticed during a pause in the rain that the tower and complex of warehouse-like buildings south of St. Martin they called the "factory" emerged from the mist less than a hundred yards away. He realized now that he had ventured out much farther than planned. A quick check of his watch revealed that it would now take twice as long to get back to Black Watch lines. It was now a race against time to get home safely before the light streamed in over Verrières Ridge at dawn.

The patrol crossed the ground in good time, but as the factory faded from view, Roulston lost his reference point. Keeping the large group together in the wheat and darkness became difficult, and he soon lost his bearings. Moving fifty yards at a time, Roulston approached what he believed to be his re-entry point. As he took one last look at his compass and map, he heard a voice yell, "Halt!" followed quickly by "Strike." Relieved that he had made it back, Roulston froze when he fumbled with his memory, searching for the countersign. Cycling like mad through all the permutations of "strike"—strike out, strike back, strike breaker—he landed on "a match." A flare went up. Taught to freeze when confronted by illumination, Roulston stood still, not daring to move a muscle. The others, skittish and lacking his experience, dove for cover or broke in all directions. A machine gun, less than fifty yards ahead, erupted.

CAPTAIN RONNIE BENNETT, FUMING AT THE DREADFUL news, summoned Benson, Hook Wilkinson, Harold Burden and Fred Delutis to accompany him out to the ditch at first light. Unsure of what they would face, the party advanced in an extended line, each man ready to hit the ground if fired upon to allow the machine guns, now fully reloaded, to resume their deadly harvest. Cautiously and deliberately, the scouts eased their way into the small corridor that had been shaved into the wheat by the heavy gunfire. They stumbled quickly upon the gruesome scene.

Bodies and body parts lay everywhere. Each man was horribly torn apart from the waist up. Some had their scalps sheared clean off, leaving the grey-yellow of brain tissue scattered in all directions, hanging from wheat stalks drenched with crimson streaks of blood. Bennett made out at least fifteen dead. To his great relief, he noticed that all the bodies lay draped in the distinctive Zeltbahn camouflage rain capes of Heer units. Some were still wearing their field caps or their telltale M42 German helmets ringed with straw. Discarded Mauser rifles, MP 40 submachine guns and *Panzerfäuste* lay strewn about the grisly scene.

Then something rustled in the wheat. As Bennett put it, "a

Hollywood scene was re-enacted . . . Two dozen figures rose out of the wheat within ten feet of our slit trenches." All had their hands up, calling, "*Kameraden*."

After hustling the prisoners to the rear for the "tactical squeeze," Benson and the scouts set about rummaging through the pockets, packs and pouches of the dead. They discovered that all the men belonged to the 980th Grenadier Regiment of the 272nd Infantry Division, comrades of the group taken prisoner the night before. Bennett pieced the events together. "We found a Company commander, one platoon officer, a Sergeant-Major, and another Sergeant huddled together with maps open all shot through the head."

From what they could gather, the German patrol, while attempting to return to friendly lines, strayed off its intended course and had become "bewildered as to their position." Hopelessly lost in the dead of night and the high grain, the company commander "halted his men and was planning a course of action" when "one of his men must have moved, which caused our sentry to challenge." Bennett, the young peacetime barrister, reasoned it "made all of his men sit up to look about" just as the massed Brens and Vickers let loose. Contented with the outcome of his prima facie inquiry, Bennett noted appreciatively, "We accepted this as a gift."

ROULSTON, ALONE AND IN THE DARK, WAITED FOR THE dust to settle for what seemed an eternity. Then he shouted the countersign: "A match! A match!!!" The voice of an English-speaking sentry just a few paces ahead beckoned him to approach with his hands up. Obeying the instructions, the Black Watch sergeant surfaced from the wheat. He too had strayed off course and away from Black Watch positions, finding himself smack in the middle of the Calgary Highlanders' position on Hill 67. Having discarded all identifying marks, as was standard practice, before the patrol went out, he could only give the password, his name, rank and serial number to the Calgarian covering him with a Sten, who was less than convinced. It took several hours before tactical headquarters established his credentials and whisked him by carrier back to Black Watch lines. Despite his homecoming, nobody ever heard from the rest of his men on the lost patrol again.

SIX STRAIGHT DAYS IN CONTINUOUS COMBAT HAD TAKEN its toll on the men in the Black Watch. Nobody had washed for over a week. Beards, generally frowned upon in the Highland unit, had grown long and filthy from a mixture of dust and mud. A few men sported a rash of pink pimples on their necks or cheeks, betraying ad hoc attempts to dry-shave. Some suffered from a slight case of dysentery—or gyppo stomach, as the British called it—brought on by the hordes of flies haunting the unburied dead. Body odours of all pungent aromas wafted about but failed to register with the men, all of whom suffered the same malady. Collectively, with no real sleep for over a week, fatigue worked down into the marrow of both man and unit alike. As John Kemp noted, "mental fatigue did not seem to occur in those kept busy, such as the officers and NCOs," but exhaustion plagued everyone.

For the first time since he arrived in Normandy, which now stretched to just under three weeks, Corporal Bruce Ducat took the time to remove his boots and peel off his matted socks. All the hygiene lessons he had conveniently ignored now came rushing back when he saw the condition of his feet: lily white and swollen, they "stunk to the high heavens." A quick review convinced the corporal his socks were a complete writeoff. Without hesitation, Ducat crushed them into a moist ball and, with smug pleasure, hurled them deep into the wheat. No sooner had he relieved himself of the offending woollen hose than he discovered, after shaking out the entire contents of his pack into the bottom of his slit, that his new pair sat safely stored with B Echelon back in Ifs. Knowing he would require a king's ransom to procure another pair from Smokey Lalonde, Ducat sat barefoot. He glanced over at the body of the kid from the Essex Scottish, whom he had managed to evict from his slit, lying a foot and a half away. "I went into his haversack and right on top was a clean pair of socks. I thought, 'Well, he won't need them now.' So, I put them on and put my boots back on, and I felt like a new man."

The rain and the mud no doubt added to the constant stress and took a toll on the men. Tempers started to grow thin, and men began to snap at each other for the slightest infractions usually ignored or completely overlooked. Bailing water from the bottoms of slits did not help morale as it took precious time away from rest, as did the constant threat of artillery, enemy patrols and the daily parade of wounded and battle fatigued. Soon, it all became impersonal. "So many guys just disappeared," Brunner lamented. "You didn't see them anymore [and] there's no bulletin board that tells you so and so has been killed. You see the guys for a few weeks, and then you don't see them."

The group that gathered around Campbell Stuart's carrier next to the church in Ifs, waiting for Cantlie to return from his meeting with Brigadier Megill and the other battalion commanders, showed the strain of battle. Each company commander stared bleary-eyed at his maps, uniforms muddy, faces unshaven and drawn and etched with fatigue. The forward observation officers from the two artillery regiments supporting the attack appeared equally grim and dishevelled, having worked almost every waking hour over the previous week, calling down fire all along the line. Gordon Powis, another old boy from Bishop's College School, who worked for the 5th Field Regiment, could barely muster more than a passing nod to his old mates when he arrived.

By contrast, Major Walter Harris from the 1st Hussars, whose tanks would support the Black Watch attack, appeared immaculate and well rested, having just arrived to take command of B Squadron earlier that day. His highly respected and decorated 2ic, Captain Jake Powell, who had fought the Germans continuously since they landed on D-Day, displayed the same strain as the officers in the Black Watch, while the oil smears on his cream-coloured coveralls testified to the recent sparring with Panthers, Tigers, Mark IVs and anti-tank guns along the ridge.

Right on time, Cantlie pulled up in his jeep accompanied by Stan Duffield and his intelligence officer, Shirley Griffin. Without any formal or informal greeting, he removed his balmoral and began his address.

The convoluted and overly complex nature of Simonds's plan demanded that Cantlie restrict his talk to the Black Watch's role. Determined to get it over with as quickly as possible, he offered only a few preliminary remarks while his officers jotted down the essentials in their field message pads, which would soon require multiple pages of notation.

Operation Spring would start in the middle of the night, at 0330 hours. The Calgary Highlanders, who had taken a beating of their own from German tanks and guns across the Orne in recent days, would get the honour of leading the attack up Verrières Ridge in the darkness towards their objective, May-sur-Orne. Supported by a heavy artillery barrage and the innovative use of searchlights directed at low clouds to create an artificial moonlight to aid navigation, the Calgarys would cross their start line—the road running out of the hotly contested St. André–

St. Martin to Beauvoir Farm—at H-hour and move south past the factory and up the slopes towards May.

At the same time, near Beauvoir Farm, the Royal Hamilton Light Infantry (RHLI) from 4th Brigade would seize Verrières village on the ridge while the North Nova Scotia Highlanders from 9th Brigade wrestled Tilly-la-Campagne from the 1st SS to complete Phase I. In Simonds's estimation, which lacked input from the frontline units, he allotted two hours to capture and consolidate these objectives before Phase II started at 0530.

As the Calgary Highlanders were fighting their way into May-sur-Orne, the four Black Watch rifle companies would snake their way off Hill 61 and skirt St. Martin, moving in single file towards their assembly area, the church on the southernmost edge of the mining town. Once in tight, they would shake out into their usual box formation at the form-up point a few hundred yards south, in a beet field next to the factory, where Harris's tanks would link up with them for the assault.

Just before Phase II began at 0530, the Black Watch would start their advance towards their start line near the crest of Verrières, a small farm track jutting out from May where they'd cross precisely at H-hour and descend upon their objective: Fontenay-le-Marmion on the reverse slope. Meanwhile, the Royal Regiment of Canada would pull an end run past Verrières village, seized earlier by the RHLI, and attack Rocquancourt to bring both towns, crucial to the success of the entire plan, into Canadian hands.

The furious flipping of field message pad pages in unison by officers taking notes in bastardized shorthand gave Cantlie a moment to pause before he turned to the complex fire plan and their tank support.

As with the previous attacks, guns from the 5th Field Regiment would lay down the concentrations, but this time they would be joined by the 25th Field Regiment, a British unit lent out to beef up the attack. All would fire a series of timed, concentrated stonks on suspected and known German positions near the crest of the ridge outside May, and on the reverse slope around Fontenay, during the Black Watch advance.

Once on the objective, the three FOOs (one with Griffin's company in the lead, another with Battalion HQ in the middle and another with Motzfeldt's company bringing up the rear) would call down defensive fire on German forces trying desperately to reclaim Fontenay-le-Marmion to re-establish their main line of resistance.

The 1st Hussars, who had six weeks of combat behind them since landing on D-Day, would provide the tank support for the Black Watch attack. Major Walter Harris, a sitting member of Canada's Parliament, would make his combat debut in Operation Spring, but luckily would have Powell, who had earned the Military Cross on D-Day, to hold his hand if necessary. Unlike the earlier attack on Hill 61, the seventeen Shermans would not follow the Black Watch up the slope for fear of being picked off by the panzers and anti-tank guns across the Orne and on the ridge. Instead, Harris would take his squadron up the road leading to May and pass through the Calgary Highlanders in the town, and then pop out from the western end of the village onto the reverse slope, just as the Black Watch closed on Fontenay. From here, they would "shoot" the rifle companies onto their objective from the right flank.

As they had done in their previous attacks at Ifs and on Hill 61, Cantlie's battalion would advance on Fontenay-le-Marmion in a box formation with Griffin's and Taylor's companies out front and Motzfeldt's and Kemp's bringing up the rear. Cantlie's tactical HQ would be in the middle. Captain Ronnie Bennett, who would patrol Hill 61 with his carriers to deceive the enemy and then catch up to the battalion along the road to St. Martin, would wait in the orchard north of the town waiting to haul his mortars, anti-tank guns, extra ammunition and supplies at the first sign of success.

None of the officers in attendance harboured any doubts, after a cursory glance at the latest defence overprint, that the job would be anywhere near as comfortable as their last two shows. The only issue that raised any hackles, however, came from Simonds's decision to use the road running through St. André and St. Martin as their "secure" start line for Phase I.[27] This decision raised eyebrows and drew comment because the twin towns remained hotly contested and anything but secure. Then Cantlie let the other shoe drop: Foulkes had transferred the Camerons to Megill's command and ordered them to secure both towns by midnight, three hours ahead of H-hour.

At that point, pens stopped writing and invective flew. "They've been hanging on by their fingernails all week," George Buch offered. "They don't have the strength to cross the bloody road, let alone clear St. Martin." When Buch asked about an alternative, Cantlie just shook his head.

Ronnie Bennett, equally alarmed by the inherent self-defeating nature of the decision, worried that the Camerons' inability to accomplish the task would throw the schedule for the operation entirely out of whack. "The timings were very important because the [artillery] program, which was very heavy and carefully planned, depended on fixed time and would be useless unless we passed our start line at H plus 120 minutes."[28]

Cantlie's officers had expressed this concern with Megill earlier in the day, when he and Lieutenant Colonel Donald MacLauchlan, commanding officer of the Calgary Highlanders, urged the brigadier to intervene with Foulkes; in their opinion, Simonds's staff, far removed from the front line, had no clear understanding of the ground. To Megill's credit, he did, but Foulkes, sensing that Simonds was out to get him, was in no mood to discuss the issue. When Megill pressed his point that the start line would cause delay and leave his battalions hung out to dry if forced to make their assault in daylight, Foulkes shot back icily, "The Corps Commander does not agree with that interpretation." To Megill, Foulkes's tone made it crystal clear that they would "carry on and get to our objectives even if not by first light." At that moment, "it was quite clear" to Megill "that no excuses would be taken for failure to try and push forward to the objective."[29]

Megill, who considered asking Foulkes to parade him before the corps commander to "tell him what I think," decided "that it wasn't worth it," as he'd "be fired and somebody else would do the job. After all, it was the Corps Commander's plan [and] nobody had the experience to say that this was the wrong way to do it. If Guy Simonds said that it could be done, it was going to be done."[30] Thoroughly frustrated and resigned to the inevitable, Megill later lamented, "We simply hitched up ourselves and did not make any formal alteration to the plan," hoping, in the end, the Maestro's "sixth sense" would prevail.

THE OPEN-TOPPED STAGHOUND ARMOURED CAR carrying Lieutenant General Guy Simonds sped through the rubble-clogged streets of Caen, bound for Foulkes's 2nd Division tactical command post, located in the basement of an abandoned brewery in Ifs. The long days of serious and urgent planning for Operation Spring had now given way to the countdown to the kickoff of the most significant battle yet undertaken in the war by Canadian forces.[31]

Fixated on his battle map, carefully marked each day by the

general's trusted aide-de-camp, Captain Marshal Stearns, Simonds absorbed the latest intelligence. Although he hoped for a clean victory, his map now displayed the formidable challenge facing the men in the assault battalions.[32] Two days earlier, Dempsey had ordered that a pair of small attacks be put in west of the Orne to either capture the German positions overlooking Verrières Ridge or, at the very least, keep the attention of the German panzers in that area fixated and out of Simonds's path. Both attacks failed to achieve those ends, and battle groups from the elite 9th SS Hohenstaufen Panzer Division and a reconnaissance element from the 10th SS Frundsberg Panzer Division had streamed across the tiny crossings over the Orne and Laize Rivers to join the veteran 2nd Panzer Division behind Verrières Ridge. Compounding this formidable array, the fresh 116th Panzer Division (which Allied intelligence failed to notice) had moved to the Cramesnil Spur and now lay in wait along the Falaise road for the next Allied move.[33]

Tending to situate the appreciation, rather than appreciate the situation, Simonds downplayed, miscalculated or outright ignored his opponent's vast skill, experience and leadership and the impact of terrain as vital force enhancers and clung instead to his material superiority in infantry, air power and tanks to carry the day.

Like a heavyweight boxer hammering away in the fifteenth round, Simonds held out hope that one decisive jab—in this case, grabbing Verrières Ridge and crushing German attempts to take it back—would weaken and unbalance his opponent and leave him ripe for a decisive knockout blow. Nothing, it seemed, would break his stride. But all this was predicated on winning the race for Verrières Ridge—a race that the intelligence map sprawled out on his lap clearly showed he was in danger of losing with each passing hour.

• • •

ON THE OTHER SIDE OF VERRIÈRES, THE MASSIVE BUILD-up in Canadian lines did not go unnoticed by Dietrich or his superiors. Alarmed by the inevitable resumption of an immense Goodwood-style attack, Field Marshal Günther von Kluge—who had just taken the reins of Army Group B following the wounding of Field Marshal Erwin Rommel in a strafing attack on his staff car—made a personal inspection of the Verrières area late on July 23. Accompanied by the German supreme commander in the west, Field Marshal Gerd von Rundstedt, and the head of Panzer Army West, Heinrich Eberbach, they arrived at the command post of the 272nd Division south of May-sur-Orne at noon.

General Friedrich August Schack, the commander of the 272nd Infantry Division, whose grenadier battalions continued to duel with Foulkes's division south of Caen, was a First World War veteran and a theologian from Breslau who had commanded the war college at Potsdam and had seen combat in Poland and Russia.

Bringing the group up to speed on developments in his sector, the highly decorated division commander proudly explained how his men had held on to their front in the face of overwhelming odds, providing crucial time for Eberbach to transfer Panzer Kampfgruppe to within striking distance of Verrières Ridge. The sacrifice, he noted, had cost his division nearly 30 percent of its fighting strength, a fact not lost on Eberbach, who later wrote that "the 272nd had proved its value."[34]

Schack's best efforts aside, von Kluge did not possess sufficient strength at that moment to launch a massive counterstroke of his own, but did plan to lash out at the Achilles heel of all Allied set-piece attacks: their delicate timings. Expecting the Allied push to resume as the weather cleared, the field marshal ordered a series of nighttime air strikes and harassing artillery fire to strike Allied command and control targets and troop concentrations right across the 2nd British Army front. Dietrich, taking his cue from von Kluge, ordered Schack to reinforce the twin towns to destabilize Simonds's drive in utero, hoping to offset the sheer numerical advantage and brute force employed by the Allies with increasing success in the recent days. If he could not stop the Canadian drive cold, at least the German forces along Verrières would make them pay the highest of costs for their success.

8

THE FOUR HORSEMEN, ACT 1: ST. MARTIN

July 25th was the most memorable day of my life. There's not a day I wake up in the morning and [do] not think of it . . . It's still a day of reckoning for me.

—HOOK WILKINSON

THE EAR-SPLITTING ROAR OF TWIN-ENGINED GERMAN intruder aircraft racing in over Verrières Ridge to fulfill Field Marshal von Kluge's orders just before H-hour brought the already escalating din on Hill 61 to new levels. From his slit, Hook Wilkinson watched the awe-inspiring light show across the entire Caen area as it marked the precise instant when two opposing armies came to life. Not even the low-hanging, patchy cloud and acrid smoke from fires burning in the valley below interfered with his vista on this momentous night. Silver flares, dropped from the attacking planes, leisurely descended in their parachutes, illuminating pockets of the countryside below, followed quickly by fluttering flashes of yellow and orange from the butterfly bombs raining down on British and Canadian positions. From the ground, Canadian anti-aircraft gunners fired wildly, spitting multicoloured tracer rounds skyward while searchlight crews scanned for targets to illuminate. "This was," as Mac Roulston put it, "the big day." Indeed, July 25, 1944, had arrived in spectacular fashion.

As feared, little had gone according to plan in the moments leading up to H-hour. Stan Duffield, who had taken on the port-folio of intelligence officer in addition to scout platoon com-mander when Megill requested that Captain Shirley Griffin join his intelligence staff earlier in the day, had just returned from a vain attempt to run the gauntlet into St. Martin to check on the progress of the Queen's Own Cameron Highlanders' attack. Radio traffic, however, made it clear that the Camerons' attempts to pacify the town had met with stiff resistance; the Germans had brought in a flame-thrower in a bid to settle the issue once and for all. Every move the Camerons made was checked in due course, and long after the wearied and battered Canadian unit reported one section cleared, they would find that the Germans had suddenly reappeared to bring down fire from behind, render-ing the secure start line anything but secure.[1]

At 0330 hours, H-hour for Phase I, over a thousand British and Canadian gun emplacements strung behind the front, from Colombelles and Caen to Verson and Carpiquet, opened fire. Hook could see bright-orange tongues lashing out, hundreds at a time, blinking in rapid succession from his position. A warm wind then blew across Black Watch lines, bringing with it the thun-derous wall of fire and steel that crashed down in the ear- and earth-shattering opening movement of Simonds's grand concerto.

In the valley below, the barrage supporting the Calgary Highlanders arrived on time, hitting German positions near their start line in St. Martin and slowly rolling through the factory area and on towards May-sur-Orne, where it sat for a time before lifting. Behind it came the four rifle companies of the Calgary Highlanders, leaning into the barrage and trying desperately to keep unit cohesion in the dark, with the artificial moonlight cre-ated by massed searchlight beams bouncing off the intermittent clouds above.

At the first sound of Allied guns, Major Eric Motzfeldt, working as Cantlie's trusted battle adjutant, ordered the Black Watch to advance. With Benson and a small group of scouts marking the route in the vanguard of the battalion, the rifle companies snaked their way off from Hill 61 in one long column, proceeding at a steady pace due west along the road leading to St. Martin. Following in the steps of Roulston's lost patrol the night before, Benson planned to turn south just before they reached the village and head overland along a large hedge directly to their waypoint at the churchyard in the southeast corner.

Marching right behind the scouts, working as the advance guard, came Taylor's B Company, followed by Cantlie's tactical headquarters, with Buch's pioneer platoon right on their heels. Strung out in a long column behind, Motzfeldt's C Company, Captain John Kemp's D Company and Major Phil Griffin's A Company rounded out the procession. While the rifle companies made their move, Captain Campbell Stuart worked his way towards an orchard off the northern fringe of the town, with the anti-tank and mortar platoons in tow, to establish the battalion radio net and main headquarters. On Hill 61, Captain Ronnie Bennett remained for a short time, noisily patrolling the rise with the carrier platoon to blind the Germans to the Black Watch move. Catching up to the rifle companies on the march, he planned to join Stuart north of the town to marshal his specialist company and prepare them to race up the ridge with the mortars, anti-tank guns, rations and extra ammunition to consolidate the newly won positions in Fontenay-le-Marmion following the battalion's assault.

Nothing so far had impeded the move west along the road to St. Martin, and the first three companies and Cantlie's tactical headquarters successfully made the turn south, moving along the hedge overland towards the church. At that point, as Captain Ronnie Bennett put it, "they ran into trouble."

218

The artificial moonlight—or "Monty's Moonlight," as the men called it—turned out to be a double-edged sword. Without a doubt, the illumination aided navigation in the dead of night, but it had the regrettable drawback of silhouetting the men moving across the open field towards the hedgerow. "It lit up the whole countryside," Private Jimmy Bennett remembered. "It scared the Hell out me . . . felt like somebody had taken all your clothes off and was shooting at you."

Within seconds, German machine-gun fire erupted, but zeroed in on fixed lines, the tracers soared above their heads. A German observation post on the ridge had a better view and quickly called down accurate mortar fire that struck Taylor's B Company. "The platoon ahead of mine . . . Number ten platoon," made up of reinforcements who had just arrived, "took a direct hit," an astonished Corporal Bruce Ducat recalled. "In an instant, they were gone."

With the left flank of his battalion now dangerously exposed to German observation and fire from the ridge, Cantlie made an understandable but ultimately fateful decision. Instead of pushing past the German fire and maintaining his axis of advance, he chose to duck the battalion into the eastern sector of what he hoped by this time would be a clear and secure St. Martin, where his men would employ the tiny lanes, high hedgerows and field-stone farm buildings for much-needed cover. Instead of finding sanctuary, the unexpected entry of the Black Watch into the town stirred up a hornet's nest.

During the night, Schack's 272nd Division, which still had plenty of fight left in it, infiltrated half a battalion's worth of infantry through the factory area and into St. Martin. When the Calgary Highlanders moved past the town at H-hour, they took fire from machine guns in the houses that hit their right flank.[2] Fearing they would lose the cover of their barrage if they took time to clear up the trouble, the Calgarys continued their advance, hoping the distraction would give the Camerons an upper hand in their struggle to pacify the town. As the Black Watch now found out, it did not. Courage and sense of duty aside, the valiant sacrificial efforts of this worn and exhausted unit sadly did not match the inflated expectations of Foulkes or Simonds—particularly when faced with an influx of fresh blood from the 272nd Division.

Moving into the once-tidy streets and close-cropped gardens of St. Martin, the men noticed, even in the dark, the pitted and torn landscape, a testimony to a week-long artillery duel in which the 2nd British Army had fired off more shells per gun than in the entire Battle of El Alamein two summers earlier.[3] Glass, roof tiles, shattered bricks and debris littered the area. Broken boughs of ancient, majestic pines lay strewn in the orchards alongside dead cattle, and smashed ammunition wagons sat tethered to dead horses. Vegetable gardens, tucked behind fieldstone houses and barns, lay crushed under the weight of shells, tanks and half-track treads. Crumpled bodies of both friend and foe lay everywhere, offering a macabre welcome for the men from the Black Watch companies flooding into the environs of St. Martin.

Catching up to the battalion along the east edge of the town, Captain Ronnie Bennett noticed "high walls and hedges surrounding orchards" littered with "three or four knocked out Panther tanks."

"The Huns had weapon slits outside the walls and hedges and dugouts and scurry holes inside," he reported, almost all "MG posts," which "had to be taken out one at a time."

"This had to be done when it was pitch black," which complicated matters, as "the artificial moonlight made night manoeuvres possible and did assist fire at great ranges [but] it did not improve close-in fighting to any degree. We were fighting in the shadows."4

Fighting immediately erupted in isolated pockets throughout the town and quickly devolved into a series of small, uncoordinated melees and vicious pitched battles for ditches, gardens, farmyards, barns, cellars, hedges, cuttings and dirt paths. With the Camerons trying to clear the start line from the west, the fighting became chaotic and confused, with the potential of "friendly fire" ever-present.

Moving at the head of the battalion, Barney Benson, Hook Wilkinson, Fred Delutis, Bobby Williams, Tommy Latham and Harold Burden cautiously picked their way forward, attempting to clear a lane leading to the churchyard. A small German patrol appeared out of the shadows, moving nonchalantly right into their line of sight. "The Jerries I saw," recalled Benson, "either had colossal nerve or were unaware that [Canadian] troops were in St. Martin, for they acted very carelessly." Equally shocked, Hook Wilkinson raised his sniper rifle and took aim dead centre on the chest of the lead man, who continued to move towards the dumbstruck Canadian with his rifle still slung. "He got within ten feet of me and he took the rifle off his shoulder," Hook recalled. Suitably alarmed, he thought to himself, "you better do something now, or he's going to." Squeezing the trigger, Hook put his shot straight into the man's chest, dropping him with one blast. "He fell dead right at my feet." His German comrades, startled by the shot, scattered into the town as Benson and the other scouts unloaded their rifles on the fleeing targets. Registering his first kill left Wilkinson momentarily awash in pride, until he passed the body of his victim. Moving now in the glow of a fire raging off to the right, Hook noticed to his horror the round, angelic face of his victim, eyes and mouth agape in astonishment. "I don't think he was 15 years of age," Hook lamented. He was just "a young German guy."

Corporal Bruce Ducat, pushing along with B Company behind the scouts, came upon one of the knocked-out Panthers that Bennett noted on the eastern fringe of the town. Still buttoned up with its hatches closed, Ducat feared its crew might still be inside, playing possum, waiting for a prize target. He considered taking on the behemoth with his section, but found to his great dismay that his PIAT team had wandered off from the platoon sometime during the advance. Furious, and with only a collection of hand grenades at his disposal, he chose instead to slip quietly behind the vehicle. When he did, he noticed to his great relief three large pockmarks on the left side of the turret, inflicted by high-explosive rounds fired by a Canadian tank or anti-tank gun. Ducat surmised that the crew had likely died instantly, victims of the metal spalling off the turret wall as a result of the shock wave of kinetic energy released with each blast.

Not long after, his section overtook the lead company and ran into the back of Benson and his scouts just north of the church. Looking down into a ditch that ran alongside the path, Ducat saw Bobby Williams, his buddy from B Company who had joined the scout platoon just before they crossed to Normandy, writhing and crying in pain. "I saw him lying there. He'd been hit through the stomach [and it was] all swollen out." Forced to keep moving, Ducat fully expected his friend to die, given the horrific nature of the wound and chaotic atmosphere preventing proper evacuation. Only after hostilities ended a year later did Ducat discover that Williams had survived the war.

• • •

PRIVATE BILL BOOTH, MOVING THROUGH AN ORCHARD in the north of the town with Sergeant Fred Janes and Private Dollard "Dolly" Lessard, had orders to get to the front of the column to prepare the form-up point for the attack. Saddled with a large spool normally wound with black signals wire, this one stood out prominently with thick white tape used to mark the formation area on the ground. The highly conspicuous trio drew the attention of a German machine gunner who opened up from a short distance. Miraculously, the burst from the MG 42 missed all three as they dove behind trees in the dead ground of the orchard for protection. "There was nothing to do but take cover where we were," a terrified Booth related. Patiently, they waited while the German gunner found a more appealing target elsewhere in the town.

The trio were perfectly content to wait things out, and everything remained calm until the carriers from Bennett's support company arrived. Knowing the vehicles would draw fire, the three men broke from cover and ran to a neighbouring ditch lined by a thick, towering hedgerow. After catching his breath, Booth wormed his way up the side to peer over as first light started to break. Through the ground mist, habitual at this time of year, "one could see the wreckage of a bomber knocked down during 'Goodwood,'" Booth noted, "and beyond it the gentle rise of the grain fields to the crest of Verrières Ridge. The grain was at least waist high."

As Booth suspected, it did not take long for the Germans to spot the Black Watch carriers in the orchard, still limbered with anti-tank guns and loaded with ammunition, rations and the battalion's mortars. The first burst of fire from an MG 42 sent everyone scrambling, including Captain Campbell Stuart, whose carrier had just entered the orchard, hauling the battalion wireless set. The massed Bren guns of Bennett's carriers returned fire immediately and silenced the German machine gun, but not before Stuart's carrier, moving at top speed, careened headlong into another parked in the orchard. Thankfully for Stuart, none of the ammunition aboard the support company carrier exploded, nor was the battalion radio set damaged or destroyed. Stuart, however, did not share the same luck. He suffered a hairline fracture of his right tibia in the collision. Refusing evacuation, he preferred to soldier on, albeit hobbled and in great pain.

Maintaining the momentum of the advance proved difficult in the tiny streets and gardens of St. Martin, and more often than not the fight came down to individual courage and initiative. Held up by what appeared to be a single machine-gun nest behind a hedgerow on the little farmer's path a stone's throw from the north side of the church, Hook Wilkinson heard another scout shout, "Barney!" and point thirty yards down the track to a German machine gun concealed in a hedgerow. Taking a quick look down the tree-lined lane, Benson, armed only with his Lee-Enfield, spun back to find himself toe to toe with a petrified teen-aged private from Kemp's company who had stumbled upon the scouts. More terrified of Benson's present demeanour than the threat of an MG 42 down the road, he readily shot his hands out when Benson barked, "Give me the Bren." He gladly exchanged his light machine gun for the scout platoon sergeant's sniper rifle. The young man sank down into the ditch, waiting, like the others, for further instructions after Benson nipped away over the hedge alone. When no sound came for nearly a minute, Hook feared the worst. Then a wild exchange of automatic weapons fire suddenly erupted, followed by dead silence and another long pause. Benson, scuffling back over the hedge from where he'd vanished moments before, swapped the empty Bren for his prized sniper rifle, uttering nothing more than "It's all over, no problem" before he ordered the astonished group to advance.

His scouts quickly learned that this seemingly cowboy move indeed had merit. Benson, quick to get into the picture and absorb the enemy's tactics, knew exactly what they would face and seized the initiative. "They tend to site the MG 42 in corners where the hedgerows meet the track or wall," he reported. "There is almost certain to be an additional MG further down a flank to cover the main one . . . and almost certain to be maintained absolutely silent until we put in a serious attempt to take the MG which is firing. Then we are caught unexpectedly in our flank." Benson, careful with the lives of his men but cavalier with his own, ensured that none of his men would fall victim and that the forward inertia of the battalion, no matter how sluggish, remained unchecked.[5]

With the fighting at close quarters, numerous actions like Benson's unfolded over the next ninety minutes. Devastating crumps from PIAT shells—customarily used to bust tanks but now blasting garden walls, thick hedges and centuries-old fieldstone buildings—mixed with the burps of Stens and Brens and the cracks of rifles, as well as the muffled thump of exploding grenades. Screams of men locked in close combat, as well as the wounded and dying, sprang up from time to time, giving a motley indication of the deliberate and challenging Black Watch advance towards the church in St. Martin.

The fight through the town, however, continued to eat up precious time, and Cantlie, doing his best to keep his strung-out unit together, could only maintain a rate of advance of one hundred yards every fifteen minutes. It would have been admirable on most occasions, given the circumstances, but it did not keep time to Simonds's schedule, and when H-hour for Phase II arrived at 0530, Cantlie found his battalion a quarter mile short of its form-up point, and over a mile from its start line with dawn about to break over Verrières Ridge.

• • •

AT 0530, TWO HOURS AFTER OPERATION SPRING BEGAN, Barney Benson finally reached the church on the southeastern fringes of St. Martin. After five days of battle, the Romanesque and Gothic structure had taken more than its fair share of pounding, and he found it in a ghastly condition. The tower that stood as a beacon in peacetime for the local miners had vanished; gaping holes in the church's southern facade facing Verrières revealed the destruction wrought inside the chapel. Shattered stained glass littered the floor; smashed oak pews and an overturned altar, all covered with masonry dust, bore witness to the ferocity of the fighting as the house of worship changed hands nearly a dozen times in a matter of days.

The graveyard surrounding the church, which sat tucked behind a ten-foot stone wall, did not escape the fury either. Dark-grey and black tombstone slabs, usually polished and adorned with flowers paying tribute to the miners lost in collapses or to black lung, lay shattered and scorched by the incessant shelling. Only five fresh white crosses, hurriedly erected to commemorate a group of local children killed on D-Day, when a British fighter swooped in and bombed the town, appeared untouched.

Major Eric Motzfeldt, whose C Company leapfrogged into the lead of the battalion, was the first to arrive at the assembly area. He followed Benson, approaching the church through a courtyard on the north side of the road. To his considerable shock, he found "groups of soldiers [from both the Calgary and Cameron Highlanders] . . . milling around in some confusion . . . while others were exchanging fire with the Germans in and around St. André and St. Martin."[6] Acting as Cantlie's battle adjutant throughout the fight in the town, the "Great Dane," wearing his balmoral instead of his helmet, ordered his men to dig in and called for the other companies to do the same while he attempted to get a grip on the fluid situation.

Given what the battalion had just experienced in its tortuous journey to the church, it came as no surprise to Motzfeldt to find men from the Camerons still fighting in the area, but what truly alarmed him were the remnants of one of the Calgary Highlander companies that, if all had gone according to plan, was to be a thousand yards ahead, tied in tight on its objective in May-sur-Orne after securing the Black Watch start line for Phase II.

Underscoring the massive confusion and chaos of the night, the young acting commander of D Company of the Calgary Highlanders only realized after the Black Watch appeared in St. Martin that he had made a grave navigational error. As Motzfeldt learned, Lieutenant Emile Michon had taken command of his company on the fly after German machine-gun fire killed scores of his mates and his company commander as they moved through the wheat field towards May-sur-Orne. Keeping the survivors together, Michon continued the push towards their objective, but without a compass to aid him, he found it difficult to fix his position on the map, particularly in the dark. After a short time trudging through the wheat, he suspected he had overshot May by nearly five hundred yards and was now on the reverse slope of Verrières, well behind his objective. In fact, in his confusion and elevated level of anxiety, time and distance compressed and he was actually five hundred yards short, stuck somewhere between the factory and the crest of the ridge. When he looked behind him, to the north, he mistook the clearing attempt by the Black Watch and Camerons in St. Martin for the other Calgary Highlander companies arriving in May. With nothing but blackness ahead of him to the south, he reasoned that his location at that moment seemed logical and ordered his company to wheel around and move north, hell-bent on arriving like the cavalry to take the German defences from behind, right in the nick of time.

With no intimate or advanced knowledge of the terrain, not even the clearing of the factory area of German forces as he approached St. Martin set off alarm bells, and he proudly moved back to the churchyard in St. Martin, thinking he had reached May. "It was not until the whole Battalion of the [Black Watch] showed up and began to dig in," recounted a highly embarrassed Michon, "that I realized from talking with them where I was."[7]

By this time, Cantlie, who had now come forward with Duffield and Buch to assess the situation up front and arrange for new orders, had put the call out for his company commanders to rally on him at the church. In minutes, Kemp and Taylor appeared, but, as Griffin's and Bennett's companies lay at the tail end of the column, close to half a mile away, it would take some time before they arrived.[8]

With the fog of war now rivalling the density of the morning mist, Cantlie proceeded to piece together the situation facing his men. The delay in moving through the town had cost his battalion precious time, and his rifle companies had sustained nearly sixty casualties, including some who required immediate attention. But as the field ambulance section attached to battalion noted, "evacuation was extremely difficult, as the road back was entirely dominated by the enemy guns from May-sur-Orne and was a graveyard for the unwary and the slow."[9]

Likewise, the handful of German prisoners they snatched up also required immediate interrogation and evacuation, which proved impossible for the moment. More pressing, however, was that Cantlie's companies lay strung out, stretching all the way from the church to the orchard area, interrupted by isolated pockets of St. Martin still in German hands. In great danger of dispersion, the Black Watch CO ordered his companies to press forward and regroup in the assembly area.

So far, the only inkling of good news came with the arrival

of the injured Campbell Stuart, who had appeared with the battalion wireless set after a hair-raising run through the town's gardens, lanes and barnyards in his carrier. Within seconds, his adept signals sergeant, Stan Ritchie, had the battalion patched back into the brigade net despite atmospheric conditions and German jamming that sounded like a "mad fiddler," which did nothing to clarify the situation ahead.

With communication spotty, Cantlie could only glean from a series of sparse and at times contradictory messages that fire from 88s on the ridge, coupled with anti-tank gunfire across the Orne River and machine guns in the factory area, had caused heavy casualties within the advancing Calgary Highlander companies as they tried to reach May-sur-Orne. Except for Michon's men dug in around the church in St. Martin, the rest of the Calgary Highlander companies had disappeared somewhere in the wheat-clad slopes of Verrières, and there was grave doubt that any had reached their objective in force.[10]

Thoroughly frustrated, Cantlie grabbed Duffield and stormed out into the field about two hundred yards south of the churchyard to "get a better look," as the latter recalled. Wading through the wheat and past the outer reaches of the fluid front line, the pair halted suddenly. "It was beginning to get light," Duffield recalled, "and there was a thick white mist [that] made visibility very poor." Realizing the fruitless nature of their brief foray, Cantlie had the good sense to return to the churchyard to join Motzfeldt at a spot he pegged out as a prime location for observation.

"We walked back to a gap in the hedge just above a sunken road near a church," Duffield related, "where we met Motzfeldt and Kemp," who ushered the group towards a small mound, crowned by a hedge, near a break in the eastern wall of the churchyard. Highly fatigued from a week of constant combat and with more pressing issues on their minds, attention to detail waned. Rifling through map cases and scanning the ground ahead with their binoculars, the small band made an elementary and fatal mistake. With dawn breaking, they silhouetted themselves against the horizon, offering an enticing target that no gun crew would pass up. As Motzfeldt recalled, "I was pointing out the situation to Cantlie and Kemp when a machine gun burst from about 50 yards in front" tore into the group, hitting Motzfeldt. At the same time, a mortar shell that struck minutes earlier—perhaps directed by the same German observation post—exploded nearby, missing Kemp and Duffield but hitting both the wounded Motzfeldt and Cantlie. Struck in the back of his skull with shrapnel, Duffield reported that the Black Watch CO "slipped to the ground, bleeding profusely from his wounds, uttering 'someone carry on' before he lost consciousness."[11]

Screams for the medics went up as Kemp and Duffield dragged their stricken brother officers behind the mound for cover. They ripped open the field dressing packages and attempted to plug the wounds on both men. Lieutenant Mackenzie-Wood, who had just arrived in the area with John Taylor, ran to Motzfeldt, who was lying on the ground, his face locked in a prolonged grimace. From under the netting that cloaked his helmet, the young lieutenant whipped out the morphine vial, snapped off the glass top and jammed it home into the major's thigh. A few seconds later, Motzfeldt's face eased as his pain subsided. A few feet away, Mackenzie-Wood witnessed Duffield and Kemp working frantically on Cantlie, trying to stem streams of blood spurting from his open wounds. The officers hoisted the stricken pair, who were in need of immediate surgical attention, onto a carrier, and with no time to waste, it sped off with Bennett's second-in-command, Lieutenant Ted Neill, leading the way, dodging enemy mortar fire as he went.

On the outskirts of Ifs, the new Black Watch padre, Canon

Cecil Royle, was hurriedly transferring the contents of a wheel-barrow he had borrowed from a French farm to haul his communion kits, typewriter and duffle bags from Juno Beach to Ifs, into a Black Watch truck for the trip to St. Martin. From behind a hedge came Neill's speeding carrier, which slammed to a halt next to Royle, who had just finished cleaning his horn-rimmed glasses. Neill, "his face white as a sheet," shouted over the grumbling engine, "Padre, do you know where the nearest medical post is?" Having passed a field dressing station located in the caves of a cliff in Vaucelles on his pilgrimage to Ifs, Royle waved for Neill to follow and jumped into the truck, which his driver jammed into gear and sped off. Within minutes, the desperate caravan arrived at the field hospital perched on the banks of the Orne.

While orderlies moved fast to unstrap the stretchers, Royle rushed in and found "everyone asleep except the orderly officer."[12] Returning to the jeep with a groggy surgeon in tow, the padre "only needed one glance to see that Motzfeldt was in extremely bad shape and that poor Cantlie was dead." In minutes, orderlies rushed Motzfeldt into the operating theatre for life-saving surgery, while others laid Cantlie's body into one of a dozen open graves, dug in anticipation of the heavy death toll expected in Operation Spring. When Royle returned to the garden, he embarked upon his first act as Black Watch padre: burying the commanding officer who had taken immense pride in his night-fighting abilities.

IN THE BLINK OF AN EYE, THE FORTUNES OF THE BLACK Watch took a drastic turn and the fog of war plaguing the battalion now transcended into the friction of war. "It was a real blow losing Motzfeldt at the same time as Cantlie," George Buch recalled. It created a "vacuum of power." The next ranking officer not left out of battle was Major Phillip Griffin, but caught up in the fighting near the northern end of St. Martin, he had yet to make it to the church. To fill the breach, Kemp, Taylor and Campbell Stuart jumped forward to bring a semblance of order and a steady hand to the helm of the unit. But without a clear plan for succession past Motzfeldt and Griffin, the triumvirate jockeyed for control, each man believing he possessed the right leadership traits needed to command under the present circumstances. With incendiary force, all of the angst, frustration and exhaustion built up over a week of continuous combat collided headlong with ego and pride, righteousness and personal ambition, which promptly bubbled up and then boiled over.

Captain Campbell Stuart assumed command immediately, believing that by virtue of his appointment as battalion adjutant he had the rightful claim to succession. Taylor, a company commander recently promoted to acting major, jumped in quickly to challenge that notion. Attempting to pull rank, Stuart at first objected, which prompted Kemp—promoted himself two days earlier to acting major—to wade into the mix. Bothered by his fractured leg, Stuart reluctantly withdrew from the fracas, leaving Kemp and Taylor to sort out the issue. In seconds, Taylor's "prickly" tone set off Kemp's mercurial temper and the two company commanders then turned on each other, going toe to toe in a verbal slugfest. Kemp pitted his superior tactical acumen against Taylor's actual, albeit limited, combat experience as the yelling escalated and each barked out orders to the men. As Arnold Williams, a private in Kemp's company, noted, confusion reigned as "order and counter-order" flew. Stunned by this unfolding spectacle, which lasted nearly forty-five minutes, none of the men knew whose instructions to obey. Paralysis descended when the men aligned themselves with their respective company commander pending a firm decision and clarification of the fluid chain of command. "I stood by and watched this thing happen," Buch recalled with great regret, and "noticed that the men seemed to be uncomfortable with it. It was embarrassing . . . but we were tired. We spent four days under fire on Hill 61 and tempers were thin."

Finally, Kemp and Taylor resorted to their pay books to establish seniority; by the slimmest of margins, Taylor emerged as the front-runner in a now-pyrrhic victory.[13]

Still seething when Griffin and Bennett finally arrived at the church after learning of Cantlie's death, Taylor, consumed now with the considerable task of regrouping the battalion, remained hostile to any notion of relinquishing command following his hard-won victory over Kemp.

Taylor, outranked by Griffin, had little choice but to acquiesce when the A Company commander, in no mood to dicker—particularly with an officer he considered less talented—pulled rank and took command.[14] Both Taylor and, to a lesser degree, Kemp indicated they would not go quietly and would instead pursue a policy of friction to effect a command by consensus. With little choice, Griffin permitted his two fellow company commanders to advise in a lopsided triumvirate, a move Bennett characterized as "superb" in "this strained and ticklish situation."[15]

"From that point on there was no vacillation," Buch recalled. In fact, as Bennett later noted, "there was no uncertainty whatsoever" in Griffin's actions as he "foresaw only delay, which would at the outside be two hours, while he rearranged timings and obtained essential information."[16]

But a quick assessment of the situation at that moment appeared bleak. As Bennett recalled, "Griffin's problem was that the Battalion was rather extended. The Companies were still intact and under good control but the threat of dispersion and of possible confusion was near. Light was breaking, and we were under heavy fire from the ridge." To make matters worse, with H-hour long gone, "Griffin had to take time to liaise with the artillery and, if possible, retime their shoot and . . . get the tank commander into the picture" and "find out the situation in St. André-sur-Orne from the Cameron of Canada and obtain what reports he could on the Calgarys and the situation at May-sur-Orne."[17]

Perhaps to mollify lingering doubts as to whether their portion of Operation Spring would continue, Stuart claimed that Griffin fired off a "lengthy message" to Megill's headquarters, citing the insecurity of St. Martin, the missed artillery support, the uncertain whereabouts of the Calgary Highlanders and the failure of the tanks to arrive as factors bearing on their fate.

There is no doubt that the insecurity of St. Martin cost the battalion its chance to assault under cover of darkness, but the extra delay produced by the squabble did nothing to mitigate the issue and served only to raise the temperature at brigade and division headquarters. Before long, a steady stream of messages started to arrive, increasing in urgency and intensity with each passing minute, urging the Black Watch to get on with their role in the operation.

FROM BRIGADE HEADQUARTERS, A MILE BEHIND THE front lines in Fleury-sur-Orne, Megill tried desperately to muddle through his own fog of war and to make sense of the confusing and at times contradictory messages flowing in from his battalions at the front. "During the night, we suddenly had a call that Cantlie had been killed and Major Motzfeldt [was] wounded," Megill recounted, "and command of the unit evolved to Major Griffin. The unit, of course, was not in action at the time—was not on its start line—it was merely formed up behind and waiting to go forward as soon as it was reasonable to do so."[18] Earlier that night, he had dispatched a pair of his staff officers down to a spot he picked from the map in what Foulkes assured him was a secure part of St. Martin to set up his new tactical headquarters. Arriving at the chosen location, the duo entered the chosen house, only to encounter German voices on the floor above. Startled, they beat a hasty retreat on foot, but only made it back to rear headquarters after first light. A second pair of officers Megill sent up failed to track down Griffin as well as to clear up the confused situation. In the meantime, he confessed, "Division headquarters was pressing to have the attack continue and that there was nothing we could do but to pass that on."

Back in St. Martin, Griffin hoped that Megill would convince Division and Corps to call the attack off, or at the very least provide some grip and clarification of the situation at hand. In short order, he found that his well-reasoned plea for instructions met with a curt response. According to the message logs, Megill told the Black Watch simply to "push on. Speed essential." As Mackenzie-Wood, assisting Griffin throughout the morning, recalled, although the message came down through Brigade, the acting Black Watch CO made it clear that "Foulkes [said] to press on."[19]

With daylight now in full bloom, the German defences on Verrières Ridge and across the Orne came to life. Sniper and shellfire started to work its way into the eastern quarter of St. Martin, making life near the church uncomfortable.

Private Jimmy Bennett, who had just screwed the cap back onto his water bottle after taking a much-needed swig of diluted rum following a nasty skirmish in a farmhouse not far from the church, sat in a ditch, his back to a hedge, soaking up the sunshine that streaked in over Verrières Ridge. Having failed to notice the sun in what seemed a lifetime since crossing the Orne

River a week before, Bennett welcomed his reprieve from the fear and the killing for a brief, fleeting moment. With his adrenalin dump now in full effect following the firefight, he could feel his anxiety return. With his heart now revving up despite his attempt to calm it with distilled fortification, the young private decided to seek the brotherly reassurance of Elie Desormeaux, seconded to another section in the platoon earlier that night. For the previous few days, nothing but the friendship of the prospector from northern Ontario had kept Bennett together, and now more than ever, he needed that tonic for his growing angst.

Working his way down the hedge, Bennett came across his mate "20 or 30 guys down the road" near the front of the column. As he approached the lead section, Bennett smiled, noticing Desormeaux resting serenely in the ditch, back against the hedgerow, finally getting some long-sought-after rest after griping for days in his almost-comedic French accent. But as Bennett moved closer, he noticed Sergeant Tommy Garvin standing over his mate with a red identity disc dangling from his fingers, freshly snipped from the cord around Desormeaux's neck. To his dread, Bennett spotted a tiny, symmetrical hole in Elie's forehead. "A sniper got him right through the head. He was dead when I got there."

The sudden landing of German shells on the road behind the church saved Bennett from complete psychological collapse. Once again, the unleashing of adrenalin served to dampen his anxiety to a degree, permitting the Black Watch private to soldier on, even with mortars raining down and the death of his best friend still fresh in his mind.

HAVING FIRST ATTEMPTED TO DIG IN NEAR A SMALL, shattered flower garden near the entrance to the church, overlooking the factory area south of St. Martin, Corporal Ducat found he could only penetrate six inches "because the chalk was so hard." Hacking at it with his entrenching tool, he "hardly made a dent," and, fearing that he remained far too exposed, he moved to the western side of the battered church and dug in along part of the wall that still stood. As usual, Smokey Lalonde and Tex Richards tagged right behind. Richards was by all accounts an excellent soldier on whom, like Lalonde, Ducat knew he could lean "when the shit hit the fan."

Nearly a decade older than his mates and recently married, the Montreal-born Richards came from lower Westmount and had no connection with the Lone Star State. Having worked as a stoker and fireman aboard Great Lakes freighters before the war, Richards had acquired a slight American drawl during his travels that his not so enlightened regimental brothers mistook for the rakish twang of a Texas cowboy.

Not long after they dug in along the churchyard wall, they realized they had made a grave mistake. From this vantage point, Ducat could see German infantry hundreds of yards in the distance, moving about the factory area, hurriedly preparing their positions or getting ready to counterattack. Soon enough, the church, which served as the main reference point for targeting in the town, drew more than its fair share of attention from the German artillery. Instead of the shells bouncing off harmlessly, Ducat quickly found out that the sloped shape of the structure facilitated the downward deflection of the falling rounds with an intensity the trio did not count on, particularly when the German artillery and mortar fire, sporadic at first, picked up in tempo and intensity. Within the hour, fully half of the German mortar and artillery rounds fired landed on the tiny road running behind the church, which the men quickly coined "Shell Alley," leaving Ducat to wonder if this was a harbinger of things to come.[20]

Across the road to the north of the church, Captain Ronnie Bennett stood in the courtyard surrounding a large, L-shaped farm building—part living quarters, part barn—where Griffin had set up shop away from the shelling. At periodic intervals, Benson's scouts ambled in, accompanied by small groups of scruffy, filthy prisoners captured throughout the town for processing and evacuation. Privates Harold Burden and Frank Balsis brought in the latest batch of six or seven, including one wounded man strapped to a stretcher to add to the motley collection that numbered close to forty. What shocked everyone was how few "German" prisoners actually spoke German; Russian and Polish predominated, followed by a mixture of central European and Baltic tongues.

Soon, however, the sheer number of prisoners became a problem. "As we knew nothing about the positions to the rear and could spare no men, we were at a loss as to how to deal with the blighters," Bennett reported. "My men were coming to me every few minutes saying, 'Where will we send them?' or 'What will we do with them?'" Consumed with getting into the new tactical picture, Bennett had little time, let alone ability, to ferry them to rear headquarters for interrogation or provide a proper holding pen.

At a loss as to what to do with this pitiful collection of humanity, Bennett spotted "a long wall completely covered by fire from a Bren in a slit trench nearby" and told his 2ic, Lieutenant Teddy Neill, to put them "against the wall, take off their equipment, and have them sit down where the chap with the Bren can cover them." Immediately, the prisoners started to wail; one dropped to his knees, begging for mercy, while the wounded prisoner confined to the stretcher shook his fist and flung a succession of foreign-language expletives at the Black Watch captain. Stupefied, Bennett failed to appreciate how his bid for expediency would play with men impressed into German service, as this "raised a great fear that they were going to be shot and it was a considerable relief to them to sit down."[21]

With the loss of Motzfeldt and Cantlie, Griffin reshuffled the battalion's leadership, turning A Company over to Lieutenant Alan Robinson and moving Taylor to cover for the severely wounded Motzfeldt in C Company, leaving B Company in the capable hands of their trusted company sergeant major, Vic Foam. Kemp's D Company, unaffected by the changes, would lead the attack down Shell Alley to the main crossroads, clearing houses on each side as they went, supported by artillery from the 25th Field Regiment. Following on their heels, the three remaining companies would fill in behind, partly to create a firm base of operations in St. Martin before tackling the ridge, and partly to allow time for High Command to correctly assess the situation and perhaps call the attack off.

Under the circumstances, the latter seemed a remote possibility, and much depended now on accurate reporting of the situation regarding the Black Watch start line running outside May. Leaving nothing to chance, Griffin leaned on Duffield and Benson to personally lead a reconnaissance patrol into the town to link up with the Calgary Highlanders and get a firm grip on the situation. Forgoing his usual preparation, Benson grabbed Private Arthur Bowmaster to join him, and Duffield and the trio set out straight away for May.

Employing the tripwire method, Benson recorded that the patrol "moved straight down the road, walking in the centre as far as the church in May-sur-Orne."[22] Covering the half-mile distance under enemy observation on what had now turned into a near-cloudless summer morning, no shots rang out, nor did they have to scurry into the deep ditches straddling the road to seek cover from enemy mortars or shells.

"Up to that point, we saw no one," Benson reported, as they

passed a row of devastated houses and the town bakery, whose chimney still stood despite its collapsed roof and crumpled walls. When the trio reached the heavily battered church that Cantlie had blasted days before with anti-tank gunfire from Hill 61, they had yet to encounter a soul—friendly, enemy or civilian—but when they moved past the church, they ran into a lone figure.[23]

"One German was on the road directly ahead, evidently expecting someone," Benson remembered. Perhaps deceived by the helmetless trio, whose camouflaged smocks somewhat resembled at a distance those worn by the SS, the German nonchalantly stood next to his VW Kübelwagen, ready to extend a welcome. Moving to within thirty yards, "he finally recognized us as enemy," Benson recorded, "and tried to get away in a jeep." His sudden departure prompted the trio to open fire at the fleeing man with their rifles. "We hit the jeep and injured him, although he did escape."[24]

Expecting the enormous racket from their gunfire to draw a prompt response, the trio leaped through a blown-out window into the remnants of a flattened butcher shop, ready to return fire on any hidden German units that opened up. Only silence followed.

Resuming their advance, the patrol turned left at the crossroads and moved east along the road towards a fork; the left branch veered off into the track running across the crest of Verrières Ridge designated as the Black Watch start line. "When we were within fifty yards, an MG 42 opened on us from the corner house," Benson recalled, prompting the men to seek cover in a laneway wedged between two dwellings that still stood untouched.[25]

Expecting to resume their advance towards the track as soon as the machine-gun fire died down, Benson reported that "Lt. Duffield felt obliged to return at once with this information" and ordered the patrol to head back towards St. Martin. Having failed to reach the spot on the map where intelligence indicated that a German vehicle bay lay, on the northern fringes of the town overlooking the ridge, the scout platoon sergeant's protests to press on fell on deaf ears.[26]

Instead of working deeper into May, the trio doubled back through the gardens and demolished houses until they reached the crossroads close to the church without encountering any further German resistance—or, for that matter, any elements of the Calgary Highlanders. Then, in one last bid to light up any German positions hidden in the town, the trio sauntered down the centre of the road as they made their way back to report to Griffin.

By the time the patrol returned to St. Martin, Kemp's company had embarked on its clearance of Shell Alley, while in the courtyard across from the church, Griffin sat in his command jeep, cycling feverishly through maps, overprints and air photos with Captain Gordon Powis to tie up the fire plan as the clock continued to tick towards his new H-hour.[27]

Unable to locate any Calgary Highlander companies in or around May, and given the report that the only enemy activity appeared to be the machine gun they discovered, Griffin concluded that the town was held neither in strength nor on a continuous basis. Rushing now to hold his orders group for the coming attack, he ordered Benson to return to May immediately with a fighting patrol to take the machine gun out before it tore into the flanks of the battalion as it moved up Verrières Ridge.

IN THE BASEMENT OF THE BREWERY THAT NOW DOUBLED as 2nd Canadian Infantry Division tactical headquarters, Simonds hovered over Foulkes, who wrestled with conflicting reports about the status of May-sur-Orne. At first, it appeared the Calgary

Highlanders had achieved their objective, but as the night wore on, it became apparent that only a small portion of the battalion had reached the outskirts and had failed to penetrate the town. He was unfazed by the news, which he had foreseen as a distinct possibility when he laid out the plan two days before. Simonds chafed to bring his masterpiece to fruition. At 0750 hours, he informed Dempsey and Montgomery of his decision to bypass the town with the Black Watch to expedite Phase II.[28]

Just over forty minutes later, a slew of unverified messages pouring into Foulkes's headquarters provided the division commander with the ammunition needed to paint an exhilarating picture of events at the front, one that complied with Simonds's desires. By 0830, it appeared that Verrières village was firmly in Canadian hands and that the lead companies of the Royal Regiment of Canada were on the move to Rocquancourt. At the same time, reports suggest that the lead elements of the 7th Armoured Division, the famed Desert Rats, now battling towards the nascent breach, would likely squeeze through should Fontenay-le-Marmion fall to the Black Watch in short order.

Five hours behind schedule, and with just under four hours until Dempsey pulled the plug on the entire operation, everything finally appeared to have fallen into place, yet there remained one sour note in the Maestro's grand symphony: the Black Watch, which sat inexplicably pinned down in part of St. Martin by machine guns and artillery on the ridge.[29]

"The next thing I knew," Megill recalled, "the gunner net called for a fire plan to be laid on at 0930 for the Black Watch. I had been reluctant to go forward because nobody knew where anybody was, and it didn't seem to be that I could do anything very much if I did go up. However, this time I decided that I must go see the Black Watch to determine for myself on the ground what the situation was before the attack went in."

Before he departed for St. Martin, Megill turned up the volume on the Black Watch. "I found myself receiving messages from Brigade to pass on to Major Griffin, demanding an immediate attack," Campbell Stuart remembered. "The frequency and the repetitious nature of the messages . . . became such that I ended up passing only about 25 percent of them to Major Griffin, who was fully occupied in attempting to clear the forming-up area." With no positive response coming back from the front, Megill then forced Griffin's hand, issuing a direct order for the Black Watch to proceed with Phase II. Undaunted, Stuart reiterated the battalion's plight, which elicited another irate reply from Megill's headquarters, which ordered him to fetch Griffin: "Understand the reason you are being held up is because of 3 MGs near burnt out tanks, have plastered them. It is essential you get on immediately. Suggest you take them on with your own guns."[30] Clearly exasperated, Megill then summoned Griffin to meet with him immediately in the forward area of St. Martin.[31] The implication was clear: the brigadier was now coming down with fire in his eyes to ensure the adherence to his orders and Simonds's timetable.

9

THE FOUR HORSEMEN, ACT II: THE RIDGE

It was perfectly clear that the attack should have been called off at a very early stage in the morning. Instead of that, the Corps Commander was pressing the Divisional Commander, and he was pressing us to get on with an attack which we knew was almost hopeless [and] under these circumstances, one does not quit. You do as much as you possibly can and hope that someone will see the light and give you some relief.

—BRIGADIER WILLIAM J. MEGILL

B Y THE TIME Brigadier William J. Megill summoned Major Phillip Griffin to rendezvous with him in
St. Martin, the acting Black Watch CO had accomplished
a near-Herculean task under the most trying of circumstances.
Neither the brigadier nor the division commander had demon-
strated a firm grip on the unfolding situation during the night,
and by default it fell to Griffin. Plagued by harassing fire, the
young major had less than two hours to regroup his strung-out
battalion, rearrange the timings for both the artillery and tanks,
send out patrols, gather intelligence, evacuate prisoners and
embark upon the clearance of Shell Alley to provide a solid base
should the attack up Verrières continue.

In addition, despite Megill's assertion that the guns of the 5th
Field Regiment had plastered centres of German resistance along

the ridge, pockets still chirped and Griffin reached out to the 1st Hussars, whose tanks had just arrived in the orchard to the north of St. Martin, to give the Black Watch some much-needed breathing room.

Major Walter Harris promptly responded, and his squadron of Shermans laid a sheet of high-explosive shells and machine-gun fire on the collection of knocked-out panzers, strung along the crest, that were suspected of housing German machine guns, camouflaged snipers and observation posts.

During this respite, Griffin did his best to clarify the confusing situation by dispatching a series of reconnaissance patrols to establish the whereabouts of the Calgary Highlanders in May and deal with reports of snipers operating near the church that had come to light in the wake of Duffield and Benson's patrol. With that done, he still had one large thorn that remained firmly embedded in his side: the factory area adjacent to the Black Watch form-up point, which continued to be a beehive of German activity.[1]

From his slit near the church, Bruce Ducat could see Germans moving in plain sight, darting in and out of the structure, shuffling boxes of what looked like ammunition into place. None of them had paid serious attention to the Black Watch, but that would change once the rifle companies approached the area. Worried that enemy machine guns hidden in the structure would bring down heavy fire on the flank or rear of his battalion as they advanced, Griffin called upon Lieutenant Emile Michon and his under-strength company from the Calgary Highlanders to pacify the area.[2]

At first, Michon wilfully undertook the task, but after he "went forward on a recce," he discovered "very heavy machine gun fire" emanating from the factory area and from "the knocked-out tanks on the high ground to the left," which made it impossible, in his opinion, for one company to pacify "without artillery or smoke."[3]

Griffin agreed. With another hurdle now thrown in his path, the acting Black Watch CO would clear the factory en route to the form-up point. To secure the start line and deal with the machine gun Benson and Duffield had discovered earlier, Griffin ordered Michon back into May to secure the start line and link up with the forward companies from his regiment that had vanished.[4] Michon, who was not under Griffin's direct command, had no obligation to act on his orders and refused to make another push towards May, suggesting instead that he try to raise his unit via the Black Watch wireless. Griffin's tone stiffened, as he was pressed for time and brooking no excuses. As Michon reported, "There was shit to pay in there," but the young Calgary Highlander platoon officer held his ground and refused to budge. Before this tempest boiled over, a runner from the Calgary Highlanders arrived with orders for Michon to report immediately to his commanding officer in St. André, at the western end of the twin towns.[5]

Griffin now had little choice but to reach out to the exhausted Barney Benson, who had gone without a break since they had come ashore on Juno Beach almost three weeks earlier. This time, the scout platoon sergeant would lead a fighting patrol that would race back up to May to take out the German machine gun before it ripped into the flank of the rifle companies during their assault. H-hour now lay less than thirty-five minutes away.[6]

Benson marshalled the freshest scouts he could muster. Young Hook and Privates Edgar Thomas and Bill Pugh were obvious choices, having just arrived after having been left out of battle since the sniper hunt at Ifs. Rounding out the rest of the patrol with three more men proved a tough choice. Those who remained had just returned from the pair of inconsequential recce patrols that Griffin had dispatched earlier to hunt down German snipers near the church in May.

For some undetermined reason—and none that his men dared to question—Benson designated Privates Mike Brunner and Dale Sharpe as left out of battle and assigned Hook Wilkinson and Jackie Jack, Syd Ayling, Harold Burden and Paul Welligan to the regimental aid post to work as stretcher-bearers. None complained. Privates Frank Balsis and Fred Delutis and Lance Corporal Melvin Cameron drew the short straws and dutifully prepped for their second expedition in less than an hour.

Immediately, Benson's group snapped up a Bren gun and a PIAT and crammed white phosphorus and high-explosive grenades into every pouch and pocket of their sniper smocks, leaving Benson to brief them on the gravity of the mission while they picked their way up the seven-hundred-yard ditch that straddled the main road leading to May.

In the meantime, Griffin, expecting to have the battalion on the move before a fuming Brigadier Megill arrived to crack the whip, called for an immediate O Group in the sunken courtyard across from the church, to commence at 0900 hours. George Buch lamented that the meeting "was the most fateful in the storied history of the Black Watch."

John Kemp, who had returned from the crossroads in St. Martin after leading the clearance of Shell Alley, recalled that Griffin delivered his orders for the Verrières attack in "great haste," but made it clear that the battalion was "operating under a direct order from higher command."[7] Griffin's curt declaration, delivered in his usual brusque and direct manner, underscored the grim nature of what lay ahead and brought lingering chatter to an abrupt halt. As the acting Black Watch CO explained, the assault companies would now face "great difficulties" as "May-sur-Orne had to be bypassed," which "forced the battalion to move up a draw, with both sides and the upper end held by the Germans."[8]

Griffin threw his map case down on the hood of his command jeep, drawing in the small circle of officers and NCOs that included his company commanders, the three FOOs and Major Walter Harris from the 1st Hussars to follow his plan with laser-like focus. Stabbing his finger down on the crossroads in St. Martin, the young major announced the battalion would proceed south along the road to May for three hundred yards, then veer left to clear the factory to avoid harassing fire from the ridge. At the same time, Harris's tanks, plunging south through the streets of St. Martin, would race past the churchyard and close the pincers by taking on the German defenders from the north while the Black Watch closed in from the west.[9]

With German resistance in the factory area pinched off, the rifle companies would then shake out at their original form-up point, a cabbage patch that lay in a small spot of dead ground tucked in between the factory and the ridge. Employing the standard box formation utilized at Ifs and on Hill 61, Kemp's D Company and Motzfeldt's B Company, now under the command of CSM Vic Foam, would be up front, with Griffin's former company, handed over to Lieutenant Alan Robinson, following right behind with Taylor's C Company right beside. Griffin, accompanied by Duffield, planned to direct the assault from his tactical headquarters sandwiched between the rear companies.[10]

To comply with the preordained caveat to bypass centres of resistance that would cause delay, Griffin decided to take the quickest and most direct route to the objective. Instead of skirting May-sur-Orne, the battalion would move straight from the cabbage patch, up and over Verrières Ridge, following a compass bearing leading directly to Fontenay. Given the horrific toll paid by the British armour in a bid to reach the long-promised "tank country" south of Caen over the previous week, moving up a wide-open slope in broad daylight with ten-foot-high Shermans was tantamount to suicide. Instead, Harris stuck to the original plan and would barrel down the road and duck into May, which by this time should have been in the hands of the Calgary Highlanders or cleared by Benson's patrol, and pop out on the reverse slope to open fire on the German defenders just as the Black Watch rifle companies descended onto Fontenay.[11]

None of this could come off unless the artillery strikes called for in the fire plan arrived on time and on target. Instead of leaning into the barrage as they had done in earlier attacks, this phase of Simonds's plan called for a series of timed concentrations designed to hit suspected German positions along the ridge and on the reverse slope near Fontenay.[12] In essence, the fire plan that Captain Gordon Powis worked out with Griffin was a repeat of the earlier one that had gone for naught that morning, and although the acting Black Watch CO considered requesting a concentration around May, the pair dismissed this notion for fear of hitting the lost Calgary Highlander company or Benson scouts currently en route.[13] To offset any surprises, Powis, along with two other forward observation officers (FOOs), would advance with the forward companies, bringing down fire missions on call and adjusting fire as needed and as they progressed up the slope.

Getting the battalion up and over Verrières Ridge was only half the problem. Piercing the German main line of resistance would, as Simonds expected and desired, provoke a swift, fierce and deadly response from Dietrich's *Kampfgruppen*, who lay in wait, ready to pinch off any embryonic breech at its base. With no intention of following in the footsteps of the South Saskatchewan and Essex Scottish Regiments, Griffin counted on Ronnie Bennett's support company to be quick off the mark, as success lay in winning the race against time to consolidate their positions before the inevitable German counterstroke arrived.

Upon receiving word that the rifle companies had reached their objective, Bennett would move at breakneck speed from the factory area, hauling the anti-tank guns, mortars and a fresh supply of land mines, ammunition and water, while the battalion rushed to dig in. At their most vulnerable until Bennett arrived, the rifle companies would have to rely on the supporting fire from the Hussars' tanks and the skill of the three FOOs to call down artillery to break up the incoming German counterattacks. If any of these elements failed to arrive on time or performed improperly, the hunters stood to become the hunted quickly.

With the reworked plan laid out, doubt still hung heavy as to whether it was wise for the show to continue. "Little on the day had gone right," said George Buch, "and there was a distinct feeling that something was off . . . no one was convinced this was a great plan, but rather the best under the trying circumstances."[14] After talking it over with John Taylor, John Kemp could find no legitimate technicality or loophole to circumvent the direct order from above. As Kemp lamented, "There was nothing wrong with the order—if it had been on schedule—but it was four hours late."[15] Although likely justified on ethical and moral grounds, failing to comply with a direct order was an "unconscionable heresy," Buch recalled, as it provoked a sense of emasculation that "brought shame on you, shame on your family and more importantly, shame on the regiment."

Beyond the seductive and magnetic concept of pride and honour came the tangible notion that, just days earlier, they had proudly laid down the law in both the moral and the physical sense when other units had faltered under the weight of intense enemy fire. Now, once they embarked, it meant that little mercy would await them on either side of Verrières Ridge.

As the clock ticked rapidly towards H-hour, a stern resignation descended upon the group as Operation Spring now took on a life of its own. As Captain Campbell Stuart noted, "Griffin had concluded that the honour of the regiment was at stake," and short of insubordination and a charge of mutiny, nothing would stop the Black Watch assault.[16] To solidify the imperative nature of his final instruction, Griffin paused and took one last look around the group to ensure his concluding remarks penetrated to their very marrow. As John Kemp described, Griffin then "ordered the Battalion to push on to its objective—at all costs."[17] Resigned to their fate, it is significant to note that there is no record (let alone suggestion) that anyone from the Black Watch, the Hussars or the artillery objected or voiced any concern.

WITHIN TWENTY MINUTES OF GRIFFIN'S ORDER, THE rifle companies, which had waited for a short spell at the crossroads following the clearance of Shell Alley, were on the move towards the factory when word came that the brigadier had arrived in St. Martin. With Griffin hurrying back to meet Megill, his acting 2ic, John Taylor, took the battalion down the road to May as prescribed, where they came under sporadic German mortar fire from across the Orne before wheeling left to pacify the factory area.

Kemp's D Company led the way, as it had all morning, his Bren gunners firing from the hip as they advanced, while his platoons swarmed the outbuildings of the pithead, moving from structure to structure to root out the German defenders. Up above, the heavy dose of Bren gun and rifle fire engulfed snipers hiding in the overhead power pylons of the tipple. One by one, Kemp's platoons raked each pylon box and connecting catwalk mercilessly, forcing the few Germans who managed to survive the initial fusillade to flee into the wheat or vanish into the buildings. Some, as the men in the lead platoons discovered, disappeared below ground down a deep mine shaft that had been discovered two days earlier, but for some unknown reason, divisional intelligence had failed to pass this crucial information to its frontline units. Hot on their heels, B Company, now under Command Sergeant Major Foam with a handful of Buch's pioneer platoon in tow, chucked phosphorus grenades and Composition C into every scurry hole and opening found. Explosions and muffled cries followed, and for the first time in a week, the factory area fell silent.

At the crossroads in St. Martin, Griffin found Megill waiting impatiently under a veranda of the only building in town left fully intact. Although rumours swirled about a heated discussion between the hard-driving brigadier and the headstrong major, their talk, although strained, remained all business, with Griffin relieved to report that he had the battalion ready to go for their 0930 H-hour, just minutes away.[18]

Poring over Griffin's map, the only question Megill asked centred around the change in the axis of advance that avoided May-sur-Orne. According to Megill, Griffin "doubted May was held on a continuous basis," but had "patrols in the town" and felt quite confident that the Calgary Highlanders would "fill in behind" and take May when the Black Watch passed their start line near the crest.[19]

At this point, if Megill harboured any doubt or trepidation about the reworked plan, he did not express it, nor did he take any action to counter it. No amount of friction kicked up from the frontline battalions could change either Simonds's mindset or the overriding desire of Megill and Foulkes to follow the music. As Megill later admitted, "Given the temper of the time, there would have been heavy casualties from much grim action before the effort would have been called off . . . We would have been ordered to continue attacking as long as troops could be persuaded to make the effort."[20] With that, Megill wilfully sanctioned the attack as planned and returned to his tactical headquarters.

WITH THE CLOCK INCHING TOWARDS H-HOUR, GRIFFIN double-timed it back to the factory following his tête-à-tête with the brigade commander. He found the rifle companies formed up, waiting for the word to go. With the steady drain of casualties over the last few days on Hill 61, plus the fighting in St. Martin earlier that night, each rifle company could muster only seventy-five men, thirty fewer than a week before. With his tactical head-quarters factored into the mix, the entire battalion numbered just over 320 men for the assault up Verrières Ridge.

On his way to rejoin the battalion, Griffin encountered Lieutenant Alan Van Vliet, one of the three forward observa-tion officers (FOOs) attached to the battalion, crouched in a ditch, feverishly fiddling with his radio, which had picked the worst time to go on the fritz. As he neared the factory, Griffin came across another FOO, Captain Oswald from the 25th Field Regiment, and his signaller wandering dazed and confused near their blazing carrier, which had been hit by a German mortar shell. With only headsets and shredded patch cords left dangling around their necks, they could no longer communicate effectively with their field regiment and Griffin had little choice but to per-mit them to return to their unit.[21]

With two FOOs down, only Captain Gordon Powis, lined up with A Company, remained to advance with the battalion. More worrisome, however, was the whereabouts of Harris's tanks from the 1st Hussars. Not only had they failed to support the clearing of the factory area but with H-hour upon them and reports that

253

the artillery fire plan had gone into effect, the Shermans had yet to appear, and Griffin could not raise Harris on the radio.

IN THE CABBAGE FIELD NEXT TO THE FACTORY, THE Black Watch rifle companies shook out in a slight depression in the ground, tucked in close to the slope, well out of sight of the Germans on the eastern part of the ridge. Some of the men stood, while others sat or took a knee, nervously rolling a final cigarette, wolfing down a bit of hardtack or a piece of chocolate, or chugging one last swig of rum. A few men prayed quietly while victims of mounting fatigue just stared out into the golden wheat fields lining the ridge. Almost all took a moment to relieve themselves; they had learned quickly at the Orne that to command nature, one must first obey it, and the last thing they wanted was to go into battle with a teeming bowel or bladder.

Like his comrades, Corporal Gordy Donald shouldered a heavy physical burden. Weighed down with extra bandoliers stuffed with rifle rounds strung across both shoulders, a shovel affixed in his webbing, with extra Hawkins grenades, Bren magazines and PIAT shells crammed into every pouch available, he complained about his plight to anyone in earshot. "You probably had an extra 50 or 60 pounds that made your manoeuvrability very limited, and the extra four pounds of body armour they issued to us just before we left Hill 61 did not help matters either."[22] This experimental covering, designed for wear under the uniform, consisted of four thin metal plates strung together by burlap straps covering the kidney, chest and pelvic regions against shrapnel and small-arms fire from long distances. Ideally, the contraption would fit under the uniform, tied snugly to the body, but with no time to strip down and re-dress, the men slung it over their heads and lashed between their webbing and their tunics. In short, its one-size-fits-all design simply did not fit all. Men of average build and height, such as Bren gunner Anthony Barbagallo, had little problem fitting it to his form. However, for Private Thanning Anderson, who stood just shy of six feet, the pelvic and chest plates rode up uncomfortably over the stomach and lower throat. The diminutive (five feet, two inches) Private Reuben Gorodetsky, however, welcomed the extra length; instead of the plate covering his pelvic region, it slung low to shield his genitals, an unintentional benefit that his section-mates now tried furiously to replicate.[23]

Although surrounded by the men in his section, Jimmy Bennett remained very much alone. Still reeling from Desormeaux's death, he sat in the dirt, right foot tapping madly while his thumb kept time on his rifle stock. Haunted by the impersonal and far too symmetrical hole in his best friend's forehead, the everlasting image continued to stoke his primal fear of going blind, a fear not even half a canteen of rum could douse. Impatiently, he muttered under his breath to get on with it, requiring a direct infusion of adrenalin to check his chronic and now escalating anxiety.

Kneeling in the middle of the small circle that included Smokey Lalonde, Tex Richards and Herb McLeod, Bruce Ducat wondered, like many others, if the show was still on. When the Black Watch had engaged in training schemes and exercises in England leading up to their arrival in Normandy, and cock-ups and delays of this magnitude occurred, it almost always led to the cancellation that many expected would happen this time. It did not.

"I didn't know what was in store," Lieutenant Mackenzie-Wood remembered. "We were just sitting around waiting for orders, we did not know if this was going to continue or what. I did not have any apprehension at the time. We were just waiting for the next move."[24] All that Gordy Donald was told was that "we're going to take the ridge," which led him and his section-mates to believe that, like the attack at Ifs and Hill 61, this would be "a piece of cake."[25]

Likewise, Sergeant Mac Roulston didn't experience the same trepidation as he had during the Orne crossing, the firefights on Hill 61 or even his ill-fated patrol a day earlier. "It was unusual not to have fear going into something that big," he recalled, but "I said these are the orders and I'm going, and my boys are coming with me."[26] Their trial by fire over the past week had created a bond unique to frontline soldiers, but for the moment, St. Crispin's Day would have to wait. No grand speeches or rallying cries filled the field to spur the men on to victory; only the clicks and clanks of weapons loaded, checked and rechecked percolated above the rumbles of fighting in the distance.

By this time, few had any idea, nor did they care, what the objective was. They only knew it lay up and over the long slope ahead. "We didn't have a word until they told us to fix bayonets," said Bruce Ducat, recalling an order that had a galvanizing effect on Jimmy Bennett because it collectively underscored the foreboding task at hand and inflamed the romantic notions of war he had devoured as a child.[27] For Bruce Ducat, however, the order left the cynical corporal incredulous: "I thought God almighty, this is fucking stupid—what are we doing? Going back to World War One?"[28]

AT TACTICAL HEADQUARTERS AT THE CENTRE OF THE battalion, Griffin checked his watch for what seemed the millionth time in the last hour. It was now one minute before H-hour and word had arrived from Powis that the fire plan had gone into effect, but Harris's tanks had yet to arrive. With Allied guns firing in support of units making their push or holding ground along the entire front, the timed concentrations fell outside of earshot of the men in the cabbage patch, leaving most with the foreboding impression that the artillery, like Harris's tanks, had failed to materialize. Undaunted and with the clock ticking, Griffin raised his right hand above his head and held it there for half a beat, then, in one motion, he dropped it to shoulder level and waved it forward, bellowing, "BLACK WATCH, ADVANCE!"[29]

Still working his fighting patrol through the long drainage ditch that led to May, Benson first caught sight of the rifle companies forming up in the cabbage field slightly off to his left and well behind his position. Minutes later, when his lead scout, Melvin Cameron, reached the northern fringes of the town, Griffin had waved the battalion forward. At that moment, Benson watched the spectacle unfold before him as the stream of riflemen waded upright into the wheat, with all, save for the men in the front rank, holding their weapons across their chests at the ready. In less than three minutes, the entire assault force, 320 men, slipped into the grain, with only heads and shoulders, rifles, bayonets and antennas from the field radios floating above the stalks to mark their advance.

"It was just a question of following the man in front of you once you started an attack like this," recalled Lieutenant William Mackenzie-Wood. "We didn't know what we were getting into either, of course—so we just moved ahead as we were asked to do."[30] Strict rationing in England had prohibited the trampling of crops during training, and although they had tackled wheat fields in their previous attack, nothing rivalled the height or density of the plots laid out on the northern slope of Verrières.

They were greeted by German harassing fire as soon as the companies started their ascent up the slope. "It was hard enough walking through it without taking fire," found Bruce Ducat. "The wheat was far thicker than I first imagined," Gordy Donald discovered, "and you could not see where the enemy was at any time . . . you just lost sight of everybody."[31] For Sergeant Mac Roulston, maintaining command and control in such terrain proved a nightmare as his men, some of whom had just arrived as reinforcements the night before, disappeared beneath the sea of grain when confronted by the odd sniper's bullet, machine-gun burst or mortar ranging round. Section and platoon leaders quickly lost sight of their charges in the chest-high wheat, and unit cohesion across the battalion front started to wane. Soon, the tight box formation started to sag and then to fold in on itself.

The momentarily sublime nature of the spectacular view unfolding half a mile from his position wore off quickly when Benson realized that he now shared this ringside seat with the machine-gun team in May. Fearing he had only moments to spare before it would tear into the flank of the battalion, he ordered his scouts to move on the double.

Weaving along the ditch, Melvin Cameron, who had taken point, slammed right into the tail end of a string of men from the lost C Company of the Calgary Highlanders, who huddled in the ditches on both sides of the road, just a few feet shy of the houses in the northern edge of the town. Darting across the street to link up with their company commander, Benson and his scouts caught the attention of a pair of MG 42s concealed near the church. The Germans had lain in wait when he passed through the town on his earlier patrol with Duffield. Instantaneously, two streams of bullets ripped down the road, filling the street with bright yellow-and-green tracers that ricocheted off the facings of the row houses and skipped up the road towards St. Martin. Benson and his scouts dove into the ditch that hugged the western side of the road, while the Calgary Highlanders pushed forward without hesitation, scurrying through the houses on each side of the road, attempting to close within grenade range of the guns.

Unimpressed by their courage and initiative, the Germans

beat them to the punch, dropping smoke onto the structures before letting loose with "every type of weapon from every direction."³² Benson wisely decided to "keep out of that scrap" and get on with his job before his "men were wiped out."³³ Using the smoke for cover, he ordered the patrol to double back and make an end run through the left-hand ditch towards their objective. Bruce Ducat, picking his way through the wheat, quite by chance caught sight of Benson and his scouts "coming back in a hurry" and suspected their retrograde movement was a harbinger of things to come.³⁴

PEERING THROUGH HIS PRIZED BINOCULARS, WHICH had served him faithfully in Poland, France, the Balkans and Russia, Lieutenant Peter Prien, a platoon commander in the crack 2nd Panzer Division, had observed the Black Watch as they steadily glided up Verrières from the turret of his Mark IV panzer, which sat carefully camouflaged in a house in the northeast quadrant of May.

For the last five days, Prien, a former *Panzergrenadier* turned tank commander, had fought in and around the twin towns, sparring with the Queen's Own Cameron Highlanders. His original tank, a forty-five-ton Panther, lay abandoned in the streets of St. Martin, the victim of an earlier run-in with a Canadian tank. Now, having taken over command of a platoon of four Mark IV panzers that formed the lead element of Kampfgruppe Sterz (named after its commander, Major Werner Sterz), Prien sat motionless in his panzer, heavily camouflaged by debris, wooden planks and straw, observing with incredulity the events unfolding in the valley below.

Beyond his boyish looks, blond hair and jack-o'-lantern smile, Prien, who turned twenty-two three days after the Allies landed on June 6, was a grizzled veteran of five gruelling years of combat who understood the benefits of proper fire discipline. Having watched as Duffield and Benson's patrol came within a hair's breadth of his position on their earlier patrol, he held his fire, maintained concealment and allowed the German machine gun down the road to take them on instead, preferring to lie in wait for a more enticing target he suspected would appear momentarily.

Sure enough, the reward for his patience came when he noticed "a body of infantry of considerable strength—about 300 to 400 men—advancing south . . . from the area of St. Martin," readying for an assault. Having learned to expect heavy artillery strikes and close tank support to accompany any Allied attack, he was gobsmacked when the Black Watch moved off by themselves into the wheat without a tank in sight and with the only Allied artillery shells falling around Fontenay, more than a mile from his position. "This was most impressive and perplexing," he recalled with incredulity. "The soldiers marched upright holding their rifles across their breasts in readiness, as if on the drill square."[35]

GRIFFIN HAD CALCULATED THAT IT WOULD TAKE TWENTY minutes to reach the crest of the ridge, and so far, although the going was tough and some of the men started to stray in the wheat—victims of sporadic German fire—their luck held. Advancing at the head of the battalion, Captain Gordon Powis, moving with his signaller, Gunner E.D. Edler, alongside, noted little more than the odd machine-gun burst, sniper fire or mortar shell plunging into the wheat field to harry the Black Watch advance. But not far from the crest, their luck ran out and "the Germans opened up with everything they had."[36]

In one furious thunderclap, the full might of German fire-power assembled over the previous five days opened up in a textbook defensive operation of war. The first salvos from their 81- and 120-millimetre mortars crashed down in a curtain of steel behind Griffin's tactical headquarters and the trailing companies, effectively cutting off the battalion from Canadian lines and any withdrawal route. From defilade positions on the flanks, machine guns, sited on fixed lines, cut swaths into the wheat at knee level and with scythe-like precision tore apart anyone in their path. On the ridge to the left, German panzers, likely mammoth Tigers from the 103rd SS Heavy Panzer Battalion, opened fire at almost point-blank range, while high-velocity shells from other Tiger tanks and anti-tank and flak guns positioned across the Orne found their mark as the promised smokescreen either proved ineffective or failed to materialize altogether. Dirt, grain, bodies and body parts flew in all directions. The ground shook with every step.

PRIEN, WHOSE PLATOON OF PANZERS KEPT A STEADY stream of fire pouring into the right flank of the Black Watch, could not believe the scene in front of him: "scarcely anybody looked for cover . . . It looked like waves of men rolling steadily forward, no sign of panic despite their visible losses. To us, soldiers with four or five years' experience, this was a most unreal sight."[37]

"IT'S THE SOUND THAT HAUNTS YOU," BRUCE DUCAT recalled. "The first thing you notice was how loud it was . . . Machine guns firing, bullets whipping through the grain that sounded like wasps, shells landing, men shouting orders and wounded screaming . . . screeching metal and the clang of bullets and shell fragments meeting body armour, shovels, picks or helmets . . . and then the smell of the cordite from the blasts . . . it just stunk."

Private Gordy Donald knew immediately the Black Watch "were in real trouble" due to the continuity of the German fire. With their machine guns registered on fixed lines, usually by a crew hunkered in a slit using a long string to trigger the weapon, a macabre game of hopscotch developed as the men advanced up the ridge. "Trying to get out of the withering fire, I jumped a cone of fire from an MG 42," Ducat remembered. "I could see it—it was tracer fire, and I skipped it like jumping a rope and kept going."

Terrified and confused, the men had no clue where the firing came from, let alone where the weapon was located. "Only the front rank could do any firing," Ducat recalled. "The rest of us had our weapons up—otherwise the bayonets would have been in the backs of the ones in front."

To make matters worse, what appeared to be German sniper fire coming from the factory area behind soon joined in. As Ducat recalled, "You were afraid to turn your head to talk to your men for fear of German snipers looking for anyone giving commands, anyone in authority, or the signallers carrying radios."

Benson, witnessing the explosions and streams of tracers lashing into the field, exhorted his men to push down the ditch to reach May. Already crowded with a handful of Calgary Highlanders and a few combat engineers sent up to clear mines and obstacles in the town, they stumbled over their Canadian brethren, which alerted the Germans to their position. As Benson recalled, "As they knew that altogether there were about eighteen of us in the ditch . . . it was not long before the Moaning Minnies opened up."[38]

The small and wiry Melvin Cameron, who had managed to squeeze past the Calgary Highlanders to reach the north end of the ditch near the houses, took the first blow from the screaming rocket shells; he was killed instantly. His body lay crumpled twenty yards away while the rest of the scouts lay pinned in the middle. To make good their escape, Benson made the heart-wrenching decision to leave his scout's body in the ditch to save the lives of his remaining men. But now, with shells and machine-gun fire continually whistling overhead, they had little choice but to crawl back towards the relative safety of Canadian lines in St. Martin.

Seeking to paralyze command and control, the Germans picked out the ten-foot-high whip antennas for special treatment, and with their first salvos systematically knocked out the battalion's communications in quick succession. Moving at the front of the battalion, Captain Gordon Powis tried desperately to adjust the supporting artillery fire to bring down smoke and high-explosive rounds on the German positions along the ridge and in May. Screaming into the handset of the wireless set strapped to Edler's back, a blast from a mortar shell knocked Powis off his feet, wounding Edler and smashing the radio. Left now with only two alternatives—wade back through two hundred yards of withering fire to the No. 19 set in his carrier, which unbeknownst to him lay blazing near the factory, or find an infantry set somewhere off to his flanks—Powis chose the latter, but failed to find one in working order.[39]

Farther behind, Griffin's tactical headquarters radio set, carried on his jeep, went up in flames when one of the first mortar rounds found its target not more than a hundred yards into the advance. The same blast caught Lieutenant Stan Duffield, wounding him severely in the right hand and forcing him to fall out of the attack. Unable to walk or run through the murderous

fire, Duffield dropped to all fours and began a long, unceremonious crawl back to the regimental aid post in the factory area.
Dragging his right arm while mortar rounds exploded all around,
he suffered two more hits, one in the same hand and another
between his legs. Thankfully, the shrapnel that ripped through
the crotch of his trousers missed all the important bits, leaving
nothing more than a superficial wound.[40] Under the intense fire,
it took the better part of an hour to move the length of a football
field before he reached evacuation.

With their escape route cut, German shells raining down, and
machine guns and tank fire ripping into their flanks, the Black
Watch could not be more alone. From Griffin's perspective, the
only hope of salvation for his men in the wheat came with reaching their objective in Fontenay. Unable to influence events with
his communications knocked out, the acting Black Watch commanding officer decided to abandon the remnants of his tactical
headquarters and dart straight up the ridge to take personal command of the battalion.

IN THE ORCHARD NORTH OF ST. MARTIN, CAPTAIN
Ronnie Bennett sat with his carriers circled, the Hussars' tanks
providing close protection and waiting for news of the advance.
Without a direct link to the battalion, except through Harris's
command tank, Bennett assumed from the cavalrymen's inactiv-
ity that either Griffin had encountered another delay or someone
had pulled the plug on the attack.

Suddenly, nearly forty minutes after the Black Watch stepped
into the wheat, the 450-horsepower engines of the Hussars'
dozen Shermans roared to life. Bennett, caught off guard by
the commotion, watched the first two troops, led by Lieutenant
Teddy Williamson and Lieutenant William Rawson, roll out of

their laager area and rumble past, pushing through the rubble in St. Martin as they headed south towards the factory.

Running to catch up with Harris, who sat in the cupola of his Sherman at the tail end of the column, Bennett shouted up at the squadron commander over the rumble of the thirty-cylinder engine and the high-pitched squeaks of the bogie wheels and treads: "Is the show still on?" Harris responded with a thumbs-up. Bennett requested the battalion's present location. "In the orchards," with "some along the road to May-sur-Orne," Harris hollered down as his tank sped off, following closely behind the lead troops.[41]

Running back to get his carriers on the move, Bennett thought the position seemed logical if Griffin had changed his mind and decided to take the battalion through the Calgary Highlanders in May before tackling Fontenay. Puzzled by the long delay, Bennett noted, "It would be simpler and more sensible in broad daylight to reach the Start line by moving down the road, where we would have some shelter from the left flank, rather than to cross the open fields to the east of the factory as we had originally planned."[42]

Just before H-hour, Harris's squadron received a direct order from Brigadier Wyman, the seasoned commander of their parent 2nd Canadian Armoured Brigade, requiring them to stay in their present location until after the Calgary Highlanders had succeeded in capturing the town.[43] What prompted this decision is unknown, but most likely it stemmed from the more experienced armoured brigade headquarters seeking to guide Harris, who was fighting his first battle as squadron commander. And without full situational awareness of what was now unfolding at the front, it threw a spanner in the works.[44]

In the interim, accurate German mortar fire found its mark, with a turret burst ripping the aerial from Harris's command tank while it was parked in the orchard, and most likely, the rookie squadron commander assumed Griffin had received the same message. Either way, B Squadron remained in a holding pattern in St. Martin long after H-hour arrived and the Black Watch went in.[45]

THE SITUATION ON THE 272ND DIVISION'S FRONT WAS dire for the Germans as well. The capture of Verrières village by the Royal Hamilton Light Infantry, coupled with the push south to Rocquancourt by the Royal Regiment of Canada and tanks of the 7th Armoured Division, had driven a wedge between the 1st SS and Schack's division that, if left unchecked, promised to turn their flank, as Simonds had hoped.

Alarmed at the developments across the Normandy front, Field Marshal Günther von Kluge telephoned General Heinrich Eberbach's Panzer Army West headquarters at 0845 hours—fifteen minutes before Griffin's O Group—to check on the situation developing in the Verrières sector. General Alfred Gause, Eberbach's highly skilled chief of staff, who had served Rommel in the desert, answered the call and quickly brought von Kluge up to speed. The lack of a heavy bombing raid to kick off the attack, as had occurred in Charnwood and Goodwood, led Gause to suspect this push up the ridge was anything but the long-sought-after breakout attempt the Allied press had pushed for in the last month. Von Kluge agreed, but maintained that an immediate counterattack was a *sine qua non*, and "under no circumstances must there be a delay."[46] Immediately, Gause contacted Dietrich's chief of staff, Oberführer Fritz Kraemer, to carry out von Kluge's command.

At the command post of the 9th SS Panzer Division, on the fringes of the Forêt de Cinglais, General Walter Harzer, the division's operations officer (who would come to fame leading the division at Arnhem during Operation Market Garden two months later), received a phone call from an excited Kraemer, who, as usual, did all the talking. "Harzer," Kraemer shouted into the receiver, "the Tommies have broken through into the sector of the 272nd. Schwerpunkt [the focus of effort] on the Caen-Thury Harcourt road by St. Martin and May . . . and by Rocquancourt. Hohenstaufen is to counterattack immediately to the north and re-establish the [main line of resistance]. Two Kampfgruppen are to be employed—Any questions? No?—Then get to it! Speed is vital!"[47]

Only Kraemer's tone came as a shock to Harzer, who had plans well under way to bolster the main line of resistance on Verrières. For days, elements of Kampfgruppe Koch who stumbled into Black Watch positions on Hill 61 had kept a finger on the pulse of the fighting, throwing in limited probes and counter-attacks to support Schack's 272nd Division in its fight for the twin towns. In need of a well-earned break following Operation Atlantic, Harzer relieved Koch's *Kampfgruppe*, moving it back for rest and refitting in the Forêt de Cinglais while Kampfgruppe Sterz of the crack 2nd Panzer Division took up positions as the mobile fire brigade, supporting Schack's division.

In the interim, two *Kampfgruppen* of the 9th SS, consisting of fifty Panther and Mark IV tanks and assault guns, accompanied by scores of half-tracks brimming with hundreds of heavily armed *Panzergrenadiers*, squeezed across every tiny span left standing over the Orne and Laize Rivers, moving relentlessly towards their form-up point south of Verrières. Preceded by their reconnaissance battalion, mobile artillery, flak and anti-tank guns, the potent force readied itself in a field south of May-sur-Orne to launch its counterattack early in the afternoon.

When Sylvester Stadler, the thirty-three-year-old career Nazi who commanded the Hohenstaufen, arrived at his command post on his Zündapp motorcycle minutes after Kraemer's call,

Harzer had already summoned Obersturmbannführers Otto Meyer and Emil Zollhöfer, his *Kampfgruppe* commanders, who waited impatiently for his orders.[48]

Without wasting any precious time, Stadler sent Meyer's *Kampfgruppe*, consisting of a panzer battalion, a company of engineers and a flak company, north to Rocquancourt to cut off Allied forces advancing in the direction of Falaise, giving them few detailed instructions other than "throw the enemy back."

Turning to Zollhöfer, whose force consisted of a regiment of *Panzergrenadiers*, Stadler ordered him to move on May and St. Martin immediately to re-establish the main line of resistance and recapture the villages of May, St. Martin and St. André. By 1305 hours, both *Kampfgruppen* were on the move towards the Canadian advance, but in the interim, Schack had thrown in his immediate reserves, and the rest of Kampfgruppe Sterz had already started to move towards the crest.[49]

COMMAND AND CONTROL OF THE RIFLE COMPANIES started to break down as casualties mounted and men went to ground, seeking cover in the wheat. Unsure of where to move or when to make the next bound, most remained isolated, confused and terrified, unable to see hand signals or sometimes hear verbal commands over the deafening roar of the German shells and bullets.

Private Jimmy Bennett, bobbing and weaving through the grain to avoid the German fire, found himself separated from the rest of his section. All around, he could hear his comrades screaming for help. "You don't see what's going on any more than 20 or 30 feet beside you . . . I didn't know all these guys were getting killed. I couldn't see them. They were just falling."

"People disappeared into the grain," Bruce Ducat recalled.

"Under no circumstances were you to stop to help anyone. You had to mark them by sticking their rifle in the ground with their helmet on top so the stretcher-bearers could find them and move on."

One shell exploded no more than five yards ahead and to the right of Ducat, Lalonde and Herb McLeod. All escaped except for Tex Richards, who lay sprawled on his back, his right leg severed, its femoral artery torn and hemorrhaging. As Ducat ran past, he caught sight of his mate sprawled on his back, clawing aimlessly at the sky, screaming, "DUKE! DUKE! I'm hit! Help me! Don't leave me!" With German bullets cutting the wheat and shells exploding, neither Ducat nor Lalonde dared stop. Under the circumstances, all Ducat could offer was a hollow promise in a futile attempt to comfort Richards: "I'll be back, Tex!" All the while, he thought to himself, "The faster you go, the faster you are going to stop the slaughter."

Sergeant Mac Roulston, trying in vain to keep his platoon together, lost sight of his men when Private George Truax from Coboconk, Ontario, disintegrated into a pink cloud, a victim of a shell that found its mark squarely on his camouflaged helmet. Soaked in Truax's blood, the horrified and now enraged Roulston continued forward. Without warning, a lone German popped up out of a heavily camouflaged slit near the crest of the ridge and "stuck his hands up" in a naive attempt to surrender. "At that stage on the attack, you don't have questions," Roulston recalled. "You can't take prisoners at that time. As I moved forward, he could have put a bullet in my back, so I shot him."[50]

By the time the battalion neared the crest of the ridge, the once-tight box formation had collapsed entirely, leaving only a glob of humanity to push forward under the withering fire.

"The only thing that kept us going," recalled Bruce Ducat, "was our orders to go and pride in the regiment. The Black Watch don't retreat. That was drummed into us every day. Perhaps we should have called it off, but once you go, you go." Not everyone shared his enthusiasm. Gordy Donald, who originally thought it would be a piece of cake, sensed once the firing started that the attack "was hopeless right from the start" and had little faith they would reach Fontenay, no matter how much courage and willpower fuelled the push. "You knew you were up against something that you couldn't handle. And running to the top of the hill was not the way to handle it. So, you got up there with three or four fellows—what are you going to do?"

Captain John Kemp, whose company had rapidly melted away in just minutes, unexpectedly found himself advancing alongside Bishop's College School old boy Lieutenant Alan Robinson, who had taken over A Company from Griffin. Scurrying with several other men into the only tree-lined area on the ridge to escape the murderous German fire, they barely reached the sanctuary before ending up under Canadian shells that fell short. The first blast killed Kemp's thirty-seven-year-old CSM, Johnny MacDougal, an American from Fulton County in upstate New York, while the second riddled the company commander's right leg with shrapnel. Having lost his rifle in the blast, Kemp pulled his father's Colt .45 from the secret pocket inside his tunic and waved it in the air, urging any men he could see to push forward. Turning to signal Robinson to keep moving ahead, another shell landed. The young platoon commander's face was sliced clean from his skull, killing him instantly. His gangly, athletic body was a victim of inertia, stumbling aimlessly forward until it collapsed and vanished beneath the grain.

Kemp sat paralyzed until Griffin suddenly appeared out of the grain, which shook the bewildered company commander back to reality. To the captain's surprise, Griffin was still in the battle and appeared as "if he was just coming on parade. He was unmistakable even under these conditions; he was calm, his bearing was great, he was totally in control, he knew exactly what he was doing." Sensing the futility of continuing, Kemp urged Griffin to call off the attack due to the "murderous" fire.[51] Griffin, knowing firsthand that the Germans had shut off any chance of retreat with a solid wall of mortars, rockets and artillery, shut Kemp down. "Orders are to attack, and the battalion will carry on."[52]

SOON AFTER HIS DEPARTURE FROM THE ORCHARD, Captain Ronnie Bennett arrived in the factory area after a hell-raising journey running a gauntlet of German shells that rained down along the main road that ran southward from Fleury, through St. Martin and onwards to May. Along the way, his carrier, skilfully driven by Jake Gemmill, managed to overtake Harris's tanks, which pushed through the gardens, trails and tiny paths of St. Martin rather than risking the enemy fire near the crossroads. However, when Bennett arrived at the still-smoking pithead, he could see "no one on the ridge or elsewhere" and "no sign whatever of the battalion."[53] In his mind, this confirmed what Harris had told him. He ordered Gemmill to head towards May, hoping to catch up with Griffin to see what the change in plan meant for his company. He waited for his orders in the orchard north of St. Martin.

About halfway up the road, Benson and his remaining scouts emerged from the ditch on the eastern side of the road, frantically waving for Bennett to stop. Running to his carrier, Benson informed him that "May-sur-Orne was in enemy hands," that "one Company of Calgarys had a weak hold on one edge just on the outskirts," but "there was no chance of getting in." Asked if he knew anything about the battalion or its location, Benson confirmed they had "gone straight from St. Martin de Fontenay to their objective and had by-passed May-sur-Orne."[54] Beckoning for Benson and the scouts to climb aboard, the group set off straight across the wheat field for Fontenay, but before long the heavy enemy fire forced them to abandon that idea, and they returned quickly to the relative shelter of the factory area.

BACK IN THE ORCHARD, CAMPBELL STUART HAD WAITED for over half an hour for Griffin's cry of success from the other side of the ridge. For the moment, the delay did not cause concern; losing wireless contact with the rifle companies during an advance was not unusual, given the fluid nature of events. The wireless silence continued, and no messages arrived long past the twenty minutes Griffin predicted it would take to reach the old start line. Harris's tanks and Bennett's carrier suddenly sprang to life and whizzed off down the road. Stuart began to worry. Grabbing his signaller, he set out on foot, despite the increasing pain in his fractured leg, anxious to re-establish wireless contact with the battalion.[55]

Fifty yards up the road to May, he encountered Lieutenant Alan Van Vliet, the FOO from the 5th Field Regiment, still in the ditch and still working on his wireless set. Van Vliet "knew nothing of the whereabouts of the Battalion." Pushing forward another fifty yards, Stuart "encountered nobody and saw no one," either in the field to the left near the factory or along the road. Following the distant sound of gunfire coming from the ridge, the pair pressed on until two machine guns—the same ones that had greeted Benson and his scouts earlier—opened fire and pinned both in the ditch alongside the road for a short spell.

The pair used the ditch as cover and worked their way back into St. Martin, eventually making it to the orchard. Here, Stuart discovered that Bennett had yet to return and nobody in his company had any clue about the fortune of the rifle companies. Limping noticeably, Stuart mounted his carrier and took off in search of the tactical headquarters of both the Calgary and the Cameron Highlanders in St. André, hoping they could shed some light. Neither unit, as he soon discovered, could offer any help.

On his return leg to the orchard, his driver cut across the fields to save time and ran smack into the lead elements of the Guards Armoured Division, which had crept forward to its start line south of Ifs, waiting for Simonds's order to move through the gap between Fontenay and Rocquancourt.

With the tanks buttoned up and engines rumbling, ready to advance, Stuart had to climb on top of the lead tank, a Cromwell from the 2nd Battalion of the Irish Guards. He banged on the hatch, and when a black beret–clad head reluctantly appeared, the Black Watch adjutant inquired if he had heard anything about the battalion on their radio net. Busy with more immediate issues, the extremely proper guardsman disavowed any knowledge of the Black Watch and then politely asked Stuart to get his carrier out of the area, as it would draw fire, and slammed his hatch shut. Stuart dismounted, and immediately the first salvo of 88-millimetre fire arrived.

Three shells exploded around him in quick succession, searching for the tanks, but miraculously, Stuart survived each blast without a scratch. Not waiting for another round, he sprinted towards his carrier, adrenalin buffeting the pain in his fractured leg, and dove inside. His driver wasted no time in getting out of the area and gunned it for the orchard area while 88-millimetre rounds tracked the carrier as it crossed back over Hill 67 and then headed southwest for St. Martin on a wild ride.

LIEUTENANT GEORGE BUCH, WHOSE PIONEER PLATOON had spent the better part of the morning lifting land mines in St. Martin following Griffin's O Group, had just packed up his carrier in preparation for the move to Fontenay when stragglers from the Calgary Highlanders appeared, looking for their shattered battalion and bringing tales of their nightmarish journey during the night. Though Buch had just mounted his carrier and given the order to advance towards the factory, the Calgary Highlanders survivors vehemently warned him that both battalions were taking a beating somewhere in the wheat and that the machine guns of the Germans were strafing the road to May. Buch gave orders for his CSM, Bob Jackson, to get the vehicles off the road and for the men to dig in. Campbell Stuart's carrier careened over a nearby hedge to announce his return. Buch only had a few minutes to bring Stuart up to speed before the 88s began to snipe the carriers and trucks parked in the orchard; they would wipe out more than fifteen vehicles by day's end.

Working his wireless from a ditch beside his carrier, Stuart fired off a series of frantic messages to brigade and division headquarters: "Being heavily mortared. No Tac Report. Do not know if infantry are on the move. Can't reach forward troops. All companies believed on left of road between St. André and May. All pinned."[56]

When no response came, Stuart sank to the bottom of the ditch in despair, calling it the "worst moment of his life." Despite the dawning enormity of the situation, he could not accept that the battalion had just disappeared. He clung to the belief that "the battalion had to be out there, pinned down somewhere," and "if only he could find out where," he could "mount some action to retrieve them."[57]

HARRIS'S SHERMANS FINALLY REACHED THE FACTORY area nearly an hour after the Black Watch had waded into the wheat. As his troop leader, Teddy Williamson, reported, the tanks had lost time pushing through the brick walls and back-yards that had exacerbated their already delayed arrival. With "so much stuff flying around," Williamson buttoned up his tank, but looking through his periscope, he failed immediately to grasp the seriousness of the situation until he spotted the first of the Black Watch wounded crawling back.[58]

Lieutenant William Rawson, whose troop had followed closely on Williamson's heels, realized right away the Black Watch was in a "very sticky position," pinned down by "terrific small arms fire [that] beat on them from the high ground."[59] Captain Jake Powell, the Hussars' 2ic, who arrived several minutes later, could see the Black Watch about three hundred yards ahead of the factory, suffering under the weight of "intense and accurate" mortar fire.[60]

The Hussars' tanks lit up the factory area. The Germans, who had taken shelter in the mine shaft six storeys below when the Black Watch passed through, resurfaced for another round, peppering the Shermans with small-arms and machine-gun fire. Fearing attacks from hand-held *Panzerschrecks* and *Panzerfäuste*, the Hussars responded immediately, encircling the structure and hosing it for minutes with their machine guns.[61] Once again, German opposition melted away, and Rawson's troop turned its guns back onto the ridge, "belting away at anything that looked like a Jerry position."[62] However, with the Germans turning in their "usual efficient job of camouflaging, [it was] mostly blind shooting," he recalled.[63]

Hundreds of yards ahead, Lieutenant William Mackenzie-Wood found himself lost after going to ground when a machine-gun bullet found him in the wheat. "Fortunately, I was carrying a rifle at the time, to make the officers look like everyone else . . . The bullet went through my rifle butt before it went into my leg."

Having lost contact with his men while he patched his leg,

the platoon commander resumed his advance, hobbling forward, following the steady incline, sure he had set a course for the centre of the ridge. To his surprise, he discovered he had strayed to one side of the bowl and had resurfaced near the northern edge of May.

Completely alone, Mackenzie-Wood then spotted a partially ruined house to the right and made a quick dash for the sanctuary. Breaking out from the wheat, he ran across a small yard to the house. He noticed the Hussars' Shermans to his right and behind him. The tanks "must have seen me duck into the house and thought I was German, because they started firing on the house, first with their .30-calibre machine guns and then their 75-millimetre main guns."

Crashing through the back door, Mackenzie-Wood landed heavily on the tiled floor of the kitchen and crawled on his stomach towards a thick cast iron wash basin in the corner. Machine-gun bullets tore "up and down the doorway" and ripped through the wall above his head. Glass shattered, cabinetry flew from its hinges and furniture exploded, engulfing the structure in showers of wood splinters, shredded linen and chunks of masonry. Desperately, the young platoon commander screamed out, "FRIEND!" but realized the futility of his plea immediately, as no one could hear him over the racket.

Squirming over onto his back, Mackenzie-Wood now stared straight up at the mosaic of punctures on the southern wall, which permitted hundreds of rays of sunlight to flicker off the swirling clouds of plaster dust. Then the top floor of the next row house exploded, a victim of a 75-millimetre high-explosive shell, and beams fell. Expecting the next round to hit home, Mackenzie-Wood rolled over and clawed at the porcelain tiles in a futile effort to escape. He lay still, resigned to his fate. He squeezed his eyes shut and braced for the final round. Only silence fol-

lowed. "Suddenly," he recalled, "they trained their fire on something else." When he opened his eyes and turned over yet again,
he found a small band of ragged, battered and unimpressed
Calgary Highlanders and a few combat engineers standing over
him. (These were the survivors of the group Benson had encountered earlier in the ditch.) Seeking refuge for their wounded, they
had arrived with a Black Watch medic, Private Allan Robson,
who, like Mackenzie-Wood, had strayed off course in the wheat.
Robson began to set up his makeshift aid station and went to
work at once.

IN THE FACTORY AREA, BENNETT'S CARRIER, OVER-
loaded by Benson and his scouts riding on the back, had just
arrived when the Hussars' tanks appeared. Soon, the Black Watch
regimental aid post arrived to set up shop in the pithead, bringing with it Dr. Rudy Ohkle, as well as members of the pipes and
drums and the remaining scouts, who immediately set to work
as stretcher-bearers. Bennett could see Panther and Tiger tanks
dug in along the ridge, firing into the wheat field ahead, presumably directly onto the men who had gone to ground and now lay
pinned. The tanks kept up their deadly rate of fire until "their
guns soon began to wear down the actual crest."[64]

Mercifully, the arrival of the 1st Hussars' Shermans diverted
the attention of the panzers, and within seconds an 88-millimetre
fire began to search for the Hussar tanks, each shell producing
a tremendous clatter when it hit the trolleys suspended from the
roof of the corrugated-iron structure.[65]

The fuming Bennett intercepted Harris, who had dismounted
his radioless tank to liaise with his troop commanders. Bennett
urged the squadron commander to move immediately into
May as planned. Harris, frazzled by the chaos of his first fight,

refused due to "the heavy 88mm fire coming from the ridge" and because of his orders, which required him to stay put until the Calgary Highlanders had cleared May. Bennett, unaware of this order, became incandescent at Harris's apparent obstinacy, but before he could rip into the squadron commander, a stray bullet found Harris, catching him in his foot. The wound ended his battle and his extremely short tenure as commander of B Squadron.[66]

Captain Jake Powell, riding in his own tank, had no idea that Harris had been wounded. When he could not raise his squadron commander on his wireless for some time, he realized something was wrong. Failing to find Harris when his Sherman pulled into the factory grounds, he seized command of the situation and immediately ordered both Williamson's and Rawson's troops to make for May.[67] As Rawson reported, "I received a message by radio stating that the Calgarys were on the East edge of May-sur-Orne and needed tank support in the worst way. I was ordered to take up a prearranged position at the east end of the town and see if I could help."[68]

By this time, the first Black Watch casualties had started to arrive in the factory area. One of the first to emerge from the wheat was Captain John Taylor, still conscious but hobbling and bleeding from shrapnel wounds to his thigh and groin. Rushing to his aid, Bennett asked about the situation up ahead.

"Don't take men up there," the company commander replied. "The battalion is absolutely pinned down. As soon as they pushed over the crest, they were pinned down by MG fire and 88mm. They cannot move, and there are too many men there now trying to dig in."[69]

Before Taylor could finish his report, more Black Watch wounded appeared, ghostlike, out of the wheat, arriving in small, pathetic groups of two or three, seeking immediate medical attention. As Bennett noted, all "were completely exhausted" and their "story made the situation forward appear an absolute massacre."[70]

THE CORE OF KAMPFGRUPPE STERZ, RESPONDING TO Prien's emergency call, moved quickly, emerging from their lair south of May not long after the Black Watch began their assault. Using the prehistoric burial mound near Fontenay, which locals said contained the remains of a beloved Roman commander slain on the ridge in ancient times, as their waypoint marker, Sterz fanned out his force into three attack groups.

On the right, a score of heavily camouflaged half-tracks brushed past the outskirts of Fontenay, carrying the men of the 304th Panzergrenadier Regiment, commanded by the wily, one-eyed Eastern Front veteran Captain Paul Scholing. To the left, fourteen Panthers from the 2nd Panzer Division's 3rd Panzer Regiment made straight up the old Roman trading road, heading for May to reinforce Prien, while Sterz, commanding his four Jagdpanzer IV tank destroyers, each armed with long, 75-millimetre guns, surged up the middle. When Scholing's *Panzergrenadiers* reached the crest, they dismounted and proceeded on foot to support Sterz's tank destroyers, which had reached the crest near May and discovered the Hussars' tanks in the factory area. Sterz's low-slung tank destroyers, still unseen from the valley below, nestled into position and waited for the Hussars to make the first move.[71]

CAPTAIN JAKE POWELL, WHO HAD TAKEN COMMAND from the wounded Harris, ordered Rawson and Williamson to move ahead in a desperate bid to support the Black Watch while his headquarters troop offered limited support from its increasingly precarious position in the factory area.[72]

Rawson, fully cognizant of the urgency of his task, gunned his four Shermans up the field alongside the ditch that Benson and the scouts had crawled back through earlier that morning. When his tanks arrived at the main road minutes later, they whipped past the house containing Mackenzie-Wood and the Calgary Highlander wounded, failing to hear their shouts above the drumming of their 400-horsepower engines.[73] But before Rawson could raise Powell on the radio, a German tank-hunting team planted a high-explosive anti-tank warhead squarely on the engine compartment of his Sherman. Following a loud thud from the hit, and then a brief, horrifying pause known only too well to tank crews, the warhead exploded, and the tank erupted in flames, forcing the rest of Rawson's troop to pull back towards the factory. With less than four seconds to escape the tank before it brewed up and immolated anyone trapped inside, the crew flung open the hatches and flopped to the ground all around the burning beast. All the crew made good their escape except for Rawson, who, wounded in both legs, fell into the hands of the same German tank-hunting team that had despatched his tank moments before.[74]

Williamson's column, moving at full tilt up the main road, also managed to reach May, where it came under intense German small-arms fire from *Panzergrenadiers* in the upper windows of houses. In the ensuing confusion, Williamson, who was fighting his first battle, lost his bearings and failed to notice that a pair of veteran Panthers had moved into position fifty yards ahead. The deafening explosions from a pair of high-velocity 75-millimetre rounds that slammed into his Sherman served notice of his rookie mistake. The shells ripped through the extra armour added to the glacis plate on the front of his tank, killing his co-driver instantly and fatally wounding his loader/radio operator, who could not escape the inferno. Williamson, separated from his crew, managed to crawl into a nearby house and, later that night, make his way back to Canadian lines. The rest of his crew, however, remained trapped in May-sur-Orne for the next twelve days, surviving on a slender diet of carrots and wine.[75]

Powell, witnessing the loss of four tanks in May-sur-Orne to a combination of concealed anti-tank teams and counter-attacking Panthers, and having seen nothing of the Black Watch for over thirty minutes, ordered his surviving tanks to pull back to the factory area, which by this time had become quite sticky, continually laced with 88s, mortars and Moaning Minnies.[76]

Sterz's Panthers and Jagdpanzers, attempting to inch forward down the slope towards the factory, came under concentrated fire from the surviving Hussar tanks and from Allied fighter-bombers that had just appeared over the ridge after supporting other operations farther to the east earlier in the morning.[77]

Lieutenant Peter Prien, still battering the Black Watch with the guns of his Mark IV panzers, watched as Powell's Shermans unleashed the "violet and red smoke" used to mark targets for air strikes. In what seemed like seconds to Prien, the Typhoon fighter-bombers swooped in to answer the call, and several of Sterz's panzers succumbed to their rockets and 20-millimetre cannons, as did one of Powell's Shermans, mistaken for the enemy in the swirling dust and smoke from shells and brush fires that had broken out due to the intensity of the fight.[78]

When Captain Ronnie Bennett joined Powell in the factory area after leading a small caravan of carriers and trucks draped with Red Cross markers to evacuate the wounded, he could see tanks on the ridge but remained uncertain whether they were friend or foe. Flagging down Powell, Bennett asked if the tanks on the ridge were indeed his and, if so, did they have any contact with the Black Watch rifle companies? Powell just shook his head and then briefly filled him in on their attempt to get forward and how, at the moment, the Hussars had "no live tanks forward."[79] Pressed for the whereabouts of the rifle companies, Powell could shed no light, and it was anyone's guess whether they had reached the crest, let alone crossed it, or gone to ground somewhere in the wheat.

With no communications open to anyone, Bennett climbed aboard a dispatch rider's Norton motorcycle. He started it up after several violent kicks of the starter and, over the chugging of the engine, ordered Benson to dig in his scouts, as they would be the only local protection for the regimental aid post. Then he sped off for the orchard in St. Martin, hoping to contact Campbell Stuart and put a plan into action to reach the men on the ridge.

10

THE FOUR HORSEMEN, ACT III:
DER HEXENKESSEL (THE WITCH'S CAULDRON)

Simonds moved through his cacophony of command like the reluctant con-
ductor, hoping the orchestra would get it together and play to his revised score.
He left the podium to visit the brass, the tympani, and the winds—gravely urging
each to do its best. He argued with Foulkes . . . and tolerantly waited for his
savaged infantry to sort things out, while two British armoured divisions were
lying in the valley before Verrières, their engines ticking over, their guns silent.[1]

—LIEUTENANT COLONEL ROMAN JARYMOWYCZ

N JUST UNDER FOUR HOURS OF INTENSE FIGHTING,
the once-tranquil and pristine western end of the Bourguébus–
Verrières feature had transformed into a ravaged, raw landscape, pockmarked with shell craters and ripped and scarred by
slit trenches, scrapes, tank tracks and scorched grain. Along the
Black Watch's axis of advance, a bloody trail of the dead, the
dying, the wounded, shocked and concussed testified to the massacre unfolding out of sight of the men in the valley below.

Up until now, only the rawest kind of courage had sustained
the men when their officers and NCOs fell, and the desire to
flee swelled. Spurred on by Griffin, who from numerous accounts
now seemed to be everywhere on the ridge, the bearded, tattered, exhausted and bloodied Highlanders savagely fought on.

Shattered now into small bands of desperate men with no chance of withdrawal, they pushed through the withering fire, some of them hit two, three or four times as they pressed on. They were continually subjected to the unyielding and punishing German fire. Fewer than half reached the crest, while fewer still made it onto the reverse slope. Those who did drove headlong into the waiting arms of the panzers and half-tracks from the surging Kampfgruppe Sterz. Not one man reached the Black Watch objective.

Captain Gordon Powis, the only officer left standing with Griffin, took command of one group of stragglers after he lost his radio to enemy fire. He made it to the crest before a wall of German fire brought his small band to an abrupt halt. "As we reached the crest of the hill," Powis recalled, "we got pinned down, and the men were very tired; we had been doubling most of the way [and] at this stage, we could not move anymore."[2]

Bruce Ducat, running ahead in yet another fifty-yard bound, had lost contact with Smokey Lalonde and Herb McLeod in the same blast that killed Tex Richard. "By the time we got up there, we were no longer in line, some were moving faster than the others [and] we were stuck. Nowhere to go. We couldn't go forward; we couldn't go backward." Resorting to a recitation of the Lord's Prayer to maintain his cadence while moving through the wheat, Ducat could not get past the refrain: "Forgive us our trespasses." The irony did not escape him as he trudged deeper into enemy territory.

Corporal Gordy Donald, who by this time had shed most of his extra equipment and body armour in a bid to gain speed and manoeuvrability, tried in vain to dig into the soil, an act that was thoroughly impossible under the present circumstances.

"The enemy was keeping up intense machine-gun fire through the wheat while heavier weapons poured down on us. The fire was just tremendous. People were dying left, right and centre, and there were enough bullets out there to kill us all."

Private Jimmy Bennett lay gasping for air, alone in the wheat near the crest. He was dogged by unquenchable thirst and drenched in sweat. "I could hear their guns firing. The shells and the bullets [were] flying by, but you couldn't see them," he lamented. "They were firing further back."

Mortar and machine-gun fire greeted any man whose pack broke the surface of the wheat. With their targets farther north in the orchard exhausted, even the 88s chimed in to hunt individual soldiers scurrying about in the grain. Mostly, however, the German fire came from the machine guns of the half-tracks and Panthers from Kampfgruppe Sterz, which for the moment stood off at a distance, content to rake the field at intervals with machine-gun fire that effectively trapped those straddling the crest.

Fire bounded in from all sides—and, most alarmingly, from behind. Many men mistook the "blind firing" of the Hussars' attempts to lend support with that of the Germans, who had briefly re-emerged from the mine shaft. The notion that the enemy had them surrounded and permanently cut off left them demoralized and distraught. Morale began to wane.

"You couldn't get out of the wheat field," an embittered Gordy Donald recalled. "They just had it too well covered. It was almost as if they knew you were coming."

Sergeant Mac Roulston, who had lost contact with most of his platoon, had gone to ground to try to catch his breath when he noticed yet another extensive line of machine-gun bullets sweeping the grain, no more than ten yards ahead. The fire moved progressively from right to left, and threatened to shear off the head of any man caught in its stream.

"The next thing I knew, Major Griffin was on my left, coming up from behind, still urging the men to move forward," recalled

Roulston. But when the Black Watch major discovered the fearsome line of tracers cutting across his front, he motioned Roulston to move left and shouted, "Let's get the hell out of here."

Roulston took off, following tightly behind Griffin, who was still pushing in the general direction of Fontenay. "Griffin was the man, everyone was following him." But only a few steps into his anxious bid, the machine-gun bullets found the Black Watch sergeant. "My leg went numb, and I went down. I was slashed clean through the right hip just about the buttock." Gripped by intolerable pain, he lay hamstrung while small groups of men scuttled past, but as per orders, none stopped. Ripping the pressure bandage from under his helmet netting, the Black Watch sergeant worked it around behind to stem the bleeding. With no way of motioning for aid, he lay helpless and terror-stricken as the sound of gunfire gave way to the evil screech and clank of panzers and half-track treads, which grew louder as Kampfgruppe Sterz closed in for the kill.

Farther ahead, Gordy Donald had already decided he had given enough. Face down in the only bit of cover on the ridge he could find—a deep rut left by the tracks of a heavy German panzer—he wondered, "What the devil do I do next?" Donald heard the thundering clomp of pounding boots and rattling kit from behind, followed by an all too familiar voice uttering words that haunted him until his dying day: "Come on, Donald, we're almost there!" Peering up, he noticed Griffin, his company commander, still moving towards Fontenay.

"Where's 'there'?" Donald thought to himself as Griffin ran past, completely alone. "There was no way in hell I was going any further because it was useless . . . I was only one person, and I could do no good."

No sooner had he reached this deliberation than Griffin, not more than twenty yards ahead, "jumped in the air . . . You could tell something had hit him, so I figured I wasn't going in that direction."

THE FEW MEN WHO HAD MANAGED TO CRAWL OUT OF the wheat near the factory arrived physically and emotionally spent and in an elevated state of fright. Some bled profusely from undressed or half-dressed wounds. All begged for water and ampoules of morphine. Under the towering steel headframe of the pithead, Padre Cecil Royle, who had come up with the regimental aid post, could not engage in anything more than a "desultory conversation" with Reverend Percy, the Calgary Highlanders' chaplain, who had come to search for stragglers from his flock.[3]

The pair flinched as shells and bullets rang off the iron structure above. They dove for cover. Royle, seconded by the Black Watch medical officer, Captain Rudy Ohkle, triaged and in some cases patched the wounded. As the morning wore on, he registered the growing number of dead brought in by the scouts, who doubled as stretcher-bearers. Although the padre planned at first to get forward, he readily admitted he was far too scared to move any farther and was more than relieved when Ronnie Bennett decided to order the regimental aid post back to the relative safety of St. Martin.[4]

Hook Wilkinson, working with Syd Ayling, Paul Welligan and Jackie Jack, had joined an army of stretcher-bearers working their way gingerly into the wheat field to retrieve the fallen. Finding it almost impossible to spot the wounded from a distance, the scouts waded into the lanes cut into the wheat by the advancing men, following the path of trampled stalks until they stumbled over the victims of the German fire.[5] After pulling his former CSM, Charlie Bolton—suffering from nasty wounds to his arm and abdomen—from the field about twenty-five yards from the factory, Hook ventured farther into the wheat and found the departure point for a long string of Black Watch wounded, dead and dying.

"It was such a horrible sight," Hook Wilkinson explained with a mixture of pity and revulsion. "Bodies and body parts lay everywhere. Corpses with heads pulverized like pumpkins, or just headless, lay next to men who had been hit in the stomach, their guts falling out around them. Others had no arms or legs; sometimes we'd only find the arms or the legs. We even found dead from the Calgary Highlanders killed during the night. Verrières was a killing field."

What haunted Hook more than the obscene picture "was the wounded who'd scream for their mothers." Indeed, "some needed to be put out of their misery," but as Hook and his mates were armed only with stretchers, "they just lay there suffering." With little morphine available, all the scouts could do was lift or roll each stricken Highlander onto the stretcher, ignoring his wails and cries for mercy. If they got lucky, the wounded man would pass out from the pain during the long run back to the aid post; if not, they would "hear them swear a bloody blue streak, cry or just whimper. It was just horrible. It was war."

Tasked with far too many journeys that morning to count, Hook was of two minds when Bennett gave the order to pull out. He was glad to get the hell out of there, but he remained sickened by the notion that his friends remained trapped somewhere out in the wheat near the crest, hanging on alone.

AN HOUR AFTER DEMPSEY'S NOON DEADLINE, A VEXED and frustrated Guy Simonds dismounted from his Staghound armoured car on the grounds of the château in Cairon, near the

Abbaye d'Ardenne north of Caen. Simonds, who had spent an infuriating morning with Charles Foulkes at his command post in Fleury-sur-Orne monitoring the fighting, had arrived at 2nd British Army headquarters hell-bent on obtaining an extension to the army commander's deadline so that he could renew his drive later that afternoon.

Precious little had gone right so far with Operation Spring. The narrative on the frightfully bloody morning now centred around mutiny, courage and massacre. In the 3rd Canadian Infantry Division sector on the left of the corps attack, the North Nova Scotia Highlanders had suffered heavily trying to wrestle the fortified town of Tilly-la-Campagne from the clutches of the 1st SS. Simonds, dissatisfied with these results, had ordered a renewed attack for later that afternoon by the survivors of the North Novas, supported by the Stormont, Dundas and Glengarry Highlanders. Both units, veterans of the fighting since they landed on D-Day, balked at Simonds's order, refusing to reinforce obvious failure. The corps commander was incensed by their disobedience and unwillingness to incur heavy casualties. He launched a court of inquiry and sacked the 9th Brigade commander and both battalion COs.[6]

The Calgary Highlanders also paid a dear price, with nearly two hundred men killed, wounded or missing, all lost while moving up the slope of Verrières at night, trying to capture and hold May-sur-Orne. Their experiences on that darkest of nights left them with under a company's worth of able bodies to continue the fight when dawn broke on July 25.[7]

The Royal Regiment of Canada, adhering to Simonds's orders to bypass centres of resistance that would eat up precious time, pushed through a wheat field towards Rocquancourt at 0600 hours, following the capture of Verrières village by the Royal Hamilton Light Infantry (RHLI). Lead companies sustained grievous losses when they hit a portion of the line held by a battalion from Schack's 272nd Division that were supported by a 1st SS *Kampfgruppe*, with at least thirty panzers sitting hull-down on the reverse slope.[8]

The only glimmer of hope for Simonds came with the performance of the RHLI, who, following the rebuff of the Royals, put in a spectacular defensive display that would go down as one of the greatest in Canadian military history. The "Rileys" were exposed on a salient and faced with repeated panzer-led counterattacks from three sides. Under the command of Lieutenant Colonel John "Rocky" Rockingham, they managed to hold Verrières, aided by artillery, tanks, anti-tank guns and rocket-firing Typhoons.

Verrières village was the only one of five objectives to fall into his hands before Dempsey's noon deadline, but Simonds remained buoyed by the RHLI's success. He ignored the unprepossessing situations on both flanks, which led to mass carnage and resolute revolt. Simonds was worried that if Dempsey pulled the plug now, Spring would die an ugly death. He remained true to the tactical mindset that he had laid out for his subordinates the week before.[9] In his estimation, if he called Spring off now, he had "achieved nothing but a waste of lives." But, like a gambler on a high, plagued by the illusion of control and the need to chase his losses, he reasoned that if he continued his attack and brought the operation to a successful conclusion, it would have been "worthwhile despite additional casualties."[10]

Dempsey, long a fan of Simonds from their time in Italy, did not deny his request outright, but, sensing the pessimistic tone bubbling up from his British armoured division commanders, decided on a compromise solution. Simonds suspended armoured operations for the day, save for an emergency intervention to stem any German breakthrough of Canadian lines. He would settle the issue on the ridge that night, "clearing May and

Tilly-la-Campagne" before "going straight" for Fontenay and Rocquancourt.[11] If all went well, by nightfall he would have a victory that rivalled Vimy Ridge, and the next morning he would resume the armoured push to the Cramesnil Spur—or, at the very least, be in tight to absorb a major panzer counterstroke.[12] If not for the horrendous casualties, which now numbered close to 1,500 men in a single day, and his complete disconnect from the human element at the sharp end, it looked like a sound plan.

ON THE REVERSE SLOPE, THE MASSIVE DEFIANCE BY THE valiant few was almost at an end. Pride in the regiment, anger, rage and the abject fear that had fused the men during their push up the slope of Verrières under murderous fire gave way. Now, the grimy, ashen-faced and exhausted Highlanders, out of ammunition and out of time, felt the noose tightening. To those trapped beneath the wheat, time seemed eternal as the panzers and half-tracks of Kampfgruppe Sterz closed in. The bullets and shells turned seconds and minutes to hours. The raw courage that had sustained the men up to this point now started to run out. In these desperate moments, fatigue that had welled up over the last week drowned out their will to fight, their will to carry on, their will to live. The men were strung out in small packets and left to their own devices. Organized resistance disintegrated.

With brief moments left before they learned their fate, the predicament of the Black Watch gave way to memories of home, a satisfying meal, a cold beer, or a fine belt of rum or Scotch. Faces of parents, siblings and close friends appeared, as did the seductive scent of a lover. In those moments, they made deals with God and pondered finality.

Gordon Powis, the only officer still active on the ridge, considered making a break for Canadian lines, but thought twice because the slightest movement in the wheat "brought down a great deal of concentrated fire from MGs and tanks." Eventually, after expending all ammunition, he told the men who wanted to escape to head back towards Canadian lines and ordered the rest to lay down their weapons to spare their lives, hoping the Germans would accommodate.

Gordy Donald briefly contemplated escape, but quickly surmised "it would have been suicide" to try. "They knew they 'had us,'" he recalled. "After the intense pounding we got from the Jerrys, there was no counterattack as such . . . they [just] came into the wheat field very cautiously." And when they did, he dropped his rifle and surrendered.

Bruce Ducat, pinned down just over the crest, saw small groups of prisoners led away under armed guard at irregular intervals as the Germans methodically broke down their fledgling position piecemeal. Farther ahead, a panzer commander, clad head to toe in black, headphones and throat microphone still in place, stood atop his turret, peering into the wheat, scanning the ground for his next victim. Between repeated bursts of directed machine-gun fire, he shouted in surprisingly good English, "Come on, all of you, the war is over for you!" and then made sure his gunner opened fire on any rustle in the grain. For fifteen minutes, he played his torturous game. Finally, after he was fully satisfied with his naked display of power and dominance, he graciously permitted the trapped riflemen to walk into German captivity.

Neither Ducat nor Bennett wanted anything to do with German hospitality, nor did they relish the idea of putting blind faith in the hands of an enemy with his blood lust at a fever pitch. The focus for each man now turned to the job at hand and survival. Both men sensed there was little chance now to snatch victory at the eleventh hour. Unlike the movies he watched on a summer afternoon at the Princess Theatre and the Kiplingesque tales he devoured as a teen, Bennett realized the cavalry was not coming to their rescue. He decided that his best chance lay in a break towards Canadian lines after sunset. He would have to sit motionless for at least eight hours until nightfall, praying that roaming German patrols would miss him or that a passing panzer or half-track would not grind him into the fine Verrières soil. Even after darkness fell, he still had to crawl more than a mile over ground inundated with German and Canadian artillery fire, sown with land mines, tripwires and slit trenches, and studded with German weapons pits, standing patrols and snipers.

Bruce Ducat never had the chance to influence his fate. A German Panther, moving towards the ridge to aid Sterz's *Jagdpanzer* on the crest, lurched to life fifty yards ahead and plunged straight for his position. Sergeant Bill Collister, a fiery redhead whom Ducat had known since childhood, grabbed the PIAT still strapped to his back, swung it around and attempted to load it with the only projectile left in his arsenal. Realizing the firing pin had shot its bolt at some point during his rush up the ridge, Collister flopped on his back, shot his feet in the air and hooked them under the shoulder pad to recock the weapon. In one violent motion, he yanked the tightly wound rod home, ending with its telltale clang. He rolled over and slammed the projectile into the open-topped bomb support. He lined up his target through the back and foresight and, with the panzer just thirty yards away, let loose.

"He missed," Ducat recalled. "The tank didn't."

The blast from the panzer's 75-millimetre high-explosive round killed Collister instantly and flung Ducat skyward, twirling him like a rag doll. "I got completely blown up in the air and then came down on my face and I thought, 'God Almighty, this is it.'" Stunned and heavily concussed from the shell and the collision with the ground, the dazed and bewildered Ducat had to take a few seconds to comprehend the gravity of his situation. The wide-eyed stares of the few men left alive around him told the tale.

"One side of my face [was] completely ripped open; the flesh just peeled back on the right side, it was blackened by the blast. One arm had been broken in two places, and the other had the nerve shot out, so it was completely numb . . . blood was spurting out. The artery had been hit, and the only thing I could think of was the Lord's Prayer. 'Forgive us our trespasses . . .' And I said the Lord's Prayer, and it stopped." Three heavily armed Germans, clad in camouflage smocks, emerged from the grain and surrounded him as he lay on the ground. "Next thing I know, I got a swift boot in the ass from a German officer. I guess he was telling me to get up—I didn't get up fast enough, so I got another boot in the ass. After that, I got up."

Thankful to be alive, but in horrible agony that his German captors seemed in no rush to alleviate, the Black Watch corporal staggered back under armed guard through the wheat, wondering if each step would be his last. Halfway into his journey, with the skin sliced from his face still dangling in the breeze, his captors brought him to a halt in the middle of the field. When one *Panzergrenadier* reached into his pocket, Ducat thought, "Well, that's it." Mercifully, the young German produced a bandage from his pocket, slapped the flailing skin back onto Ducat's cheek, and then wrapped the dressing tightly, turban-like, around his head, leaving only one eye uncovered.

Resuming the journey to the German aid station, Ducat noticed the still-potent might of the German Army in this sector south of Verrières Ridge. Fire trenches, dug in a zigzag pattern, littered the field west of Fontenay, while weapons pits for machine guns lay intertwined with mortars farther back. On the roads, trucks, panzers, motorcycles and armoured cars were parked along hedges, all carefully camouflaged with branches or scrub to conceal them from Allied photo reconnaissance and roving fighter-bombers. Vehicles in the open fields sat piled high with straw to resemble haystacks; ammunition and fuel dumps were tucked in along the shoulder of the old Roman trading route, covered with camouflage netting. Men scurried about in the fields, restocking ammo from horse-drawn wagons, while self-propelled artillery of the 9th SS Panzer Division sidled into position for the coming counterstroke.

The German aid post sat in plain view in a field not far from the Black Watch objective of Fontenay. Next to it, a confiscated French bus draped with a large off-white sheet marked with a giant Red Cross waited to evacuate both wounded and prisoners for treatment and interrogation.

When Gordy Donald arrived, he joined a group of thirty men sitting or lying in various stages of undress, some missing helmets, webbing and even trousers, cut off or otherwise dispensed with to tend to their wounds. All sported bandages soaked with varying shades of crimson. Mac Roulston, lying on a stretcher near the bus, saw Ducat arrive not long after and take his place with the macabre group. Captain John Kemp, his right leg mangled by shell fragments from the knee down and in obvious pain, sat with his fawn balmoral perched firmly on his head. "Name, rank, and number. Don't tell them anything," he barked when Ducat arrived, which earned him a "swift kick" in his torn-up leg from his all too eager teenaged guard. Kemp was rendered unconscious by the excruciating pain.[13]

CAPTAIN SHIRLEY GRIFFIN SPENT THE MORNING AT Megill's new command post in a ruined building north of the crossroads in St. Martin, assembling bits and pieces of information that were pouring in over the wireless and from a litany of runners and liaison officers, as well as Major Torchy Slater. Periodically, Captains Ronnie Bennett and Campbell Stuart arrived at separate intervals giving transitory updates of the menacing situation at the front area and seeking information about the rifle companies. Distressed over the predicament of the regiment and what his friends and his kid brother likely now faced on the ridge, Griffin could do little but pass on the dismal picture to Brigadier Megill. Megill found himself "in limbo," waiting for the issue to resolve itself, when Foulkes and Brigadier Young appeared at his command post.

Foulkes wasted no time laying into Megill, telling him that the corps commander was "furious" with him for failing to reach Fontenay or, at the very least, capture May-sur-Orne. As a direct result, Simonds had now ordered a renewal of the assault that evening in a desperate bid to capture Fontenay by sending the Régiment de Maisonneuve along the same path as the Black Watch.[14] Sensing Megill's hesitation and his less than enthusiastic reception, Foulkes summoned the brigadier to an adjoining room and ripped straight into him.

"Are you disobeying my orders?" Foulkes demanded. Tersely, Megill replied that he was not, but added that he "had lost two battalions as a result of plans . . . laid [down] by division and corps, on information that was inaccurate." Before Foulkes could launch into orbit, Megill quickly added that he was quite prepared to use the Régiment de Maisonneuve if he could make the plan and put it into effect, as he could choose the line of advance "better than anyone else."[15] As Megill put it, Foulkes "hostilely agreed," but admitted "he didn't think much was going to happen" with the assault and departed for his command post with Brigadier Young in tow.[16]

With the Maisonneuves' attack now set for 1900 hours, it became imperative to withdraw both the Calgary Highlanders and whatever remained of the Black Watch to a perimeter in the southern end of St. Martin and the factory area before the artillery supporting the attack crashed down on the ridge. As Ronnie Bennett discovered, Megill's plan called for a short-lived smoke-screen to cover the withdrawal. This allowed enough time for the Calgary Highlanders to withdraw from the northern fringes of May, but precious little for the Black Watch, given that they had almost three times as much ground to cover.[17]

Confusion ensued when the smoke came down just after 1600 hours, and as one Calgary Highlander officer reported, "Some of the [Black Watch] got shot up by ourselves and by a tank on our left flank. They were bringing in some prisoners, and we mistook the party for the enemy."[18] Instead of pulling back into the factory area as ordered, the withdrawing Calgary Highlanders, accompanied by Mackenzie-Wood and a slew of their wounded, went straight back up the road and into St. André, leaving Bennett, Benson, his scouts and the remaining tanks of Powell's B Squadron alone and exposed on a vulnerable salient.

No sooner had Bennett realized his predicament than Benson and the scouts sounded the alarm. A German infantry platoon, likely a reconnaissance element of Zollhöfer's *Kampfgruppe* from the 9th SS, made for the factory. They started an aggressive probe of the Black Watch position. "Jerry did not seem to be in sufficient strength to be planning a serious counterattack," Bennett reported, "but he seemed to know where he was going and intended to get there."[19] Attempting to sow despondency and increase the fear of encirclement in an already reeling enemy, Bennett noted that "Jerry came through the wheat fields . . . in about one platoon strength using the old pepper pot method," firing and moving as they went. Powell, fearing the vulnerability of his tanks to hand-held anti-tank weapons in the wheat, pulled the remnants of his three troops back to the southern end of the churchyard in St. Martin, where he engaged the German patrol with his machine guns. Meanwhile, Bennett used the distraction to pull Benson and his scouts, along with the regimental aid post, back into the fields and farmyards straddling the church in St. Martin. As Bennett noted with satisfaction, "This worked very well, but dusk was closing in, which would soon make the tanks take off, and I was not happy about holding so large an area without them."[20]

Jumping onto a dispatch rider's Norton motorbike, he kicked its 450 cc engine into gear and sped off to brigade tactical head-quarters. There, he found Megill's staff had "a plan drawn up for the Calgarys to hold the southern part of the town, the Camerons to wedge in from the north, and the Black Watch to hold the southeast sector."[21] Looking over the plan, which appeared solid on paper, he noticed it did not conform to the reality faced by his men at the front.

"We spread ourselves extremely thinly over the ground . . . I had thirty men with which to hold the entire eastern sector of the town, which meant one or two men in each orchard . . . This was obviously impossible."[22]

To remedy his precarious situation, Bennett requested per-mission to shrink the Black Watch perimeter into a "collection of two or three houses" across from the church that would "com-mand the sector."[23] Megill agreed and ordered the Calgarys to hold the western and central sectors of the twin towns with their depleted companies while the long-suffering Camerons tightened the grip from the north. Without wireless or line communication, however, "Bennett's commandos," as the press would come to coin them, had to rely on "an elaborate system of defensive fire tasks and report centres" that, Brigade assured, would form the solid base Bennett's band of "odds and sods" would need to fall back upon should things take a nasty turn in St. Martin.[24]

SEVEN DAYS IN HELL

Bennett realized he needed to put Campbell Stuart, who remained out of touch with the fluid situation, back into the picture and round up his surviving carriers to haul the battalion mortars and anti-tank guns to bolster his position in St. Martin.

THROUGHOUT THE MORNING AND EARLY AFTERNOON, Private Bill Booth of the battalion's intelligence section sat pinned by German mortars and 88s in the orchard to the north of St. Martin. The field, now strewn with abandoned and burning vehicles, displayed the destruction wrought by German guns, whose operators possessed an almost perfect view of proceedings south of Caen.

The orchard itself, in full summer bloom just hours before, now lay almost flat, devoid of its thin apple trees, clear-cut by the red-hot shell splinters from the constant pounding of German artillery. What saplings still stood did so limbless, with broken boughs amid a checkerboard of craters of varying sizes and girth that hosted a multitude of abandoned carriers, jeeps, trucks and armoured cars, most with thick shrouds of smoke billowing from their engine compartments or blazing from fuel tanks punctured by shrapnel. The bodies of their crewmen were strewn beside them or had been immolated in the fiery heaps. Their vital cargo— the ammunition, land mines, ration packs and rum, destined for Griffin's companies in Fontenay—had exploded or continued to cook off in the flames, while the vital anti-tank guns and mortars sat horribly mangled from direct hits.

Hours earlier, as Booth lay in the ditch, keeping a keen eye on the crest of the ridge and the crashed British bomber in the field off to the left, German mortar fire arrived just moments after the tanks had departed, with Bennett and the vehicles of the regimental aid post in tow.

"The first mortar rounds—three of them—dropped on the airplane wreckage in the field to the east of the road," Booth remembered. "We guessed that they were either ranging shots or were intended to kill or drive out our snipers." Suddenly, the scrape the young private inhabited appeared far too shallow for his comfort. Booth decided to hollow out a deeper shelter, but struck a thick root that his shovel could not cut. Moving back up the ditch about six feet, he resumed his furious excavation not far from two battalion signallers who "had dug quite a deep trench for themselves."

Across the road, Padre Cecil Royle observed Lieutenant George Buch, who had a reputation for loving his explosives as much as his men, preparing their plastic explosive charges to blast a hole for the regimental aid post when it reached Fontenay.[25] They shared a passing word with Sergeant Fred Janes of the intelligence section. Janes, who found himself serving under the newly minted intelligence officer, Stan Duffield, his former subordinate at the Bank of Montreal in peacetime, had started to dig a slit next to his section carrier but decided the ditch not far from Booth made better sense than beside such an obvious target. As Booth recalled, "He had not been long digging when we heard the approach of a mortar shell. We knew it was coming in on us when the feathery sound it makes when it descends changed to a roar." Royle heard it too, and "in that split-second decision which means the difference between life and death," as he put it, he dove into the carrier, which in hindsight he marked as "truly a foolish thing to do." Janes, not far from Booth, dove into the ditch.

Booth found his nascent slit far too shallow when the round exploded in a blinding flash. He was engulfed by the overpressure and the intense shock wave that followed. He thought "a giant foot had stepped on [his] back and driven the air out of [his] lungs." Royle, face down in the carrier, his feet flailing above, had managed to pull his "tin hat down over [his] ears" when the shell arrived, and he could hear the shrapnel "rattle against the side of the carrier."

Booth looked over to where Janes had started to dig, only to find that "a blackened depression remained." A millisecond later, the "recognizable half" of the intelligence sergeant's corpse crashed back to earth a few yards away. Turning around, Booth found the two signallers, motionless in their trench, "both dead, but not a mark on their bodies." Booth pondered the fickle nature of fate, wondering "if, on the next round, a slight adjustment of the sights on the mortar would have made it a clean sweep?" Shaken by the grisly episode, Royle could not escape the irony, either, as "poor Janes and his friends were lying dead in the ditch and those of us in the carrier survived."

Janes and the signallers would not be the only ones to die in the orchard that morning. As Booth reported, "the Germans had the entire area under observation and made the most of it." Within seconds, they started walking their mortars up and down the ditch and the hedgerow, a terrifying and highly effective tactic that continued at regular intervals throughout the day. The arrival of Campbell Stuart's carrier careening in at breakneck speed, chased and bracketed by 88-millimetre fire, only made matters worse; their shells, a terrified Booth observed, "came in on us with a shriek and a near simultaneous explosion."

By mid-afternoon, Booth noted that a pall of smoke and dust hung over the park, but they received no word about the situation with the rifle companies, nor had anyone stepped up to organize and direct those left in the orchard after Buch moved forward with his carriers.[26] Assessing their dismal situation, Booth and the rest of the intelligence section, including Dollard "Dolly" Lessard and Private Ray Dubuc, decided to make a break for it during a lull in the German firing.

"Lessard, who was a little way down the ditch towards St. André, shouted to me," Booth remembered, "and we both ran across the road to the truck. The driver and Ray Dubuc ran over from their trenches. The steel frame that supported the canvas canopy had been cut in two on one side by shrapnel. Jerry tins of gas had been spilled but had not caught fire. The tires on one side, I remember, had been blown, and there was a large hole in the engine hood, but no critical part had been damaged. We jumped in, the driver floored the accelerator, and we raced up the hill to Fleury-sur-Orne."[27]

WHEN CAPTAIN RONNIE BENNETT ARRIVED IN THE orchard, not long after the German shelling had reaped its own whirlwind, he found Campbell Stuart "with his burning carrier beside him." On this extraordinary day, the Black Watch adjutant had emerged unscathed yet again, save for his throbbing leg, when the 88 rounds finally caught up to his ride moments after he dismounted. This, however, was the only good news; when his carrier went up in flames, it took with it the sole surviving wireless set, instantly severing communications with Brigade, the artillery and the tanks. The loss of the vital equipment quashed any hope of re-establishing contact with Griffin and the rifle companies, who Bennett and Stuart believed lay pinned somewhere on the ridge and in need of rescue.

Bennett, worried about the perimeter he had to hold with the scratch force that remained, sent word by runner back to Ifs, rallying anyone who could walk to grab a rifle and get up to St. Martin to hold ground. Dale Sharpe and Mike Brunner, whom Benson had designated earlier as left out of battle, answered the call immediately and doubled back to St. Martin. Other men, many of whom had not fired a shot in months, let alone in anger, raced up too, shouldering Lee-Enfields, Stens, Brens and any captured German machine guns and machine pistols scooped up along the way. They dutifully answered Bennett's call to hold the farm building across from the church on Shell Alley—the last bastion of the Black Watch.

11

ODDS AND SODS

There are rumours tonight, not entirely confirmed, of large armoured forces assembling on 2nd Canadian Corps front. An attack on our position is held to be not unlikely and is contemplated, in higher circles at least, with satisfaction, however unhappy it might make the fighting men who would bear its brunt.

—2ND CANADIAN FIELD HISTORICAL SECTION[1]

AFTER A WEEK OF CONSTANT FIGHTING, LESS THAN one-tenth of St. Martin stood unscathed. The town, increasingly pounded into a shambles over the last twenty-four hours, was no longer serene. Wood and steel splinters that had been torn from houses, fences and sheds lay everywhere. A thick coat of red brick dust covered the ground, sprinkled with thousands of spent bullet casings. The massive iron gates barring access to courtyards swung aimlessly, riddled and pockmarked by shrapnel. Everywhere, doors hung grotesquely from their frames while the singed and tattered curtains of blown-out windows fluttered in the breeze.

Along Shell Alley, a line of blackened trees and dismembered stumps interwoven with abandoned jeeps and burned-out carriers paved the way to the collection of vernacular stone farmhouses Bennett selected as their bastion. "We held three gardens, a large L-shaped house and a barn connected to the house with a smaller

ST. ANDRÉ · HILL 67 · CROSSROADS · THE "FACTORY" · HILL 61 · THE CHURCHYARD · BLACK WATCH FORM-UP POINT (FUP)

This photo, taken from the northernmost end of May-sur-Orne, shows the rubble (on the far right) where Lieutenant William Mackenzie-Wood took refuge during the assault up Verrières after he was wounded. DEPARTMENT OF NATIONAL DEFENCE

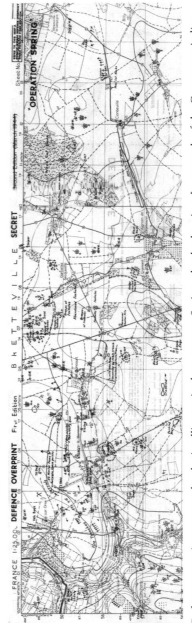

Defence overprint put together by intelligence in the run-up to Spring, clearly showing the strength of the German main line of resistance on the reverse slope of Verrières Ridge, leading to the Black Watch objective of Fontenay-le-Marmion. DEPARTMENT OF NATIONAL DEFENCE

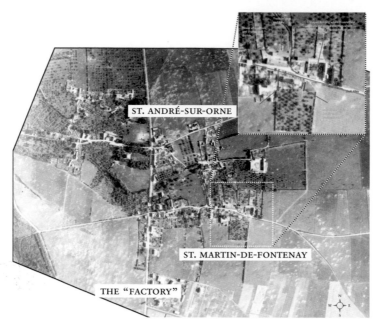

Aerial photograph of the "twin towns" of St. André and St. Martin, taken days before the battle engulfed the area. The "factory" is visible to the south, as is the arrow-straight road that led from the crossroads in St. Martin to May-sur-Orne to the south. LCMDS

A cutaway of the photograph of the twin towns, focusing on St. Martin. Note the church, surrounding orchards and the farmyard with the L-shaped house that formed the bastion for Captain Ronnie Bennett's "odds and sods" when they made their stand against elements of Kampfgruppe Zollhöfer from the 9th SS Panzer Division. LCMDS

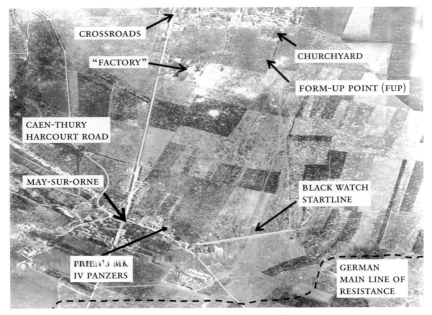

CROSSROADS

"FACTORY"

CHURCHYARD

FORM-UP POINT (FUP)

CAEN-THURY
HARCOURT ROAD

MAY-SUR-ORNE

BLACK WATCH
STARTLINE

PRIEN'S MK
IV PANZERS

GERMAN
MAIN LINE OF
RESISTANCE

Aerial photo taken after the battle, showing the vast scarring of the stretch of land that comprised the Black Watch axis of advance during their ill-fated assault on Fontenay-le-Marmion. LCMDS

Above: This photo, taken of British troops earlier in the Normandy campaign, gives a good idea of the type of terrain the Black Watch had to fight through on their way up Verrières Ridge. IWM, B-6119

Left: A Canadian soldier from the 3rd Canadian Division, waiting for H-hour in Phase II of Operation Spring, displays the typical load carried by the men in the Black Watch rifle companies. LAC, PA-163403

Left to right: Captain Shirley Griffin, an intelligence officer and the brother of A Company commander Major Phillip Griffin; twenty-two-year-old Lieutenant William Mackenzie-Wood, who arrived as a reinforcement platoon officer seventy-two hours before the attack up Verrières Ridge; and Lieutenant Alan Robinson, who took command of A Company when Griffin took the reins of the battalion. BWA

Left to right: The battalion adjutant, Captain Campbell Stuart, who fought all day on a broken leg; Captain John Taylor, who took command of B Company after the Orne crossing; and Captain John Kemp, an officer with a mercurial temper, who kept his father's Great War Colt .45 pistol stitched into a secret pocket inside his battledress tunic. BWA

Corporal Bruce "Duke" Ducat (*left*) from B Company and Private William "Bill" Booth from the intelligence section attached to battalion headquarters. BWA, Ducat and Booth families

Captain Edwin Ronald "Ronnie" Bennett, the support company commander who jumped into the breach and took command of the remnants of the battalion when the rifle companies disappeared on Verrières Ridge. A young lawyer by profession, he was the nephew of the former Canadian prime minister R.B. Bennett. BWA

Left to right: Lieutenant Stan Duffield, scout platoon commander, who would earn the Military Cross for his courage in the last weeks of the war; Lieutenant John "Jock" McLennan, who at six foot four towered over the entire battalion; and Lieutenant George "Booby Trap" Buch, the pioneer platoon commander. BWA

Major Werner Sterz, who commanded Kampfgruppe Sterz of the veteran 2nd Panzer Division, and his panzer commander, Lieutenant Peter Prien, who watched the Black Watch form up for the attack from his position in May-sur-Orne. DIDIER LODIEU

C Company commander Eric Motzfeldt, the "Great Dane," who spoke five languages fluently and acted as Cantlie's battle adjutant. He and Phil Griffin were widely considered to be the best of the Black Watch company commanders. BWA

Lieutenant Colonel S.S.T. Cantlie had served in the regiment since he was a teenaged cadet. An RMC graduate, Cantlie was on the fast track for a staff position to high command when he took the reins of the battalion for the second time in 1944. BWA

Major Phil Griffin, A Company commander, who took over command of the battalion after Cantlie's death and Motzfeldt's wounding and led them up Verrières Ridge on the morning of July 25, 1944. BWA AND GRIFFIN FAMILY

Major Otto Meyer from the 9th SS Panzer Division (*left*), who led Kampfgruppe Meyer, and Major Emil Zollhöfer, who commanded Kampfgruppe Zollhöfer, which hemmed the remnants of the Black Watch into the farmyard in St. Martin.

BUNDESARCHIV, BILD 146-1985-036-08, AND ARCHIV WOLFGANG VOPERSAL, BUNDESARCHIV-MILITÄRARCHIV

Dr. Rudy Ohkle (*left*), the Black Watch medical officer who continually risked his life to treat the vast majority of the battalion's wounded in the forward areas, and Captain Gordon Powis, FOO with the 5th Canadian Field Regiment, who took command of what was left of the battalion after the death of Major Phil Griffin.

GORDON OHKLE AND MCGILL ARCHIVES 0000-0481.04.430

Just some of the more than a thousand artillery pieces that opened fire as Operation Spring kicked off on July 25, 1944. LAC, PA-166804

Storm boats with Evinrude outboard motors attached, similar to those used by the Black Watch during the Orne crossing on the night of July 18–19, 1944. JOHN SLIZ

barn," Bennett noted. Although the building had taken its share of the damage, its thick fieldstone walls and concave windows came as close to a fortress as one could find in the ravaged town.

Much had changed in the farmyard since Teddy Neill had herded the German prisoners into it nearly twelve hours earlier. At the north end, only part of the barn remained, its roof holed by a shell. A dead cow, swarmed by flies, gave off a pungent and vile stench. Overturned and demolished furniture lay everywhere in the main building, which was strewn with discarded uniforms, equipment and weapons that belonged to both sides. The shards of smashed household crockery lay mixed in with books and scattered magazines, overturned lamps and ripped wallpaper. In another corner, partially uneaten campo rations indicated that either Canadian or German soldiers had broken bread at one point during the week in an all too infrequent respite from the fighting.

A Black Watch jeep, missing tires and its spare, sat next to a carrier apparently in pristine condition, surrounded by empty jerry cans but missing its crew. On the road out front, the battered tower of the church overlooked a hedge lined with Canadian dead pulled from the wheat field and the factory area. Padre Royle moved down the line, methodically confirming identities where possible from the red discs, pay books or, when necessary or when in doubt, a witness statement. He scrawled their names, ranks and service numbers, followed by the suffix KIA, on a growing stack of white chits. He lamented, "Never, never, never, had a day been so long . . . I felt I had lived not one day, but one thousand years."[2]

Bennett's scratch unit was a motley affair, to say the least. In addition to his 2ic, Neill, Benson and his scouts, and Buch and his pioneers, he scrounged up two quartermaster sergeants, Red Langford and Jack McInnes; a cook, Private Albert Johnson; a driver, Private Albert Reed; and Private Clair Atherley, a shoemaker who had just arrived to replace Private Bleau, who had been killed at the abbey ten days before. With the padre and the medics of the regimental aid post, a quick count of Bennett's odds and sods put his full complement at "about 50 with many weapons, especially Brens and 3 MG42s"—all that the proud regiment could muster.

The arrival of Sharpe and Brunner came as a welcome surprise to Benson, as four of his scouts who'd acted as stretcher-bearers had yet to return. Thomas Edgar and Tommy Latham—who had revenge for his brother's death on his mind—who had ventured out into the wheat to collect the wounded, the dying and the dead, had disappeared. Likewise, Arthur Bowmaster and Harold Burden—the division's middleweight champ—who had hauled out several men from D Company and had gone back for more, failed to make it back by the time the sun began to set.

Bennett relied now on the scout platoon, along with Buch's pioneers, as the only combat-tried veterans available. He parcelled out his snipers in teams to each of the three buildings, expecting they would provide the backbone of the defence of his impromptu citadel.

Young Hook, Balsis, Delutis and Pugh took up positions in the loft of the barn across from the church, where they would use the perforations through the roof that had been made by shell fragments and bullets. They would have a clear line of sight to any movement on the ridge. Benson distributed the rest of his snipers among the houses on both sides of the farmyard to protect the sentries and to prevent surprise. Hook Wilkinson took Syd Ayling, Paul Welligan and Jackie Jack to the west, setting up shop in the fieldstone dwelling on the other side of the hedge that lined the westernmost part of the farmyard. On the eastern fringe, Dale Sharpe and Mike Brunner, aided by a pair of Buch's pioneers, held the ruins of the house to the east, in the courtyard where Griffin had delivered his fateful orders hours earlier. Benson, making the rounds to shore up holes in the perimeter, found Brunner and Sharpe and tossed them a bandolier of rifle ammunition, a set of grenades and a canteen of rum and said, "You're going to need these. We might get a counterattack. You're the left flank."

Although the Black Watch perimeter was smaller than initially assigned, plenty of gaps still existed in the walls surrounding the farm and needed immediate attention, but Bennett remained "happy in the thought" that three companies from the other battalions stood close by, "ready to support us."

Bennett then divvied up his collection of Bren guns and captured MG 42s. He placed the majority around the farmyard to cover any apparent approaches, but maintained a pair of Brens to act as a mobile reserve ready to rush to any threatened location when summoned. With insufficient firepower to cover the entire sector, he relied heavily on CSM Peter Young to provide real-time communication from an observation post installed in the loft between the sniper teams. From this perch, Young would relay enemy movements to Bennett, stationed a floor below, permitting him to adjust his fire and rush his meagre reserve to a threatened flank at a moment's notice.

Throughout the farmyard, men worked briskly and frantically to ready for the coming storm. They set up obstacles and booby traps and dug slits in the courtyards to act as shelters from artillery. Buch's pioneers quipped in distinctive gallows humour that the shelters were "ready-made graves."

The men cleared lines of sight and buttressed their fire positions by punching holes into walls, roofs and fences; stripping timber from ceiling beams and walls for extra cover; and jimmying cupboards and doors from their hinges to place over windows or any visible opening that was sure to draw German fire.

They smashed windowpanes and tore plaster from walls to prevent flying glass and clouds of choking dust from impeding their performance in the upcoming fight. To provide protection inside, they disconnected gas stoves, overturned dining room tables and sofas, and filled cedar credenzas, steamer trunks and even a stand-up piano packed with earth to act as makeshift barriers against a rogue enemy grenade or shell. To fight the potential of fires, they scrounged anything that could hold water or dirt. Buckets, wash basins, toilets, pots, bedpans, discarded German helmets and even an uprooted bathtub came to the rescue.

To aid movement and maintain voice communication, they burrowed mouse holes between interior walls and smashed openings in the floors with their picks to create a break large enough to shout orders through—or, in desperate times, drop grenades down upon an unwelcome intruder.

Medical officer Dr. Rudy Ohkle, aided by Padre Royle and a set of cooks doubling as medics, set up a triage centre amidst the stalls in the cellar of the long barn, ready to tend to casualties from the impending fight or stragglers from the ridge they hoped would appear at any moment.

Buch and CSM Bob Jackson feverishly laid anti-tank mines and daisy chains of Hawkins grenades at choke points along the roads to ambush approaching panzers. Then they set booby traps in ditches and gaps in the wall on either side to foil their infantry support. Although Bennett possessed an impressive cache of weapons, given the size of the force, he had only one PIAT, and it had a faulty spring and no ammunition, which left Buch's defensive artistry as their only safeguard against armour.

Before they could catch their collective breath and Benson could finish his rounds, CSM Young raised the alarm. The *Kampfgruppen* of the 9th SS had arrived.

CSM Young and the sniper teams could see Otto Meyer's

panzers and half-tracks skirting the ridgeline off to their left, making for Verrières village at top speed. To the right, coming down the road from May, they spotted a sizable contingent of Zollhöfer's *Panzergrenadiers* in their distinctive SS pea-dot uniforms, brazenly moving in the open to swarm into the southern reaches of the twin towns. More alarming, the grain in the wheat field dead ahead now shimmered like a breaking wave making for the shore. The Hohenstaufen men reoccupied the factory area in seconds without a shot fired.

Having no line or wireless communication, Bennett stood helpless, unable to call down artillery and mortar fire on Zollhöfer's men. Near Verrières village, however, Meyer's *Kampfgruppe* ran into a maelstrom of the combined firepower from dug-in infantry, anti-tank guns and hull-down tanks, all backed by artillery and rocket-firing Typhoons.

THE ROYAL HAMILTON LIGHT INFANTRY'S DEFENCE OF the village was a textbook example of what should have occurred had the Black Watch reached Fontenay in good order earlier that day. From their vantage point in the loft, CSM Young and snipers witnessed a spectacular visual display on the ridge ahead with red, green, orange and gold tracers darting back and forth as the RHLI clung desperately to Verrières village. Every few minutes, a mushroom cloud of flame and smoke billowed high from an exploding panzer or half-track, testifying to the deadly fire from the Canadian anti-tank screen. Expecting that he would quickly roll up the Canadian line, Meyer's panzers suffered in a deadly crossfire compounded by the Sherman tanks from C Squadron of the Hussars and the Typhoons swooping in from above. Meyer, realizing his panzers had run into an immovable roadblock, called off his attack at 1750 hours, reporting that "whoever crosses the ridge is a dead man." With his effort permanently checked, he swung his support behind Zollhöfer, who intended to drive the Canadians back beyond St. Martin, steamrolling them past the high ground to the north and hopefully back to Caen.

The only temporary break in Zollhöfer's stride came with the sudden appearance of the Régiment de Maisonneuve, who arrived in the field south of the crossroads to shake out for their attack on Fontenay. Sub-units from Schack's 272nd, still hanging on in small pockets, sent up an emergency SOS—"Where is Zollhöfer?"—not realizing the Hohenstaufen men had noticed the development too and now lay in wait for the Maisies to make their assault.

Unaware of the SS presence, the Maisonneuve attack went in as scheduled at 1900 hours. From the factory, Zollhöfer watched the Canadian rifle companies advance unmolested past his position before he opened fire on them from behind. In less than an hour of murderous combat, the Maisies' attack came to a grinding halt with horrific casualties, and Simonds's renewed bid for the ridge collapsed.

For Bennett and the men who lay behind the farmyard walls, the unintentional sacrifice of the Maisonneuves brought a brief respite and much-needed breathing room. Instead of pushing on immediately, Zollhöfer chose to infiltrate small units into the streets of St. Martin as darkness fell, with an eye towards isolating the farmyard, which he planned to tackle at dawn. In the interim, he continued to harass Bennett's men with sniper fire, which knocked out Lieutenant Teddy Neill. Although the medics reached him quickly and lashed off his wound after a bullet severed his femoral artery, he went into shock and needed immediate attention from the surgeons at the field hospital on the banks of the Orne. Realizing they could not save his life in the farmyard, a cook and a baker volunteered to make the perilous run back to

Fleury, carrying the stricken Neill strapped to the only stretcher they could find—a farm door jimmied off its hinges—for the mile-long run. The trio made it through, but Neill did not have long to live. The young officer, who had joined the Black Watch as a private in 1940 and had been commissioned from the ranks, a distinct rarity in the regiment, never stabilized. Unresponsive even after shock therapy, he failed to regain consciousness and died, his body buried in a temporary plot alongside Cantlie near a walled garden overlooking the bend in the Orne near Fleury.

IN AND AROUND THE FARMYARD, HOLLOW-EYED HIGH-landers, who by now had gone a week without proper sleep and had long since expended their supply of Benzedrine, found fatigue a more daunting and immediate enemy than the Germans. Thoughts and time blurred; men started to drift off. Overcome by exhaustion, they willingly risked death at the hands of the SS for the sake of a few minutes of rest.

Following Bennett's orders, Hook Wilkinson, Syd Ayling, Paul Welligan and Jackie Jack moved into a large fieldstone dwelling no more than fifty yards to the west of the farmyard down Shell Alley. They passed a pair of Black Watch carriers—abandoned earlier, during the clearing of the route—that lay in the courtyard outside the main door. They conducted a quick check for German occupants and booby traps before seeking respite from their exhaustion in the cellar. Worn out from multiple trips to recover the wounded and the dead from the factory and the wheat field, Hook ordered Welligan to stand guard in the upstairs window.

Descending into the grimy cellar using his Ronson to light the way, Hook's boots gave off a voluble ripping sound from coagulated rivulets of blood trickled across the stairs. As Hook recalled, the sound "would have woken the dead." At the bottom of the short staircase, the trio encountered a pile of discarded German field dressing packages, soiled bandages and stained brown gauze spread amongst a collection of empty bottles of rubbing alcohol and wine, half-eaten apple cores and crushed vials of medicinal cocaine, paraffin and adrenalin. "In the back of the basement," Hook noted with disgust, "there was a German stretched out on the table. He stunk; he was dead for I don't know how long." Too tired to remove yet another body and fearful of booby traps, the men curled up in the far corner of the cellar, hoping to sleep their own "sleep of the dead." No sooner had they drifted off, however, than Welligan busted down the stairs, alerting them that a sizable SS patrol had just entered the grounds, making for the house.

Still nauseous from the abrupt rousing and regretting the moment he surrendered to exhaustion, Hook and his fellow snipers propped a large steel plate against the cellar door as a makeshift barrier just as the stomping of German boots trampled past on the floor above their heads. Taking shelter in the darkness behind the stairs, each man at the ready, they anxiously waited as the thumping reached the cellar door. "Any second," Hook thought, "I expected a bloody German grenade would come bouncing down the stairs and we'd be goners." While his fellow snipers relieved themselves of any trinkets "liberated" from German dead or prisoners that would give the SS cause for retribution, Hook remained fixed on the door, firm in his decision that if the enemy penetrated the barricade, surrender would not be an option.

BY MID-EVENING, SERGEANT JACK MCINNES HAD ARRIVED at the farmhouse for what seemed the tenth time in just the last few hours. Working under orders from Campbell Stuart, who remained north of the town, the battalion orderly clerk relayed much-needed supplies of water, ammunition, bandages, and what rations and rum he could scrounge from the carnage in the orchard to the men trapped in the farmyard. Unable to take a carrier or jeep laden with stores through the tiny streets for fear of hitting a land mine or drawing fire from 88s and mortars still lurking in the distance, each journey on foot became increasingly dangerous since lead elements of Zollhöfer's unit had infiltrated the town. Forced to weave in and out of lanes and ditches, crawl through gardens and sprint past gaps in hedges to reach the farmhouse, the wily sergeant narrowly escaped death and capture, making it back alive each time to offset rapidly dwindling stocks in the meagre arsenal in the farmhouse.

When McInnes returned to the orchard on his final run just after dusk, he discovered Stuart lying on the ground not far from his blazing carrier, the victim of an 88 round. A pair of dispatch riders had discovered the Black Watch adjutant, still breathing but in critical condition, in the moments after his legendary luck had run out. While one zoomed back on his Norton motorbike to fetch a jeep ambulance, the other attached tourniquets to Stuart's thighs just above the knees on both legs shredded by the blast. The quick action by two men whose names Stuart never discovered saved his life and one of his legs. The other leg, the fractured one he had fought on all day, required amputation once he reached the field hospital at Fleury-sur-Orne.

BACK AT THE FARMHOUSE, AN UNEASY STANDOFF HAD developed by the time light faded on July 25. Zollhöfer's stormtroopers had used the cover of darkness to creep into position on the southern edge of the churchyard, and had tucked in so close to the Black Watch lines on the farm that they could not call in mortar fire for fear of hitting their own men. Satisfied nonetheless, the *Panzergrenadiers* from the 9th SS settled in for the night, ready to resume the fight with Bennett's Black Watch band at first light.

From the farmyard, Bennett and his men could hear the battle raging around Verrières village several miles away, and the artillery pounding German lines on and behind the ridge in a display that eclipsed the expenditure of shells that Montgomery had dished out two years before at El Alamein.[3]

Once again, the Luftwaffe launched an air strike that hit Canadian gun positions around Caen just before midnight in the largest German air attack since the invasion had begun almost eight weeks earlier. Once again, flares fluttered to illuminate targets, this time near the stadium in Caen and the château used by the Black Watch seven days earlier during the Orne crossing. While the exhausted service corps personnel, who had dumped one thousand rounds for each artillery piece in Foulkes's division earlier that day, sat watching the film *One Dangerous Night*, German intruder aircraft swooped down to bomb and strafe.

Nothing stirred on the immediate Black Watch front, however. As Ronnie Bennett noted, "The worst part [came] when we had six hours of absolute quiet [as] it was really eerie waiting for something to happen."

The men cleaned weapons, rechecked ammunition stocks, primed grenades or found a spot to relieve themselves to ease the mounting tension. Some, if they still had any, lit up smokes or tracked down a splash of rum or bit of chocolate McInnes had brought their way. Any of the chatting between men mostly centred on what they would do when they got home, or at least out of their present predicament. All, however, battled with fatigue, as very few could sleep despite levels of near-paralytic exhaustion. Some did catch a few moments of restless sleep, interrupted at 0300 hours when, as Bennett put it, "Jerry . . . started to play tricks."

At that moment, Zollhöfer decided to increase the pressure on the Black Watch and embarked on a spirited exercise in psychological warfare calculated to draw tighter the already overstretched nerves of his Canadian foes.

For the next hour, the SS *Kampfgruppe* commander ran a single tank up and down behind the ridge, to give the impression that his entire 20,000-man division had begun to arrive in the area.[4] To increase the effect, which Bennett recognized immediately as a ruse, Zollhöfer "kept his men shouting as if to imitate a whole battalion." Not long after, three Panther tanks clanked up the road overlooking the farmyard one hundred yards to the east and fired several softening-up rounds into the Black Watch positions. "They did no damage," Bennett reported, "except to our peace of mind."

A few hours earlier, Dempsey had summoned Simonds to his headquarters once again following the failure of his second attempt to seize the ridge. Thoroughly convinced now of the futility of continuing the push, he shut Spring down, telling Simonds to "hold where he is, hold all ground gained, and carry out no further attacks without reference to me."[5] As a result, orders came down the line for the Calgary and Cameron Highlanders, the Régiment de Maisonneuve and the Black Watch to pull back to the northern fringe of the twin towns to take up defensive positions along the ridge connecting Hills 61 and 67.

Bennett never received the message. Perhaps the mounting travails that McInnes encountered getting to and from the farmyard should have alerted Bennett to their increasingly precarious situation, but instead the acting Black Watch CO remained blissfully ignorant, confident that if hard-pressed, he could fall back on a solid base that by midnight, unbeknownst to him, had ceased to exist.

THE PROBE OF THE BLACK WATCH PERIMETER BY THE Panthers, coupled with overnight rain and hazy conditions, put every man in the farmyard on high alert near dawn in anticipation of a German counterattack. For close to two hours, every eye strained through telescopes, binoculars or sniper scopes, peering into the ground fog, hoping to pick out the first indication of a German move.

Near 0730, when the mist began to burn off and lift, sounds of growling panzer engines brought the Black Watch positions to life. From the loft in the barn, Benson and his two sniper teams, along with CSM Young, caught sight of three Panthers, heavily camouflaged with brush and tree branches, rumbling out of the factory and heading directly for the farm. Two platoons of *Panzergrenadiers* accompanied the panzers. Some rode on the Panther's engine grille, huddled up behind the turret, while the rest approached on foot.

Because ammunition was limited, Bennett had ordered the men to hold their fire until presented with a prime target and at short range. Barney Benson, having learned from his experience in May, watched patiently as the SS men sauntered into the churchyard not more than fifteen yards from his position. Likely fuelled by a potent mixture of amphetamines, adrenalin and alcohol, "they came in shouting, hollering and calling," Benson reported. One platoon of Zollhöfer's *Panzergrenadiers* peeled off towards the graveyard spot where Cantlie and Motzfeldt had fallen a day earlier. Part of the other platoon, riding on the backs of the panzers, moved around to the east, where Mike Brunner, Dale Sharpe and a handful of Buch's pioneers sat on picket duty in the house in the sunken courtyard. All three Panthers, creeping along, flanking the farmyard, dropped off pairs of camouflage-clad SS grenadiers every twenty yards in what Benson suspected was an attempt to seal off escape routes and trap his men before the main attack went in.[6]

The sniper teams in the loft tracked every move through the holes and cracks in the roof while CSM Young calmly relayed their progress through a hole in the floor to Bennett below. Content to let the SS overextend themselves, Bennett waited for a few excruciatingly long moments, and then barked his order to open fire. Jackson, getting the word, nodded to Benson and he in turn unleashed his scouts.

Flashes and retorts from scoped .303s rang out from the loft as the Black Watch snipers found their marks, "picking off the odd one," as Bennett recalled. Their accurate and deadly fire forced the SS to scatter behind a hedge rigged with Buch's booby traps. More *Panzergrenadiers* fell. In the confusion, one accompanying Panther, devoid of its infantry shield, failed to spot the daisy chain of Hawkins grenades slung across the road.[7] The corresponding blast severed the treads under the front sprocket wheels and immediately rendered the panzer immobile.[8] The crew, no doubt fearing an impending second hit and a "brew up," or perhaps a swarming mob of bloodthirsty Highlanders, slithered out of the hatches and fled on foot, leaving the abandoned panzer for the salvage teams to rescue.

While CSM Young continued to scan the countryside for other German units closing in on their positions, Benson kept an eye on the few Germans who survived the opening fusillade and had taken cover behind a large hedge. Soon they crawled back to the top and readied, as Bennett termed it, to make "a rather stupid attempt to attack us from that side."[9]

Dale Sharpe and Mike Brunner spotted the same group a few

seconds earlier, but failed to register a shot when the scattering SS grenadiers disappeared behind the hedge, in the grass. Now, however, they spotted them when they sprang back into action and made their headlong rush over the hedge and through a neighbouring field towards the duo's hide in the sunken courtyard. In his perch, CSM Young, watching this unfold, waited until the Germans enfiladed themselves before he gave the order to unleash the massed machine guns. In seconds, thousands of searing-hot rounds from the collection of Brens and captured MG 42s tore into the German squad, ripping off limbs, shattering skulls, slashing bowels and dropping nearly the entire platoon in one fusillade. The few *Panzergrenadiers* who survived managed to scramble back behind the hedge and into cover, where Benson noted with dismay that "without mortars to tackle them," the Black Watch could not go in for the kill.[10]

This triumph proved momentary, as one of the Panthers suddenly appeared right in front of the house occupied by Brunner and Sharpe. The first 75-millimetre high-explosive round it fired at point-blank range cleaved the front facing of the building right off, and the two snipers found themselves on the run. Darting through the rubble and out the back door, the pair raced through a garden, down a ditch and through a gap in a hedge to another farmhouse a short distance away. The farmhouse had been partly crushed by a Sherman tank that lay in the collapsed half of the structure, knocked out.

Brunner and Sharpe wasted little time jumping into the rubble before diving into the cellar just as the panzer clanked into view. "Luckily for us, the knocked-out Sherman grabbed the panzer's attention," Brunner recalled. "He put four or five shells into it as we made our escape into the basement." Like Hook and the others trapped on the other side of the farmyard, Sharpe and Brunner found themselves in a makeshift field dressing station alongside three decomposing bodies of South Saskatchewan men killed days earlier. Brunner wondered if they'd be next. Then, as quickly as this developed, everything went silent for the next hour as the two Panthers withdrew, leaving the infantry screen surrounding the farmyard. CSM Young spotted another push forming up, this time from the opposing flank. Bennett rushed his mixed team of eight MG 42s and Brens to the wall in the south-west corner, with McInnes trailing the pack, pouches filled with Bren magazines, belts of ammunition draped around his neck and boxes of MG 42 ammunition in each hand. In seconds, the cooks, drivers, signallers, bakers, pipers, drummers and clerks kicked the bipods down and had set up their guns to unleash another broadside into the SS.

"My guys aren't supposed to have much firsthand experience in battle," Bennett boasted, "but I never asked for men to act more coolly than they did."[11]

Bennett's men, armed and ready, tracked the German platoon as it broke from cover in a clumsy attempt to move through the wheat in a wide circle. When the SS men appeared in an open expanse in the middle of the field, Bennett's massed machine guns opened up, slicing through the wheat as easily as they did through flesh, tissue and bone. All but four of their targets went down, while the rest managed to squirm away amidst the screams, misery and confusion.

Before the barrels of their weapons had a chance to cool, Young bellowed out yet again, pointing down Shell Alley towards the crossroads in the centre of St. Martin. Working their way up the road, yet another SS platoon closed in on the farm, leapfrogging past the house where Hook and the other snipers remained trapped. Unable this time to get all his machine guns into position, Bennett's men failed to dole out the same volume of punishing fire, but brought down enough to halt their advance after a few of

Zollhöfer's men managed to breach the west end of the barn. In a nasty, close-quarters fight, the Highlanders rooted them out in no time flat, which brought the third SS assault on the farmyard in just over an hour to an end, just as Black Watch ammunition started to run out.[12]

DOWN IN THE CELLAR, HOOK, JACK, WELLIGAN AND Ayling had listened intently when the firing started and the floor above them suddenly came to life. Not sure if the Germans had discovered them and were making a rush to the cellar, Hook and the others gripped their weapons tighter, pointed at the door and took aim—"ready," as Hook succinctly put it, "to take as many of the bastards with us as we could."

The stampede above, although furious, proved brief. To their great relief, the SS *Panzergrenadiers* shot past the cellar and out the main door into the courtyard. Hook and his fellow scouts remained perplexed by the sudden scuttling up above but suspected the worst had befallen the men in the farmyard. For several minutes nobody spoke and nobody moved, until Hook broached a less than subtle escape plan.

Looking over at Ayling, he asked, "How many carriers outside?"

"Two, I think," answered Ayling.

"Okay, you and Jack take one. Welligan and I will take the other. Ready?" As Hook admitted, "It was not the most cunning plan," but the group cared little, as they did not relish sitting tight any longer, hoping that the storm would lift on its own.

Without missing a beat, they sprang into action, removing the steel plate blocking the cellar door. Hook popped his head out to make sure no SS remained in the house. Satisfied they had fled, he waved his fellow snipers forward. One by one they emerged from the cellar, each squinting in the bright sunshine that filled the house. After a cautious slither through the kitchen and into the main foyer, they arrived at the front door, where, after a cursory glance in each direction, they darted out into the garden and leaped into the carriers.

In their impetuousness, none had considered the state of the vehicles. Were they gassed up? Would they start? To their horror, neither fired up at the first try, leaving all with a sinking feeling of despair and dread. Then, after a series of furious attempts and plenty of cursing, both engines roared to life in unison. With a hefty jerk, both carriers were off, plowing through a fence and a series of hedges before reaching open ground and the safety of the new Canadian lines north of town.

Their abrupt exit from the battle, although wholly understandable in the swirling fog of war, was a potentially fatal mistake. With nothing to stand in their way, it left the western flank of the farm wide open to a renewed German attack.

ZOLLHÖFER, FRUSTRATED BY THREE FAILED ATTEMPTS to dislodge Bennett's men from the farmyard, decided to employ his firepower rather than manpower to bring the Highlanders to heel. Pulling his men back into their positions ringing the town, he sent the two remaining Panthers back to rearm and refuel, and brought up machine guns and mortars to pound and harass the Black Watch.

For Bennett, their sudden appearance proved nothing more than a nuisance, as he countered with a quick redeployment of his tiny force. But soon, fire erupted from the area Hook and the scouts had just vacated. As Bennett noted, "This did not encourage me."[13] Believing the rest of St. Martin to be in Canadian hands, he ordered Barney Benson to contact the

Calgary Highlanders and the Camerons to see if they had come under attack as well.

With nobody to spare, Benson had to go it alone. Crawling out of the farmyard on his stomach through a gap in the hedge, the scout platoon sergeant slunk along a series of ditches but did not get far before he found himself surrounded. "Two Jerrys passed me noisily," he reported, "and I stayed down by the sides of the road until they passed." Sitting tight until the Germans moved out of earshot, he crawled forward again, this time more cautiously, but he found no one in the area, friend or foe.

Continuing to push northward, Benson finally stumbled into a Camerons observation post, whose startled sentries informed him that their tactical headquarters had pulled out the night before and had moved farther up the road, past the orchard. Realizing that the Black Watch sat alone, exposed on a fragile salient, surrounded on three sides by the SS and separated from Canadian lines by more than half a mile of no man's land, the scout platoon sergeant returned immediately through the labyrinth of ruined houses, muddied fields, inundated ditches and SS posts and patrol to deliver the dire news to Bennett.

By the time he arrived back at the barn, Benson noted that "Jerry had posted snipers on all [of the] buildings surrounding the farmyard and was harassing us with fire."[14] Without wireless communications, but now fully aware of their desperate situation, Bennett decided to run the gauntlet in an effort to find brigade headquarters and impress upon them the urgency of the Black Watch's plight. Leaving Buch in charge, he followed Benson's route and found, like the scout platoon sergeant, that "the Hun was all through the town," but thankfully, for the moment, "not in strength." Crawling through St. Martin, Bennett squeezed past German pickets parcelled out and managed to find brigade headquarters. Upon arrival, he learned that Megill was in the midst of planning for the Régiment de Maisonneuve to clear the town, but that it would take four more hours before Lieutenant Colonel Lefort Bisaillon's battered battalion could reach the farm. Given what had transpired so far on this horrific day, Bennett remained highly skeptical that any promised help from Brigade would come to fruition, let alone arrive on time and on target. With little confidence that his men could successfully hold off the SS without reinforcements or a proper replenishment of food, ammunition, water and medical supplies, he urged Brigade to move fast before it became a "sticky job" later in the day. Unmoved, Brigade staff told the Black Watch support company commander to hold out until relief came. Convinced that both time and the luck of his men would run out in the interim, Bennett raced back down through the gauntlet to rejoin his "odds and sods" in the farmyard, only to find when he returned that the fighting, as he feared, had flared up yet again.[15]

The first salvo caught George Buch standing next to a jeep, peppering the severely myopic pioneer platoon commander with minuscule slivers of shrapnel up and down his legs, back and arm, which required medical attention from Ohkle, but not evacuation. The blast shattered Buch's only pair of eyeglasses, and as such rendered him effectively blind and, in his own estimation, "thoroughly useless" to anyone in the farmyard.[16]

From the loft of the barn, CSM Young continued, as he had all morning, to direct the Black Watch fire with determination and steadfast courage, even while exposed to increasing levels of enemy machine-gun, mortar and sniper fire. When Bennett returned, Young shouted down from his perch that, since his departure, things had become "distinctly warm."[17]

During Bennett's absence, Zollhöfer's mortars had spent the good part of the intervening hour "pitching bombs into the garden." Bennett also noticed a lone German machine gun on the high ground on the ridge who had kept his men under constant fire, "noisily throwing lead over our heads."[18]

The steady trickle of casualties that filled the lower extremities of the barn, where Dr. Rudy Ohkle and Padre Royle had frantically patched the wounded, concerned Bennett, as did the waning supply of ammunition. In the absence of anything close to surgical facilities, the severely wounded stood little chance of survival unless evacuated immediately. This meant bargaining with the devil during a brief lull to permit stretcher-bearers to pass unmolested, always a dicey proposition at best, particularly amidst the fighting. Yet, for a reason that defied proper explanation, a bizarre dynamic developed between Zollhöfer's SS *Panzergrenadiers* and the Black Watch.[19]

"It was curious, really," George Buch recalled. "The Germans, as Churchill said, were either licking your boots or at your throat, and the SS seemed to respect us more the harder we fought. They actually acted 'humane.' Given what we learned about them earlier, that was a pleasant surprise, but they were SS, so we knew it only went so far."[20]

Bennett noticed the same phenomenon and he reluctantly acknowledged that "the Hun in some ways was very good."[21] During one lull, when Padre Royle held a funeral service for Privates Henry Bobbitt and Bernie Spencer—the cook and baker who doubled as medics, both killed instantly by the same mortar round—the group "stood out in the open with helmets off near a gap in the orchard wall," and nothing happened. "Jerry may not have been looking," Bennett commented, "but in any case, he did not shoot."[22]

Shortly after this incident, Private Fred Noftall "got a burst from machine gun at about 25 yards range" and was lying exposed to German fire in the courtyard. Immediately, CSM Young jumped from the loft of the barn. Whether through fate, luck or "the consideration of the machine gunner," Young dragged the young Newfoundlander to cover.[23] Bennett now had to take his chances with the odd display of honour and chivalry to send the severely wounded young private "back on a door," as he had with Neill earlier that morning.[24]

Taking his chances with the SS, Bennett arranged a temporary truce to evacuate the wounded, and then watched as "two awkward cooks . . . walked right out in the open, unarmed past five Jerrys armed to the teeth." As Bennett noted, "They, of course, had no arm bands with them and no red cross, but the Hun signalled them on, and they walked forward, stealthily placing each foot on the ground and expecting a round between the shoulder blades."[25] No shot followed, and the trio made it unscathed back into Canadian lines. Shortly after arrival, Noftall, who celebrated his twentieth birthday fighting for his life in the farmyard that morning, succumbed to his injuries.[26]

Then the SS resumed their attack.

Bennett's massed machine guns continued to command approaches into the gardens and orchards, but stocks of ammunition ran low and they had to hold their fire, waiting for the final German push. Benson's sniper teams went to work from the loft again, hoping their marksmanship would offset the dwindling supplies of ammunition. As they had done all morning, the snipers exacted a hefty price until the Germans found the range "and started working on the top floors with rifle and hand grenades," which changed the complexion of the battle. As Bennett reported, "Mortars and shells and aimed fire from machine guns sighted just outside the long, broken wall defined the front."[27] Zollhöfer's men systematically doused the structure with a steady stream of machine-gun fire and rifle grenades, forcing CSM Young, Benson and the scouts down to the main floor. From that point on, Bennett was effectively blind. Every time he tried to send Benson and his scouts back up, the Germans sniped at them with rifle grenades. Soon, Sharpe and Brunner, who had experienced the same treatment in their new perch in a nearby farmhouse, came running into the farmyard, signalling the urgency of the situation.

For the second time, Zollhöfer's men penetrated the western edge of the farmyard, but once again the Highlanders pushed back, forcing the SS to retreat, but not before twenty-four-year-old Private Ernie Dooley, a Boston Irishman who usually worked the wireless at rear headquarters, and twenty-six-year-old Private George Shea, a Maritimer who had arrived in Normandy early on the morning of the twenty-fifth, suffered severe wounds. With the SS out of patience and empathy, and no doubt smelling blood, no truce followed to arrange for the evacuation of either, and before long they succumbed to their wounds.[28]

"We stood off every one of Jerry's attempts to get into our positions," reported Bennett with pride. He planned now for a breakout with his remaining men to Canadian lines in lieu of a Götterdämmerung battle for the farmyard, even though the inevitable seemed at hand.[29]

Before he could arrange for the escape, a series of machine-gun bursts from behind appeared at first to signal that all was lost. As he prepared for his own private Götterdämmerung at any moment, relief came when scouts from Bisaillon's Régiment de Maisonneuve arrived with the rest of the Maisies in tow, having moved heaven and earth to reach Black Watch lines.

Zollhöfer, apparently satisfied that his men had not only restored the main line of resistance on Verrières Ridge but had pushed the Canadians back past their start line, decided to end the siege and pull back to the ridge, leaving outposts in the church and the southern parts of the twin towns to carry on the fight.[30]

As suddenly as it had begun, the Black Watch battle for

Verrières Ridge ended at precisely 1430 hours on July 26 without notice and without fanfare. With relief at hand, Bennett's small band of Black Watch brothers picked up their wounded, weapons and kit and worked their way back to Fleury to pick up the pieces of a shattered regiment, hoping that some of those trapped on the ridge had made it back alive.

12

THE ABACUS WAR

In the fog of battle communications become disrupted, and units become separated, and when the "survivors" start coming in, they report that their section, platoon, or company has been wiped out. It must always be realized that when a soldier is separated from his comrades, he feels that he is the sole survivor, and it is only after the reorganization, possibly three or four days later, that one realizes that casualties have been far less than at first feared.

—LIEUTENANT GENERAL GUY SIMONDS, JULY 16, 1944

JIMMY BENNETT MADE IT BACK ALIVE TO CANADIAN lines near Fleury by midday on the twenty-sixth, but could offer no rational justification for his miraculous escape from the carnage on Verrières, save for a modicum of good luck or perhaps divine intervention. For close to eight hours after his company vanished on the ridge, the Black Watch private had lain prone in the wheat, listening to the white noise of the battlefield, waiting for the right moment to make his move. After darkness fell, Bennett set out on his desperate gambit, crawling over nearly a mile and a half of hotly contested ground. Picking his way through the wheat and moving north, he used the thud of artillery, the sporadic cracks and burps of rifle and machine pistols, or the bellows of the SS rounding up his Black Watch brothers to guide him away from danger.

For some unexplained reason, his chronic angst remained at bay for the entire sixteen-hour journey on hands and knees, and not once did a shell land near him, nor did a panzer or German patrol chase him, nor did he trigger a land mine or a nervous German or Canadian sentry. "I don't know how I escaped with my life," he recounted incredulously. "I should have been dead."

When he reached the Black Watch lines—a small pear orchard littered with shell holes, shattered branches and broken boughs—tea laced with rum and a bar of chocolate awaited, as did a resupply of ammunition doled out by a brawny, fresh-faced reinforcement who had arrived earlier that morning.

Still clad in his soiled uniform, trouser knees muddied and torn and knuckles bleeding from clutching his rifle during his long crawl, Bennett drifted in and out of his post-battle daze. Looking around the orchard for any familiar face, he counted "only twenty" riflemen. Failing to grasp the significance of this minuscule number, he asked the private hovering over him, offering a selection of rifle magazines and grenades from a khaki satchel, "Where is everyone?" Taken aback by the disconnected nature of Bennett's query, the young private, who had watched the parade of ambulance jeeps haul out the wounded and dead all morning, paused; then, in a hushed tone, he responded, "They're gone. Hundreds and hundreds of them. Just gone."[1]

Thirty-six hours earlier, Griffin had given the order for 320 men to advance up Verrières Ridge, but only these twenty, including Bennett, could report fit for duty. Fit, of course, was at best a relative term; although physically unwounded, each man in the orchard had suffered intense psychological trauma that left them scarred by a debacle that, next to Dieppe, would go down as the deadliest day for the Canadian Army in the entire Second World War.

Propped up on the fender of a Bren gun carrier, Lieutenant

William Mackenzie-Wood, tending to his superficial leg wound, did not initially grasp the full weight of the calamity either, until he saw how few other "stragglers" had arrived in the pasture. Hook Wilkinson remained "stunned" and could "not visualize the enormity of the loss" incurred by the rifle companies, while Mike Brunner remained "numb to it all" at first, but soon came to realize that he had "used up all [of his] nine lives" evading the clutches of the Panther in St. Martin with Dale Sharpe.[2]

Although the score of survivors sat in a tight packet, all remained very much alone, locked in their thoughts and plagued by varying degrees of bewilderment and despondency, thoroughly unsettled by the scale of the day's tragic events. On the lip of one shell hole, Smokey Lalonde pined over the loss of Tex Richards and the disappearance of Duke Ducat, while Herb McLeod continued to shake long after the firing stopped. Reuben Gorodetsky, swamped by his oversized body armour, feverishly cleaned his Sten gun while Sergeant Tommy Garvin, who took command of No. 17 Platoon in D Company during that attack and, like Bennett, had filtered back through the wheat, endeavoured to slice off a week's worth of facial hair. Private Thanning Anderson, wearied and drained after fleeing the wheat with a wounded comrade pasted to his back, tried to surrender to his exhaustion, but recurring nightmares jolted him back to consciousness on each attempt. Restless and traumatized, he decided to channel his grief by chatting with his best friend, Private Kris Krause, propped on a stretcher, the victim of a gunshot wound to the leg. Although their conversation centred on wild nights spent on leave in London, his effort proved short-lived when the jeep ambulance arrived to whisk Krause off to Juno Beach, making him the sixtieth man evacuated from the battalion that day. In a heavily self-censored letter home, Anderson sought cathartic release, telling his parents little more than that he had just endured "the most strenuous and hardest time" he had ever experienced in his short twenty-two years of life, leaving them to read between the lines.[3]

Like Anderson, each man in this pathetically small group strove to cope with waves of remorse and fear tinged with unwarranted shame and guilt. Knowing that war does not stop for anyone, they sought to "keep it together," knowing full well they'd be back on the line in short order, expected to "soldier on." The response to Bennett's facile query had provoked serious ruminations about the capricious nature of fate and luck. One right or wrong move in any direction, one moment of boldness or hesitation, could have spelled the difference between life and death—between a minor scratch and maiming, or complete psychological collapse. Then the guilt surfaced. Why had he survived when his friends did not? What had he done to deserve this fate? No clear-cut or satisfying answer followed; there was no logic, no fairness, no justice, only hopeless, malicious randomness. Like Brunner, Bennett felt he had spent his entire share of good fortune and was thoroughly terrified to return to the line, suspecting that if he did, he would not last a day.

Adrift in this cruel ambiguity, Bennett weighed his competing fears—neither of which, he found, held a clear-cut advantage. Now, with the far too sobering outcome of the push up Verrières lying naked before his eyes, a greater appreciation for the fine line between self-preservation and sacrifice appeared. As Bennett reasoned, "Bravery can be ridiculous and can be stupid," but to be "so brave that you get yourself killed" no longer held its once-seductive draw. Still, as the young prairie boy put it, "You don't have to run away, either. A coward will leave his friend, and I'd sooner be dead than a coward." Sensing that the distinction between ecstatic vision and sinful frenzy is all too vague, Bennett actively sought out any path, short of desertion and cowardice, that would prevent his return to the line and another round of nightmarish combat with the rifle companies.

FOLLOWING HIS MAD DASH TO THE SAFETY OF CANADIAN lines with Ayling, Jacks and Welligan, Hook Wilkinson was relieved to find that his kid brother had escaped death at the farmyard along with Benson, Brunner, Sharpe, Delutis, Pugh and Balsis. Tasked once again, with Tommy Garvin, to restock the scout platoon, Hook had to scrounge up candidates to fill the spots left by Alex Duncan (lost on the Orne), Charlie Lee (on Hill 61) and Melvin Cameron (killed in May during Benson's fighting patrol). Although Latham, Harold Burden and Arthur Bowmaster had failed to return after venturing into the wheat to pull out the wounded, hopes remained high that the trio would, as Garvin had done, make it back through the grain in the next few days or even hours.

By evening on the twenty-sixth, Padre Cecil Royle had assembled a weighty stack of casualty chits that registered the names of the Black Watch killed, wounded, sick and missing. As required, he placed each name under its appropriate column in his ledger— two-thirds of which ended up in the "missing" category—and then proceeded to pound out the first of three hundred letters to the next of kin on his Corona 3 typewriter. Short on details, Royle tried his best to comfort and console, but being a recent addition to the regiment, his letters were all too brief and at times painfully generic. For the families at home or for friends with the battalion, more news would have to wait until German reports arrived through the Red Cross office in Switzerland or until the ridge fell into Allied hands.

Two days later, Captain Shirley Griffin, working as Brigadier William Megill's brigade intelligence officer, noted sombrely in the war diary, "There is still no news of the missing Black Watch Boys." Worried about his brother and his friends, Griffin ignored army regulations and dispatched a special telegram to his family to fill them in on the bleak situation before the official notice of his brother's disappearance arrived: "In a recent show, Phil along with some others went missing. Personally, I am convinced that he is safe and unwounded as a prisoner. I have investigated every possible source of information, and I am now positive in my own mind that this is the case. It is hardest when you don't know. In the statement 'missing' is pretty vague, so I wanted you to know what I feel after an exhaustive search and questioning so as to relieve your mind a little at any rate. You may even get this before the official notice, but I don't see any harm in that. I have hesitated to write till I was 100% positive, but then I will probably never be while I am here, and I wanted you to have what information I was able to get, and that is simply that from all reports he is a prisoner. So, don't worry too much—'the little major' will show up all right somewhere, or you will hear from him soon."[4]

GENERAL MILES DEMPSEY PERMANENTLY SHUT DOWN Simonds's Operation Spring on July 26 and tucked its horrific cost and less than pleasing results under the cloak of the dramatic and historical events unfolding elsewhere in the bridgehead. While Dietrich's 1st SS Panzer Corps turned Simonds's bid for glory into the greatest defensive victory for the Germans in Normandy, farther west, General Omar Bradley's 1st US Army had launched Operation Cobra, which after two days of hellish fighting in the hedgerow country broke the German line near the town of St. Lô. With the majority of the German panzer reserves pinned to the Verrières sector, Bradley's massive rupture quickly turned into a full-fledged breakout, and by week's end,

General George S. Patton's 3rd Army had plunged straight into the vitals of the German lines near Avranches, a development that permanently altered the nature and complexion of the battle for Normandy.

By early August, it only took one look at his situation map to convince Field Marshal Günther von Kluge that the entire German Army in Normandy now stood on the precipice of defeat. Montgomery's attritional policy had taken its toll on the Germans as well, and von Kluge requested permission to pull his armies back to the natural defensive barrier of the Seine River to avoid disaster. Hitler refused. Left with no alternative, von Kluge continued to fight on. In the interim, 5th Panzer Army commander Heinrich Eberbach urged von Kluge to take advantage of the shaky condition of Simonds's 2nd Canadian Corps and launch Dietrich's panzers in a headlong offensive designed to crush the Allied forces caught between the ridge and the Orne River. At Hitler's direction, von Kluge chose instead to shift the panzers west, away from the Verrières sector, in a bid to cut the supply lines of Patton's army, which had turned the corner at Avranches and now barrelled eastward with its sights set on Paris. In the second week of August, Hitler ordered a pair of ill-fated panzer-led counterattacks near Mortain that backfired spectacularly, prompting von Kluge's suicide and the collapse of the German front. By the end of the month, Allied forces had liberated Paris and destroyed a vast amount of the retreating German Army in Normandy in a pocket around Falaise, forcing the remnants to flee unceremoniously across the Seine.

In Allied minds, these momentous events appeared to usher in the war's climactic final movement, arousing expectations of a German surrender at any moment, and certainly by Christmas at the latest. In the interim, the 1st Canadian Army, under the command of General Harry Crerar, had taken over the Verrières

Ridge sector from Dempsey's 2nd British Army after Operation Spring. Immediately, and at Montgomery's direction, Crerar ordered Simonds to embark on a series of small-scale "holding attacks" along the Verrières feature designed to pin the German panzers to the ridge and away from the surging Americans, while he restocked his depleted battalions and prepared for yet another colossal crack.

On August 8, twenty-six years to the day after the Canadian Corps helped smash the German line at Amiens and delivered what the German High Command called "the blackest day for the German army," Simonds launched his colossal crack: Operation Totalize. Backed by copious amounts of artillery and heavy bombers, the operation proved to be the third and concluding chapter in the Verrières trilogy. After seventeen days of bitter, brutal and unrelenting combat that took the lives of over 1,300 Canadians and left another 4,500 men physically, emotionally and psychologically scarred, not only did Simonds have his ridge, but the capture of the blood-soaked heights brought the fate of the lost Black Watch rifle companies into sharper focus.

FIVE DAYS AFTER THE RIDGE FELL, BENSON AND HIS scouts found themselves in the back of a 60-hundredweight truck, rumbling back into May-sur-Orne, accompanied by their new commanding officer, Lieutenant Colonel Frank Mitchell, and the battalion's new intelligence officer, Lieutenant Mackenzie-Wood.

With the Canadian front line six miles to the south, Benson received a distinctly different welcome than on his previous visits. Little had changed in the town since July 25, as most of the bombs destined for the village during Totalize had fallen wide of their mark. With the rapid departure of the Germans, a few locals who had hidden in the caves along the Orne River had come out of hiding, and now they floated like apparitions from house to house, picking through the rubble in a vain attempt to restore their disrupted lives. Not one structure in May had escaped damage, and almost all of the tightly packed row houses had lost their red-tiled roofs and their walls. For the skeletons left standing, massive punctures in fragile facades betrayed the contents of former kitchens and bedrooms now entombed under heaps of red bricks, twisted metal and snapped timber in the collapsed cellars below.

Approaching the crossroads near the church whose clock hands had frozen at precisely five o'clock, Benson, Mitchell and Mackenzie-Wood hopped off the truck when it slowed to make the turn onto the road towards the Black Watch start line. As the vehicle disappeared in a cloud of dust, Benson took the trio down the same path he'd trudged with Duffield early on the morning of July 25. The nightmares of that day, the second-guessing, and above all a profound sense of guilt for not challenging Duffield's decision to turn back seemed to weigh heavily on the mind of the scout platoon sergeant. Always a student of war, Benson had come back to May in part to learn, in part to commiserate, and perhaps to seek some form of forgiveness. Working their way past the burned-out remnants of the Hôtel Louis XIV, which sat kitty-corner to the church across the Route d'Harcourt, the men picked their way gingerly through the ruins, mindful of uncleared mines and booby traps, and soon discovered just how well prepared the town had been to receive the Allied attack on the twenty-fifth. As Benson noted, "each of the buildings was carefully sealed" with "doors that could not be opened," with "every window and doorway along the road covered by fire." Benson marvelled at the "extraordinarily good" German "fire control," which permitted his recce patrol "to walk all the way through May-sur-Orne."[5]

Farther on, after moving through the vehicle bays that housed Prien's panzers, Benson realized that the Black Watch had learned the toughest of lessons in the hardest of schools from the wily veterans of Sterz's *Kampfgruppe*. It was "evident," he reported, "that the enemy was most anxious that we see this small display of strength and that we return and report it."[6] Benson now suspected that the lone figure they encountered at the crossroads, and the single machine gun that opened up on them, represented a deliberate ploy to paint the impression that the town could easily be taken out by a fighting patrol, when in reality it demanded a full-scale battalion attack supported by tanks and artillery. But Benson could not forgive himself for not pushing Duffield to press on when the young officer ordered their return without a thorough check of the town. May-sur-Orne was anything but "lightly held," and had they indeed pushed forward just a few more yards, they would have bumped into Prien's panzers concealed in the rubble. Whether the patrol lived to tell the tale or not, their discovery might have radically altered the complexion of events on the day—and, consequently, the fate of the Black Watch. This revelation was the heaviest of burdens for any man to carry.

ALONG THE RIDGE EAST OF MAY, THE SMALL CONVOY pulled off the dirt track that led to Fontenay and stopped to allow the remaining scouts to dismount in the grain field that marked the farthermost advance of the Black Watch on the twenty-fifth. The weather was hot and sticky with no breeze and the humidity hung in the air. Immediately, the men noticed a parade of jeep ambulances queuing up along the track facing May. Alongside, teams of Canadian engineers decked out in mine-clearing gear stood smoking, taking a much-needed break from their chores in the stifling heat. "I had no idea what was going on," Brunner recalled, until the men dismounted the truck and found "a lot of bodies lying there."

Padre Royle appeared and briefed them on the most delicate task that lay ahead. Several days earlier, the Black Watch padre had joined a small cohort of chaplains from Division and Corps who had embarked on a systematic recovery of the men who had fallen in all three of Simonds's bids to take the ridge. The task proved daunting and unsettling because most of the bodies lay in areas sown with land mines that first needed to be swept. As one chaplain noted, after "exposure to heat and flies" for several weeks, "the bodies are in an advanced state of decomposition." Another, affected just as profoundly by the grisly scene, remarked, "It's the worst we have seen . . . mostly lads from the Black Watch and the South Saskatchewan Regiment."[7] Plodding up and down the slopes of Verrières, Royle had followed a carefully marked grid, tucked in close behind the engineers, who swept the ground from side to side in a wide arc with their metal detectors. Each time they came across a body, the bespectacled padre would beckon for a stretcher team to join him while the sappers doused the remains with DDT to kill disease-bearing insects. After a cursory inspection for identification, the stretcher teams lifted each body and placed it on one of the dozen ambulance jeeps to take them to a temporary resting place staked out in a field between St. Martin and the "factory."

"We began to stack Black Watch bodies from the ridge four at a time onto the back of each jeep," Brunner recalled, a task the stifling heat made all the more horrific. "The smell was unbearable," Bennett recalled. "We had about fifteen guys start; when it ended up, there was only three of us left that could do it. Just three; the rest all got sick to their stomachs."

With the remains loaded, the solemn procession made its way

slowly back through the clogged streets of May, down the main road and through the factory to the temporary graveyard—quite fittingly, between the cabbage patch and the church. When the convoy arrived, a trio of bulldozers had just finished tilling a series of communal plots. Pulling the bodies off the stretchers, the snipers "put them side-by-side, lined them up, and got them ready to bury."[8] As Royle recalled, they were "laid out in rows of 40 to a grave," with successive services conducted for each row. Although Royle did his best to ensure "the interment was carried out as reverently and respectfully" as possible under the prevailing circumstances, the lead chaplain could only remark that "it was all very grim."[9]

Following the last interment, an army cameraman stepped forward from the shadows and shot a photograph of the makeshift cemetery, showing row upon row of crosses set against a backdrop of shattered trees and the remnants of St. Martin, with a "Union Jack, taken from the possessions of a deceased padre" flying above. Then a lone piper played the lament.

Royle shifted close to ninety names from "missing" to the "killed in action" column in his ledger—among them, scouts Harold Burden, Arthur Bowmaster and Tommy Latham, all of them found not far from the factory area along the Black Watch axis of advance. With these discoveries, what little hope had remained for their deliverance vanished and a deep flood of loss and mourning swept over the Black Watch. In just four hours, the carefully crafted Black Watch rifle companies, whose men had grown so tight as they honed their skills during months and years of training in England, had taken 94 percent casualties. That scale of loss far surpassed anything their fathers might have experienced while trudging down their own Voies Sacrées and rivalled the rate suffered by the Royal Newfoundland Regiment at Beaumont Hamel on the disastrous opening day of the Somme offensive on July 1, 1916.[10] During the four-hour ordeal, one Black Watch man fell every twelve seconds. Every two minutes, one Highlander died in the withering German fire as they pushed up the ridge in a bid to fulfill their duty to higher authority, honour, regiment, manhood and, as some would say, destiny. Nearly half of these casualties, 126, proved fatal, with most of the fallen found straddling the crest of Verrières. Only a handful, it appears, made it to within a hundred yards of their objective in Fontenay-le-Marmion. None reached it. "They didn't have a chance; they simply died where they fell," Royle recalled in a fitting epitaph. "More than a hundred of this fighting unit, which up to this point had been together for years and knew each other's tricks inside out, now lay dead upon that wheat field."[11]

Five weeks earlier, the 1st Battalion of Canada's Black Watch had arrived jubilantly on Juno Beach, sporting a full complement of thirty-six officers and 815 NCOs and men, all brimming with confidence and anxious to "get at 'em" after four monotonous years of training on the English downs.[12] After twelve days of "battle inoculation," they went into combat for the first time late on July 18 but stumbled out of the blocks in a classic case of opening-night jitters. In this case, an elementary and unforgivable mistake in the coordination of timings cost eighteen men their lives, with another sixty wounded when they bumped their heads crossing the Orne River. Then, after delivering a textbook attack on the hamlet of Ifs, followed by an overnight sniper hunt, their pride soared. But before they could catch their breath, an emergency call to restore the line arrived, which they answered with ruthless efficiency—and then paid the price for that success by inheriting an exposed position in an unforgiving wheat field on Hill 61.[13]

For the next four days, the men withstood constant rocket, mortar and artillery fire while playing a deadly cat-and-mouse game with enemy snipers, patrols and panzers that inflicted an unrelenting stream of casualties to mind, body and soul. Without the ability to hit back at German lines, they had to sit and take the pounding from crack panzer and *Panzergrenadier* divisions and from Schack's 272nd Infantry Division—which by all accounts punched far above its weight class. Adding to their misery, they had no sleep, rum or hot meals to help check their rising anxiety. Plagued with stifling heat by day and bouts of torrential rain and marrow-penetrating dampness by night, they fought near-paralytic fatigue and persistent gut-wrenching fear as hard as they did the Germans. Those gruelling days on Hill 61 cost the Black Watch 166 casualties. Remarkable as it may be that fewer than twenty men died, close to a hundred others suffered physical wounds from shell splinters, concussive blasts and gunshots that ranged from minor to life-threatening. More alarming, forty-eight men euphemistically listed as "sick" in the casualty returns had suffered severe psychological scarring and, in some cases—such as that of Lieutenant Jock McLennan—complete breakdown. Known to their fathers as shell shock and to them as battle exhaustion, these cavernous unseen wounds—now known as post-traumatic stress disorder—would plague the Verrières survivors, leaving men like McLennan unjustly stigmatized and emasculated long after peace returned.

The reward for this purgatorial chapter came with an all-out assault up and over Verrières Ridge on July 25. Neither a breakout operation, as initially planned, nor the holding attack that Simonds called it after the disaster, Spring was an attritional contest designed to grind down the German line to create the conditions for another of Montgomery's colossal cracks. Although Montgomery, Dempsey and their veteran British armoured division commanders held out little hope that the operation would succeed, given the steady and increasing buildup of the German

DAVID O'KEEFE

line along the ridge, Simonds fully expected to come away with
Verrières and was willing to give it everything he had.

Fatal flaws undercut his plan from the start. Unnecessarily
complex, complicated and grounded in strict adherence to
unreasonable timings, his preordained order to push past centres
of resistance to meet the noontime caveat imposed by Dempsey
effectively sealed the fate of all the regiments taking part in the
operation before the first shot was fired. Inflaming matters,
Simonds's autocratic command style, which inculcated a culture of blame, prevented his subordinates on the ground from
seizing the initiative. This, in turn, fuelled Foulkes's sycophantic
permissiveness and Megill's blinkered and obstinate approach,
all of which conspired to create a blueprint for disaster for the
units at the sharp end on the front. Despite the initial indecision,
infighting and delay, which arose in large part from the insecure
start line, and the fog of war that contributed in no small part
to the death of S.S.T. Cantlie and the wounding of Major Eric
Motzfeldt, the battalion, when finally under Griffin's control,
managed to regain its composure and consolidate its position
in St. Martin. In the interim, the Little Major reorganized every
aspect of the assault without any meaningful input, guidance or
grip from higher command, save for a series of unhelpful whip
cracks and chides for the battalion to "push on."

As a result, a spent and overstretched battalion, couched in
history, legacy, honour and pride, responded dutifully to a blind
call for obedience from Simonds, who with the clock ticking
gambled that he could get his forces over Verrières Ridge, only to
find to his horror that he had lost the race for time. As a result,
wholesale slaughter on an unimaginable scale ensued, leaving
the entire Allied position south of Caen in jeopardy and leaving
Benson's scouts to anchor Bennett's "odds and sods" in a fight
for their lives to hold on to a desolate farmyard in St. Martin

342

against overwhelming odds. In those seven days of hell, the Black Watch suffered nearly five hundred casualties—161 of whom remain entombed for eternity in the lush and windswept fields of Normandy. Buried at first in a makeshift cemetery in St. Martin, where each plot sat adorned with a handmade, whitewashed wooden cross emblazoned with name, rank and service number, their final resting place in the Bretteville-sur-Laize cemetery came with one ironic twist. In an attempt to gather the fallen together, the war graves concentration units exhumed and reinterred the men in a picturesque field on the fringe of the tiny town of Cintheaux on the Falaise road—the same village that Simonds had marked as the ultimate objective of Operation Spring.

THE MAJORITY OF THE BLACK WATCH DEAD CALLED Montreal and its environs home, and it was not hard for city boys like Brunner and Hook Wilkinson to envision the impact on families throughout the city. In less than a week, bicycle-bound couriers would arrive at the doors of brownstones and mansions in Westmount and the Town of Mount Royal, cottages and apartments in Notre-Dame-de-Grâce, and row houses of the working-class districts in Rosemount, Verdun, Griffintown and Pointe-Saint-Charles, armed with the dreaded telegrams that would shatter their worlds.

Montreal, however, did not stand alone in this world of grief and mourning. Every province in the country sacrificed a son to the Black Watch attack on Verrières Ridge.[14] Next to the province of Quebec, Ontario provided the most men in the Black Watch, with about half of those—such as Henry Jones, from Toronto, and Private Ray Hazell, from Hamilton—coming from urban centres. Others resided in rural and remote locations—including Bob Barrie, from Powassan, Tom Johnston from Thornloe, and

Harvey Mahaffy from Nestleton. Indeed, large and small communities right across the country made the sombre list: High River, Alberta, gave up Lloyd George Jackson, who worked the family farm, as did Private J.J. Pruden from Big River, Saskatchewan. Sergeant Morley Wachnow, a Jewish lad from Winnipeg who worked as a store clerk in North Battleford, Saskatchewan, died not far from Jimmy Cockburn, from Briercrest, Saskatchewan.

The Maritimes gave up Dan Hinkley, from Pleasant Bay at the foot of the Cabot Trail on Cape Breton Island in Nova Scotia, only a ferry ride away from Hugh MacInnis, who called Antigonish home. Wally Duncan was the pride of Cardigan, Prince Edward Island, while Joe McLaughlin lived in Grand Falls, New Brunswick, a few hours north of Mervell Stickells, an African-Canadian lumberjack from Fredericton.

Canada's First Nations also forfeited part of their future with the deaths of mortarman Carmen Barnhardt from the Six Nations Reserve in Caledonia, Ontario, and Augustine Johnny from Williams Lake, British Columbia.

The breadth and depth of the losses to Canada were indeed enormous, and so were those to the Allied cause. Newfoundland, which had yet to join Confederation, gave up Fred Noftall, while Glasgow, Scotland, lost Private Robert Hugh Baker, and Devon, England, lost George Alexander Brown. John Howard Farrell, who survived one massacre at Dieppe, was born and raised in Flushing, on Long Island, and like George Dale of Daytona Beach and Ernie Dooley of Boston, he had come north to get in on the action. Each of these men now lay in a Norman pasture alongside immigrants or first-generation Canadians from Russia, Ukraine, Latvia, Estonia, Lithuania, Czechoslovakia, Hungary, Poland, Denmark, Sweden and even Italy, from which John Bisaro of Trieste had escaped Mussolini's Fascistic grip.

None of these men had made soldiering his lifelong profession. They had wilfully volunteered to leave the safety of their homes and risk their lives to defeat the vilest scourge humanity has known. This citizen army, made up in part of mechanics, bookkeepers and accountants, chemists, bakers, machine fitters, carpenters and heavy machine operators, went off to war ready to shoulder the load with truck drivers and deliverymen, railwaymen and farmers, lawyers, medical students and stockbrokers. Harry Best tended bar at a private golf club; Harvey Booth worked as a plumber. John Bichard, who served with Jimmy Bennett and Elie Desormeaux on the Kiska operation in 1943, died in the same field that claimed the battalion signals officer, Lieutenant Hubert Pedlar, a budding journalist with the *Midland Free Press* who perished along with sailors, stewards, salesmen, medical supply technicians and even a bushman who specialized in "mucking and drilling."[15] Many of these men stood poised to play roles in building and maintaining Canada upon their return—a return that would never come.

The average age of the Black Watch soldiers who died during these seven days of unrelenting combat was just twenty-three. Twenty-one of these "men" could not legally purchase a drink or vote in elections at home. The oldest man to die on the slopes of Verrières was forty-six-year-old Private William Des Cotes, who had joined the army to escape the Depression and provide for his family of six.[16] The youngest to perish, Private Ernest Armstrong Wilson, lied about his age when he joined the army at age sixteen. His death, however, brought his surreptitious act to light, and authorities soon discovered that he did not die at age twenty, but rather a month and a day after his eighteenth birthday.[17]

At the time, the burial of Canadian soldiers overseas perpetuated the British tradition, which meant that, unlike today, when the fallen come home, the battlefield upon which these men fell would forever be their home. Few of the grieving families would see their graves; sometimes only a solitary photo of the temporary cemetery in St. Martin or a snapshot of the individual grave augmented the sanguine telegram that opened with an impersonal "Minister of National Defence deeply regrets to inform you . . ."[18]

The only remaining tactile connection came with the personal effects parcelled up to be sent home. As Royle recalled, the few items he drew from the pockets and pouches of the dead in the fields joined what he retrieved from kit consigned to B Echelon and amounted to no more than "a little bundle; a watch perhaps, fountain pen, a pay book, a letter or two." These "pathetic little remnants," as Royle sorrowfully called them, now formed the eternal bond for families and provided a final glimpse of their lives forever frozen in time. Stripped of costume and rank, these vestiges of youth and promise lay bare and partially exposed quirks of their nature that shed light on who these men were, who they hoped to be, what they planned, desired and dreamed, all ensconced in the soul-destroying notion of permanent forfeiture of youth and promise.

Vic Foam, the consummate company sergeant major who died leading his company from the front, left his leather wallet, a trusty penknife and his pair of highly polished black oxfords. A stack of letters from home formed part of the collection of Private George Crogie, along with a Waterman pen and pencil and an Eveready flashlight—used, no doubt, to scrawl letters home after lights out. Corporal Bill Herd's collection included an address book and a rail and bus guide from what must have been a most memorable leave in London.

A math textbook and a collection of short stories betrayed John Henry Harper's desire to better himself, while Private Harvey Mahaffy left a set of leather gloves, a toothbrush and his personal identification bracelet (a gift from his family), which matched a personalized cigarette case. Lieutenant Alan Robinson left his kilt, his fawn balmoral and his prized cribbage board, a veteran of many a tussle in the officers' mess with the Bishop's College School "old boys." A rosary and a photo of Anthony Barbagallo, mugging for the camera with his Bren gun slung around his shoulder and a machete tucked into his pack, formed a lasting visual reminder of the job that took his life. Private Reg Long, Cantlie's batman, left a sleeveless sweater that maintained the scent of his aftershave, while Cantlie himself left a trunk containing over 150 items very much befitting a Black Watch CO, including a silk dressing gown, badminton racquets, a blue blazer and lampshade sans lamp, and a rubber ball.

Corporal William Steel, recommended for the Military Medal for saving countless lives during the Orne crossing, did not live long enough to receive it, and provisions existed for only two posthumous awards: a mention in dispatches and the Victoria Cross. Killed trying to repeat his heroic efforts on July 25, his effects contained a 10,000-franc souvenir note, a personalized Bible and a lock of hair.[19] Lance Corporal George Truax, a former ring opponent and sparring partner of scout/ sniper Harold Burden and Frank Balsis, blown apart on the ridge, left only a pair of boxing shoes, his fighting trunks and his jockstrap. Burden, who died with Bowmaster and Latham trying, like Steel, to pull men out of the fire to safety, left only a leather belt and a Bible. Arthur Bowmaster's effects included the Ronson lighter he employed during the sniper hunt at Ifs, an autograph album and two hundred French francs, while Melvin Cameron's comprised letters, snapshots and a deck of cards. The family of Tommy Latham, who had lost another son the previous March, received nothing—his kit, stored with B Echelon, disappeared mysteriously, and his pay book was the only item retrieved from his body.

The last set of effects gathered by Royle brought a sense of finality to this sorrowful chapter in Black Watch history: a pipe, a set of gold cufflinks and the prized Kodak Six-20 camera and personal diary of Major Phillip Griffin.

In the last pass of the day, Royle discovered Griffin's body buried in the wheat, struck down on the reverse slope. As the regiment would learn from a series of patchy accounts given months later by repatriated Black Watch prisoners, Griffin had indeed pushed past Gordy Donald on the reverse slope, moving towards the objective in Fontenay. Nevertheless, following their encounter, where Donald witnessed his wounding, Griffin finally accepted the hopelessness of the situation and reluctantly ordered what few men remained on their feet to make it back to Canadian lines as best they could. Moments later, he stepped on a German land mine and died.[20]

The discovery of his brother's body abruptly curtailed the hope that Shirley Griffin was holding out for the safe return of the Little Major. Likewise, his death hit Captain Ronnie Bennett hard; along with Eric Motzfeldt, who lay in a hospital bed in England, Bennett counted the A Company commander as his closest friend in the regiment. For years, the trio had trained together, worked together and spent time on leave together, indulging in whatever young officers might do. Now, after the deaths of Cantlie, Fraser, Robinson and Teddy Neill, the wounding of Stevenson, Taylor, McLennan and Stuart, and the capture of Kemp, only Lieutenants George Buch and William Mackenzie-Wood remained as "battle-hardened" and able-bodied combat veterans.

Every man who survived the attack, whether still with the battalion, lying wounded in a hospital bed or languishing in German captivity, harboured a mixture of sorrow, resilience and resentment. "It was upsetting to see your boys, your friends, go down, because we were one big family," Bruce Ducat recalled. "Many of us were with each other for four years; we lived in the same bunks, shared slits, ate the same meals, drank together. Hell! We even chased the same women! You got to be terrific friends, real buddies. Moreover, now they were gone. There is not a bloody thing you can do about it."

Thoughts for many centred on the faces, the laughs and the quirks of nature of those lost. Moments of conflict, friendship and kindness all came storming back. There were good days and bad, while in training and while at the front. All took time to reflect on those lost, and the stories flowed: the personality traits, the jokes they pulled, the bonding moments while breaking bread, drinking and even brawling—all of the "rituals of manhood" that brought them together as a group, and which they took for granted, now came surging back. As Mac Roulston succinctly put it, "We didn't always get along, but we were family."

Soon, thoughts turned again to the fickle nature of war. Gordy Donald, who by late August would find himself in a German POW camp in Poland, remained grateful despite his current bleak situation. "By the luck of somebody I survived, and a few others survived. I guess that bullet just happened to go in the wrong direction." Mike Brunner, equally grateful, finally discovered why Barney Benson had tapped both him and Dale Sharpe to sit LOB (left out of battle) on the morning of the attack. Although locked in a desperate life-and-death struggle, Benson never lost his compassion, sense of decency or grip on humanity. As Brunner discovered later, their scout platoon sergeant had cut them a break because Sharpe was "married with a couple of kids" and Brunner, swept up in the momentous events, forgot that July 25, the day the regiment died, was also his twenty-second birthday.

• • •

WHEN LIEUTENANT COLONEL FRANK MITCHELL, THE newly promoted Black Watch CO, rushed up to take the reins of the battalion and bring "some semblance of order" to the chaotic situation on July 26, there was little he could say that would in any way assuage or mitigate the sting of defeat and loss. "In all its history," he told the few survivors who remained in the field, "never has the honour of the 'HACKLE' been higher than it is today."[21] Few men paid attention to Mitchell's words, not out of disrespect or as an indictment of his talents, but because no words or actions could stir or console. Only time would accomplish that task.

The ten days that followed provided the men with a brief respite from fighting and a chance to relax, restock and clean up on the banks of the Orne River. Soon, a sense of normalcy prevailed despite the proximity to the front lines. The Orne reminded some of the streams, brooks and tiny lakes in the Laurentian Mountains north of Montreal—or, for Dale Sharpe, the Napanee River, where he learned to hunt and fish—and provided the men with their first bath parade since leaving England. For the first time in weeks, they shaved, showered and washed soiled uniforms, disturbed only occasionally by a stray shell or enemy air raid. Gone were the beards and the matted hair. Mike Brunner, who landed, like the other scouts, with a closely shorn head, once again sported a full head of hair, but for some reason it grew back curly this time.

The cleansing process, like everything else in the army, was systematic and orderly—but only to a point. Before sauntering into the Orne, the men stripped down and dumped their trousers in one pile, shirts in another, tunics in another, and there was one each for underwear and socks. When they emerged half an hour later, having scrubbed off layers of dirt and grime, they discovered that army efficiency had led to a free-for-all to reassemble uniforms fresh from the laundry. For the men who had taken the time to stencil their names and service numbers inside their tunics and trousers, they usually scored their own, but those too lazy to mark their property ended up with a size too big or small or with a pair of socks that needed darning in the worst way. Underwear, however, posed a unique problem. Lacking name tags, an entire company's worth of "clean" undergarments ended up in one generic and less than antiseptic pile, and it was anyone's guess as to which pair belonged to any given soldier.

The caves and quarries and the river itself provided a much-needed playground of sorts for souvenir hunting and cavorting. Although Drunner failed to obtain his prized Luger, others made off like bandits, coming away with everything from "aftershave to half-tracks." In a "strange paradox of war," as the war diarist recorded, some enterprising Highlanders discovered a set of canoes and now paddled the Orne, mindful of the bodies of friend and foe alike that floated aimlessly in the waterway.[22]

Yet amid lingering death, life of a sort returned. On the shore, baseball games broke out yet again, and meals were hot and plentiful, with compo rations augmented by pears and apples, fresh meat, milk and eggs from local farmers. Rum, wine and other spirits flowed. Sleep returned too, but only for the veterans of Verrières—after their experiences, nothing but the heaviest of enemy shells could wake them from the sleep of the dead.

However, this fleeting sense of "normalcy" lasted only for a brief moment. High in the sky, a pair of Typhoons appeared, in distress after tangling with a German heavy-flak battery in the area and losing. The pilots of both aircraft prepared to either crash-land or bail out. One plane suddenly burst into flames and its pilot let go with his guns, calling attention to his now-desperate plight. As the other continued overhead past their position, the flaming fighter-bomber nosed down sharply. "We all held our breath," the war diarist recorded, "until we could see a figure emerging from the flaming airplane." In due course, the pilot managed to wriggle his way out of the cockpit, raising hopes on the ground of a most miraculous escape. "To our dismay," the war diarist added, "for some reason, his parachute failed to open, and he followed his plane down. This incident cast a pall over the battalion that evening."[23]

It did not take long for Jimmy Bennett to find a solution to his dilemma. Having lived a rather solitary existence within his platoon, which in the wake of the attack no longer existed in any real sense of the word, he had no bonds to friends or comrades left to maintain. Alone now, he had to start over and seek out a new niche and establish new friendships that would permit him to fulfill his duty and, ultimately, to survive.

When Hook Wilkinson called out, "Who wants to join the scout platoon?" it resonated with many of the survivors sitting in the field in much the same way that a failed carnival barker exhorted the passing public, describing the attractions to the most fabulous show on earth. Initially, nobody bit; then Bennett piped up, "What do you have to do?" The others looked at Bennett, stupefied.

"Well," Hook said, "I might as well tell you the truth, it's dangerous—but you don't have to do guard duty, you don't have to carry packs, we've got a half-ton truck that will carry all your ammunition, weapons. You don't have to carry a whole bunch of crap on your back . . . but it's dangerous; you have to work in the dark."

Having few qualms about night work, Bennett jumped at the chance of not having to fight all day and then pull guard duty at night. For him, guard duty denoted a solitary existence devoid of any initiative, the worst of which he witnessed in the days on Hill 61. Put out on the line alone, fixed in place, the solitary soldier appeared more as pawn or bait than sentinel. He now preferred to play the role of hunter rather than hunted.

Within the hour, Bennett had a new scoped Lee-Enfield, a used balaclava and a freshly minted sniper's smock that contrasted sharply with the faded brand worn by the rest. Struggling to slip it over his head and then snap it shut under his legs, Bennett crowned his new garb by sticking a collection of slender twigs in his helmet netting for scrim and propped it awkwardly on his head. He remembered sage advice imparted by a former sergeant: "Even if you guys are nothing, try and look like something!" His attempt, however, left the private looking, in his estimation, less like a fierce Highland warrior and more "like a prairie chicken."

Although they had spent over half a year in the same battalion and he knew them by sight, Bennett had never exchanged words with Dale Sharpe or Mike Brunner, but their shared experiences over the last few weeks had, by default, swept away the trad-itional courtship rituals and vaulted them into an exclusive club— that of Verrières survivors. From Brunner's perspective, neither he nor Dale knew what to make of Bennett at first—"He was dark-haired, good-looking and reminded me of Dean Martin— although not as tall—but he survived the ridge in a rifle company, so it was all good with me."[24] Nor did Bennett have qualms about the pair. "Certain people you take to straight away," he recalled of his initial meeting with the two men who would become his closest friends. He warmed to Brunner immediately—"He was not the worrying type" or "excitable like me." Neither was Dale Sharpe, whose imposing six-foot, two-hundred-pound frame and large moustache gave Bennett a sense of confidence. He was a "very serious guy" and "didn't talk foolishness," Bennett remem-bered; he was "very cool and smart."[25] Indeed, Bennett quickly came to recognize what the rest of the scout platoon had come to rely upon: Sharpe's stoic and steadying demeanour that, along with Benson, Garvin and the Wilkinson brothers, now formed the pillars of the scout platoon.

Within days, Bennett had carved his place within the tight fabric of the eccentric unit. What he loved the most about his new occupation was the combination of independence and mystique associated with the platoon. The rest of the rebuilt battalion, all newcomers, viewed the scouts as rebels and renegades—men who refused to conform, working by night, forgoing sleep, heading into no man's land or behind enemy lines in lightly armed pairs or trios, sneaking and stalking the foe with little hope of mercy if wounded or captured.

For Bennett, however, the risks had their rewards: they did not have to put up with the usual army BS, given that they bypassed the traditional command hierarchy and dealt directly with the battalion's senior officers. They lived a separate existence from the men in the rifle companies and played mainly by their own rules, dressed as they thought fit, and even had a cook of their own, who travelled with them to prepare their meals. As he later put it, "We lived free and easy" compared with life in the newly reformed rifle companies, leaving him to chuckle on many occasions when men would pass on foot while he sat perched on a carrier and shout up at the scout platoon private, "Wouldn't want your job." More importantly, however, Bennett found the friendships amongst his peers—for the moment, he had found a home.

TASKED WITH REBUILDING THE BATTALION, MITCHELL assured the regimental elders that he would maintain the "very high standards" that Cantlie had set, but with only sixteen veterans left in the scout platoon, he had little to work with.

Leadership at every level throughout the unit, the skeletal system that holds a unit together, had vanished.[26] Built up and honed over months and years in training in England, it now stood decimated by the difficult attritional process that started with the Orne crossing and culminated a week later on a ridge in Normandy. In just one week of combat, the battalion had lost its commanding officer, his temporary replacement, and all rifle company commanders and their 2ics. Griffin and Fraser lay dead; Motzfeldt, Stevenson and Taylor were seriously wounded; and Kemp was wounded and a prisoner.

Only George Buch, whose wounds suffered in the farmyard healed quickly, and Ronnie Bennett remained, the former promoted to captain and the latter to major, each of them given command of two of the four vacant rifle companies. These two men now stood alone as Mitchell's "senior" company commanders.

Along with finding a new adjutant to replace Campbell Stuart, who had lost his leg, and a scout platoon commander to fill Duffield's shoes, all of Mitchell's companies and platoons needed a complete rebuild from the ground up. Finding new company and platoon officers in a hurry proved difficult enough, but his most daunting challenge came with the need to restock the depleted ranks of the battalion's core of NCOs. The attack up Verrières tore the spine out of the battalion as twenty-two corporals and lance corporals died, along with ten sergeants and warrant officers, while dozens of others fell wounded, sick or missing or were taken prisoner.

The loss of the senior NCOs, whose experience and gritty leadership formed the essential glue that kept the fabric of the unit together, hit the battalion hard. Highly trained NCOs ensured the implementation of orders from above and made the fighting engine of the battalion run smoothly.

To make good the grievous losses, men from right across the country poured into the ranks of the Black Watch. The territorial exclusion, long considered the centre of gravity of the entire regimental system, went out the window in the new version of the battalion. When the Highlanders had landed in Normandy a month earlier, almost three-quarters of the officers and men came from Montreal and its environs; now, only half. The "reinforcements" met a stern rebuff from the scouts—whom Mitchell parcelled out temporarily to each company to lend their experience—when they mistakenly referred to themselves as "replacements."[27] One could not simply "replace" the lost men; they had benefited from months and years of intimate training and combat; they knew each other inside out and had absorbed all the finer points of life found in the daily slog in the brotherhood of the Poor Bloody Infantry. Familiarity, in this case, did not breed contempt; rather, it built confidence and fostered co-operation on a thousand little points that soldiers need to take for granted while in combat.[28]

Obtaining infantry-trained reinforcements was one thing; integrating them into a battalion and re-forming them into a cohesive fighting unit was another—particularly when the training of the reinforcements appeared subpar, which Eric Motzfeldt had noted as early as July 20.[29] "We received one draft of about 40 men half an hour before the attack on Hill [61]," he wrote, and later discovered that that "1 man had less than six weeks training in Canada and one week in England while another only had three months" of military service in total.[30] As Mitchell lamented after taking command, "Typical story is the lad who saw the invasion pictures of D-Day and thought the time had come to join up . . . we got them with 6 to 8 weeks' total service. We had an accident last week, man changing a Bren gun did not know you could take the magazine off. Do you wonder that we become balder and greyer."[31]

Megill commiserated with Mitchell's plight to a point and agreed that under normal circumstances, a battalion could suffer 10 percent casualties per month and keep fighting, while 20 percent casualties would require one month of retraining, 30 percent a full two months, and so on.[32] These, however, were not normal times. Despite assurances that Mitchell would have all the time necessary to absorb reinforcements into a battalion that had suffered 94 percent casualties on July 25, the scouts headed out with the lead company just ten days later as the Black Watch moved down the road towards May-sur-Orne once more.

EPILOGUE

===

THE BITTER HARVEST

I find analysis of an operation like the attack of the Black Watch at May-sur-Orne a most distasteful task, for it means criticism of some, who, whatever mistakes they made, made them in good faith and paid the supreme sacrifice in the course of their duty.

—LIEUTENANT GENERAL GUY SIMONDS, 1946

TEN DAYS AFTER THE MASSACRE ON VERRIÈRES Ridge, the new Black Watch CO, Frank Mitchell, stood with George Buch and Ronnie Bennett, watching the newly reconstituted A Company head down the road to May-sur-Orne yet again with the scout platoon in support. This hastily conceived operation, spurred by Lieutenant General Guy Simonds, Major General Charles Foulkes and Brigadier William J. Megill, called for the Black Watch to push their necks out to see whether the 1st SS Panzer Division had fled from the village and ridge, since intelligence indicated it had pulled out to join the counter-attack against the Americans at Mortain, to the west.[1] As the men of A Company found out to their horror, intelligence had miscalculated. Instead of pulling out in its entirety, the 1st SS Panzer Division moved piecemeal, and while a good portion had gone west, potent elements remained south of Caen. In minutes, A Company was wiped out to a man, caught on the march to

May by a lone Panther that barrelled down the road with guns blazing. Forced to take shelter in the same ditch that Benson had used on the twenty-fifth, the men sat trapped, mowed down by the Panther, which killed or wounded nearly half of them and forced the rest to surrender.

During the attack, the Germans fired ranging shots for their mortars, searching for Black Watch tactical headquarters, which lay five hundred yards behind. Mitchell, who had quickly developed a reputation for good luck or divine providence, survived several close calls; the others, however, did not share his good fortune. One of the last shells to crash down took the life of the newly promoted Major Ronnie Bennett, who died instantly without drama or fanfare. "One minute he was talking to us; the next he was dead," Buch lamented. "That's all there was to it really."

Nine days later, Ronnie's brother Harrison, who had joined the Black Watch with Ronnie and whose machine gun supported the battalion on Hill 61, died too, leaving their mother, Elva, to suffer as so many mothers would. Six months later, she died too, reportedly of a broken heart, as the doctors could find no physical reason for illness.[2]

Bennett was not the only hero of Verrières to die in the weeks following the attack.

On September 10, in the hamlet of Grand-Millebrugghe, the Black Watch had come under shellfire from the surrounded German garrison in nearby Dunkirk. Turning their massive naval guns landward, the Germans hit back fiercely like a cornered animal.

When the cry of a wounded man went up, Barney Benson, true to form, broke from the cover of his slit to drag the man to safety. He didn't make it. Cut almost in half by chunks of white-hot metal from the large-calibre naval shell, Benson died on a stretcher before he reached the aid station. In a most unusual and telling move within a regiment where few dared to cross the demarcation line that separated officers from NCOs, Captain John Kemp, recovering in a hospital bed, put pen to paper when he heard of Benson's death. He reached out to Benson's fiancée, whom he knew only as Ruth:

> *During the last five years I saw a good deal of Barney at Aldershot, Nova Scotia, in England and France; he was, of course, always a very popular and prominent figure, but it was when we reached France that he really came into his own. He was completely fearless and was an inspiration to every man in the battalion; time and again I have seen him expose himself in order to draw fire from a machine gun that we had been unable to locate; and there was no job too difficult or dangerous for Barney to have a try at it. When I heard of his death my first thought was of sorrow at the loss of a friend, and then the more I thought about him, the more I realized what his loss meant to the battalion; there are many of us who will never forget "Benson and his Scouts."*

BITTERNESS AND RECRIMINATION WENT HAND IN HAND in the aftermath of the Black Watch attack on Verrières Ridge, and they proved far-reaching. Headlines in British papers screamed of a "serious setback" for Anglo-Canadian forces south of Caen, but provided little detail, leaving Prime Minister Winston Churchill, who had just arrived back in England from his cross-Channel junket, to address the issue in Cabinet.[3] With the Soviet Red Army rampaging on the Eastern Front and the

Americans swanning south after their breakout from St. Lô, the heavy losses and limited gains on the front south of Caen sat in stark contrast to their successes.

The failure of Operation Spring to grab the coveted land south of the ridge for airfields had provoked another round of attacks on Montgomery by his fuming detractors. Churchill, however, did not bite. Instead, the British PM chose to back the 21st Army Group commander to the fullest, and push the unfolding narrative that Montgomery had penned long before the Germans stopped Simonds's drive dead in its tracks. Placing the disaster in the best possible light, the PM disavowed any knowledge of a setback. Churchill explained that the Germans had driven the Canadians back from one thousand yards of hard-won ground, an event entirely understandable given their role in holding the Germans in that sector to facilitate the American breakout to the west.

Except for the broad headlines, detailed word of what the failure meant for Canadian units had yet to reach the hometown newspapers an ocean away. In early August, the dreaded telegrams arrived at soldiers' homes, first in dribs and drabs and then in a flood. When regimental family members started connecting the dots, and whispers of a massacre arose, Colonel Paul Hutchison, the regimental commandant who had seen action at Vimy during the Great War, began to search for answers. He wrote to Captain F.C. Smith, his regimental adjutant:

> *Understand that Matthew Halton in "News Roundup" broadcast over CBC gave a "commentator on the spot" talk about an attack in Normandy which people have taken to have been our show on July 25th and that he was critical about the way the Battalion was handled . . .*

Is there any news through yet from any of the officers as to exactly what did happen July 25th to the Battalion? It looks as though very few officers were left.[4]

ON THE MORNING OF AUGUST 12, THE DAY BEFORE THE scouts recovered the bodies from the ridge, a series of sensationalist press reports broke the grim news in Canada, and the Verrières saga erupted. These reports, written by some of the country's finest war correspondents and run in all major dailies, laid bare the unsettling facts, and did little to alleviate the impact of the losses on the families at home. Based primarily on interviews with a handful of the Black Watch who had survived Verrières and an exhausted Captain Ronnie Bennett, who sat down with war correspondent Ralph Allen less than twenty-four hours after the fight in the farmyard, the headlines blazed: TRAPPED BLACK WATCH UNIT FIGHTS UNTIL LAST MAN: ASKS FOR NO AID and BLACK WATCH UNITS DIED ALONE IN TRAP.[5]

At the time of his interview, Ronnie Bennett still clung to a thin thread of hope that his fellow officers and their men had indeed survived, but the extensive nature of the casualties and the initial reports gave a good indication of the steep price paid by the Black Watch. "Trapped on a barren ridge," wrote Ralph Allen of the *Globe and Mail*:

[A]ll that was left of their gallant spearhead was swallowed up, platoon by platoon, section by section, finally man by man. Their ammunition ran out as a ring of German heavy guns and lighter automatic weapons went about its deadly work with the calculated precision of a firing squad. Finally, even the thin trickle of wounded, half-walking, half-crawling to the rear, came

to an end . . . the last man out . . . bore this message from the battalion's 24-year-old acting commanding officer—"don't send reinforcements."

IN AN ATTEMPT TO TEMPER THIS EXCEEDINGLY DARK chapter, Allen and other correspondents fell into line with the narrative coming down from Montgomery's headquarters and falsely attributed John Taylor's dramatic directive to Bennett not to take any more men up the ridge as the final words of Phil Griffin, a passage he now scripted as an epitaph for the regiment.

The long delay between writing and publication came at the order of 1st Canadian Army commander General Harry Crerar, who imposed an embargo on the stories, suspecting at first that journalistic exaggeration, rather than sound fact, might be at play. After a cursory examination of the war diaries and after-action reports, however, he realized that, despite the salacious tone of the correspondents, the basic facts of the stories rang true. Nevertheless, understanding the potential hot potato he had in his hands, Crerar dragged his feet for seventeen days to "lessen the effects on the public at home."[6]

When Hutchison first read the reports in August, the regimental commandant was in a state of disbelief. Not even his days on the Western Front in the Great War had prepared him for losses such as these, and he could not fathom the depths of the tragedy. Initially, he dismissed the accounts as gross exaggerations and was incensed by their tone. In his opinion, they created the wrong impression in the minds of the general public and did nothing but cause great distress among the next of kin at home.[7] But when the never-ending stream of telegrams continued to arrive and the casualty returns swelled, he strove to put the massacre into some semblance of context to "ease the minds" of the mothers and the widows of the fallen. Soon, the weight and nature of the grief proved overwhelming, to such a degree that Hutchison ordered a public memorial service held for the battalion. This unprecedented display of mourning culminated with an enormous candlelight vigil on an early-fall night that packed the seven-thousand-seat Percival Molson Memorial Stadium at McGill University, a mere stone's throw from Ronnie Bennett's mansion near the crown of Mount Royal. Despite this cathartic release, questions remained. When the stories finally broke, they fused with the litany of telegrams and letters home and instantly set off a firestorm of controversy. Politically well-connected members of Canada's most storied and celebrated regiment sought answers. The regimental elders lodged complaints with Douglas Abbott, the member of Parliament for St. Antoine–Westmount who had become minister of national defence in the fall, demanding a formal investigation, or at the very least a ministerial statement. With the world still at war, that would have to wait, leaving the families to deal with their loss, anger and a multitude of unanswered questions.

VERY FEW OF THE MEN WHO SURVIVED THE ASSAULT fully understood the multitude of factors that conspired to influence their fate on July 25. Their visceral appreciation, drawn from their personal experiences of that morning, whose scope remained little more than fifty yards wide and fifty yards deep, concluded that High Command had dropped the ball in the most spectacular fashion. Jimmy Wilkinson went right to the top, blaming, as he called him, "Montgomery the Rat" for his lack of martial ability. Jimmy Bennett put Simonds in his crosshairs: "He eventually got his 'victory,' but at what price?" Lieutenants George Buch and William Mackenzie-Wood pointed to Foulkes for failing to ensure the security of the start line, and his reluctance to intervene when Simonds ordered the attack to continue despite the little hope of success. "Foulkes says to press on, Foulkes says to press on" remained the nightmarish refrain that haunted Mackenzie-Wood in the decades that followed. To him, this "proved the moment of no return" and had become, in his view, a "fitting epitaph for the Black Watch attack." As Bruce Ducat, who succinctly characterized the intense frustration, put it so eloquently, "We went through four years of training for that horseshit?"

Even Major Phil Griffin, who approached beatification with calls for his posthumous awarding of the Victoria Cross for valour, did not escape a measure of scorn. Private George Alexander, who praised Griffin for fulfilling his duty, questioned why something "so suicidal had to be done" and "why higher up authorities allowed such a murderous attack to proceed."[8] Private Maurice Montreuil offered a more direct indictment: "Despite orders from Brigade, Major Griffin should have shown better judgment and called off the attack. It was just a plain case of suicide."[9]

Gordy Donald's criticism proved more stinging: "A lot of men got killed over somebody's stupidity—for not knowing enough to say when. The attack, one, should never have taken place, and when it did, it should have been stopped. It was hopeless right from the start. You knew you were up against something that you couldn't handle, and running to the top of the hill, I don't think, was the way to handle it. So, you got up there with three or four fellows—what are you going to do?"

With the war still raging and the material witnesses confined to either hospital beds, POW camps or the battlefield, any holistic and dispassionate assessment of the question would have to wait until war's end, when C.P. Stacey's historical team began to conduct its investigation in the summer of 1945.

As a professor of history at Princeton University before the war, Stacey had enjoyed full academic freedom, but now, as a major serving in the Canadian Army, the results of his inquiry would be subject to the chain of command and the comments and massaging of Guy Simonds and Charles Foulkes.

Once again, Foulkes shocked everyone with his meteoric and thoroughly unexplainable rise to power. Instead of losing his job following Spring, he gained a promotion and took over the 1st Canadian Corps, which fought in Italy and later in the North-West Europe campaign. When peace came, General Harry Crerar named him, rather than Guy Simonds, as the first postwar chief of the Canadian general staff. As such, the subordinate on July 25 now became the master, and Stacey's investigation became trapped within this unfolding saga at the highest levels of the Canadian military.[10]

Simonds, smarting from the slap in the face from his own government, did not rise to the occasion; instead of accepting responsibility for the failure of the operation and its high cost as both the architect and conductor, he strove to distance himself from the debacle. Immediately, he tried to influence the narrative by pressuring Stacey to conform to his wishes and downplay the losses to the Black Watch.[11] Stacey, for his part, resisted as best he could, but given his lack of academic freedom, his attempt only went so far. All that the adept military historian could do was leave footprints in his files for future generations of historians to follow in a bid to unravel the corps commander's intentional obfuscation. Sensing Stacey's reticence, and perhaps an allegiance with his arch-enemy Foulkes, Simonds took a further step and penned a series of petulant comments intended for the record, but not for publication, which blamed the fate of the Black Watch directly on certain aspects he believed would never meet a challenge: ultra-secret classified signals intelligence and the late Phil Griffin.

Taking advantage of the cloak of secrecy attached to the upper-echelon intelligence, which he had been told would remain hidden for eternity, Simonds blamed the "eleventh-hour" German reinforcement of the Verrières line for the compromise of what he claimed was an otherwise sound plan.

At first, this appeared a deft ploy, until the declassification of ultra-secret signals intelligence files following his death showed that he, like Dempsey and Montgomery, was fully aware of the buildup and the increasingly formidable German defences straddling Verrières from July 20 onward.[12] In fact, these releases made clear that Simonds was anything but surprised and that he had seized upon the fruits of this intelligence in his first attempt to grab the heights in Operation Atlantic, when reports showed a rip in the German line. Scorned by that failure, he planned to renew the breakout called for in Atlantic and Goodwood with the initial incarnation of Operation Spring. When intelligence showed that the German line had thickened over the next few days (a development that caused concern and skepticism for Dempsey and Montgomery and resulted in the noontime caveat on July 25), Simonds scaled the operation back, falling in line with Monty's request to grind down and "write off" German panzer reserves as a precursor to another colossal crack. Undaunted, Simonds clung to his belief that, at the very least, he would pocket the ridge as part of the bargain despite the mounting German threat. Without a doubt, when Spring kicked off in the early morning hours of July 25, the evidence was clear that he had lost the race for time, but he obstinately refused to accept that fact.

Equally, Simonds took the same approach when dealing with the touchy issue of the massacre of the Black Watch. Here, he placed the full responsibility squarely on the shoulders of those who could not answer back—in particular, Phil Griffin. "It has been a source of deep regret to me that a fine battalion like the

Black Watch suffered so heavily in this attack," he recorded. "I would prefer to make no statement on the subject for I dislike even suggesting criticism of those who lost their lives, but if a statement is required from me as a matter of record, I consider that the losses were unnecessarily heavy and the results achieved disappointing. Such heavy losses were not inherent in the plan nor in its intended execution. The action of the Black Watch was most gallant but was tactically unsound in its detailed execution."[13]

According to Stacey, Foulkes objected strongly to these assertions and prepared his own set of comments that took exception to Simonds's claims of faulty minor tactics on the part of the Black Watch. Their disagreement set off a historical tempest that embroiled the two most powerful men in the postwar Canadian Army.[14] Before this could boil over and become public, both men agreed to have their comments withdrawn and destroyed. For some unknown reason, only Foulkes's met the shredder, while one copy of Simonds's remarks survived in Stacey's files.

Although initially rankled by the overtly callous nature and tone of Simonds's remarks, historians and other critics have reluctantly accepted them; no matter how cutting, sharp, unsettling and distasteful, it was felt that, in essence at least, the corps commander had told the cold, hard truth. But alas, he had not.

At no time did Simonds mention the ticking clock that Dempsey imposed in direct response to the thickening of the German defences on Verrières, and the corresponding pessimism. Nor did Simonds factor in his preordained instructions to bypass centres of resistance to ensure he achieved his timing. This, of course, meant that no matter what Benson and Duffield had discovered in May-sur-Orne, or what route Griffin planned to take, Simonds had already sealed the fates of not only the Black Watch but all his units on the day, well before Griffin gave the order to advance.[15]

In later years, Brigadier Megill chafed at any suggestion that High Command had dispatched the Black Watch "unthinkingly into the maelstrom like the Light Brigade of Balaclava fame."[16] However, in mounting such a spirited defence, the brigade commander unwittingly offered a *mea culpa* for the entire chain of command, admitting that their decision did not come by chance or by accident, but rather as a consequence of ruthless and calculated design.

Of course, many of the Verrières survivors went to their graves before the evidence needed to solve this conundrum appeared in the public domain. In the interim, Megill became the main culprit and villain in the Black Watch saga. Already held in contempt, the brigadier remained within arm's reach, unlike Foulkes and Simonds, and although not blameless, he bore far too much of the brunt of their ire.

To the officers and men, Megill had failed to show grip. Instead of exercising initiative and thinking things through, he acted like an automaton, coming down from on high with fire in his eyes to blindly enforce orders for Griffin to "press on." Of course, none could know, let alone fathom, the depths of the command dysfunction at the corps, division and brigade levels fostered by Simonds's autocratic command style, which promoted near paralysis. Nor did they know of Dempsey's caveat, which sealed their fate long before Benson failed to push Duffield to go farther into May-sur-Orne or Griffin, with the honour of the regiment at stake, launching the men straight up and over Verrières Ridge.

Right across the front, Simonds had wedded his divisions to an unrealistic and overly rigid timetable, where the infantry and the tanks were forced to march to the beat regardless of the reality facing them along the line. Stripped of their initiative and flexibility, they could not "call an audible" or play a variation.

Instead, Simonds inculcated an atmosphere of fear that precluded independent action, which in turn ensured that when Spring took on a life of its own and became akin to a runaway locomotive, nobody felt confident to find the emergency brake, let alone pull the lever. Instead, an "all costs" culture and mentality arose—which, as it turned out, was exactly the price his subordinates paid on July 25, 1944.

But did Simonds have a viable alternative? Because the main objective of Spring was to draw the Germans into a costly battle of attrition, Simonds should have consolidated the meagre gains that his divisions achieved in the first phase of Spring, for it was clear by first light that despite Foulkes's division stumbling out of the blocks, the attack had provoked the desired German reaction. Instead of forcing the Royal Regiment to bypass Verrières village and the Black Watch to swing out past May-sur-Orne, creating the conditions for a breakthrough between Rocquancourt and Fontenay-le-Marmion that he, and only he, reasoned had a solid chance of success, Simonds should have opted to reinforce the RHLI at Verrières and Calgary Highlanders at May with the Black Watch. Failing that, he could have consolidated in St. Martin to await the counterattack from Dietrich's panzers. Quite likely, as witnessed by the RHLI's gallant stand at Verrières, he would have achieved his primary objective over the course of the twenty-fifth without needlessly risking everything in a race up Verrières in broad daylight. Equally, with the back of Dietrich's panzer reserve snapped, he could have resumed his advance with his armour on the twenty-sixth to capture Rocquancourt and Fontenay. Instead, Simonds, swept up in delusions of grandeur and riding a gambler's high, found himself seduced by misplaced pride in his bid to deliver the Vimy Ridge of his generation. Instead of achieving a monumental victory, he came away from Verrières with a bloody defeat that, next to the disaster at Dieppe, would go down as the deadliest day in Canadian history.[17]

Although unwise, some will argue that his actions fell well within the purview of a field commander, no matter how distasteful it may have been to the men at the front who had to bear the brunt of his actions. Perhaps so. But what is inexcusable, and can only be interpreted as an egregious act of cowardice and disloyalty to his subordinates, is Simonds's choice to turn his back on the men who faithfully obeyed his authority and executed his plan as prescribed. Sadly, as he had done in the past with other of his flawed plans and misadventures, he wilfully offered up Griffin and the Black Watch (among others) as the sacrificial lambs for his failure on July 25 to protect his career and reputation.

A STRING OF BITTER VICTORIES AND HARD-SLOGGING engagements continued as the war unfolded over the next nine months. By the end of hostilities, the Black Watch and the Calgary Highlanders vied for the dubious record of highest casualty totals suffered by the Canadian Army in the Second World War.

Some of the men who had fought and survived Verrières came back to fight another day. Eric Motzfeldt rejoined the battalion in the Rhineland and took temporary command of the battalion after Brigadier Megill fired his second Black Watch CO in less than five months. Before Megill could confirm him in the post, he fell wounded yet again, ending his war. Motzfeldt would come back to Montreal and start a successful insurance company. He died with his wife in a fiery car accident near Gananoque, Ontario, in 1967. John Taylor returned after six months in hospital, rehabbing from wounds to his upper thigh. Taylor's injuries had not fully healed, however, and he could not maintain the hard-slogging pace through the Reichswald forest. Within two weeks of rejoining the battalion, Taylor found himself on a ship, heading back to England. His war was over.

Stan Duffield also came back after his wounding and took command of a rifle company, where he lived up to his promise, steering it superbly in battle. Ten days before the war ended, he earned the Military Cross for bravery, coolness under fire and determined leadership in the Battle of Delmenhorst on the Weser River in April 1945.[18] Campbell Stuart, who lost a leg and never returned to combat, earned a mention in dispatches and the Croix de Guerre for his exploits at Verrières.[19] He came back to Canada and embarked on a career with C-I-L chemicals before moving on in his later years to the Department of External Affairs, where he worked as a Canadian negotiator on several major trade agreements. In 1995, Stuart, not long after his seventy-fifth birthday, died at the hands of his housekeeper, who stabbed him in a botched robbery attempt.

Bruce Ducat, John Kemp, Mac Roulston and Gordy Donald, who had all fallen into enemy hands, shared different fates. Ducat and Kemp saw their captivity curtailed abruptly when the Germans collapsed in Normandy and the Americans overran their hospitals. They returned to Canada long before Roulston and Donald. Kemp never regained the full use of his leg, while Ducat, permanently scarred on the right side of his face and lip, suffered from night terrors throughout his life. Roulston ended up in a German POW camp in Poland, not far from Gordy Donald. In January 1945, both embarked on the forced march westward, used as human shields by their German captors as the Soviets rampaged towards Berlin. Both survived the arduous eight-hundred-mile trek in the dead of winter with little food and were liberated in late April by the Americans. Upon their return to Canada, the two men took vastly different paths. Roulston married his sweetheart and used his paltry pension to get his university degree before embarking upon a lifelong career in sales. Donald, by his own admission, "crawled into a bottle" for the first five years after his homecoming, in response to the devastating results of the trauma he endured. Luckily, the strength of the woman who would be his second wife pulled him from the pits of despair and permanently put him back on the rails to sobriety and a happy, productive life.

Jock McLennan eventually pieced his world back together and returned to Montreal, where he met and married Helen Lake, a graduate of Queen's University who pursued a career promoting social justice with the International Labour Organization. They went on to have two children and lived in Winnipeg for years following Jock's transfer with the Bank of Montreal in the 1970s. In 2007, after sixty-one years of marriage, Jock passed away, having eventually regained the dignity—and, for the most part, the peace of mind—stolen abruptly from him on Hill 61.

The war would continue for Hook and his kid brother, as well as Sharpe, Brunner, Jimmy Bennett, Frank Balsis, Fred Delutis, Bill Pugh, Thomas Edgar, Paul Welligan and Syd Ayling. They would become the backbone of the regiment as its trials and tribulations continued. Some made it home in one piece—physically, at least—while others were wounded or died at the hands of the enemy, in accidents, and even as a result of friendly fire.

True to their legacy, the battalion fought on throughout France, Belgium, the Netherlands and Germany. By the end of the war, members of the regiment had won more than two hundred battle honours and awards and fought a wide range of foes: SS, Wehrmacht and fanatical German *Fallschirmjäger* (paratroopers); security forces; Luftwaffe personnel; and, near the end of the war, Dutch Nazis. They liberated many towns, from France to northern Holland, including Bourgtheroulde, Hoogerheide,

Goes, Xanten, Groningen and Oldenburg. In their finest moment, they not only liberated the Dutch from the tyranny and oppression of Nazism, but delivered them from the depths of hunger and famine as well.

Yet, along with the long left flank of the Allied advance, they had their setbacks too: the Battle of Spycker on the Dunkirk perimeter; another full-blown disaster in a beet field outside Woensdrecht, in the soggy Battle of the Scheldt, on "Black Friday," October 13; and the bloodbath on the Walcheren Causeway two weeks later. In its final act of the war, the battalion took the fight to Germany, battling through the Reichswald and Hochwald Forests before bouncing the mighty Rhine River and heading north into Holland proper. On the way, they liberated Groningen in a tense city struggle and were chasing the Germans into Oldenburg when the guns mercifully fell silent.

ACKNOWLEDGEMENTS

T HE RESEARCH FOR THIS BOOK UNFOLDED SLOWLY over a period of nearly two decades, and I would like to begin by thanking everyone who helped to make it possible. One of the best aspects of this historical research journey has been meeting a wide range of people who have influenced my work and become colleagues—and in some cases, lifelong friends.

First, I have to thank C.P. Stacey's historical team, who risked their lives during the war to record history, and of course the officers and men—dog-tired, beaten, battered and torn—who sat down and gave hours' and days' worth of their recollections of the most tumultuous moments of their lives. In many cases, these testimonies represented their last words on the subject.

I am also grateful to Dr. Stephen Harris, from the Directorate of History and Heritage in Ottawa, and his team at DHH who have generously helped me over the years: Serge Bernier, Alec Douglas, Bill McAndrew, Bob Caldwell, Bill Rawling, Donna Porter, Isabelle Campbell, Mike Whitby, Richard Gimlett, Sean Hunter, Ken Reynolds, Michelle Litalien, Jean Morin, Greg Donaghy, Bill Johnston, Yves Tremblay, Jim McKillop, Mike McNorgan, Carl Kletke, Andrea Schlecht and the late Ben Greenhouse, among others.

I would also like to thank the two generations of historians who have contributed to our understanding of the Canadian military experience during the war, and in Normandy in particular. Contextually, the many publications by J.L. Granatstein, David Bercuson, Holger Herwig, Desmond Morton, Jack English, Doug Delaney and Terry Copp have been invaluable to my research, as have Steve Prince, Andrew Godefroy, Denis and Shelagh Whitaker, Alex Fitzgerald-Black, John Nelson Rickard, Dave Grebstad, David Patterson, Geoff Hayes and Mike Bechthold.

This list also includes a historian's best friend—the archivist. In this case, without the support and expertise of Owen Cooke, Warren Sinclair, Lauren Butler and Valerie Casbourn at DHH and the wisdom, friendship and advice of Paul Marsden, Kevin Joynt and Alex Comber and the entire archival staff at Library and Archives Canada, this research would never have been possible.

I must thank Dr. Roger Sarty, who was a friend, mentor and boss all those years ago when I was a tiny cog in the machine that created the official history of the Royal Canadian Navy in the Second World War. In addition, I would like to thank Professor Emeritus Terry Copp at Wilfrid Laurier University, who gave me sage research advice and plenty of material throughout the course of this project.

This research could not have been completed without "bird dogs" on the ground—the researchers at various archival facilities, particularly Simon Cawthorne, James Ellis, Fiona Isaacson, Greg Hill, Joanne McCutcheon, Cal Kufta, Adam Simatos, Ines Khanna, Laird Niven, Jaimie Chausse, Joel and Marianne Stoeppels, John Sliz, Richard Long and Nigel Griffin. Additional thanks go out to the specialist historians André Grard in St. Martin, France; Kristian Gravenor, for his vast knowledge of the history of Montreal; Doug Nash and Didier Lodieu, for help with the 272nd Division; and Charles Trang, for his work on the 9th SS.

For translation, I must thank Lorina Walker and Peter Berg,

who handled the French and German, respectively, in the volume, and John Vincent for his literary eye for descriptive detail.

An additional note of thanks goes to Andrew MacLaughlan, Lewis Evans and François Tessier for their commitment to history and their most generous help on a very difficult and painful chapter in the grand history of Bishop's College School.

To the Black Watch Regiment and its extended family: Colonel Steve Angus, Colonel Tom Price, Lieutenant Colonel Vic Chartier, Lieutenant Colonel Ian McCulloch, Lieutenant Colonel Gordon Lusk, Lieutenant Colonel Daniel O'Connor, Lieutenant Colonel Bruno Plourde, Lieutenant Colonel Bruce Bolton, Lieutenant Colonel Hal Klepak, Lieutenant Colonel Tom MacKay, Lieutenant Colonel Bill Sewell, Lieutenant Colonel Chris Phare, Major Mike Boire, archivist Mike Cher, historian Earl Chapman, Lionel Chetwynd, pipe majors Cameron Stevens, Andy Kerr and Brian MacKenzie, drum major Mike Lanno, Preston McIntyre, Stephanie Cyr, Jim Conway, Maciej Jonasz, Mike Walker, Sergeant Brian Hill, Cal Kufta, Andy Kerr, David Patterson, Andrew Godefroy, John Nelson Rickard, Bob Clarke, Dan Cunningham, Charles Bierbrier, Ted Bird, Gary Young, Peter Gannon, John Barron, Oscar Kontorsky, Jean and Cal Wilson, Andrew Lindsay, Hugh Lawson, Andy Melville, Enrique Munizaga, Eric Maura, Jim Quesnel, Jeff McCarthy, Steph Gaines and "the corps": Peter Danyluk, André Demers, Carl Rowland and Mark MacIntyre. Special thanks goes out to Mike Dorosh from the Calgary Highlanders, Gord Ritchie, Bill Carlisle and Tom Irvine for their tireless efforts on behalf of the Black Watch veterans and Lady Catherine Hamilton for the help she offered on multiple occasions. I would also like to thank Lieutenant Colonel Roman Jarymowycz for his friendship and constant debate over the years, and my best friend in uniform, Colonel Keith Lawrence, for all your help, friendship and support.

ACKNOWLEDGEMENTS

What took me on many occasions to battlefields around the world was the filming of nearly twenty documentaries for History Television in Canada and UKTV in England. These projects would never have happened without the support of the crew, past and present, at History Television: Sarah Jane Flynn, Nick Crowe, Andrew Johnson, Cameron Mask, Steve Gamester, Michael Kot, Lynne Carter, Sydney Suissa, Lisa Godfrey, Doug Murphy, Christine Shipton, Robin Neinstein, Rachel Nelson, Cindy Witton and Robin Hutt. I have happily worked in conjunction with them for nearly twenty years, and have been so proud and appreciative of their support for groundbreaking historical research on their network.

Special thanks go to my "partner in crime" in several documentary productions, the talented producer/director Wayne Abbott, who has traipsed across many a battlefield with me, from Hong Kong to Europe, in our effort to bring history to life on the small screen, starting with *Black Watch: Massacre on Verrières Ridge* in 2005. I also want to thank the War Junk team—Dan Stevenson, Andrew Sheppard, Dallas Boyes, Joanna Maracle, Craig Mitchell and Keon Abbott—for the many hair-raising and death-defying scrapes we managed to escape while on set, and all that time we spent in Arras. I would also like to thank Elliot Halpern, Elizabeth Trojan, Derek Rogers, Anja Sobkowska and director Robin Bicknell and the entire team at Yap Films who produced *Black Watch Snipers*.

Having taught history at the university, college and high school levels for close to twenty-five years, I would like to thank my fellow historians, faculty, administration and staff at Marianopolis College in Westmount for all that you've done to support me during this project, and particularly my office mate, Maria Salomon, for putting up with me.

To put a complex book together requires a team of experienced and talented professionals. My literary super-agent, Rick Broadhead, who ensured everything came together, and the excellent team at HarperCollins, particularly my editor, the incomparable Jim Gifford, as well as Craig Swinwood, Iris Tupholme, Leo MacDonald, Michael Guy-Haddock, Cory Beatty, Noelle Zitzer, Lauren Morocco, Melissa Nowakowski, and copy editor Lloyd Davis. They all have my deep respect and admiration for a job well done.

A special note of appreciation goes out to the veterans and their families who generously gave of their time to talk to me and granted permission to quote from their letters, diaries, journals and unpublished memoirs—all of which add to the drama and human reality of this story. They include Jimmy and George Wilkinson, George Buch, Gordon Donald, Sandy Sanderson, Dale Sharpe, Jim Bennett, Phil Griffin, Bill Booth, Bill Mackenzie-Wood, Cal Wilson, Bruce Ducat, John Kemp, Captain Campbell Stuart, Eric Motzfeldt, John Taylor, Bill Davis, Stan Matulis, Thanning Anderson, Gordon Ohkle, Ian Mitchell, Joe Nixon, Bill "Boots" Betteridge and the Black Watch Associations in Montreal, Toronto and New Brunswick. Additional thanks go to Kate Catterall, André du Chastel de Montrouge, Philippa Duchastel de Montrouge, Hanna MacDuff, Dugal MacDuff, Nicola Danby, Frank Royle, Rod Hodgson, the team at Project 44, Steve Lehman, Drew Maynard and Will Hannenberg, Nicola Beaucourt, Fred Jeanne, David Zelden, Tim Weingard, Jayne Poolton-Turvey, Jim Hanna and Alex Fitzgerald-Black.

To the friends and family I have put on hold for the last year—Greg Hill, the boys from the Black Sox, Geoff B. and the Knights, my former colleagues at LBP and the Black Watch, John, Liette, Pat, Lorina, Dave, Carly, Stephanie, James and all of my nieces and nephews—I thank you for your patience, understanding, love and friendship.

ACKNOWLEDGEMENTS

Finally, I would like to thank my mother, Imelda "Millie" O'Keefe, for everything you have done and continue to do in your most remarkable life, and of course my wife, Carolyn, my children, Jessica, Andie and Kevin, and our boxador, Poppy (who acted as part muse, part foot warmer as she curled up for hours at my feet while I penned this work)—thank you so much for your support throughout this remarkable journey. I love you all.

ENDNOTES

—

CHAPTER 1: LA VOIE SACRÉE

1. The Black Watch War Diary notes that Eisenhower addressed the entire
    5th Brigade on May 29, 1944: "After a warm march to the camp, the
    troops appreciated his punctuality and off-handed manner, as the
    orders were to 'stand easy' for the inspection. His jovial and honest-
    looking countenance soon won the hearts of the troops and after
    addressing them from atop of a Jeep as to what support would be given
    for the impending invasion both from the air, land and sea; how much
    he thought of the Canadians in Italy; and generally how confident of the
    outcome; a spontaneous thundering applause was given him before the
    prosaic and usual three cheers were offered."

2. LAC, Personnel file of Mike Brunner.

3. NAUK, WO 231/289, Army Training Instruction No. 9: The
    Organization, Training and Employment of Snipers, 1944; WO
    204/7584, Training Snipers; WO 279/833, Sniping, 1946; WO 179/3969,
    War Diary, 1st Cdn Corps Sniper School, June 1944.

4. BWA, Roman Jarymowycz Collection, Questionnaire for Bill Pugh.

5. LAC, Personnel file of Maj. E.S. Duffield.

6. BWA, Letter from John Kemp to Ruth (fiancée of Barney Benson),
    November 25, 1944.

7. LAC, Personnel file of Sgt. Bernard Benson.

8. Dinesen was the brother of author Karen Blixen, who penned *Out of
    Africa* and also wrote under the name Isak Dinesen. Thomas earned his
    VC during the opening of the Last Hundred Days. One of the first duties
    I had as a young subaltern in the Black Watch was to help find a home
    for his VC when his family decided to part with it in the early 1990s.
    Eventually, it ended up in the Lord Ashcroft Medal Collection at the
    Imperial War Museums in London.

9. LAC, Personnel file of Lt. Col. Eric Motzfeldt.

10. LAC, Personnel files of Maj. George C. Fraser and Maj. Alan Stevenson.

11. LAC, Personnel file of Maj. F.P. Griffin.

12. BWA, John Kemp interview with Roman Jarymowycz and Brian McKenna, 1990.
13. BWA, 1st Bn BWC CASF, Confidential Memo for OC 1st Battalion the BW (RHR) of C (CAA) Concerning Officers Sent Forward on Draft from the Reserve Units of the Regiment, circa 1940.
14. Ibid.
15. "Alpha Psi Remembers," Zeta Psi–Alpha Psi Chapter, http://www.zetapsimcgill.com/history/alpha-psi-remembers/.
16. LAC, Personnel file of Maj. Edwin Ronald Bennett.
17. *Gazette* (Montreal), March 23, 1940.
18. *Gazette* (Montreal), October 14, 1940.
19. BCS Archives, Personnel files of Ronnie Bennett, Harrison Bennett, George Buch, John Kemp, Campbell Stuart, Alan Robinson, George MacKay, Bill Doheny, Gordon Powis and Sydney Radley-Walters.
20. Hal Miller, "Builder of Men," *Saturday Night*, 1942.
21. BCS Archives, BCS Bulletin, February 1995.
22. LAC, Personnel file of Crawford Grier.
23. BCS Archives, BCS Yearbook, Winter 1931.
24. Bethan Bell, "Jutland Jack: The Life and Death of a Boy Sailor," BBC News, May 27, 2016, https://www.bbc.com/news/uk-england-36386665.
25. BWA, Letter from John Kemp to his father, Collin, July 1944.
26. Howard Margolian, *Conduct Unbecoming*, 123.
27. L.S.B. Shapiro, "Black Watch Warriors Horrified at Hun Murder of 19 Canadians," *Gazette* (Montreal), August 4, 1944.
28. BWA, Letter from Capt. J.P. Taylor RHC to Lt. Col. D.H. Taylor, August 15, 1944.
29. Alexander McKee, *Caen: Anvil of Victory*.

CHAPTER 2: ALBATROSS
1. Lieutenant General Guy Granville Simonds, the 2nd Canadian Corps commander, was also awarded the Sword of Honour on his graduation in 1925. Lieutenant Colonel Robert Guy Carrington-Smith, who wrote Cantlie's yearbook entry, was a lifelong diplomat and former high commissioner to Trinidad and Tobago and Canadian ambassador to the United States. Cantlie's other classmates from 1929 include Brigadier Ted Beament, who ran the show for General Harry Crerar at the 1st Canadian Army, and Lieutenant Colonel Cecil Merritt, who earned the Victoria Cross for valour during the deadly Dieppe raid. Major General Herbert Alan "Sparky" Sparling became vice-chief of the general staff. Douglas Cunningham served as brigade major at Dieppe and then com-

manded the 9th Infantry Brigade in Normandy on D-Day. He earned
the Distinguished Service Order for gallantry and distinguished service.
Maxwell Charles Gordon Meighen, who rose to colonel in the Corps of
Royal Canadian Electrical and Mechanical Engineers, was the son of
Canadian prime minister Arthur Meighen. Colonel Robert Theodore
DuMoulin was a battery commander with the 15th Field Regiment
in Italy and North-West Europe. Lieutenant Colonel Allan Kitchener
Jordan, commander of the 3rd Reconnaissance Regiment, Governor
General's Horse Guards, earned the DSO for "courageous leadership,
bravery and outstanding leadership" at the battle of the Gothic Line and
later during the capture of Cervia. George Dyer Weaver served with the
South African Army and later the Royal Canadian Corps of Signals during the Second World War, then went on to become the Liberal member
of Parliament for the Manitoba riding of Churchill. Less distinguished
was Squadron Commander Fowler Morgan Gobeil, who commanded
242 Squadron during the disastrous fighting in France in June 1940. The
242, an "all-Canadian" squadron cobbled together for public relations
purposes, included the flying ace Douglas Bader. Gobeil's command was
as disastrous as the campaign, and he was promptly relieved of command at start of the Battle of Britain.

2. The regimental *cri de coeur* came in the wake of the unceremonious
sacking of his older cousin Stephen Cantlie as battalion commander
in the spring of that year. The name Cantlie was synonymous with the
Black Watch. Stephen's father, George, was viewed as the real father of
the regiment. Unsubstantiated rumours, typical of army scuttlebutt when
few know the truth, flew wide and fast that the division commander,
Major-General Hamilton "Ham" Roberts, had sacked Stephen after
finding him drunk on duty during an inspection. Although it appeared
suddenly, his dismissal did not come overnight, nor was it unexpected.
For nearly a year, his superiors had Stephen Cantlie on their radar
following an inspection of the division's fighting capabilities, conducted
by Field Marshal Montgomery before he left to assume command of
the Eighth Army in North Africa. After observing Cantlie in operation
for a little over an hour, "it became quite clear," Monty wrote, "that he
knows nothing whatever about how to command and train a battalion.
He is possibly a good Company Commander. It is a great pity he was
given command of this fine battalion. He is quite unfit for it. He inspires
no confidence." Montgomery's damning measurement carried much
weight and proved a hill too high to climb. Despite repeated warnings
to improve in a multitude of areas, the slide continued for nearly a year

before Stephen was axed and sent home. Although a harsh assessment, the decision to remove him from command likely proved a blessing in disguise. In the estimation of his superiors, by the time he was relieved, the stocky, now-balding forty-year-old appeared older than his age. Although "co-operative and sincere," they viewed him as "a plodding type with little brains," who was "sadly lacking in drive, personality and spark."

3. LAC, Personnel file of Lt. Col. S.S.T. Cantlie: "An excellent type of officer who inspires confidence and will do well on the staff or in command . . . Reliable, hardworking, and possesses a good deal of energy. He works well as a member of a team but also has the ability to take charge when appointed as leader. He expresses himself very well, both verbally and on paper. He has a pleasing personality. His brain works quickly and he shows more than the average amount of common sense. He has a good knowledge of his arm and his knowledge of the other arms has improved since the beginning of the course and is now good. He always produces good work, even though pressed for time. He is sturdily built and should be able to stand a good deal of physical effort. He has the personality and ability to make a very good staff officer."

4. BWA, Farewell Address of Lt. Col. S.S.T. Cantlie, given to the men of the 1st Battalion RHC (Black Watch) on relinquishing command, England, October 9, 1943.

5. Ibid.

6. Paul Hutchison, *Canada's Black Watch: The First Hundred Years, 1862–1962* (Montreal: Black Watch of Canada, 1962).

7. In Stephen Cantlie's case, his attention to detail started to wane, then morale (the primordial ingredient in any organization) dipped to dangerous levels. Requests from some of his best officers and men for transfer ensued, as did a rise in disciplinary issues that manifested in a marked deficiency in performance during a series of training exercises. Finally, his nerves started to fray, and it was not long before both his officers and men realized something was not right with the "Boss." Lieutenant George Buch, the bespectacled, oval-faced commander of the pioneer platoon, recalled, "He would hide if Brigade people were coming down. He would hide. 'Don't let them know where I am' or 'tell them I have gone to lower Slobovia' or something like that." It should not have come as a shock when Stephen's relief came; unlike SST, he did not view command of the battalion as the culmination of a professional or personal goal, or even passion, but rather a family obligation.

8. BWA, Letter from Lt. Col. S.S.T. Cantlie to Col. P.P. Hutchison, June 5, 1943.

9. BWA, Farewell Address of Lt. Col. S.S.T. Cantlie, given to the men of the 1st Battalion RHC (Black Watch) on relinquishing command, England, October 9, 1943.

10. Letter from Cantlie to Hutchison, June 5, 1943.

11. LAC, Personnel file of Lieutenant Colonel S.S.T. Cantlie.

12. Cantlie's farewell address.

13. Letter from Cantlie to Hutchison, June 5, 1943.

14. BWA, Letter from Cantlie to Hutchison, as quoted in the Black Watch Officer's Bulletin No. 1, November 20, 1943: "We have progressed a considerable amount. We have had one large exercise on which the unit did very well and we were awarded a considerable amount of favourable comment. We were leading unit in an approach march and A Company distinguished itself by making a naked attack (literally speaking) across a river. It was a very stout effort because their instructions were to get ahead at all costs and they did. The GOC even went so far as to ask if my leading company had recovered its pants when I saw him the next day. I had rather expected a racket for such behaviour, but on the contrary we were complimented for our ingenuity and initiative."

15. BWA, Letter from Lt. J.L. McLennan to Col. P.P. Hutchison, May 27, 1944.

16. The infamous Kurt Meyer commanded the 25th SS Panzergrenadier Regiment of the 12th SS Panzer Division. Known as "Panzer Meyer," he was convicted of war crimes by the Canadian government after the war for the actions of his men in Normandy. Sentenced to death at first and then commuted to life in prison, he served five years in Nova Scotia's Dorchester Penitentiary, where he petitioned for clemency. In 1951 he was transferred to a British military prison in Germany and was released in 1954. He became a leading apologist for the SS until he died of a massive heart attack in December 1961.

17. Much to his dismay, the censor seized them and they never arrived in Canada.

18. The 2nd SS Das Reich Panzer Division committed a series of atrocities while making its march from southern France to Normandy, first at Tulle and then the most notorious: the sacking of Oradour-sur-Glane, where they murdered hundreds of French civilians. The other SS unit in Normandy, the 1st SS Leibstandarte Panzer Division (Hitler's bodyguard), had a string of ruthless actions on its record on the Eastern Front, while the 17th SS Panzergrenadier Division had committed atrocities against French civilians and American servicemen alike. The newly arrived 9th SS Hohenstaufen Panzer Division and the 10th SS

Frundsberg Panzer Division had yet to make their marks, but it was assumed they too would follow suit.

19. Michael E. Sullivan, "Combat Motivation and the Roots of Fanaticism: The 12th SS Panzer Division in Normandy," *Canadian Military History* 10, no. 3 (2001); LAC, RG24 Vol. 10427, Supplementary Report of the Supreme Headquarters Allied Expeditionary Force Court of Inquiry Re: Shooting of Allied Prisoners of War by 12 SS Panzer Division (Hitler-Jugend) in Normandy France, 7–21 June 1944; Howard Margolian, *Conduct Unbecoming*, 123.

20. DHH, Biographical File, Robert Elliot Rogge.

21. BWA, Letter from Capt. J.P. Taylor RHC to Lt. Col. D.H. Taylor, August 15, 1944.

22. BWA, Letter from Sgt. J. McOuan to his parents, August 2, 1944.

23. Robert, born in 1905, served with the Seaforth Highlanders in Italy. Herbert, born in 1910, served with the Royal Canadian Artillery and earned the Military Cross for valour, serving as a forward observation officer with the 15th Field Regiment in September 1944. Shirley, born in 1915, served with Phil in the Black Watch as battalion and later brigade intelligence officer, and his sister Eileen, born in 1908, worked at Canadian military headquarters in London as a social worker dealing with war brides.

24. Author's notes on interview with Eileen Griffin in Morrisburg, Ontario, March 27, 2005.

25. BWA, Kemp interview with Jarymowycz and McKenna, 1990.

26. LAC, Personnel file of Maj. Fredrick Phillip Griffin. So impressed was he with Griffin that the commander of the tactical school recommended that he be made battalion second-in-command following some seasoning as a company commander—or, failing that, his successor as commandant of the company commander's course, where he would be responsible for teaching all the company commanders in the Canadian Army their craft.

27. BWA, 1st BN BWC CASF, Confidential Memo for OC 1st Battalion the BW (RHR) of C (CAA) Concerning Officers Sent Forward on Draft from the Reserve Units of the Regiment. The full comment reads: "Extremely efficient and smart. Excellent instructor. Full of confidence. Used to taking responsibility. Shut-in nature making it difficult to get to know him well personally. Really brainy. Too 'Regimental' in dealing with Canadian type of other ranks. Needs to be drawn out more in Mess. Considered here probably most efficient subaltern we have ever had."

28. DHH, 145.2R15011 (D11), "Account of a Search for Verson as told by Maj. F.P. Griffin, A Coy, RHC, 16 July 44."

29. Author's notes on conversation with George Buch, May 10, 1992.
30. Author's notes on conversation with Bruce Ducat, March 2005.
31. Richard Lawrie, "Narratives of Collaboration."
32. Author's notes on a conversation with Jimmy Wilkinson, May 2005.
33. BWA, Letter from Capt. John Kemp to Ruth (last name unknown—fiancée of Sgt. Bernard "Barney" Benson), November 25, 1944.
34. DHH, 145.2R15011 (D11), "Account of a Search for Verson as told by Maj. F.P. Griffin, A Coy, RHC, 16 July 44."
35. Ibid.

CHAPTER 3: INOCULATION
1. LAC, RG24 Vol. 15188, War Diary, Régiment de Maisonneuve.
2. BWA, Letter from John Kemp to his father, July 8, 1944.
3. J.L. Granatstein, "The Old Boy Networks."
4. University of Toronto Archives, B90-0020/017/041, C.P. Stacey, "Impressions of Guy Simonds, Fall 1945"; Stephen Ashley Hart, Montgomery and "Colossal Cracks."
5. Stacey, "Impressions of Guy Simonds"; Imperial War Museums, Erskine Papers, Erskine Diary, July 21, 1944; LAC, RG24 Vol. 17506, War Diary, 2nd Field Historical Section, 1000, July 21, 1944. In Stacey's remarks from the fall of 1945, he wrote, "Part of General Simonds' success may well have been due to his capacity for taking decisions which some might deem ruthless—decisions in which the needs of the tactical situation were placed before 'human' considerations." On July 16, 1944, Simonds addressed the officers of the 3rd Canadian Infantry Division and 2nd Canadian Armoured Brigade at the château near Cairon: "The Russian offensive in the East is going extremely well. From the latest reports, the Russians are some thirty to forty miles from the East Prussian frontier. Here in the West, the German formations are all committed, including two which arrived recently from Russia. As far as we can determine, the Germans are short of men and equipment, and we have not so far encountered any fresh formations, nor do there seem to be any in sight. Opposite us is the 'works,' so to speak. I think you will remember General Montgomery's remarks when he spoke to all formations prior to D-Day and said that we had the war 'in the bag' if we made an all-out effort. My view is that we will have the war 'in the bag' this summer, or at least in a matter of weeks, if we pursue the advantage we now hold. I cannot stress too highly what effect this all-out effort will have on the enemy and its advantages to us particularly from the point of view of our own troops. If the war drags out, normal wastage will ensue and casualties will mount up. On the other hand, by making use of an all-out

effort, our casualties may be initially high, but in the long run they will be less. I think that it is safe to compare the enemy in his present situation to a boxer who is groggy on his feet, and needs but the knockout blow to finish him off. I ask all commanders here present to put first and foremost into their minds the idea of the all-out effort. You must always remember that if you rest, so does the enemy; and the final outcome takes considerably longer. You must therefore call on your troops for this all-out effort . . . I want it to be absolutely clear in your minds that occasions will arise when I will make heavy demands from you at a time when your troops are tired, but the enemy is groggy. This produces great results and saves casualties. There is always a tendency on our part to look at our troops after a particularly stiff engagement and consider them tired, without appreciating, at the same time, that the enemy is more so. I think that the German's position as a whole is not far from the point of cracking up unless he produces fresh formations. His prospects of producing fresh formations from Russia are at present very slim, although he may produce some from Italy. There is no doubt that he may have a certain amount of reinforcements to draw from but they cannot materially alter his present position."

6. J.L. Granatstein, *Weight of Command*, 19.
7. Douglas Delaney, *Corps Commanders*, 190.
8. Author's notes on conversation with Brigadier Elliot Rodger in Ottawa, March 1997.
9. LAC, MG30 E374, Vol. 2: Reginald Roy Papers, Interview with Lt. Gen. R. Moncel, June 3, 1982.
10. J.L. Granatstein, *The Generals*, 201.
11. LAC, Personnel file of Maj. Gen. Charles Foulkes.
12. John Buckley, *British Armour*, 204.
13. BWA, Letter from John Kemp to his mother, July 11, 1944.
14. BWA, Letter from Lt. J.L. McLennan to Col. P.P. Hutchison, July 15, 1944.
15. Ibid.
16. LAC, Personnel file of Pte. Elie Desormeaux.
17. Dave Grossman and Bruce K. Siddle, "Psychological Effects of Combat"; Dave Grossman, *On Killing*; Dave Grossman, *On Combat*.
18. LAC, Personnel files for Pte. Jean Jacques Bleau, Pte. Thomas Watt and Pte. Robert Garrett. Watt was Anglican, Garrett a Protestant, while Bleau had converted from Roman Catholicism to the Church of England to marry his sweetheart from Sussex fifteen months earlier. Although the Black Watch war diary lists a fourth man, by the name of Wood, who was killed along with these three, there is no such indication in the records.

There was a soldier named Wood who was listed as wounded effective July 17, which raises the possibility that he was wounded in this incident, but survived—much to the surprise, I am sure, of the war diarist.

19. Ibid.
20. LAC, Personnel file of Maj. Gen. William J. Megill.
21. University of Calgary Archives, Bercuson Papers, Interview of George Hees by Jeffery Williams for *The Long Left Flank*, June 6, 1985. Hees, who attended RMC with Cantlie, served under Megill during the Battle of the Scheldt in the fall of 1944 before being wounded by a sniper. After the war, he went into politics and became a minister in the Diefenbaker government until he resigned during the Bomarc missile scandal. Later in his career, he was appointed to serve as veterans affairs minister in the Mulroney government.
22. Terry Copp, *The Brigade*, 35.
23. Ibid.
24. LAC, Personnel file of Maj. Gen. William J. Megill.
25. Hees interview by Jeffery Williams.
26. Ibid.
27. Ibid.
28. Ibid.
29. Author's notes on conversation with George Buch, May 10, 1992.
30. Field Marshal Helmuth von Moltke, the chief of the Prussian general staff, created a matrix of officer attributes, based on whether they were smart or dumb, lazy or energetic. Officers who were smart and lazy or smart and energetic would bring success on the battlefield. Even dumb and lazy would not hurt. But the combination of dumb and energetic was to be avoided at all costs, as it was sure to court or usher in disaster. "Field Marshal Moltke's Four Types of Military Officer," *I Was Just Thinking* (blog), July 16, 2011, http://old-soldier coloncl.blogspot.com/2011/07/field-marshal-moltkes-four-types-of.html.
31. James Wood, *Militia Myths*.
32. LAC, Personnel file of Maj. Robert Gordon Slater.
33. Author notes on conversation with Lt. Warren Trudeau, May 2005.
34. BWA, 1st BN BWC CASF, Confidential Memo for OC 1st Battalion the BW (RHR) of C (CAA) Concerning Officers Sent Forward on Draft from the Reserve Units of the Regiment. "Doheny, W.—Excellent officer, keen, capable, and efficient. Has plenty of initiative. Has brains and a leader. Handles men extremely well and very popular with junior officers. Wants to make Army his career. Considered here one of ablest junior officers we have ever had. Sloppy in his dress and very Irish in many

ways, but most effective nevertheless and gets things done. Not afraid of responsibility. Has some signalling experience and worked 5 months in orderly room full time. Was particularly good Regt Orderly Officer."

CHAPTER 4: BOUNCE THE ORNE

1. Roman Jarymowycz, *Tank Tactics from Normandy to Lorraine.*
2. NAUK, WO 205/1121, Operation Goodwood: 2nd Army Plan Break Through to South of Caen, July 1944.
3. DHH, AHQ Report No. 58.
4. Ibid.
5. BWA, Black Watch War Diary, July 1944.
6. LAC, RG24 Vol. 14109, 5th Brigade War Diary, "Operational Order No 1—Operation Atlantic. July 18, 1944."
7. BWA, Black Watch War Diary, July 1944.
8. LAC, Personnel file of Sgt. Fred Janes.
9. Kemp interview with Roman Jarymowycz and Brian McKenna.
10. LAC, Personnel file of Pte. Alex Duncan.
11. LAC, Personnel file of Cpl. Dale Sharpe.
12. LAC, Personnel file of Sgt. Bernard Benson; author's notes on conversation with Jimmy Wilkinson, March 2005.
13. Author's notes on conversation with Mike Brunner, December 21, 2014.
14. Author's notes on conversation with Jimmy Wilkinson, March 2005.
15. NAUK, WO171/221, Second British Army Intsum No. 44, July 18, 1944. Both the 1st and 8th British Corps were expecting that the 10 SS would come east of the Orne; WO171/221, Second British Army Int Log.
16. NAUK, HW 41/416. The regulations concerning Ultra prohibited its distribution to any unit lower than army level. As such, Montgomery and Dempsey received this precious information, while Simonds, thanks to Montgomery's patronage, could view the material at Dempsey's headquarters, though his staff at 2nd Canadian Corps headquarters remained officially in the dark.
17. BWA, Letter from Maj. Alan Stevenson to Lt. Col. S.D. Cantlie, September 7, 1944.
18. Author interview with George Buch, March 7, 1992.
19. LAC, RG24 Vol. 9879, Battle Experience Questionnaire, Major J.P.G. Kemp, 1st Battalion RHC, October 14, 1944; author's notes on conversation with George Buch, May 10, 1992.
20. BWA, Black Watch War Diary, July 18, 1944.
21. This boulevard was renamed after Yves Guillou, the first postwar mayor of Caen, who died in 1963.

22. BWA, 1st BN BWC CASF, Confidential Memo for OC 1st Battalion the BW (RHR) of C (CAA) Concerning Officers Sent Forward on Draft from the Reserve Units of the Regiment.
23. Author's notes on conversation with George Buch, May 10, 1992.
24. LAC, RG24 Vol. 14109, 5th Brigade War Diary, "Operational Order No. 1—Operation Atlantic. July 18, 1944."
25. Victor Turner, "Liminality and Communitas," in *The Ritual Process*, 94–113, 125–30.
26. Kemp interview with Roman Jarymowycz and Brian McKenna.
27. Author's notes on conversation with George Buch, May 10, 1992.
28. Ibid.
29. In 1961 the Lycée Malherbe moved to its present location, about five hundred yards south of the Abbaye aux Hommes on the Boulevard Albert Sorel.
30. DHH, A Company RHC, Report on Storm Boat Training by A Coy RHC (17–18 April 1944) by Major F.P. Griffin.
31. Ibid.
32. Ibid.
33. BWA, Black Watch War Diary, July 1944.
34. LAC, Personnel file of L. Cpl. Robert George MacKay.
35. Author's notes on a conversation with Jimmy Wilkinson, May 2005.
36. LAC, Black Watch War Diary, Pt. II: Orders, July 1944.
37. *Ottawa to Caen*, 119.
38. LAC, Personnel file of Pte. Arthur Campbell Wilkinson; *Ottawa to Caen*, 119.
39. Author's notes on conversation with George Buch, May 10, 1992.
40. Letter from Stevenson to Cantlie, September 7, 1944.
41. LAC, Personnel file of Lt. Robert Austin; BWA, Letter from Lt. E.S. (Stan) Duffield to Col. P.P. Hutchison, August 30, 1944.
42. LAC, Personnel file of Lt. Robert Austin.
43. Letter from Stevenson to S.D. Cantlie, September 7, 1944.
44. DHH, 1st Bn Black Watch RHR of Canada, "The Crossing of the River Orne" by Maj. Alan Stevenson, September 12, 1944; author's notes on a conversation with Bruce Ducat, March 2005.
45. Author's notes on a conversation with Bruce Ducat, March 2005.
46. LAC, Personnel file of Pte. Leo Lalonde.
47. LAC, RG24 Vol. 13750, Message Log, HQ 2nd Cdn Inf Div, 19 July, 0100hrs, from 2nd Cdn Corps to 2nd Cdn Inf Div: "Make sure 5 Cdn Inf Bde cautioned re move across; 7 Cdn Inf Bde thinks that some RHC shooting up Regina Rifles already."

48. LAC, RG24 Vol. 9879, Battle Experience Questionnaire, Capt. V.E. Traversy, 1st Battalion RHC, August 18, 1944.
49. LAC, RG24 Vol. 15885, War Diary of 18th Field Ambulance, July 1944.
50. Private Albert Warburton, an American from Massachusetts, had come north of the border in 1942 after being rejected for service by the US Navy in the rush to enlist following the Japanese attack on Pearl Harbor. Openly gay—a distinct rarity for the period—Warburton proudly informed the navy doctor of his sexual orientation and was failed immediately on medical grounds. When he arrived in Canada, it appears his sexuality did not matter, and he successfully joined the Canadian Army and transferred into the Black Watch in 1943, although he did cite his next of kin as his "fiancée" named Marion, suggesting that he operated under an informal "don't ask, don't tell" policy.
51. LAC, Personnel file of Lt. Robert Austin.
52. Author's notes on conversation with Bruce Ducat, March 2005.
53. LAC, RG24 Vol. 10973, Honours and Awards, 5th Canadian Brigade (Mention in Despatches).
54. Letter from Stevenson to S.D. Cantlie, September 7, 1944.
55. LAC, RG24 Vol. 15885, War Diary of 18th Field Ambulance, July 1944. The medical officer of the 18th Field Ambulance, Major Letourneau, wrote: "The Orne River at this point of crossing was about 60 feet wide. Special rope used by the section was strung across the river in the early stages of the crossing, [and] about 12 men pulled themselves to safety when their boats sank. I feel that more men would have been rescued if we had more ropes—about 10 men drowned in the river, possibly more."
56. Author's notes on conversation with George Buch, May 10, 1992.
57. Ibid.
58. Ibid. Although witnessed by others, Buch's feat was attributed in the war diary to another officer. The author found independent verification of his action in a letter he wrote to his wife, as well as in a letter written by Bill Doheny to BCS, which indicates support for his claim.
59. LAC, RG24 Vol. 13750, Message Log, HQ 2nd Canadian Infantry Division, 0100hrs, July 19.
60. Author's notes on a conversation with Jimmy Wilkinson, May 2005.

CHAPTER 5: IFS
1. LAC, RG24 Vol. 14116, War Diary, 6th Cdn Inf Bde: "20 July 1000hrs Bde commander attended Corps Commanders O Group. Corp Commander reviewed our situation which had not materially changed.

Presumption was that the opposition on our front was not great and that quick offensive action should break through readily the enemy screen."

2. LAC, RG24 Vol. 14116, War Diary, 6th Canadian Infantry Brigade Corps Commanders O Groups Held at 6th Canadian Infantry Brigade 1000 hrs.
3. Douglas Delany, *Corps Commanders*, 223.
4. LAC, RG24 Vol. 14116, War Diary, 6th Canadian Infantry Brigade Corps Commanders O Groups Held at 6th Canadian Infantry Brigade 1000 hrs.
5. Ibid. Simonds ordered, "All guns to be turned on St. Andre for three mins from 1200hrs. Fighter-bombers to seek targets of opportunity in area Fontenay le Marmion at H plus 90 minutes. Fighter-bombers to attack targets in gun areas near Rocquancourt south of the 59 grid line from H to H plus 3."
6. George Blackburn, *Guns of Normandy*, 181.
7. According to the history of the 1st SS Panzer Division, the 6th Brigade attack, supported heavily by artillery and air power, blunted their initial attempts to counterattack the advancing infantry. However, when the rains came, they pounced with tanks and assault guns. "Our attack caught a Canadian anti-tank unit just as it was trying to shift position," the history recorded. "Our forces drove it back altogether."
8. John S. Edmondson and R.D. Edmondson, "The Pawns of War: A Personal Account of the Attack on Verrières Ridge by the South Saskatchewan Regiment, 20 July 1944," *Canadian Military History* 14, no. 4 (2005), http://scholars.wlu.ca/cmh/vol14/iss4/6.
9. Ibid.
10. Ibid.
11. Ibid.
12. LAC, RG24 Vol. 14287, War Diary, 27th Canadian Armoured Regiment, July 1944.
13. LAC, RG 24 Vol. 14559, War Diary, 2nd Canadian Anti-Tank Regiment, July 1944. The 2nd Canadian Infantry Division history noted, "Later, a call came in for a load of British mines for 5 and 6 Bde fronts, and there was little doubt in anyone's mind that the Div was having grave difficulties in holding its front against continuous German pressure." Just how badly the 6th Brigade battalions had been mauled was brought home when the companies were called upon later in the day to supply twenty trucks to bring what was left of the South Saskatchewan Regiment back to DMA for reorganization. Fewer than four hundred men were brought back, many of them minus equipment and personal weapons.
14. LAC, RG24 Vol. 14116, War Diary, 6th Canadian Infantry Brigade.

15. Author interview with George Buch, March 7, 1992.
16. LAC, RG24 Vol. 9879, Battle Experience Questionnaire, Capt. G.M. Hunter, 4th Field Regiment RCA, October 13, 1944.
17. BWA, Notes on the Action of 25 July 1944 by Capt. Campbell Stuart, Adjt, 1st Bn RHC, May 29, 1990.
18. BWA, Memoirs of Bill Booth; author's notes on conversation with Bill Booth, March 2005.
19. Author interview with George Buch, March 7, 1992. Although no more than unsubstantiated rumour, the perception that this action did occur, or could have easily occurred, effectively made it the reality for some. With a lighting bolt, the story, due to its salacious nature, attained the status of urban legend within the division.

CHAPTER 6: HILL 61

1. The reconnaissance units of the 1st SS then proceeded to "pursue the enemy about five hundred yards north," which gave Canadian High Command the mistaken impression that a counterattack of major proportions was either under way or about to happen. On the German side, their depleted ranks forbade any major push, and the panzers retreated over the ridge, satisfied they had re-established balance on their HKL. See Rudolf Lehmann and Ralf Tiemann, *The Leibstandarte* IV/1, 161.
2. LAC, RG24 Vol. 9879, Battle Experience Questionnaire, Capt. V.W. Jewkes, 6th Canadian A Armoured Regiment, November 25, 1944; Maj. G.W. Gordon, 6th Canadian Armoured Regiment, January 28, 1945; LAC, RG24 Vol. 14287, War Diary, 27th Canadian Armoured Regiment. During the clearing of Ifs, the Sherbrooke Fusiliers reported, "After an early recce by the CO, the RHQ tks and scout cars moved to a posn alongside HQ 6 Cdn Inf Bde in the orchard west of Ifs at 036636, which had been taken by the inf during the night and which was then being cleared of Snipers by the Black Watch (RHC). During this the Regiment HQ was constantly being shelled and the CO's tank was hit on the turret and later evacuated. No one was injured."
3. LAC, RG24 Vol. 10450, Battle Experience Questionnaire, Capt. W. Doheny, 1st Battalion RHC, August 5, 1944.
4. LAC, RG24 Vol. 9879, Battle Experience Questionnaire, Maj. J.P.G. Kemp, 1st Battalion RHC, October 14, 1944.
5. LAC, RG 24 Vol 10906, History of RCASC, 2nd Canadian Infantry Division, June–December 1944.
6. Simonds's corps was now bloodied, but it paid a high price: 3rd Division lost 386 men, but Foulkes's division lost 1,149 casualties in

the Atlantic—which put them on par with the losses for 8th Corps in Goodwood. Seventy-six percent of casualties came in the infantry, and only seven percent for armour—as men had a better chance of walking away from a knocked-out tank to fight another day.

7. LAC, RG24 Vol. 9879, Battle Experience Questionnaire, Maj. J.P.G. Kemp, 1st Battalion RHC, October 14, 1944.

8. Author interview with Jim Wilkinson. See Edgar Jones and Stephen Ironside, "Battle Exhaustion: The Dilemma of Psychiatric Casualties in Normandy, June–August, 1944," *Historical Journal* 53, no. 1 (March 2010), 109–28.

9. Terry Copp and William J. McAndrew, *Battle Exhaustion*. As Copp writes in a follow-up article, exhaustion casualties for Atlantic alone numbered "[m]ore than 300 battle exhaustion cases evacuated to the Exhaustion Unit." As Copp noted, the diary of Major Burdett McNeel, who commanded the 1st Canadian Exhaustion Unit, notes that on July 22 alone, "One hundred and one cases of exhaustion were admitted . . . our ward and the 'morgues' are filled. Those in the morgues have had to sleep on blankets spread on the ground. The rain has been pouring down and the majority of men are wet and muddy." Fortunately, two thousand capsules of sodium amytal arrived and full sedation was possible.

10. Junior officers tended to be more susceptible to combat fatigue, which came with the intense pressure to perform that was exacerbated by the Black Watch legacy and expectations. Another aggravating factor was that they got less sleep than the men as they spent their time planning, checking on their men and worrying about their decisions. It made for a toxic mixture when added to normal stressors such as lack of food, poor morale and discipline, or damp, wet conditions. Those of a more reflective bent, like McLennan, proved more susceptible because they could envision the impact in advance. Empathy, a most desirable trait in any human being, was ironically a curse on the battlefield in its uncontained form.

11. Corporal Eric Hibbert, a printer from Valleyfield, Quebec, who had just gotten engaged to his fiancée, Joyce, prior to arriving in Normandy, was one of those men who required evacuation immediately. Two days after the incident, he wrote, "I have just got out of hospital. Nothing serious—knocked out by blast. Of course, I had the shakes when I came to, but there are so many fellows suffering from shock that it is common. I felt like an ass at first, to be in hospital with nothing wrong with me, so to speak, but I felt better when I met others the same way. I hope you can read this; my hand is still shaking, and my mind isn't at its best, but

at least it will let you know that I'm still OK. I lost all my stuff except for what I had in my pockets, so this will have to go ordinary mail. I don't feel too bad now, still at times, I get a punchy feeling." Three weeks later, the stigma associated with the wound had hit home. "It's a shame the way some of the poor devils are being treated. Fellows who practically ruined their lives fighting for their country and can't even buy a packet of fags at our Canadian canteen."

12. David French, "Discipline and the Death Penalty in the British Army in the War Against Germany During the Second World War," *Journal of Contemporary History* 33, no. 4 (October 1998), 531–45; Todd C. Helmus and Russell W. Glenn, *Steeling the Mind: Combat Stress Reactions and Their Implications for Urban Warfare* (Santa Monica, CA: Rand Corporation, 2005); S. Kirson Weinberg, "The Combat Neuroses," *American Journal of Sociology* 51, no. 5, Human Behaviour in Military Society (March 1946), 465–78; Simon Wessley, "Twentieth-Century Theories on Combat Motivation and Breakdown," *Journal of Contemporary History* 41, no. 2 (April 2006), 269–86; Brian H. Chermol, "Wounds Without Scars: Treatment of Battle Fatigue in the U.S. Armed Forces in the Second World War," *Military Affairs* 49, no. 1 (January 1985), 9–12.

13. LAC, RG24 Vol. 14455, 6th Canadian Infantry Brigade, Message Log, July 1944.

14. Wilhelm Tieke, *In the Firestorm*, 134.

15. LAC, Personnel file of Lt. Thomas Dorrance.

16. LAC, RG24 Vol. 14455, War Diary, 6th Canadian Infantry Brigade, July 1944.

CHAPTER 7: MAESTRO

1. Author's notes on conversation with William Mackenzie-Wood, March 2004.

2. Ibid.

3. Letter from Dwight D. Eisenhower to BLM, July 21, 1944.

4. NAUK, CAB 106/1120, The Airfield Controversy, Capture of Caen, Montgomery's Intentions and Relations with SHAEF.

5. Imperial War Museums, BLM Papers, BLM Diary, July 22, 1944.

6. BLM Diary, July 20, 1944.

7. Ibid.

8. NAUK, CAB106/1061, Notes Made by Captain Liddell-Hart on His 21/2/1952 Interview with General M.C. Dempsey, Operation "Goodwood," July 18, 1944. "By striking first on one side of the Orne

and then on the other," Dempsey told Liddell-Hart, "we should force
him to bring divisions across, and be able to hit them with our air force
in the process of crossing, when they were particularly vulnerable."
Also, LHCMA, Liddell-Hart Papers, LHP 1/679, Liddell-Hart to Lord
A. Tedder, with attached questionnaire of interview with General Miles
Dempsey, May 1, 1952.

9. LAC, RG 24 Vol. 10790, Operational Policy, 2nd [Canadian] Corps,
February 17, 1944. On February 17, Simonds told his subordinates at
the 2nd Canadian Corps that he considered that "a sound, simple plan"
was based upon: "(a) The ground; (b) Enemy dispositions and probable
intentions; (c) The support available; (d) The characteristics and capabilities of our own arms and troops. And, pressed home with resolution,
will usually succeed. Complicated, involved plans seldom succeed."

10. In addition to the units listed above, Simonds had the 2nd Canadian
Armoured Brigade, along with the usual corps and divisional artillery
allotment and one Army Group Royal Artillery. In the air, he could call
upon support from the medium bombers and Typhoon aircraft from the
RAF's 2nd Tactical Air Force.

11. Planning for Operation Spring proved anything but smooth, however,
as Simonds's chief of staff, Brigadier Elliott Rodger, related decades
later. "Haven't you heard it has all been changed" became the constant
mantra within 2nd Canadian Corps headquarters. Impossibly demanding, Simonds expected everything "yesterday" and showed no mercy for
failure, employing a "high-strung" command style based on fear and a
quick trigger finger to get things done.

12. LAC, RG24 Vol. 13711, 2nd Canadian Corps Intsum No. 13, 2000, July
23, 1944; LAC, RG24 Vol. 13750, 2nd Canadian Infantry Division Intsum
No. 5, Part I, July 23, 1944. As with the 2nd Canadian Corps summary,
2nd Division intelligence concurred with Corps's assessment of German
strength, but offered a tempered prediction of the expected conduct of the
German defence in its intelligence summary: "The confused state of the
enemy order of battle in our sector suggests very strongly that elements
of the above formations [272 Inf Div, 1 SS, 9 SS, 2 Pz Divs.] which have
suffered casualties, together with lesser elements of the severely mauled
12 SS and 21 Panzer Divisions, have been formed into battle-groups . . .
There must be no misconception, however, regarding the fighting effectiveness of such battle groups. Mustering all they can from wherever they
can, they will contest our advance hill by hill, village by village." This
counsel was echoed again in the second part of the intelligence summary:
"Although there have been definite reports of the enemy digging in along

new defensive lines as indicated in part I of this summary, it appears that the scarcity of infantry will require him to depend more upon rapid and aggressive defensive tactics of his army." With this in mind, divisional intelligence inferred that German intentions were designed to keep its battalions deployed along its present line on the foot of Verrières Ridge in order to facilitate preparations of a defensive line running through May-sur-Orne, Fontenay-le-Marmion, Rocquancourt, Garcelles-Secqueville and the woods to the east. While this position was fortified, intelligence suspected that the enemy would be "gathering his scattered armour for a heavy counterattack based upon Bretteville-sur-Laize." An officer from the 272nd Division offered his Canadian captors an ominous warning about future German operations. He reported that he had been told to expect a large-scale counterattack on the Canadian front between July 24 and July 28, spearheaded by large numbers of SS troops brought in from the Eastern Front. This claim of an impending movement of SS troops from the Eastern Front to Normandy was deemed possible by operational intelligence. The 2nd Canadian Corps Intsum No. 12, for July 22, warned of the sudden appearance of the Totenkopf, Wiking and Hohenstaufen divisions at any time. The 2nd Canadian Corps Intsum No. 13, on July 23, reported that "Panther tanks of SS Totenkopf might easily turn up anytime." LAC, RG24 Vol. 14334, War Diary, 4th Canadian Infantry Brigade, July 23, 1944; 2nd Canadian Corps Intsum No. 13, July 23, 1944.

13. NAUK, WO171/439, 7th British Armoured Division Special Intelligence Summary No. 43, July 24, 1944.

14. LAC, RG24 Vol. 14334, War Diary, 4th Canadian Infantry Brigade, July 23, 1944; LAC, RG24 Vol. 13750, 2nd Canadian Infantry Division Intsum No. 5, Part I and Part II, July 23 1944; 2nd Canadian Corps Intsum No. 13, July 23, 1944.

15. DHH, AHQ Report No 58.

16. NAUK, WO171/376, Guards Armoured Division Intsum No. 14, 2000, July 23, 1944.

17. LAC, RG24 Vol. 10808, Notes from Corps Commander's O Group, 1000 hrs, July 23, 1944; David O'Keefe, "'No Waiting for George.'"

18. Author's notes on conversation with Mike Brunner.

19. Ibid.

20. LAC, RG24 Vol. 13750, 2nd Canadian Infantry Division Intsum No. 4, July 18, 1944.

21. Ibid.

22. LAC, Personnel file for Pte. Thomas Charles Lee.

23. Ibid.

24. LAC, Personnel file for Maj. J.P.W. Taylor.
25. BWA, Interview of Capt. John Kemp by Brian McKenna and Roman Jarymowycz, September 30, 1989.
26. BWA, Interview with Bruce Ducat.
27. As he had done with all the battalions, Simonds had set their objectives, timings and start lines without serious input from his division or brigade commanders. Megill came up against questions from his battalion COs, who did not feel that there was any sense in the start line that had been laid down by Corps headquarters far removed from the front lines. Instead of working the problem out, Megill admitted defeat. "There was nothing left to the discretion of Brigade commanders in arranging the details of a fight on either the left or right flanks . . . so we simply hitched up ourselves and did not make any formal alteration to the plan."
28. DHH, Account by Major Bennett, RHC, of the Attack by the Black Watch on May-sur-Orne, July 25, 1944, as Given to Capt. Engler at Basse, 1 August 1944 (hereafter referred to as the Bennett Report).
29. Interview of Brigadier William J. Megill by Terry Copp, January 1988.
30. Calgary Highlanders Archives, Megill Interview with Calgary Highlanders, May 1992.
31. Ibid. According to Simonds's chief of staff, Brigadier Elliot Rodger, the situation leading up to Spring was both "serious" and "urgent." Also, letter from Elliot Rodger to the author, February 29, 1996; LAC, Reginald Roy Papers, MG30 E374 Vol. 2, Letter from W.J. Megill to Reginald Roy, 22 Nov 1981; Museum of the Regiments, Interview with Lt. Emile Michon, Calgary Highlanders, March 1992.
32. NAUK, WO171/439, 7th British Armoured Division Special Intelligence Summary No. 43, 24 July 1944.
33. NAUK, WO171/310, War Diary, 12th British Corps, 22 July 1944. On the night of July 22-23, the 12th Corps carried out two limited operations: Express and Pullman. The object was to gain ground west of the River Orne in step with the 2nd Canadian Corps's advance on the east side. Pullman was an extension of Express, with the dual objects of straightening the line west of the Orne between Hill 112 and Maltot and establishing the whereabouts of the 10th SS in the Esquay area. In response to a question posed by Chester Wilmot as "to what extent was failure due to 12 Corps's inability or slowness in clearing the W(est) bank of the Orne High Ground around Maltot," Simonds answered that it was "an embarrassment but not a decisive factor." LHCMA, Wilmot Papers, Queries for General Simonds, n.d.
34. ETHINT B-840 Panzer Gruppe West Eberbach Report, p. 30.

CHAPTER 8: THE FOUR HORSEMEN, ACT 1: ST. MARTIN

1. Reginald Roy, 1944: *The Canadians in Normandy*, 119.
2. LAC, RG24 Vol. 14109, Message Log, HQ 5th Canadian Infantry Brigade: At 0710 hours, the 5th Brigade received word that "272nd Div 980&981 regts came in to line Sunday/Monday night. 230 strong."
3. LAC, RG 24 Vol. 10906, History of Royal Canadian Army Service Corps History. 2nd Canadian Division, June–December 1944.
4. Bennett Report.
5. As John Kemp remarked, "There was no job too difficult or dangerous for Barney to have a try at it . . . when we reached France, he really came into his own." Moving now at the head of his company, given the ultra-conservative culture of the Black Watch, where officers, NCOs and men remained three distinct solitudes, Kemp's praise is quite telling. "Time and again," he wrote, "I have seen him expose himself in order to draw fire from a machine gun that we had been unable to locate . . . he was completely fearless and an inspiration to every man in the battalion." As Hook Wilkinson put it, "Barney Benson was a tremendous soldier, he simply had no fear at all."
6. BWA, Memo of Col. Hutchison's Questions and Lt. Col. Eric Motzfeldt's Answers, 8 June 1945 [hereafter referred to as the Motzfeldt Memo].
7. DHH, Account of the Attack by the Calgary Highlanders on May-sur-Orne During the Night of 24–25 July 1944, Given by Lt. E.A. Michon, D Coy, to Capt. Engler at Basse, 29 July 1944 [hereafter referred to as the Michon Report].
8. BWA, Memo of Col. Hutchison's Questions and Lt. Col. Eric Motzfeldt's Answers, 8 June 1945. In the memo, Motzfeldt mentions that it was members of the Camerons and the Régiment de Maisonneuve that were in the area. This recollection, however, is slightly off: the R de Mais were held in reserve farther to the north, while there is plenty of evidence that puts at least one company from the Calgary Highlanders in the same area at that time.
9. LAC WD 18th Field Ambulance.
10. Ibid.
11. Motzfeldt Memo; LAC, RG24 Vol. 14406, Message Log, HQ, 2nd Canadian Armoured Brigade, 8 June 1945; LAC, RG24 Vol. 13750, Message Log, Main HQ, 2nd Canadian Infantry Division; LAC, RG24 Vol. 14406, Message Log, HQ, 2nd Canadian Armoured Brigade.
12. BWA, Memoirs of Canon E.C. Royle, *circa* 1988 [hereafter referred to as the Royle Memoirs].

13. Author interview with Lt. George Buch, pioneer platoon commander, January 1993. BWA, War Diary, July 1944. Acting Majors John Kemp and John Taylor were the two officers on the scene. Taylor, who was promoted to major on July 19, "outranked" Kemp by all of five days—the latter was promoted to company commander on the twenty-fourth.

14. According to Bennett, Griffin took over at 0530, which is clearly in error because the message log has Taylor in command at that time. Benson claims that Griffin took over at 0730, which is likely some time after the A Company commander actually took over. Buch's claim, based on his memory sixty years after the fact, was that it was not long after first light, but that Taylor had command first—something that Mackenzie-Wood confirmed. John Kemp recalled in a report that Griffin took over near 0700, while Stan Duffield, also in a postwar report, claimed it was 0500 (five minutes after the duo were hit), which was impossible because Brigadier Megill confirmed that Taylor (the nearest company commander) took over the battalion originally until Griffin, the senior surviving officer, arrived on the scene, but he does not provide a specific time frame. The clearest indication comes at 0600 hours, when the Black Watch sent a message to 5th Brigade that "CO a casualty and E3 taking over." Given the timeline, this likely denotes the outcome of either the Kemp–Taylor dispute or when Griffin finally arrived to take over. Compounding the confusion, there is no indication what "E3" denotes, and whether this is a typo or a genuine designation for someone in the chain of command. So far, "E3" remains a mystery.

15. LAC, RG24 Vol. 14109, Message Log, HQ, 5th Canadian Infantry Brigade. According to the message log, at 0645 Foulkes ordered the Calgary Highlanders not to dig in, but instead to "go wide and keep going." Two minutes later, Brigadier Megill told the Royal Highland Regiment to "push on," as "speed was essential." Half an hour later, at 0715, came a direct order from Megill to Griffin to "go ahead." This evidence is corroborated by Captain G.D. Powis, the artillery FOO attached to the Black Watch, who reported in an interview a year later that after Griffin sent his message, the response was simply to "push on." Stuart, "Notes on Action"; BWA, Notes of Interview with D-81761 CQMS F.E. Ritchie, B Coy 1 RHC, April 17, 1945 [hereafter referred to as the Ritchie Interview]; DHH, 92/252, February 1946 Statement of Capt. Powis, 5th Canadian Field Regiment FOO with Left Forward Company During the Attack Up Verrières Ridge on July 25, 1944 [hereafter referred to as the Powis Report]; Bennett Report.

16. Stuart, "Notes on Action"; Ritchie Interview; Powis Report; Bennett Report.
17. Bennett Report.
18. Interview of Brigadier Megill by Terry Copp, January 1988. In his post-battle report (DHH, Outline Report on Battle May-sur-Orne–Fontenay-le-Marmion, 25 July 1944, by Brigadier W.H. Megill, Commander, 5th Canadian Infantry Brigade, 16 August 1944—here-after referred to as the Megill Report), Megill explained that the command of the unit went to Taylor before Griffin took over.
19. LAC, RG24 Vol. 13750, Message Log, Main HQ, 2nd Canadian Infantry Division. Captain Gordon Powis, one of two FOOs from the 5th Field Regiment attached to the Black Watch for the assault, corrob-orated this message in his 1946 report to Colonel C.P. Stacey's historical inquiry. Interview with William Mackenzie-Wood by David O'Keefe for *Black Watch: Massacre on Verrières Ridge*.
20. Michon Report; Author's notes on conversation with Bruce Ducat.
21. Bennett Report.
22. DHH, 145.2R15011 (6), Account by Sgt. Benson, Scout Pl, RHC of the attack by the Black Watch on May-sur-Orne 25 July 1944 Given to Capt Engler at Basse, 2 August 1944 [hereafter referred to as the Benson Report].
23. Ibid.
24. Ibid.
25. Ibid.
26. Ibid.; DHH, 145.2B1 (D1), Notes on Movement of the RHC at May-sur-Orne, 25 July 1944.
27. Stuart, "Notes on Action"; Ritchie Interview; Powis Report.
28. NAUK, WO171/112, 21st Army Group, TAC HQ Log, 25 July: "TOR 0750hrs from Second Army: 2nd Cdn Div. 5th Cdn Bde one Coy in May-sur-Orne. Mopping up continues in St. Martin. One Bn by-passed May-sur-Orne and moving on Fontenay. 4th Cdn Bde—one bn just south of Verrières, one bn just north of the village; bn by-passed town and going on to Rocquancourt. 3rd Cdn Div—9th Cdn bde still mop-ping up Tilly-la-Campagne. 7th Armd Div. 22 Armd bde with two regts up met enemy tanks 0360. Four enemy tanks brewed up: others with-drawing . . . 1025hrs from Second Army: RHC of 5th Cdn Bde started moving towards Fontenay by passing May-sur-Orne at 0830hrs. Royal Regt of C of 4th Cdn Inf Bde making slow progress South of Verrières in face of hy mortar fire. 7th Armd Div engaging enemy inf at 035595. Gds Armd Div now at 2 hrs notice to move. Corps Comd will decide by 1200hrs whether Gds Armd Div will be employed today."

29. Unknown to the Black Watch and the Hussars, units of the veteran 3rd Canadian Infantry Division, engaged with the elite 1st SS Panzer Division at Tilly-la-Campagne, balked at Simonds's orders to bypass, refusing to carry out what seemed to be a "hopeless action." However, in Foulkes's division, which was fighting its first major engagement since Dieppe, there is no record of any outright refusal to conform to Simonds's orders.

30. LAC, RG24 Vol. 13750, Message Log, Main HQ, 2nd Canadian Infantry Division.

31. Ibid.: "July 25 0823hrs serial 2222 from 5th Cdn Inf Bde to RHC: Intercept—Fetch Sunray—I must see Sunray at once have your wireless comn with him. Can you relay a message for us? (Passed to Command post.)"

CHAPTER 9: THE FOUR HORSEMEN, ACT II. THE RIDGE

1. Bennett Report; Michon Report; LAC, RG24 Vol. 14406, Message Log, HQ, 2nd Canadian Armoured Brigade.

2. Ibid.

3. Ibid.

4. Ibid.

5. DHH, Account of the Attack by the Calg Highrs on May-sur-Orne Carried Out on 25 July 44 as Given by Lt. Col. MacLaughlan, OC at Fleury-sur-Orne, 28 July 44 [hereafter referred to as the MacLaughlan Report].

6. Benson Report; Michon Report.

7. Megill Report. According to Megill, Cantlie decided to change the axis of advance after assessing the situation in St. Martin. However, there is no other evidence to corroborate this version of events.

8. BWA, Report on the Actions of Major F.P. Griffin, 1st Bn, The Black Watch (RHR) of Canada, C.A.O. on 25 July 1944 by Major J.P.G. Kemp, 26 February 1945 [hereafter referred to as the Griffin Report].

9. LAC, RG24 Vol. 12745, Memorandum of Interview with Lt. Col. J.W. Powell, DSO, MC, RC Armd C at Cdn Military HQ, 9 January 1946 [hereafter referred to as the Powell Interview]; LAC, RG24 Vol. 12745, Memorandum of an Interview with Major W.E. Harris MP, Formerly OC B Squadron 6 Cdn Armd Regt. At Historical Section GS, Department of National Defence, 24 January 1946, Re: Attack on Fontenay-le-Marmion, July 25, 1944 [hereafter referred to as the Harris Interview].

10. Megill Report.

11. Powell Interview; Harris Interview. Tank crews had become painfully aware that the country south of Caen was "gun country," rather than

the promised "tank country." The great fear for crews stemmed from the accuracy and penetrating power of German 88- and 75-millimetre anti-tank guns, which could pierce the thin skin of a Sherman tank at long distances with relative ease. Compounding this, most Canadian Shermans ran on gasoline rather than diesel, leaving the crews with the impression that they were more susceptible to quick "brew ups"—catching fire if hit by armour-piercing shells—than those running on diesel, with an average escape time of just four seconds for the former, compared with fifteen for the latter. See George Kitching, *Mud and Green Fields*.

12. Powis Report; Benson Report.

13. Powis Report. This is likely the reason so many of the Black Watch who survived the assault reported after the war that artillery support had been non-existent. Unlike in training and in their earlier, albeit brief, experiences in Normandy, the focus on distant targets was unlikely to be seen, let alone heard, in the heat of battle as they plunged down on the reverse slope of the ridge.

14. Griffin's decision was due to the fact that neutralizing fire by the British 12th Corps and a smokescreen put on by the 2nd Canadian Division had both proved ineffective, leaving the western approach to Verrières in full view of German positions on the heights west of the Orne River. LAC, RG 24 Vol. 13750, War Diary, 2nd Canadian Infantry Division, Operational Order No. 1, 24 July 1944.

15. BWA, Interview of Captain John Kemp by Brian McKenna and Roman Jarymowycz, September 30, 1989.

16. Stuart, "Notes on Action."

17. Griffin Report.

18. Terry Copp, *The Brigade*.

19. Ibid.

20. LAC, Papers of Reginald Roy, Letters from W.J. Megill to Reginald Roy, 2 March 1980 and 22 November 1981.

21. Powis Report; NAUK, WO 171/970, War Diary, 25th Field Regiment Royal Artillery, July 1944.

22. Interview of Gordy Donald by David O'Keefe for *Black Watch: Massacre at Verrières Ridge*, directed by Wayne Abbott, written by Wayne Abbott and David O'Keefe, aired November 10, 2006, on History Television.

23. Ibid.

24. Interview of William Mackenzie-Wood by David O'Keefe for *Black Watch: Massacre at Verrières Ridge*.

25. Author notes on conversation with Gordy Donald.

26. Interview of MacGregor "Mac" Roulston by David O'Keefe for *Black Watch: Massacre at Verrières Ridge*.
27. Interview of Bruce Ducat by David O'Keefe for *Black Watch: Massacre at Verrières Ridge*.
28. Ibid.
29. Author's notes on conversation with Gordy Donald.
30. Interview of William Mackenzie-Wood by David O'Keefe for *Black Watch: Massacre at Verrières Ridge*.
31. Interview of Gordy Donald by David O'Keefe for *Black Watch: Massacre at Verrières Ridge*.
32. Benson Report.
33. Ibid.
34. Ibid.
35. Didier Lodieu, *L'Enfer au sud de Caen*, 188.
36. Powis Report.
37. Helmut Ritgen, *Western Front 1944: Memoirs of a Panzer Lehr Officer* (Winnipeg: Fedorowicz Publishing, 1995), 88.
38. Benson Report.
39. Powis Report.
40. LAC, Personnel file of Maj. Ernest Stanley Duffield.
41. Stuart, "Notes on Action"; Ritchie Interview; Powis Report; Bennett Report.
42. Bennett Report.
43. LAC, RG 24 Vol. 13750, Message Log, Main HQ, 2nd Canadian Infantry Division.
44. Michael R. McNorgan, *The Gallant Hussars*, 168.
45. Powell Interview; Bennett Report.
46. DHH, War Diary, 5th Panzer Army (Panzer Army West), July 25, 1944.
47. Wilhelm Tieke, *In the Firestorm*, 137.
48. Ibid.
49. Roman Jarymowycz, "Der Gegenangriff vor Verrieres."
50. Interview of MacGregor "Mac" Roulston by David O'Keefe for *Black Watch: Massacre at Verrières Ridge*.
51. DHH, Interviews with RHC Survivors of Operation Spring conducted by Major Brissette from the Army Historical Section (*circa* December 1945). The exchange was witnessed by Private Maurice Montreuil, who had advanced the entire way with Kemp.
52. Ibid.
53. Bennett Report.
54. Bennett Report.

55. Stuart, "Notes on Action."
56. LAC, RG24 Vol. 14109, Message Log, HQ, 5th Canadian Infantry Brigade.
57. Stuart, "Notes on Action."
58. DHH, Letter from T.E. Williamson, Troop Leader, B Squadron, 6th Canadian Armoured Regiment (1 Hussars) to DHS, January 23, 1946 [hereafter referred to as the Williamson Letter].
59. LAC, RG24 Vol. 12745, Letter from William Rawson to Lt. Col. G.F.P. Stanley, Historical Section, January 24 1945 [hereafter referred to as the Rawson Letter].
60. Rawson Letter; Powell Interview; McNorgan, *The Gallant Hussars*, 168.
61. MacLaughlan Report.
62. Rawson Letter.
63. Ibid.
64. Bennett Report.
65. Ibid.
66. Williamson Letter.
67. Powell Interview; Bennett Report.
68. Rawson Letter.
69. Bennett Report.
70. LAC, RG24 Vol. 14109, Message Log, HQ, 5th Canadian Infantry Brigade. "1512–1805hrs from G3 (De Salabery liaison officer) to Megill: Capt Bennett just came back from 024605. States about 50% casualties. Said this is not confirmed but the general opinion of the lads who have come back. Incl Capt Taylor he states the troops in the forward localities are pinned down and not moving forward. Tks have come back from the crest where they say it."
71. Jarymowycz, "Der Gegenangriff vor Verrieres."
72. Rawson Letter; Powell Interview; Bennett Report.
73. Ibid.
74. Ibid.
75. Ibid.
76. Powell Interview.
77. The skill of Powell's surviving tank gunners temporarily saved the day. Faced with a Panther that sported thick frontal armour that proved more than a match for the underpowered 75-millimetre gun on the Sherman, Canadian tank crews employed a desperate measure to knock out at least two of the beasts and make the rest think twice about bounding down the slope with abandon. The "trap shot" was the "Hail Mary" of the armoured world, and it required crews with nerves of steel and

excellent marksmanship—and a hell of a lot of luck—to intentionally bounce an armour-piercing round off the underside of the Panther's gun mantlet, making it deflect downward through the lighter armour on the deck, where it would kill the crew instantly.

78. Foster M. Stark, *A History of the First Hussars Regiment, 1856–1945* (London, ON: Hunter, 1951), 93; McNorgan, *The Gallant Hussars*, 168. By the end of the day, B Squadron was left with seven tanks, while only twenty-eight remained in the entire regiment.

79. Bennett Report.

CHAPTER 10: THE FOUR HORSEMEN, ACT III:
DER HEXENKESSEL (THE WITCH'S CAULDRON)

1. Roman Jarymowycz, "General Guy Simonds: The Commander as Tragic Hero," in *Warrior Chiefs*, 119.

2. Powis Report.

3. Royle Memoirs.

4. Ibid.

5. Author's notes on interview with Jimmy Wilkinson.

6. Lieutenant Colonel Charles Petch of the North Nova Scotia Highlanders, Lieutenant Colonel George Christenson of the Stormont, Dundas and Glengarry Highlanders and Brigade Commander Dan Cunningham were sacked for refusing to carry out the corps commander's orders. Petch, although commanding the North Novas, was a Black Watch officer who, after the war, married the widow of S.S.T. Cantlie. See John A. English, *The Canadian Army and the Normandy Campaign: A Study in the Failure of High Command* (New York: Praeger, 1991).

7. See David Bercuson, *Battalion of Heroes*.

8. English, *The Canadian Army in the Normandy Campaign*, 191.

9. This trait was not lost on the legendary army historian C.P. Stacey, who wrote: "Part of General Simonds' success may well have been due to his capacity for taking decisions which some might deem ruthless, in which the needs of the tactical situation were placed before 'human' considerations."

10. LAC, RG24 Vol. 17506, Report on the Address by Lt. Gen. G.G. Simonds, CBE, DSO, GOC 2nd Cdn Corps, to Officers of 3rd Canadian Infantry Division and 2nd Canadian Armoured Brigade at the Château Near Cairon by Major A.T. Sesia: "But for the operation which is worthwhile, and I call it off with 50% casualties incurred, then I have achieved nothing but a waste of lives; if I continue, and incur a

further 20% casualties and bring the operation to a successful conclusion, then the operation is worthwhile. I speak of casualties in grossly exaggerated figures. In no operation yet have I participated where casualties were not between 15 and 25%, and even at that, 25% is still a grossly exaggerated figure."

11. NAUK, WO171/439, 7th Armoured Division, Message Log, July 1944: "1630hrs. The Corps Commander intends to clear May-sur-Orne and Tilly and continue attack on Fontenay-le-Marmion and Rocquancourt today. 7th Arm Div will support this attack but will not be involved in a major battle. Gds Armd Div have been told to stand down until tomorrow."

12. NAUK, WO171/439, 7th Armoured Division, Message Log, Rear HQ: "1325hrs Germans active up to Tilly and May-sur-Orne. Corps Commander to clear May-sur-Orne first then on to Fontenay. Not pressing Verrières and Rocquancourt for us." NAUK, WO171/118, 21st AG Intelligence Log: "1430hrs phantom reports from 2nd Cdn Div that heavy fighting continues, and that new plan now being made for 5th Cdn Inf Div."

13. The translation of the German report of Kemp's interrogation shows that the Black Watch commander heeded his own advice. Revealing nothing of import to his captors, the only note they made came in reference to the sidearm they found stitched into his uniform.

14. In a January 1988 interview with Terry Copp, Megill mentions St. André, but this must be an error because it does not conform to the overwhelming evidence available. Megill claims he argued with Foulkes to go to May-sur-Orne and not to Fontenay, because he was sure the Régiment de Maisonneuve could take the former if it followed the axis of advance laid out by him. Megill states that he planned the second assault on Fontenay by the Maisonneuve and was not surprised that "it got nowhere."

15. Interview of Brigadier W.J. Megill by Terry Copp, January 1988.

16. NAUK, WO171/439, 7th Armoured Division, Message Log, Rear HQ, 1917hrs: "G1 to G2 1900 attack going straight for Fontenay."

17. MacLaughlan Report.

18. DHH, Account of the Attack by the Calgary Highlanders on May-sur-Orne, 25 July 44, given by Lt. Morgandeen, A Coy, to Capt. Engler at Basse, 29 July 44, 145.2C1011 (D5).

19. Bennett Report.

20. Ibid.

21. Ibid.

22. Ibid.
23. Ibid.
24. Ibid.
25. LAC, Mary Buch Papers, Letter from Buch to Marion Strang, Dean of the Women's Residence at Macdonald College, Ste. Anne de Bellevue, Quebec, August 19, 1944.
26. BWA, Memoirs of Bill Booth.
27. Booth Memoirs; Author notes on conversation with Bill Booth.

CHAPTER 11: ODDS AND SODS
1. LAC, RG 24 Vol. 17506, War Diary, No. 2 Canadian Historical Section, March–July 1944; War Diary of Capt. J.R. Martin, Historical Officer, 3rd Canadian Infantry Division, Entry for July 25.
2. Royle Memoirs.
3. LAC, RG 24 Vol. 10906, History of R.C.A.S.C., 2nd Canadian Infantry Division, June–December 1944.
4. Bennett Report.
5. NAUK, WO285/9, Personal War Diary of General Miles Dempsey.
6. Benson Report.
7. Bennett Report; Ralph Allen, "Commandos from Rear Take German Platoon from Behind," Globe and Mail (Toronto), July 27, 1944.
8. Author notes on conversation with George Buch, March 1992.
9. Bennett Report; Allen, "Commandos from Rear."
10. Bennett Report; Allen, "Commandos from Rear."
11. Bennett Report; Allen, "Commandos from Rear."
12. Bennett Report; Allen, "Commandos from Rear."
13. Bennett Report.
14. Benson Report.
15. Lieutenant Colonel Frank Mitchell, who took command of the battalion late on the twenty-sixth, dubbed the men in the farmyard "Ronnie B's Odds and Sods" in a letter home to the regimental commandant (found in the BWA) in Montreal in the summer of 1944.
16. Author's notes on conversation with George Buch, March 1992.
17. Bennett Report.
18. Ibid.
19. Although this is purely speculation, one potential reason for the different attitude amongst members of the 9th SS towards their enemy (something that was prevalent two months later during their fight at Arnhem in Holland) stemmed from their upbringing. Although elite in every sense of the word, the 9th SS were not volunteers, but men conscripted into

service with the Waffen SS in 1943. As such, an argument can be made that they did not possess the same level of indoctrination or murderous fanaticism displayed by the 1st SS, 12th SS or 2nd SS units. Of course, in the heat of battle, nobody on the Black Watch side of the line would have any idea of this nuance.

20. Author notes on conversation with George Buch, 1992.
21. Bennett Report.
22. Ibid.
23. Ibid.
24. Ibid.
25. Ibid.
26. LAC, Personnel file of Pte. Fred Ann Noftall.
27. Bennett Report; Allen, "Commandos from Rear."
28. LAC, Personnel files of Ernest Swanson Dooley and Henry George Charles Shea.
29. Allen, "Commandos from Rear."
30. Jacques Dextraze, "The Attack on the Church in St. Martin-de-Fontenay: 31 July–1 August 1944," *Canadian Military History* 15, no. 3 (2006), 113–19; Bennett Report.

CHAPTER 12: THE ABACUS WAR

1. Author's notes on conversation with Stan Matulis, April 2004; Patricia Burns, *They Were So Young*, 168.
2. Brock Weir, "'You Were Numbed': Second World War Sniper Shares Story in New Documentary," *Shelburne (ON) Free Press*, November 10, 2016; Author's notes on conversation with Mike Brunner, December 22, 2014.
3. Letter from Thanning Anderson to his mother, August 2, 1944 (courtesy of Anderson family).
4. BWA, Copy of cable from Captain S.E. Griffin to his parents, August 1, 1944.
5. Benson Report.
6. Ibid.
7. LAC, RG 24 Vol. 15633, War Diary, Principal Chaplain Overseas (P), 2nd Canadian Corps, August 1944.
8. Interview with Jim Bennett for *Black Watch Snipers*, directed by Robin Bicknell, written by Michael Allcock, aired 2016 on History Television.
9. LAC, RG 24 Vol. 15635, War Diary, Senior Chaplain, 3rd Canadian Division, August 1944; War Diary, Principal Chaplain Overseas (P), 2nd Canadian Corps, August 1944.
10. According to the Department of Veterans Affairs, "So far as can be ascertained, 22 officers and 758 other ranks were directly involved

in the advance. Of these, all the officers and slightly under 658 other
ranks became casualties, but exact figures are not available as casualties
were reported for the day as a whole. Of the approximately 800 men
who went forward only about 110 survived unscathed, of whom only
sixty-eight were available for roll call the following day. The Battalion's
War Diary on July 7 states that on July 1 the overall casualties for the
Battalion were 14 officers and 296 other ranks killed, died of wounds
or missing believed killed, and that 12 officers and 362 other ranks
were wounded, a total of 684 all ranks out of a fighting strength of
about 929. About 14 of the wounded subsequently died from their
wounds. Afterward, the Divisional Commander was to write of the
Newfoundlanders' effort: 'It was a magnificent display of trained and
disciplined valour, and its assault failed of success because dead men can
advance no further.'" "The Opening Day, Battle of the Somme, 1916,"
Veterans Affairs Canada, https://www.veterans.gc.ca/eng/remembrance
/memorials/overseas/first-world-war/france/beaumonthamel/somme.

11. Royle Memoirs.
12. Author's notes on conversations with Bruce Ducat and Jim Wilkinson.
13. BWA, Letter from Maj. Gen. H.A. Young (former Brigadier of 6th
    Canadian Infantry Brigade) to Col. P.P. Hutchison, January 2 1945. "It
    is indeed true that I saw quite a bit of the Black Watch, both in England
    and in France. In the fighting which took place in the outbreak from
    Caen, between the 19 and 25 of July, I had the Battalion under my
    command. I must say the Unit under Steve Cantlie fought exceptionally
    well. On one occasion, the 21 July, the Unit put in the most spectacular
    attack; one of the most efficient I have ever seen. The Unit reverted from
    my command to the 5th Brigade on the 24 July, just before that sad
    episode of the 25th."
14. See the personnel files for the named men, available at LAC.
15. BWA, Letter from Fred Pedlar to Col. P.P. Hutchison, June 28, 1946.
16. Having lost both legs in a mortar blast, Des Cotes ended up in
    the hands of the SS, and for a while it appeared he would survive.
    Transferred to a German hospital in the French town of Alençon,
    no amount of treatment could save him, and he died in their care.
    Agonizingly for his family, no sign of his remains or a grave appeared
    when the French 2nd Armoured Division overran the town in late
    August. With no known grave, there is no headstone for Des Cotes and
    five others who died. Rather, their names were etched on the Bayeux
    Memorial, not far from Juno Beach.
17. LAC, Personnel file of E.A. Wilson.

18. LAC, Personnel file of Fred Noftall. In the summer of 1946, Noftall's mother, Annie, wrote to the Canadian War Graves Commission, "Would it be possible to obtain some little particle of sod, leaves or anything from the grave of my late son? The desire to secure this is becoming almost unbearable. To you it is just one more soldier over there but to me a loved lost son, whom while I live, I shall always mourn for. About the same time this son was killed I buried here a daughter, a trained nurse, 23 years old. To her grave I can expect a memorial and kneel in prayer for consolation but my son's grave is so far away."

19. Like Cantlie, Fraser and numerous others were recommended for gallantry awards such as the Distinguished Service Order, Military Cross or Military Medal. Only two, the mention in dispatches and the Victoria Cross (the highest award for valour), could be awarded posthumously. As such, if a soldier did not live long enough, as was the case with Steel, his recommendation for the Military Medal would by default become a mention in dispatches—unless, of course, his actions warranted the rarest recognition of all, the Victoria Cross. Despite the regiment's best efforts to have Phil Griffin awarded the VC for his actions, he received the MID instead as the attack, although gallant, did not succeed and therefore did not merit the highest award.

20. Buried now alongside his men, the detailed circumstances of Major Griffin's demise had to remain shrouded in mystery for the moment, as very few of the men who reached the crest with him made it out alive, and those who survived ended up in German hands. None of the wounded had reached the reverse slope with Griffin, and their post-battle testimony was spotty at best. What is known is that Griffin was still on his feet, moving forward, when he reached Gordy Donald on the reverse slope, and he entertained no thoughts of calling off the attack in that moment, which lines up with testimony of Kemp and others who saw him before he reached Donald's position on the reverse slope. Seconds after their encounter, Donald witnessed Griffin shake and shudder, as if hit by something, but by what, and to what extent, he did not know. Given that several witnesses testified that Griffin gave orders to withdraw, this could only have happened following his encounter with Donald. The details of his death remained with men like Gordy Donald and Gordon Powis and the others who survived the attack unscathed and who, by the second week of August 1944, were nearly a thousand miles from Normandy, parcelled out in German prisoner of war camps spread across Poland and eastern Germany.

21. BWA, Black Watch War Diary, July 1944.

22. Ibid.
23. Ibid.
24. Author's notes on conversation with Mike Brunner, December 21, 2014.
25. Ibid.
26. BWA, Letter from Lt. Col. F.M. Mitchell to Col. P.P. Hutchison, August 2, 1944.
27. The quality of reinforcements was lacking compared with the original cadre that arrived on July 6 and had no knowledge of battalion operations and traditions. Certainly, the latter could be excused under the extraordinary circumstances, but deficiencies in the individual training in the art of the infanteer was a fundamental problem that plagued both British and Canadian armies during the latter stages of the Normandy campaign and throughout the liberation of North-West Europe.
28. Basing their wastage projections for the Normandy campaign on their experiences in the desert and Italy, the British concocted reinforcement tables that called for large reinforcements in the armoured corps, as tank losses had been heavier than infantry losses in those two campaigns. This, however, was not the case in the early weeks of the Normandy campaign because the battle did not unfold into the armour duel that General B.L.M. Montgomery had envisioned, but devolved into an infantry struggle reminiscent of the last year of the Great War. Following the British wastage tables, the same phenomenon occurred in the Canadian Army. As a result, manpower reinforcements, in general, were ample, but what was lacking was the specially trained infantry replacement. It is hard to say whether the events of July 25 caused the need or simply revealed the weakness in the system, but either way, the infantry reinforcement crisis was beginning to rear its unprepossessing head. See C.P. Stacey, *Arms, Men and Governments: The War Policies of Canada, 1939–1945* (Ottawa: Queen's Printer, 1970) and *The Victory Campaign* (Ottawa: Queen's Printer, 1960). According to Stacey, the first ripples of the reinforcement crisis came on August 4 in the wake of the casualties suffered on July 25.
29. War Diary, Black Watch 1st Battalion RHC July 1944. For the most part, Mitchell was able to scrape the proverbial "bottom of the barrel" for infantry-trained replacements from other Canadian units in the Normandy bridgehead and the generic No. 2 Canadian Base Reinforcement Group in England.
30. BWA, Memo of Col. Hutchison's Questions and Lt. Col. Eric Motzfeldt's Answers, June 8, 1945.

31. BWA, Letter from Lt. Col. Frank Mitchell to Lt. Col. A. Wright, dated September 26, 1944.
32. Terry Copp, interview with Brigadier William J. Megill, 1988. Courtesy of Terry Copp.

EPILOGUE: THE BITTER HARVEST
1. David O'Keefe, "Pushing Their Necks Out."
2. Bishop's College School, File of Ronald Bennett.
3. Nigel Hamilton, *Monty*; NAUK, CAB121/370 and CAB/65, War Cabinet, Minutes 44/97, Conclusions, July 27, 1944; Imperial War Museums, BLM Papers, BLM Diary, July 27, 1944.
4. BWA, Letter from P.P. Hutchison to Capt. F.C. Smith Adjutant Black Watch Montreal Aug. 7, 1944.
5. Both headlines denoted the same article by Ralph Allen, the former with the Montreal *Gazette* on August 12, 1944, and the latter in the *Globe and Mail* on the same day.
6. Richard S. Malone, *A World in Flames*. According to Malone, head of public relations at the 1st Canadian Army, Crerar sent a message back to National Defence Headquarters in Ottawa to prepare them for the release of a "lurid" story about the Black Watch that would appear in the coming days.
7. BWA, Letter from P.P. Hutchison to Lt. Col. Frank Mitchell, October 3, 1944.
8. DHH, Interviews with RHC Survivors of Operation Spring, conducted by Major Brissette from the Army Historical Section (*circa* December 1945).
9. Ibid.
10. David O'Keefe, "Bitter Harvest."
11. C.P. Stacey, *Victory Campaign*, 195. The casualties in Operation Spring were always a controversial point. In 1983, Stacey wrote about his 1945 account of Spring that "he [Simonds] particularly didn't like the emphasis on the losses," when precise figures were not known. For the Victory Campaign, the "statistical experts," as Stacey calls them, had "ground out" a total of 1,500 dead, wounded, missing and prisoners—one-third of these were from the Black Watch alone. Standing his ground, Stacey told Simonds, "I have greatly shortened the reference to the losses of the Black Watch in 'Spring.' I have felt, however, that it would not be good policy to omit all reference to them, in view of the considerable amount of newspaper publicity in Canada at the time."

12. David O'Keefe, "Fortune's Fate: The Question of Operational Intelligence for Operation 'Spring,' Normandy, July 25, 1944," *Canadian Defence Quarterly* 24, no. 3 (March 1995).

13. DHH, CMHQ Report No. 150, Appendix A.

14. DHH, 83/269, Stacey, Comments Regarding Official History Second World War—General Charles Foulkes, 24 April 1959. Foulkes went on to comment that "General Simonds wrote a very blasting account of the failure of the Black Watch to capture Andre-sur-Orne and he and I had some strong words about this, as he had accused the Black Watch on the day of this battle of surrendering to the enemy because there were so few left. However, after we finally captured Andre-sur-Orne, I took General Simonds to the ridge where the Black Watch had been stopped and had him count with me the casualties. He then, some years later, pointed out that this was due to lack of management and junior officer leadership This remains a very gruesome memory with the Black Watch." This was not the only occasion on which Simonds tried to blame the failure of an attack on his frontline troops, much to the resentment of some of his fellow officers. In 1987, Lieutenant General Howard Graham, who served under Simonds in Sicily as a brigadier in the 1st Canadian Infantry Division, wrote his memoirs, which included a "categorical denial" of Simonds's remarks about the outcome of his brigade's attack at Nissoria. Graham confided that he "resented" Simonds's "effort to justify a bad plan by putting blame for its failure on the backs of the troops," which made it quite clear that this bitterness had still not waned forty years later. See Lt. Gen. Howard Graham, *Citizen and Soldiers: The Memoirs of Lt. Gen. Howard Graham* (Toronto: McClelland and Stewart, 1987), 174.

15. According to plan, the Royal Regiment of Canada bypassed the fighting in Verrières village to maintain Simonds's timetable and paid a heavy cost as well.

16. LAC, Reginald Roy Files, Letter from W.J. Megill to R.H. Roy, 16 April 1980.

17. C.P. Stacey, *The Victory Campaign*, 194. Stacey lists the fatal casualties for Operation Spring at "about 450," while fatal casualties for Canadians at Dieppe were 907.

18. DHH, Military Cross Citation of Major E.S. Duffield, Black Watch. April 26, 1945.

19. DHH, Mention in Despatches and Croix de Guerre, July 25, 1944.

BIBLIOGRAPHY

ABBREVIATIONS USED IN BIBLIOGRAPHY AND ENDNOTES

BCS   Bishop's College School Archives
BLM   Bernard Law Montgomery
BWA   Black Watch Archives
DHH   Directorate of History and Heritage
LAC   Library and Archives Canada
LHCMA   Liddell Hart Centre for Military Archives—King's College, London
MOTR   Calgary Highlanders Archives—Museum of the Regiments, Calgary
NAUK   National Archives of United Kingdom
UVIC   Archives of the University of Victoria

PRIMARY SOURCES

PUBLISHED

Bradley, Omar N. *A Soldier's Story.* New York: Simon & Schuster, 1951.
Bradley, Omar, and Clay Blair. *A General's Life.* New York: Simon & Schuster, 1983.
Canada. Senate of Canada. *The Valour and the Horror: Proceedings of the Standing Subcommittee on Veterans Affairs of the CBC Series* The Valour and the Horror. 1992.
Clausewitz, Carl von. *On War.* Harmondsworth, UK: Penguin, 1968.
De Guingand, Maj.-Gen. Sir Francis. *Generals at War.* London: Hodder & Stoughton, 1964.
Eisenhower, Dwight D. *Crusade in Europe.* London: Heinemann, 1948.
Graham, Howard. *Citizen and Soldier: The Memoirs of Lieutenant-General Howard Graham.* Toronto: McClelland & Stewart, 1987.
Graham, Dominick. *The Price of Command: A Biography of General Guy Simonds.* Toronto: Stoddart, 1993.
Hinsley, F.H., and Alan Stripp. *Codebreakers: The Inside Story of Bletchley Park.* Oxford: Oxford University Press, 1993.

Horrocks, Sir Brian. *A Full Life*. London: Leo Cooper, 1974.

Kirby, Norman. *1100 Miles with Monty: Security and Intelligence at Tac HQ*. London: Alan Sutton, 1989.

Kitching, George. *Mud and Green Fields: The Memoirs of Major-General George Kitching*. St. Catharines, ON: Vanwell, 1993.

Montgomery, Bernard Law. *Normandy to the Baltic*. Boston: Houghton-Mifflin, 1958.

———. *The Memoirs of Field-Marshal, the Viscount Montgomery of Alamein, K.G.* Cleveland: World Publishing Co., 1958.

Pyman, Sir Harold. *Call to Arms*. London: Leo Cooper, 1971.

Richardson, Charles. *Flashback: A Soldier's Story*. London: William Kimber, 1985.

Stacey, C.P. *A Date with History: The Memoirs of a Canadian Historian*. Ottawa: Deneau Publications, 1983.

Tedder, Arthur William, Baron. *With Prejudice: The War Memoirs of Marshal of the Royal Air Force, Lord Tedder*. London: Cassell, 1966.

United States National Research Council. *Psychology for the Fighting Man*. Washington: Penguin, 1943.

Winterbotham, F.W. *The Ultra Secret*. New York: Harper & Row, 1974.

UNPUBLISHED

CANADA

DHH, 83/269, Stacey, C.P. "Comments Regarding the Official History of the Second World War," 1959–1962.

DHH, AHQ Report No. 50: "The Campaign in North-West Europe: Information from German Sources, Part II: Invasion and Battle of Normandy (6 June–22 August 1944)," October 14, 1952.

DHH, AHQ Report No. 58: "Canadian Participation in the Operations in North-West Europe, 1944: Part II—Canadian Operations in July," February 15, 1953.

DHH, AHQ Report No. 95: "Historical Activities within the Canadian Army," May 21, 1962.

DHH, CMHQ Report No. 131: "Operation 'Overlord' and Its Sequel: Canadian Participation in the Operations in North-West Europe, 6 June–31 July 44 (Prelim Report)," February 12, 1945.

DHH, CMHQ Report No. 150: "The Black Watch (Royal Highland Regiment) of Canada in Operation 'Spring,' 25 July 1944," February 12, 1946.

DHH, CMHQ Report No. 162: "Canadian Participation in the Operations in North-West Europe, 1944: Part II—Canadian Operations in July," November 8, 1946.

DHH, Simonds, Maj-Gen. G.G. "Report on Visit to Eighth Army, June 10, 1943."

LAC, RG24 Vol. 9873, Sanford, Lt. Col. S. "GSO 1's Report on Fourth Canadian Junior War Staff Course."

LAC, RG24 Vol. 10799, Simonds, Lt. Gen. G.G. "Operational Policy, 2nd Canadian Corps."

LAC, RG24 Vol. 12756, Historical Officer CMHQ (London). "Progress Reports, 1944."

University of Toronto Archives, B91-0013/00, Stacey, C.P. "Stacey's Impressions of Simonds, September 1945."

UNITED KINGDOM

Imperial War Museums, BLM Papers, Sir Edgar Williams, "Appreciation of Monty" written for Sir Dennis Hamilton, 1975.

NAUK, HW11/8, Government Code and Cipher School, "Air and Military History, Vol. VIII: The Western Front, Part I."

NAUK, CAB 65, War Cabinet, "Minutes (44) 97, Conclusions," July 27, 1944.

NAUK, WO208/3575, Williams, Brig. E.T. "Notes on the Use of Ultra at 21 Army Group," 1945.

War Office. "Current Reports from Overseas" series, 1943–45.

War Office. "Infantry Section Leading," 1934.

War Office. "Infantry Section Leading," 1938.

War Office. "Infantry Section Leading and Platoon Tactics," 1950.

War Office. "Infantry Training: Training and War," 1937.

War Office. "Infantry Training, Pt. 1: The Infantry Battalion," 1944.

War Office. "Infantry Training, Pt. 8: Fieldcraft, Battle Drill, Section and Platoon Tactics," 1944.

War Office. "The Instructors' Handbook on Fieldcraft and Battle Drill," 1942.

UNITED STATES

NARA, Center for Captured German Records, MS#B-470, Stadler, Sylvester. "Combat Report of the 9 SS Panzer Division: Period 3–24 July 1944."

NARA, Center for Captured German Records, MS#B-540, Schack, Friedrich. "272nd Infantry Division Normandy from 5–26 July 1944."

United States Army, Military Intelligence Division. *German Doctrine of the Stabilized Front*. Washington, DC: War Department, August 1943.

CORRESPONDENCE

Rodger, Brig. N.E.H., to the author, January 2, February 17 and March 26, 1996.

Williams, Sir Edgar, to the author, April 19, 1995.

PERSONAL PAPERS AND DIARIES

Crerar, Gen. H.D.G. (LAC).

Dempsey, Gen. M. (Public Records Office, Kew, and LHCMA).

Erskine, Maj. Gen. G. (Imperial War Museums, London).

Grigg, Sir James (Churchill College Archives, Cambridge).

McNaughton, A.G.L. (LAC).

Montgomery, Field Marshal B.L. (Imperial War Museums, London).

O'Connor, Gen. Sir Richard (LHCMA).

Pogue, Forrest C. (US Army Military History Institute, Carlisle Barracks, Pennsylvania).

Roy, Reginald (LAC).

WAR DIARIES

CANADA

LAC, RG24 Vol. 10715, 3rd Canadian Special Wireless Intelligence Section Type A, July 1944.

LAC, RG24 Vol. 13645, 1st Canadian Army Intelligence, September 1943–December 1944.

LAC, RG24 Vol. 13712, 2nd Canadian Corps, July 1944.

LAC, RG24 Vol. 13750, 2nd Canadian Infantry Division, July 1944.

LAC, RG24 Vol. 13765, 3rd Canadian Infantry Division, July 1944.

LAC, RG24 Vol. 14212, 9th Canadian Infantry Brigade, July 1944.

LAC, RG24 Vol. 14221, 5th Canadian Infantry Brigade, July 1944.

LAC, RG24 Vol. 14334, 4th Canadian Infantry Brigade, July 1944.

LAC, RG24 Vol. 14345, 2nd Canadian Armoured Brigade, July 1944.

LAC, RG24 Vol. 14455, 6th Canadian Infantry Brigade, July 1944.

LAC, RG24 Vol. 14991, 2nd Canadian Wireless Intelligence Section (Type B), July 1944.

LAC, RG24 Vol. 17506, 2nd Canadian Field Historical Section, July 1944–December 1945.

LAC, RG24 Vol. 17515, Director of the Historical Section (Col. Stacey), July 1944–December 1945.

UNITED KINGDOM

NAUK, WO171/131, 21st Army Group, July 1944.

NAUK, WO171/221, Second British Army, July 1944.

NAUK, WO171/310, 12th British Corps, July 1944.

NAUK, WO171/376, Guards Armoured Division, July 1944.

NAUK, WO171/439, 7th British Armoured Division, July 1944.

NAUK, WO171/620, 22nd Armoured Brigade, July 1944.

SECONDARY SOURCES

BOOKS

Addison, Paul, and Angus Calder. *Time to Kill: The Soldier's Experience of War in the West, 1939–1945*. London: Pimlico, 1997.

Ahrenfeldt, Robert H. *Psychiatry in the British Army in the Second World War*. London: Routledge & Kegan Paul, 1958.

Ambrose, Stephen E. *Band of Brothers: E Company, 506th Regiment, 101st Airborne from Normandy to Hitler's Eagle's Nest*. New York: Simon and Schuster, 1992.

Bartlett, F.C. *Psychology and the Fighting Man*. Cambridge: Cambridge University Press, 1927.

Belfield, Eversley, and H. Essame. *The Battle for Normandy*. London: Pan, 1983.

Bercuson, David. *Battalion of Heroes: The Calgary Highlanders in World War II*. Toronto: Penguin, 1994.

Bessner, Ellin. *Double Threat: Canadian Jews, the Military, and WWII*. Toronto: Canadian Jewish Press, 2018.

Biddle, Stephen, and Stephen Long. "Democracy and Military Effectiveness: A Deeper Look." *Journal of Conflict Resolution* 48, no. 4 (August 2004): 525–41.

Blackburn, George. *The Guns of Normandy: A Soldier's Eye View, France 1944*. Toronto: McClelland & Stewart, 1995.

Blake, George. *Mountain and Flood: The History of the 52nd (Lowland) Division, 1939–46*. Glasgow: Jackson, 1950.

Bourke, Joanna. *An Intimate History of Killing: Face to Face Killing in Twentieth-Century Warfare*. London: Granta, 1999.

Brière, Daniel, et al. *Saint-Martin-de-Fontenay: Un XXe siècle tourmenté*. Cabourg, France: Éditions Les Cahiers du temps, 2002.

Brode, Patrick. *Casual Slaughters and Accidental Judgments: Canadian War Crimes Prosecutions*. Toronto: University of Toronto Press, 1997.

Buckley, John. *British Armour in the Normandy Campaign, 1944*. London: Frank Cass, 2004.

———. *Monty's Men: The British Army and the Liberation of Europe*. London: Yale University Press, 2013.

Bull, Stephen. *World War II Infantry Tactics: Company and Battalion*. Botley, UK: Osprey, 2005.

Burns, Patricia. *They Were So Young: Montrealers Remember WWII*. Montreal: Véhicule Press, 2002.

Callahan, Raymond. "Two Armies in Normandy: Weighing British and Canadian Military Performance." In *D-Day 1944*, edited by Theodore A. Wilson. Lawrence: University Press of Kansas, 1994.

Campbell, Ian J. *Murder at the Abbaye: The Story of Twenty Canadian Soldiers Murdered at the Abbaye d'Ardenne*. Ottawa: Golden Dog, 1996.

Carafano, James Jay. *After D-Day: Operation Cobra and the Normandy Breakout*. Boulder, CO: Lynne Rienner, 2000.

Chandler, Alfred, ed. *The Papers of Dwight David Eisenhower, Vol. III*. Baltimore: Johns Hopkins University Press, 1970.

Chandler, David G., and James Lawton Collins, Jr., eds. *The D-Day Encyclopedia*. New York: Simon & Schuster, 1994.

Cohen, Eliot. *Citizens and Soldiers: The Dilemmas of Military Service*. Ithaca, NY: Cornell University Press, 1985.

Collins, Robert. *You Had to Be There: An Intimate Portrait of the Generation That Survived a Depression, Won World War II, and Re-invented Canada*. Toronto: McClelland & Stewart, 1997.

Cook, Tim. *Clio's Warriors: Canadian Historians and the Writing of the World Wars*. Vancouver: UBC Press, 2006.

Cooper, Matthew. *The German Army, 1933–1945: Its Political and Military Failure*. Chelsea, MI: Scarborough House, 1991.

Copp, Terry. *Fields of Fire: The Canadians in Normandy*. Toronto: University of Toronto Press, 2004.

———. *Cinderella Army: The Canadians in Northwest Europe, 1944–1945*. Toronto: University of Toronto Press, 2006.

———. *Guy Simonds and the Art of Command*. Kingston, ON: Canadian Defence Academy Press, 2007.

———. *The Brigade: The Fifth Canadian Infantry Brigade in WWII*. Mechanicsburg, PA: Stackpole, 2007.

Copp, Terry, and Mark Humphries, eds. *Combat Stress in the 20th Century: The Commonwealth Perspective*. Kingston, ON: Canadian Defence Academy Press, 2010.

Copp, Terry, and Bill McAndrew. *Battle Exhaustion: Soldiers and Psychiatrists in the Canadian Army, 1939–45*. Montreal: McGill-Queen's University Press, 1990.

Copp, Terry, and Robert Vogel. *Maple Leaf Route*. 5 vols. Alma, ON: Maple Leaf Route, 1982–88.

Delaney, Douglas. *Corps Commanders: Five British and Canadian Generals at War, 1939–45*. Vancouver: UBC Press, 2012.

D'Este, Carlo. *Decision in Normandy: The Unwritten Story of Montgomery and the Allied Campaign*. London: Collins, 1983.

Dickson, Paul. *A Thoroughly Canadian General: A Biography of General H.D.G. Crerar*. Toronto: University of Toronto Press, 2007.

Dixon, Norman. *On the Psychology of Military Incompetence*. London: Pimlico, 1994.

Douglas, W.A.B., and Brereton Greenhous. *Out of the Shadows*. Toronto: Oxford University Press, 1977.

Ellis, John. *Brute Force: Allied Strategy and Tactics in the Second World War*. London: André Deutsch, 1990.

Ellis, L. F. *Victory in the West*. 2 vols. London: Her Majesty's Stationery Office, 1962.

Engen, Robert. *Strangers in Arms: Combat Motivation in the Canadian Army, 1943–45*. Montreal: McGill-Queen's University Press, 2016.

English, John A. *The Canadian Army and the Normandy Campaign: A Study of Failure in High Command*. New York: Praeger, 1991.

———. *Marching Through Chaos: The Descent of Armies in Theory and Practice*. Westport, CT: Praeger, 1996.

———. *On Infantry*. New York: Praeger, 1981.

———. *Patton's Peers: The Forgotten Allied Field Army Commanders of the Western Front, 1944–45*. Mechanicsburg, PA: Stackpole Books, 2009.

———. *Surrender Invites Death: Fighting the Waffen SS in Normandy*. Mechanicsburg, PA: Stackpole Books, 2011.

Evans, Chris. "The Fighter-Bomber in the Normandy Campaign: The Role of 83 Group." *Canadian Military History* 8, no. 1 (1999): 21–36.

Farran, Roy. *The History of the Calgary Highlanders, 1921–1954*. Calgary: Bryant Press, 1954.

Fennell, Jonathan. *Combat and Morale in the North African Campaign: The Eighth Army and the Path to Alamein*. Cambridge: Cambridge University Press, 2011.

Foster, Tony. *Meeting of Generals*. Toronto: Methuen, 1986.

French, David. *The British Way in Warfare, 1699–2000*. London: Allen & Unwin, 1990.

———. *Military Identities: The Regimental System, the British Army, and the British People, c. 1870–2000*. Oxford: Oxford University Press, 2005.

———. *Raising Churchill's Army: The British Army and the War against Germany, 1919–1945*. Oxford: Oxford University Press, 2001.

Fussell, Paul. *Wartime: Understanding and Behavior in the Second World War*. New York: Oxford, 1989.

Goodspeed, D.J. *Battle Royal: A History of the Royal Regiment of Canada, 1862–1962*. Toronto: Royal Regiment of Canada Association, 1962.

Gouin, J. *Bon Coeur et Bon Bras: Histoire du régiment de Maisonneuve, 1880–1980*. Montreal: Cercle des officiers du régiment de Maisonneuve, 1980.

Granatstein, J.L. *Canada's Army*. Toronto: University of Toronto Press, 2002.

———. *Canada's War: The Politics of the Mackenzie King Government, 1939–1945*. Toronto: Oxford University Press, 1975.

———. *The Generals: The Canadian Army's Senior Commanders in the Second World War*. Toronto: Stoddart, 1993.

———. *Weight of Command: The Voice of Canada's Second World War Generals and Those Who Knew Them*. Vancouver: UBC Press, 2016.

Granatstein, J.L., and J.M. Hitsman. *Broken Promises: A History of Conscription in Canada*. Toronto: Oxford University Press, 1977.

Greenhous, Brereton. *Semper Paratus: The History of the Royal Hamilton Light Infantry (Wentworth Regiment), 1862–1977*. Hamilton: RHLI Historical Association, 1977.

Grossman, Dave. *On Combat: The Psychology and Physiology of Deadly Conflict in War and in Peace*. 3rd ed. Mascoutah, IL: Warrior Science Publications, 2008.

———. *On Killing: The Psychological Cost of Learning to Kill in War and Society*. Rev. ed. New York: Little, Brown, 2009.

Hamilton, Nigel. *Monty: The Making of a General, 1887–1942*. London: Hamish Hamilton, 1981.

Hargreaves, Richard. *The Germans in Normandy*. Barnsley, UK: Pen & Sword, 2006.

Hart, Russell A. *Clash of Arms: How the Allies Won in Normandy*. Boulder, CO: Lynne Rienner, 2001.

Hart, Stephen Ashley. *Montgomery and "Colossal Cracks": The 21st Army Group in Northwest Europe, 1944–45*. Westport, CT: Praeger, 2000.

———. "Indoctrinated Nazi Teenage Warriors: The Fanaticism of the 12th SS Panzer Division, *Hitlerjugend* in Normandy, 1944." In *Fanaticism and Combat in the Modern Age,* edited by Matthew Hughes and Gaynor Johnson. New York: Frank Cass, 2005.

Hayes, Geoffrey. *Crerar's Lieutenants: Inventing the Canadian Junior Army Officer, 1939–45*. Vancouver: UBC Press, 2017.

———. *The Lincs: A History of the Lincoln and Welland Regiment at War*. Alma, ON: Maple Leaf Route, 1986.

Henderson, William Darryl. *Cohesion: The Human Element in Combat*. Washington: National Defense University Press, 1985.

Horn, Michiel, ed. *The Dirty Thirties: Canadians in the Great Depression*. Toronto: Copp Clark, 1972.

Horn, Bernd, and Stephen Harris. *Warrior Chiefs: Perspectives on Senior Canadian Military Leaders*. Toronto: Dundurn Press, 2001.

Jackson, Paul. *One of the Boys: Homosexuality in the Military during World War II*. Montreal: McGill-Queen's University Press, 2010.

Jarymowycz, Roman Johann. *Tank Tactics: From Normandy to Lorraine*. Boulder, CO: Lynne Rienner, 2001.

———. "General Guy Simonds: The Commander as Tragic Hero." In *Warrior Chiefs: Perspectives on Senior Canadian Military Leaders*, edited by Bernd Horn and Stephen Harris. Toronto: Dundurn Press, 2001: 107–42.

Kite, Ben. *Stout Hearts: The British and Canadians in Normandy 1944*. Solihull, UK: Helion and Company, 2014.

Lackenbauer, P. Whitney, and Chris M.V. Madsen, eds. *Kurt Meyer on Trial: A Documentary Record*. Kingston, ON: Canadian Defence Academy Press, 2007.

Lehmann, Rudolf, and Ralf Tiemann. *The Leibstandarte* IV/I. Winnipeg: J.J. Fedorowicz, 1993.

Leleu, Jean-Luc. 10. *SS-Panzer-Division Frundsberg: Normandie 1944*. Bayeux, France: Éditions Heimdal, 1999.

Lodieu, Didier. *L'Enfer au sud de Caen*. Caudebec-lès-Elbeuf, France: Éditions La Poche de Falaise Chambois, 2015

Longden, Sean. *To the Victor the Spoils: D-Day to VE Day, the Reality behind the Heroism*. Gloucestershire, UK: Arris Books, Great Britain, 2004.

Luther, Craig W.H. *Blood and Honor: The History of the 12th SS Panzer Division "Hitler Youth," 1943–1945*. San Jose, CA: Bender, 1987.

Malone, Colonel Dick. *Missing from the Record*. Toronto: Collins, 1946.

Malone, Richard S. *A Portrait of War, 1939–1943*. Toronto: Collins, 1983.

———. *A World in Flames, 1944–1945: A Portrait of War, Part Two*. Toronto: Collins, 1984.

Marchand, Gérard. *Le Régiment de Maisonneuve vers la victoire*. Montreal: Les Presses libres, 1980.

Margolian, Howard. *Conduct Unbecoming: The Story of the Murder of Canadian Prisoners of War in Normandy*. Toronto: University of Toronto Press, 1998.

McAndrew, Bill. "The Canadians on Verrières Ridge: A Historiographical Survey." In *The Valour and the Horror Revisited*, edited by David Bercuson and Sydney F. Wise. Montreal: McGill-Queen's University Press, 1994.

McKee, Alexander. *Caen: Anvil of Victory*. London: Souvenir, 1964.

McNorgan, Michael R. *The Gallant Hussars: A History of the 1st Hussars Regiment, 1856–2004*. London, ON: 1st Hussars Cavalry Fund, 2004.

Messenger, Charles. *Hitler's Gladiator: The Life and Times of Oberstgruppenführer and Panzergeneral-Oberst der Waffen-SS Sepp Dietrich*. London: Brassey's Defence Publishers, 1988.

Meyer, Hubert. *The History of the 12th SS Panzerdivision "Hitlerjugend."* Winnipeg: J.J. Fedorowicz, 1994.

Milner, Marc, ed. *Canadian Military History: Selected Readings*. Toronto: Irwin, 1998.

Mitcham, Samuel W. *The Panzer Legions: A Guide to the German Army Tank Divisions of World War II and Their Commanders*. Westport, CT: Praeger, 2000.

Nicholson, G.W.L. *The Gunners of Canada: The History of the Royal Regiment of Canadian Artillery*. Vol. 2, 1919–1967. Toronto: McClelland & Stewart, 1972.

O'Keefe, David. *One Day in August: The Untold Story behind Canada's Tragedy at Dieppe*. Toronto: Knopf, 2013.

Ousby, Ian. *The Road to Verdun: World War I's Most Momentous Battle and the Folly of Nationalism*. Toronto: Doubleday, 2002.

Perras, Galen Roger. *Stepping Stones to Nowhere: The Aleutian Islands, Alaska, and American Military Strategy, 1867–1945*. Vancouver: UBC Press, 2003.

Reid, Brian A. *No Holding Back: Operation Totalize, Normandy, August 1944*. Toronto: Robin Brass Studio, 2005.

Reynolds, Michael. *The Devil's Adjutant: Jochem Peiper, Panzer Leader*. New York: Sarpedon, 1997.

———. *Sons of the Reich: The History of II SS Panzer Corps in Normandy, Arnhem, the Ardennes and on the Eastern Front*. Havertown, PA: Casemate, 2002.

———. *Steel Inferno: 1 SS Panzer Corps in Normandy*. New York: Sarpedon, 1997.

Rosado, Jorge, and Chris Bishop. *Wehrmacht Panzer Divisions, 1939–1949*. London: Amber, 2010.

Roy, R.H. *1944: The Canadians in Normandy*. Toronto: Macmillan, 1984.

Ryan, Cornelius. *A Bridge Too Far*. London: Book Club Associates, 1975.

Sheffield, R. Scott. *The Red Man's on the Warpath: The Image of the "Indian" and the Second World War*. Vancouver: UBC Press, 2004.

Stacey, C.P. *Six Years of War*. Ottawa: Queen's Printer, 1957.

———. *The Victory Campaign*. Ottawa: Queen's Printer, 1960.

Stevenson, Michael J. *Canada's Greatest Wartime Muddle: National Selective Service and the Mobilization of Human Resources during World War II*. Montreal: McGill-Queen's University Press, 2001.

Tieke, Wilhelm. *In the Firestorm of the Last Years of the War: II SS Panzerkorps with the 9 and 10 SS Divisions Hohenstauffen and Frundsberg*. Winnipeg: J.J. Fedorowicz, 1999.

Turner, Victor. *The Ritual Process: Structure and Anti-Structure*. Chicago: Aldine, 1969.

Walther, Herbert. *Die 12. SS-Panzer-Division HJ: Eine Dokumentation in Wort und Bild*. Friedberg, Germany: Podzu-Pallas, 1987.

Weigley, Russell F. *Eisenhower's Lieutenants: The Campaign of France and Germany, 1944–1945.* Bloomington: Indiana University Press, 1981.

Weingartner, James J. *Hitler's Guard: The Story of the Leibstandarte SS Adolf Hitler.* Nashville, TN: Battery Press, 1996.

Wieviorka, Olivier. *Normandy: The Landings to the Liberation of Paris.* Cambridge, MA: Harvard University Press, 2008.

Wilkinson, Alta R., ed. *Ottawa to Caen: Letters from Arthur Campbell Wilkinson.* Ottawa: Tower Books, 1947.

Williams, Jeffery. *The Long Left Flank: The Hard-Fought Way to the Reich, 1944–45.* Toronto: Stoddart, 1988.

Wood, James. *Militia Myths: Ideas of the Canadian Citizen Soldier, 1896–1921.* Vancouver: UBC Press, 2010.

Zetterling, Niklas. *Normandy 1944. German Military Organization, Combat Power and Organizational Effectiveness.* Winnipeg: J.J. Fedorowicz, 2000.

ARTICLES

Brown, Ian M. "Not Glamorous, but Effective: The Canadian Corps and the Set-Piece Attack, 1917–1918." *Journal of Military History* 58, no. 3 (July 1994): 421–44.

Cook, Tim. "The Politics of Surrender: Canadian Soldiers and the Killing of Prisoners in the Great War." *Journal of Military History* 70, no. 3 (July 2006): 637–66.

D'Amours, Caroline. "Reassessment of a Crisis: Canadian Infantry Reinforcements during the Second World War." *Canadian Army Journal* 14, no. 2 (2012): 72–89.

Delaney, Douglas. "Knowing Enough Not to Interfere: Lieutenant-General Charles Foulkes at the Lamone River, December 1944." In *Canada and the Second World War: Essays in Honour of Terry Copp*, edited by Geoffrey Hayes. Waterloo, ON: Wilfrid Laurier University, 2013.

Dykstra, Ralph. "The Liberation of Groningen—An Urban Battlefield." *Army Doctrine and Training Bulletin* 5, no. 3 (Fall 2002).

Fitzgerald-Black, Alexander. "Investigating the Memory of Operation Spring: The Inquiry into the Black Watch and the Battle of St. André-sur-Orne, 1944–46." *Canadian Military History* 21, no. 2 (Spring 2012): 21–32.

Granatstein, J.L. "The Old Boy Networks—Lieutenant General William A.B. Anderson Interview, Ottawa, 21 May 1991." *Canadian Military History* 23, no. 2 (2014).

Grossman, Dave, and Bruce K. Siddle. "Psychological Effects of Combat."
In *Encyclopedia of Violence, Peace and Conflict*, edited by Lester Kurtz.
Academic Press, 2008.

Humphries, Mark. "War's Long Shadow: Masculinity, Medicine, and the
Gendered Politics of Trauma, 1914–1939." *Canadian Historical Review*
91, no. 3 (September 2010): 504–32.

Jarymowycz, R. "*Der Gegangriff vor Verrières:* The German Counterattacks
along Verrières Ridge, July 25–26, 1944." *Canadian Military History* 3, no.
3 (1993): 46–53.

Lewin, Ronald. "A Signals Intelligence War." *Journal of Contemporary
History* 16 (1981): 501–12.

Liedtke, Gregory. "Canadian Offensive Operations in Normandy Revisited."
Canadian Military Journal 8, no. 2 (Summer 2007): 60–68.

McAndrew, William J. "Fire or Movement?: Canadian Tactical Doctrine,
Sicily—1943." *Military Affairs*, July 1987: 160–65.

McNorgan, M.R. "Between Strawberry and Raspberry: An Examination of
the Action Fought at Le Mesnil-Patry on June 11, 1944." *The Rifleman:
The Journal of the Queen's Own Rifles of Canada* (1997).

Milner, Marc. "Stopping the Panzers: Reassessing the Role of 3rd Canadian
Infantry Division in Normandy, 7–10 June 1944." *Journal of Military
History* 74 (April 2010): 491–522.

O'Keefe, David R. "Double-Edged Sword Part 1: Ultra and Operation
Totalize, Normandy, August 8, 1944." *Canadian Army Journal* 12 (Winter
2010): 85–93.

———. "'No Waiting for George': The Question of Support for the Black
Watch Assault on Verrières Ridge in Operation Spring, Normandy, 25 July
1944." *Canadian Army Journal* 16 (Winter 2016): 11–30.

———. "'Pushing Their Necks Out': Ultra and the Black Watch at May-sur-
Orne, Normandy, August 5, 1944." *Canadian Military History* 15 (Spring
2006): 33–44.

———. "'With Blinders On': The Black Watch and the Battle for Spycker,
September 12–14, 1944." *Canadian Army Journal* 11 (Spring 2008): 98–109.

Perrun, Jody. "Best Laid Plans: Guy Simonds and Operation Totalize, 7–10
August 1944." *Journal of Military History* 1 (January 2003): 137–73.

Simonds, Capt. G.G. "An Army That Can Attack, a Division That Can
Defend." *Canadian Defence Quarterly* (July 1938): 413–17.

———. "What Price Assault Without Support." *Canadian Defence Quarterly*
(January 1939): 142–47.

Stacey, C.P. "The Life and Hard Times of an Official Historian." *Canadian
Historical Review* 51, no. 1 (1970): 21–47.

———. "Canadian Leaders of the Second World War." *Canadian Historical Review* 66, no. 1 (March 1985): 64–72.

———. "The Staff Officer: A Footnote to Canadian Military History." *Canadian Defence Quarterly* (August 1990): 21–29.

MASTER'S THESES AND DISSERTATIONS

Durflinger, Serge. "City at War: The Effects of the Second World War on Verdun, Quebec." PhD dissertation, McGill University, 1997.

Hart, S.A. "Field Marshal Montgomery, 21st Army Group, and North West Europe, 1944–45." PhD dissertation, King's College London, 1995.

Hutchinson, W.E.J. "Test of a Corps Commander: Lieutenant General Guy Granville Simonds, Normandy—1944." Master's thesis, University of Victoria, 1982.

Hull, C. "A Case Study in Professionalism in the Canadian Army in the 1930s and 1940s: Lieutenant General G.G. Simonds." Master's thesis, Purdue University, 1989.

Lawrie, Richard. "Narratives of Collaboration in Post-War France, 1944–1974." PhD dissertation, School of Modern Languages and Cultures, University of Durham, 2013.

MacDonald, John A. "In Search of Veritable: Training the Canadian Army Staff Officer, 1899–1945." Master's thesis, Royal Military College of Canada, 1993.

O'Keefe, David. "Bitter Harvest: A Case Study of Allied Operational Intelligence for Operation Spring, Normandy, July 25, 1944." Master's thesis, University of Ottawa, 1997.

Sauer, E.J. "Germany's I SS Panzer Korps: Defensive Operations June–September 1944." PhD dissertation, Boston College, 1992.

INDEX